Embracing the Spirit

**The Bishop Henry McNeal Turner/Sojourner Truth Series
in Black Religion**

Previously published in the Turner Series:

1. *For My People* by James H. Cone
2. *Black and African Theologies* by Josiah U. Young
3. *Troubling Biblical Waters* by Cain Hope Felder
4. *Black Theology USA and South Africa* by Dwight N. Hopkins
5. *Empower the People* by Theodore Walker, Jr.
6. *A Common Journey* by George C.L. Cummings
7. *Dark Symbols, Obscure Signs* by Riggins R. Earl, Jr.
8. *A Troubling in My Soul* by Emilie M. Townes
9. *The Black Christ* by Kelly Brown Douglas

In the Turner/Truth Series:

10. *Christianity on Trial* by Mark L. Chapman
11. *Were You There?* by David Emmanuel Goatley
12. *My Sister, My Brother* by Karen Baker-Fletcher and Garth (Kasimu) Baker-Fletcher

Editor: Dwight N. Hopkins
The University of Chicago, The Divinity School

Associate Editors:
James H. Cone, Union Theological Seminary, New York
Katie G. Cannon, Temple University
Cain Hope Felder, Howard University, School of Divinity
Jacquelyn Grant, The Interdenominational Theological Center
Delores S. Williams, Union Theological Seminary, New York

The purpose of this series is to encourage the development of biblical, historical, theological, ethical, and pastoral works that analyze the role of the churches and other religious movements in the liberation struggles of black women and men in the United States, particularly the poor, and their relationship to struggles in the Third World.

Named after Bishop Henry McNeal Turner (1843-1915) and Sojourner Truth (1797?-1883), the series reflects the spirit of these two visionaries and witnesses for the black struggle for liberation. Bishop Turner was a churchman, a political figure, a missionary, and a pan-Africanist. Sojourner Truth was an illiterate former slave who championed black emancipation, women's rights, and the liberating spirit of the gospel.

The Bishop Heny McNeal Turner/Sojourner Truth Series
in Black Religion, Volume XIII

EMBRACING THE SPIRIT

*Womanist Perspectives on Hope, Salvation,
and Transformation*

Emilie M. Townes
editor

ORBIS BOOKS

Maryknoll, New York 10545

Copyright © 1997 by Emilie M. Townes

Published by Orbis Books, Maryknoll, NY 10545-0308

Manufactured in the United States of America

Library of Congress Cataloging-in-Publication Data

Embracing the spirit : womanist perspectives on hope, salvation, and
    transformation / Emilie M. Townes, editor.
        p.   cm.—(Bishop Henry McNeal Turner/Sojourner Truth series
    Includes bibliographical references.
    ISBN 1-57075-140-4 (alk. paper)
    1. Womanist theology.   2. Spiritual life.   I. Townes, Emilie
Maureen, 1955-   . II. Series.
BT83.9E47   1997
230'.082—dc21   97-25111
                                                         CIP

for my bestest

to embrace the spirit
is to be led
again
again
again
to the holiest of holies

Contents

PART III
LOVES THE FOLK

INTRODUCTION

On Creating Ruminations on the Spirit

Emilie M. Townes

As I sit writing the introduction to this anthology, I do so in my mother's hospital room waiting for her to return from surgery. There is a myriad of emotions welling up, but the one that I find returning again and again is hope. Since my father's death in 1990, I have sometimes joked with my sister about our being one mother away from being orphans. I realize now that such joking is serious.

I am blessed to spend my time waiting with two lovely women, one of whom is waiting for her own surgery. They are Linda Keith and Frances Fletcher, mother and daughter. We pass the time waiting for my mother to return from surgery and for Linda to go to surgery talking about today's youth, the need for discipline, the kinds of pride mothers have in their children, the lessons Linda learned from the Depression and how she tried to teach her children "to do right." As we sit in this Durham, North Carolina, hospital room, I think of the ways that the South has changed and the ways it has not from my birth. Here sit three women—two White and one African American—passing time and sharing thoughts about our lives, frustrations, joys, and hopes.

I am hopeful that Mom's surgery will go well and that the test results will come back negative. This will be good news for our family. Yet this hope that I have is indescribable ultimately. I can point to it, I can even walk around in it and be comforted by it, but I cannot convey to you the reader how it is holding me in a place of calm, of peace.

Such is the hope that the contributors to this anthology try to describe. It is often yoked, as we have done, with notions of salvation and transformation. The volume is designed to continue the conversations begun in *A Troubling in My Soul: Womanist Perspectives on Evil and Suffering*. I am convinced that evil and suffering should never be our last or only word about the nature of humanity and the way in which the divine works in our lives. This was brought home to me when I was receiving feedback from my best friend on chapter drafts of *In a Blaze of Glory: Womanist Spirituality as Social Witness*. As she paused before telling me what she thought, she asked, "Em, when are you going to do happy?" My response, without thinking, was, "I'm an ethicist—I don't do happy!" After we laughed and went on with our conversation, it began to haunt me. In parts of the African American faith tradition, being haunted is not considered bad or negative. It simply means that God is trying "to get a word through" to you, and one needs to be still and listen. What occurred to me is that in my preaching, I am almost always speaking a strong word of hope, a promise of salvation, a yearning for transformation. It dawned on me that *A Troubling in My Soul* needed a companion volume.

So often, Black life in the United States is painted in absolutely grim and hopeless colors. If all one knows is what media images portray of African Americans, one would be tempted to think that there is nothing healthy or whole in the lives and witnesses of those folks whom I know as relatives and kinfolk, friends and acquaintances, colleagues, brothers and sisters in Christ. It became a necessity, in my eyes, that womanist thought go on record about the hope, salvation, and transformation we have in our lives and in our academic and intellectual musings.

There is a blend of new voices and returning voices in this anthology. Time, commitments, and the dailiness of life prevented all of the contributors of the first volume to return for this one. As with the first collection, however, the essays in this volume are both theoretical and practical. The contributors are Protestant (American Baptist, African Methodist Episcopal, African Methodist Episcopal Zion, Christian Methodist Episcopal, Episcopalian, Missionary Baptist, Presbyterian, United Church of Christ, and United Methodist) and Roman Catholic, lay and ordained, academicians and practitioners, and a range of ages of women, from their thirties to their sixties.

The themes of hope, salvation, and transformation point to the liberating promises of God through the gospel of Jesus Christ found in traditional theo-ethical discourses. These themes move beyond history to help us imagine and then work to create spaces of justice. The aim of this volume is to explore some of the many dimensions possible in this search for justice through a womanist commitment to an interstructured analysis employing race, gender, and class. The challenge is both academic and practical. Academically, a womanist search for new and more fulfilling images and realities for hope, salvation, and transformation enters the lively dialogue created in the modern-postmodern dialogue. The contributors deal with questions of rationality, objectivity, historicity, value-free established knowledge, social location, institutionalized radical doubt, and knowledge as hypothesis. Practically, United States society (and African American society in particular) stands at a precarious crossroads. The forces of conservative and liberal political ideologies and theologies offer ill-conceived panaceas for entrenched sociopolitical problems. The church needs more than a religiosized civil religion if it seeks to remain faithful to its pastoral and prophetic call. The contributors to this volume offer new, and in some cases rethought, avenues for the church to explore and employ in living into its mission and witness.

As in *A Troubling in My Soul*, this anthology is divided into parts that bear phrases from Alice Walker's definition of *womanist* in her 1983 collection of essays, *In Search of Our Mothers' Gardens: Womanist Prose*. The first part of the anthology, "Serious," centers on the primary theme of hope. The reader will find that several contributors also intertwine themes of salvation and transformation. This will be the case in the other parts of the anthology as well. There is something about hope, salvation, and transformation that often compels them to be natural dance partners. At times, there will be a razor-thin difference between these notions, and at times it may appear that any distinction among the three is arbitrary. Such, I believe, is natural to discourse centered on seeking to understand how justice and wholeness can and should prevail in our world and in our societies.

The lead essay in this anthology, "Looking to Your Tomorrows Today," by Mary M. Townes, is an adaptation of a college commencement address delivered to graduates of North Carolina Central University (NCCU) on December 16, 1994. NCCU is one of the historical traditionally Black colleges in the South. This was the first December graduation ceremony for the school. The administration and graduating class asked Townes, as immediate past dean of the College, to be the commencement speaker for this important event. She draws on history, sociology, cultural studies, and economic common sense in her address. Ultimately, Townes argues that hope is found in discovering and remembering roots as one seeks to move into the uncertain realities as we face the turn of the century at a time of tremendous unrest and fearfulness.

In chapter 2, Diana L. Hayes explores the aftermath of one of the worst "uprisings" in recent United States history, the Los Angeles rebellion after the first Rodney King verdict. She notes that people of color are facing a future in which they, although they are increasingly the majority in all but the uppermost levels of society, are being scapegoated for our nation's ills. The question that drives Hayes's exploration is, What reasons have we, as African Americans, to hope? To continue to hope in the face of the many crises facing the Black community today is to challenge the status quo, both religious and secular. Hayes responds that such a hope is found in practicing the subversive love we find modeled in the life and ministry of Jesus Christ. Hayes presents a Black Catholic womanist perspective on the continuing faith of African Americans which not only serves to transform Black lives and communities but also recognizes the need to build coalitions across racial, ethnic, and gender barriers.

Rosita deAnn Mathews explores in chapter 3 the Latin American idea of susto, deep despair, as it relates to the lives of African Americans. In her essay, "Overcoming Susto," Mathews works with the notion that losing one's soul or losing hope in oneself or in God is a common predicament for many. When paired with systemic oppression, this constant onslaught against mind, body, and soul can gradually erode our hope to the point of loss of self. For Mathews, keeping hope alive is vital. She argues that one must bring the perpetrator to account, to make her or him confront the incident. Further, Mathews argues that to ignore acts of oppression is to condone them and encourage their repetition. Her goal is healing—one forged from honest storytelling that is found in a hope that sustains and undergirds our movement to save our souls and spirits to live in a better tomorrow.

In chapter 4, "Womanist Work and Public Policy," Rosetta E. Ross explores public policy implications of womanist theology and ethics, which she calls "womanist work." The tradition of Black women's activism in the United States demonstrates a focus of these women on the needs of the most disenfranchised segments of society. Historically, these women, who were active in the public sphere, often saw themselves not only as working in behalf of African Americans, but also as legitimate participants in the public discourse. As participants in public discourse, they were making assertions about public policy. Ross focuses on the work of Victoria Way DeLee, a civil rights activist in South Carolina, as a representative of this tradition. Her chapter begins with an analysis of voting rights and school desegregation work as civil rights practice designed to change public policy and as activity with which Victoria Way DeLee's local community work resonated. Ross then presents the particular instances of DeLee's civil rights work as efforts to address specific policies. Next, she investigates general policy implications of DeLee's work. Finally, Ross lays the framework for future directions for womanist work.

Linda E. Thomas, in chapter 5, examines the life and ministry of Mother Christinah Nku, the founder of the second-largest African-initiated church in southern Africa. Thomas places Mother Nku's story in the Black South African understanding of *ubuntu*, peoplehood, as a response to their domination by Whites. She yokes *ubuntu* with Alice Walker's understanding of community in Walker's four-part definition of *womanist* in *In Search of Our Mothers' Gardens: Womanist Prose* and with Delores Williams's understanding of the wilderness in *Sisters in the Wilderness*. Thomas presents a compelling portrait of life in South Africa during apartheid, the multiple categories of race, class, and gender that Black South African women faced and continue to face in postapartheid South Africa, and the healing ministry of Mother Nku. Thomas asserts that Nku was a womanist who provided a place for the suffering masses of Black South Africans to find hope and comfort. The church of Mother Nku created a religion of the oppressed that acted as an alternative health care system for people who suffered from illnesses that were the result of social malice caused by apartheid. The creation of this religion and the development of an alternative health care system reflect the power of rituals of rebellion and a theology of power.

In the concluding chapter in part 1, Teresa L. Fry draws on her rich experience in the local church and in the academy. At Shorter Community African Methodist Episcopal Church in Denver, Colorado, Fry developed the Sisters Working Encouraging Empowering Together (S.W.E.E.T.) program over a six-year period that eventually touched the lives of five hundred to six hundred women in the Denver area. The goal of S.W.E.E.T. was to be a network for sharing womanist perspectives and for providing a support system for Black women's spiritual and social liberation. Fry found that as she ministered within African American women's groups and that as she talked about the importance of finding one's voice as a means to empowerment, the women were trying to find the breath to begin the process of speech. Using the powerful image of asphyxiation, Fry notes that although the women attempted to speak, to articulate their positions, oppressive stumbling blocks, overdependence on others, fear of isolation, lifelong inferiority beliefs, mistrust and resentment of women in the academy, and lack of knowledge caused them to suffocate slowly. Fry provides a practical model for sharing womanist thought with "ordinary" African American women, families, churches, and community organizations. The model focuses on the transformative power of individual and small group discussions of African American women's social, theological, occupational, psychological, and health concerns; ethnographic studies of womanist relatives and friends; composition of womanist sermons; and African American women's literature and liturgical study groups as means of avoiding asphyxiation. For Fry, if womanist thought and practice fails to address the material needs and concrete concerns of African American girls and women, it will only serve to increase Black women's inability to breathe in the breath of life and live.

Part 2, "Committed to Survival and Wholeness of Entire People," focuses on salvation. In chapter 7, "Straight Talk, Plain Talk," Delores S. Williams explores dimensions of social salvation. She writes out of a sense of the shared experience of civil rights/community building. Williams provides a piercing synopsis of the rise of White hate groups and the phenomenon of White supremacy in the late twentieth century. For her, the only way to combat such threats to the body, spirit, and souls of Black folk is the full resurrection of the Black civil rights movement. Rather than providing a nostalgic look at this movement, Williams pushes for a rigorous "in-house" conversation in the African American community using "Black common sense." This common sense is the collective knowledge, wisdom, and action Black folk use to survive and develop productive and creative lives in the midst of crushing inequality. She develops three in-house strategies: reactivating and sustaining the memory of the activity of Black heroes and sheroes; cultivating a Black community consciousness and actions that promote the work of getting beyond the obstacles of oppressive systems; and encouraging constructive critical thinking and careful planning rather than emotional reaction to issues affecting Black life. For Williams, such a multifaceted strategy will confront the fragmentation the Black church must address in the lives of the Black community in the United States.

In chapter 8, Karen Baker-Fletcher draws on Black women's literature, film, personal narrative, scripture, the historical eschatology of Anna Julia Cooper, and contemporary womanist scholarship. This compelling interweave explores the Black church hymn "The Lord Is My Light and My Salvation," based on Psalm 27 as a metaphor for God as empowering Spirit. Baker-Fletcher lifts up richly textured resources to highlight this theme as an eschatological one concerned with a God who empowers in the fullness of time, which is in the past, present, and immediate future. God as the strength of life transforms fear into hope, ignorance into the light of wisdom and knowledge, and brokenness into salvation. Such a God empowers Black women and humankind to engage in transformative ethics of courage, survival, risk, and liberation.

Cheryl A. Kirk-Duggan argues in chapter 9 that Black music, including gospel and blues, which are the younger sisters of the spirituals and work songs, offers responses to life. Black gospel and blues emerged as creative Black women and men blended their consciousness, visions, interpretive grasps of the Bible, glimmers of God's grace, hopes for freedom and equality, and contemporary life experiences into a melodic potpourri of song. Kirk-Duggan explores a message of hope, salvation, and transformation contained within certain gospels and blues created and/or performed by African American women. She uses the lives and works of singers, composers, arrangers, and blues singers Ma Rainey, Alberta Hunter, and Tracy Chapman. Her gospel composers, singers, and arrangers are Lucie Campbell, Roberta Martin, and Shirley Caesar. The life and music of Aretha Franklin complete her cavalcade of voices. Kirk-Duggan presents a rich synthesis of their messages and the impact of their performances, and summarizes and critiques their views of hope, salvation, and transformation as these parallel certain tenets of womanist theory.

In chapter 10, "Woman at the Well," Mozella G. Mitchell focuses on the inner and outer spiritual transformation of Mahalia Jackson. Jackson, one of the twentieth century's preeminent gospel singers, represents the "singing something" of Anna Julia Cooper. This "singing something" is the voice of God in every human being as we cry out against injustice. For Mitchell, Jackson literally becomes the "singing something." Mitchell focuses on the song "Jesus Met the Woman at the Well" as representative of Jackson's own spiritual experience of salvation and conversion. Mitchell argues that Jackson focuses on gospel songs because of the personal spiritual growth they provide. Gospel songs reflect the personal trials, testimonies, and direct conversations with God and Jesus in ways that spirituals or hymns could not do for Jackson. When Jackson sang, she experienced her own growth and spiritual encounters *and* spread the gospel message of salvation to her audiences. The intimate yoking of personal and communal transformation through salvation is the hallmark of Mahalia Jackson's legacy and witness for Mitchell.

My own essay, in chapter 11, " 'The Doctor Ain't Taking No Sticks,' " uses the health and health care debate to frame health issues in the African American community. With the extremely troubling case of the Tuskegee experiment as the backdrop, I look at the complexity of issues regarding health care for Blacks and the ways in which hope can remain a compelling theo-ethical impulse that can help all of us address the inequities of health care in the United States. The book of Joel helps frame my essay. Joel urges Judah to plead publicly for Yahweh's help, but it is not seen as an act of penitence, but as a plea for assistance. As we move through Joel, we do not see the crisis as a punishment for disobedience, but it is a deeply distressing reality that Judah longs to correct (1:5-14). The only way to get there is to repent. There is an urgent flavor to repentance in Joel, and it must be more than a set of external rites; it must be a matter of the heart— for the God who judges sin is the God of compassion and mercy. Communal lament happens in community, and this corporate experience of calling for healing is made bearable and manageable in the community. When we grieve, when we lament, we acknowledge and live the experience rather than try to hold it away from us out of some misguided notion of being objective or strong. All of us live in structures of evil and wickedness that make us ill. We must name them as such and seek to repent—not out of form—but from the heart. It is only then that we can begin to heal in hope.

In chapter 12, Marsha Foster Boyd's brief yet compelling sketch of a womanist pastoral theology, or "WomanistCare," begins part 3, "Loves the Folk." She emphasizes the importance of listening to the stories of other women, therefore providing a helpful step to begin the final focus of transformation. Foster Boyd articulates the importance of exploring healthy images for African American women and the roles which they play. For her, the image of the wounded healer is not helpful or healthy for Black women. Rather, she turns to the image of the "empowered cojourner" as one who faces the difficulties and defeats of life as a cojourner with others. Foster Boyd outlines five components of a pastoral theology of WomanistCare: communication, affirmation, confrontation, accountability, and healing. These components function in a dynamic tension pointed toward finding place, healing, and voice for African American women. For Foster Boyd, WomanistCare functions best in small group settings and through the cultivation of friendships and interdependent relationships between Black women.

In chapter 13, Barbara J. Essex describes how she comes from a long line of strong Black women—women who made choices and decisions outside the norm; women who worked farms without men; women who made livings without husbands; women who left inadequate and abusive men and forged on alone; women who by their examples opened new possibilities for her. Essex notes that sociologists would describe these women's lives as marked by hardship, menial jobs, and poverty. She argues that what they fail to see in the lives of her great-grandmothers, her grandmothers, her aunts and cousins are strength, beauty, and the power of making "a way out of no way." She focuses on the story of her mother, Archie Mae Simmons Essex. She died one year and one month after her husband, twenty-eight days after Barbara Essex's graduation from seminary and six days before Barbara's thirty-fourth birthday. This is a story of movement—physical, emotional, and spiritual. It is a story of transformation, as Essex's mother moved from the country to the city and again to the country and to the city; from shy little girl to sometimes awkward teenager to complex adult to mature and confident woman; from wife and mother to woman of substance and power.

In chapter 14, "Paul and the African American Community," New Testament scholar C. Michelle Venable-Ridley explores the elements of the Pauline texts and biography that have proved and continue to prove troublesome for many African Americans. Venable-Ridley proposes a perspective "detached from the assumptions and interpretations of slavocracy" to do so. Her project is straightforward. First, she joins other New Testament scholars who struggle to correct the distortions of the New Testament text. Second, she attempts to reclaim the writings of Paul as a religious source for the African American community. Finally, she reintroduces the religious legacy, theology, call, mission, eschatological hope, and vision of Paul. Her chapter ends with an exploration of the tradition of Black spirituals as a tangible source of an eschatological theology that can be a liberating yoking of Paul with the African American community.

In chapter 15, Kelly Brown Douglas explores some sociopolitical and religiopolitical issues that surround African American sexuality in her essay, "Daring to Speak." Douglas explores the hesitancy she sees in the value of most womanist theologians to address issues of sexuality in a straightforward way. Her aim is to broaden the theological discourse of womanist theology to address the profound heterosexism and homophobia in the Black Church and the African American community. For Douglas, womanist theology must address the connections between White racism and Black sexuality to explore the ways in which power and privilege are magnified when placed within a patriarchal, racist, classist, and heterosexist synthesis. Such an analysis is informed by Black faith in a God who is with us in the struggle for wholeness. This God is empowering and liberating and calls each of us to transformation and wholeness. This call, in part, requires that womanist theology and theologians engage in comprehensive and candid sexual discourse.

Toinette M. Eugene's essay, " 'How Can We Forget?' " addresses the ethical and theological problems connected to responding to HIV/AIDS in relation to the Black family. In chapter 16, she takes a pointed look at the role of African American women in this issue. She concludes by exploring a womanist praxis that will provide a model for the Roman Catholic Church ministry to Black families living, surviving, and dying because of the onslaught of HIV/AIDS. Eugene's powerful contextualization of the problem is set in the poetry of Imani Harrington, a Black woman who is HIV positive.

Harrington's poem "Aid of AMERICA" weaves in and out of Eugene's analysis and insights as she calls the Roman Catholic Church to remember its historic role in ministering to those whom others have pushed out. For Eugene, the role of the church is to stand with and be in ministry with those who die of, suffer with, or live with HIV/AIDS—in love, through justice, and with the care of God.

The final chapter, by sociologist Cheryl Townsend Gilkes, is a transformatory reading of hope. Gilkes explores Alice Walker's novel *The Color Purple* as a subversive and critical ethnography. For Gilkes, Walker's work is not "anthropologically correct" but does reveal the webs of significance concerning race and class in the rural South of the earlier part of the twentieth century. Gilkes looks at *The Color Purple* as a sociologist to recover the details of everyday existence to understand our humanity more fully. She argues that the subversive dimensions of Walker's ethnography can free us to liberate and transform our communities and our very lives. We are, as Gilkes so rightly points out, "products of our history, but our spiritual journeys also make us shapers of history."

This anthology offers no final solutions. Rather, it is an attempt to expand the current discussions within the academy and the church as each seeks to understand and offer solutions to the thorny issues of our day. The attempt in this volume is to provide methodological musings and praxeological constructs that are centered on justice and on a richer vision for our lives together.

PART I

SERIOUS

1

Looking to Your Tomorrows Today

North Carolina Central University,
December 16, 1994

Mary M. Townes

I am pleased to have this opportunity to speak to the graduates of North Carolina Central University's first Fall Commencement Exercise. One of my first thoughts when Dr. Marvin Duncan asked me to consider this assignment, and to allow him to recommend me to the Commencement Planning Committee and, with that group's concurrence, to make the recommendation to Chancellor Chambers, was that no one would want or expect a full-blown Commencement speech at noontime. Then I read in the November 25 issue of the *News and Observer* that some seniors were concerned that this program would not be as full of pomp and circumstance as the annual May Commencement, because it would be much smaller. This was my cue that today's honorees would be disappointed with anything less than a full-blown Commencement address. So, in spite of the hour, I do not plan to disappoint our honorees. Hope you will not be sorry! I intend to give a full Commencement speech in spite of the fact that, to paraphrase a line of Abraham Lincoln's Gettysburg Address, you will little note nor long remember what I say here.

When I sat in the B. N. Duke Auditorium forty-five years ago at the Commencement Exercise for the Class of 1949, the graduating group was about the same size as this one. We were graduates of the quarter system. This institution was North Carolina College at Durham. Tuition was $75.00 a year for residents of North Carolina. Room and board was $27.50 a month, and most of us had a very hard time paying it. The Alexander-Dunn Building was the cafeteria, and service was family style. B. N. Duke Auditorium had an organ, but it was not the present Moeller Organ that currently is insured for $350,000. The whole student population of about five hundred was a fairly closely knit group of persons who tried to help one another. If

3

you did not dress right, they would let you know it—those were not the days when it was fashionable to mix polka dots, plaids, and stripes. Those who did not know this were politely informed. And for the first two of my undergraduate years, Dr. Shepard, the president and founder, ruled with an iron fist that was not in a velvet glove. There was no due process. If the decision was made to suspend or to expel a student, Dr. Shepard or Dean Rush gave you a one-way bus ticket, and informed the student that "there were no specific charges." There were no security officers when I was an undergraduate—no campus police. We had one night watchman. Lights in all rooms were to be turned off at 11:00 P.M. Mr. Jeff, the night watchman, reported all rooms that were lighted after 11:00 P.M. We were fined one dollar for each violation. How did we study after 11:00 P.M.? We used the hallways and the bathrooms.

My, my. How times have changed.

In those days, Nat King Cole was one of our heroes in the entertainment world. His song "Straighten Up and Fly Right" was one we used often to admonish those we thought were not doing right. Now you have Whitney Houston, among others. The lyrics of one of Ms. Houston's hit songs, "One Moment in Time," read as follows:

I want one moment in time
When I'm more than I thought I could be,
When all my dreams are a heartbeat away,
And the answers are all up to me.

"And the answers are all up to me." And the answers are up to each of you! I am here to say to the graduating class that you must desire, expect, and hope for the very best for yourselves.

If you expect nothing, if you desire nothing, if you hope for nothing, you will get nothing! Oswald McCall wrote the following words many years ago:

Remember that while you are seeking, you are also being sought. You will not be lost, you will not miss the gate. You will be found. You will be led. You will enter in. Look for that. Expect it. Expect shells to break in their season. Expect boats to ride as the tide comes in.

This is hope, to desire and to expect. To desire but not to expect is not hope, for though you may desire the moon, you hardly hope for it. To expect but not to desire is not hope, for who that expects his or her loved one to die could be said to hope for it?

But to *desire*, and to *expect* the desire's fulfillment, that is *hope*.

And we are saved by hope.

When hope is in the heart, it is as prophetic as the song of a young stream on the mountains. It is set for far destinies.

I am here to say to this graduating class: If you are going to be more than you think you could be, you will have to *stand tall*, to *smile tall*, to *live tall*, and to *think tall*. In the physical side of your life, you must *stand tall*; in the social side of your life, you must *smile tall*; in the spiritual side of your life, you must *live tall*; in the mental side of your life, you must *think tall*. You owe it to yourself, to your parents, and to others who have supported and encouraged you to *stand tall*, to *smile tall*, to *live tall*, and to *think tall*.

What do I mean by *standing tall*? In this physical aspect of your life, your parents and guardians have provided for your physical development. No doubt they anxiously await the day you will be able to provide for yourself—things like food, housing, clothing, transportation, insurance, and taxes. When you do become self-supporting, remember that it would be nice to send your gratitude home in the form of a certified check.

Standing tall also means radiating self-confidence and high self-esteem. It means having pride in your person and your decorum or manner—the image you project. When you go out to seek a job, do not look as though you are begging. Put on your best clothes—do not go to a job interview in sneakers, jeans, chomping on chewing gum, britches hanging off your hips. You should hold your head up, look the interviewer in the eye, and tell him or her in your best English (not your dormitory English) what you have to offer. Tell the interviewer that you are willing to work hard and long, and that you are willing to learn the things you do not know how to do. Don't ever put the lowest price tag on the service you can offer. Employers know that they are not likely to get more than they are willing to pay for. People who make it a habit to give more than is asked or required are people who *stand tall*.

What does it mean to *smile tall*? It means you should always be as cheerful as possible. Nothing is more depressing than to run into a person who is a constant complainer. Things always are wrong with them—their toenails ache, their hair hurts, their ears pop all the time. When you meet these chronic complainers early in the morning, do not let them ruin your day! We have to remember that everybody has troubles and problems. Everybody has at least one cross to bear—and we are all lucky if we have just one cross.

Learn to carry your burdens like a mature person and to present your best front to your publics. Take yourself seriously, but do not be grim about it. Be serious but not tense, focused but not obsessive, confident but not cocky.

We know that our young people are not all going to hades in a basket. Your presence here today indicates that you are not. So we have to discredit, to some extent, what Socrates wrote in the fifth century B.C. These are his words:

> Our youth now lives in luxury. They have bad manners; contempt for authority; they show disrespect for their elders and love chatter in place of exercise. They no longer rise when others enter the room. They contradict their parents, chatter before company, gobble their food and tyrannize their teachers.

Do those words sound familiar?

Let us now consider *living tall*—the spiritual side of our lives. Acceptance has been called the first law of personal growth. Acceptance is seeing something the way it is and saying, "That's the way it is." John-Roger and Peter McWilliams have given the following description:

> Acceptance is not approval, consent, permission, authorization, sanction, concurrence, agreement, compliance, sympathy, endorsement, confirmation, support, ratification, assistance, advocating, backing, maintaining, authentication, reinforcing, cultivating, encouraging, furthering, promoting, aiding, abetting, or even *liking* what it is.[1]

Acceptance is saying, "It is what it is, and what is is what is." When you are in a state of nonacceptance, it is difficult to learn. Relax. Accept what has already taken place—whether done by you or something outside of you. Then look for the lesson. You might not enjoy everything that happens in life, but you can enjoy the fact that no matter what happens, there is a lesson in it. Look for the lesson!

There is a children's play that is accompanied by a group of choral readers. The play is based on the thirty-first chapter of Jeremiah. In this play, the children dance out the journey of struggle, survival, despair, and hope as they move toward the land of great mountains, a land fertile and holding great promise and opportunity for all. In their journey, the children move through periods of doubt and disbelief, periods of being lost and on unfamiliar ground. But the choral readers keep repeating the stories that remind them of who they are, of the power surrounding them, and of the reason they are on their journey. Finally, they catch a glimpse of the mountain, but before that mountain is a chasm.

The more they look at the chasm, the more anxious and fearful they become. They can see the danger *and* the promise before them, but they need a word of hope. The choral readers begin their song again, and they retell the story—the story that reminds them of their identity, purpose, and power. And suddenly, a child rises and positions herself in an act of faith and leaps into the air. As she leaps, she reaches forward to the land of promise and also extends a hand back to grasp the hand of a brother to take with her. He follows her example while holding onto her hand and reaches back to clasp the hand of a sister to take with him.

The stage explodes with a human chain leaping over the chasm to the land of promise. But the joy is shattered when the last person, preparing for the leap, puts down her baby in order to get a firmer grip on her before they move across the chasm. The momentum of the human chain reaches her before she is ready; her hand is grasped before she can grasp her child, and she is taken over the chasm. Her child is left, alone, on the other side, a chasm separating her from her mother, her people, her hope, her future.

The child wanders toward the edge of the chasm. The community, who no longer need the choral readers to tell them their story, call the child by name. The community tell her *their* story and her story. The community encourages her to leap.

You watch as the child gathers courage and confidence and is empowered by the community. She keeps her eyes on the great mountains and leaps into the air over the chasm and into the arms of the waiting community.

It is said that one night there was an old man sitting in the audience. And for him, this was no longer a play; it became real. He rushed to the stage, picked up the child, held her high in the air, and proclaimed with the voice of wisdom and vision—"Thank God almighty! Even our children know how to fly!"

That child flies right here in the midst of us.

You, the members of this graduating class, must be a part of that community of welcome and justice that defies the great abyss of despair and destruction and violence, that dares the chasm of hatred and inhumanity.

Finally, I dare you to *think tall*. In your individual minds, please answer these questions for me: What happens to some people that causes them to declare themselves *done* when they receive a bachelor's degree? What is it about renting or buying a cap and gown and getting a diploma that makes some of us think our learning days are over?

It is not that there is nothing left to learn. Far from it. "Commencement does not just mean graduation; it means a new beginning. Commencement is a time to make a commitment to life long learning."[2]

Education has been described as the ability to listen to almost anything without losing your temper or your self-confidence. The Earl of Chesterfield said, "Wear your learning like your watch, in a private pocket: and do not pull it out and strike it, merely to show you have one."[3]

What will you do with your degree? Will you grow in wisdom and in understanding? Will you be a good citizen, informed about the world with its variety of government, but loyal to America? Will you have a special ability of understanding and caring for people, any people, all people? Will you strive to reach higher levels of maturity? Maturity is a necessary part of excellence and success. It is stick-to-it-iveness, the ability to stick to a job and to work on it and to struggle through until the job is done. It is endurance of difficulties, unpleasantness, discomfort, frustration, and hardship. The ability to size things up, to make one's own decisions, is a characteristic of maturity. The mature person is not dependent unless ill. The mature person shows tolerance and can adapt to different situations and can compromise, unlike Newt Gingrich. But we must hope that Newt will learn.

Like the children I described in the play based on Jeremiah, you must reach back and help others to rise. There is a rising cry that the mission of institutions like ours is redundant, that we should not have a future. This institution will have to be the very best it can be if it is to survive into the twenty-first century and give others a chance to strive to reach the "promised land." To this end, it is very important that all of us support NCCU with our financial resources. Don't worry about whether or not your donation is too small. All donations will be welcomed!

Thinking tall demands that you continue to resist the old racist belief that African Americans are genetically and intellectually inferior to White Americans. A recently published book entitled *The Bell Curve* and subtitled *Intelligence and Class Structure in American Life* is getting a lot of attention and providing fodder for the conservatism that has swept this land.[4] *The Bell Curve* is an 845-page book that costs thirty dollars plus tax. It presents arguments based on such shaky premises as (1) intelligence can be depicted by a single number, the IQ score, (2) this single number can be used to rank people in linear order, and (3) the score is genetically based and can't be changed. The book's authors, Charles Murray and the late Richard Herrnstein, claim that race and class differences are largely caused by genetic factors and are therefore essentially not capable of or susceptible to change. In other words, they are immutable.

The Bell Curve contains no new arguments and presents no compelling evidence for its claims. It has gained attention at this time because it reflects the ungenerous and depressing temper of the times. It supports the idea that it is OK to slash selected social programs such as Head Start, because the beneficiaries, mainly African Americans, can't be helped due to inborn limitations expressed by low IQ scores. We have always had to run faster, kick harder, jump higher, think better, hang tougher, live livelier, hate slower. And we cannot stop now! I agree with William Raspberry's assessment that *The Bell Curve* confuses brains with social advantage.[5]

Finally, "Only the curious will learn and only the resolute overcome the obstacles to learning. The quest quotient is much more exciting than the intelligence quotient!"[6]

Merry Christmas, Happy New Year, and God bless you.

Thank you.

Notes

1. John-Roger and Peter McWilliams, *Life 101: Everything We Wish We Had Learned about Life in School—but Didn't* (Los Angeles: Prelude Press, 1990), 105.

2. Ibid., 13.

3. Quoted in ibid., 12.

4. Charles Murray and Richard J. Herrnstein, *The Bell Curve: Intelligence and Class Structure in American Life* (New York: Free Press, 1994).

5. William Raspberry, "Is IQ Really Everything?" *Washington Post* A, 23 October 12, 1994. Raspberry criticizes the authors, charging that the book is a "stink bomb." Raspberry notes that Murray and Herrnstein use largely discredited views regarding heritability, measurability, and immutability of intelligence. Ultimately, they may be confusing brains with social advantage.

6. Ibid.

2

My Hope Is in the Lord

Transformation and Salvation
in the African American Community

Diana L. Hayes

The Lord is my light and my salvation
The Lord is my light and my salvation
The Lord is my light and my salvation
Whom shall I fear?

Psalm 27

Introduction

The many cataclysmic upheavals which have taken place in our nation and around the world in the last few years have led many to look with ever-growing trepidation toward the *eschaton*, the End-time. As we approach the Third Millennium, many envision the signs of God's judgment appearing all around us, the footprints of the Horsemen of the Apocalypse embedded in the dust, dirt, and mire of our seemingly rapidly deteriorating society.

The cataclysms that have taken place—the Los Angeles uprising, quickly followed by earthquakes, mudslides, floods, forest fires, bombings of innocent people, rampant violence in our cities and suburbs—have been called both acts of a humanity which has named itself divine and acts of an angry God using nature as the instrument of divine punishment to smite all, calling to mind the ancient story of the Tower of Babel (Genesis 11:1-9).

Commentators world-wide have debated these issues, and self-proclaimed prophets have arisen to spread the good and/or bad news of the approaching end of the world far and wide. We have witnessed the fall of the U.S.S.R., the horrors continuing in the former Yugoslavia, the peaceful reunification of Germany accompanied by a violent emergence of neo-Nazism, hope for peace in the Middle East rising and falling, the long-prayed-for overthrow of apartheid in South Africa and the return of President Aristide, accompanied, hopefully, by a final peace, to Haiti.

Yet throughout, one critical voice has not been heard to speak clearly or forcefully in any organized or united way: the voice of institutional religions. Where are the voices of the Catholic bishops of Haiti decrying the murders openly taking place in their streets? Where are the voices of the Christian and Muslim spiritual leaders of Bosnia and Serbia, of Israel's rabbis and the Islamic nations, calling for what they all proclaim as doctrine: peace, justice, and love of neighbor? In the echoing silence, the questions must be asked: What reason do we have to hope in today's chaotic world? What is and should be the role of the Christian churches and all faiths in attempting to heal the wounds—mental, physical, and spiritual—with which our cities and our world have been and are being inflicted on a seemingly daily basis? What hope is there in attempting to rebuild our cities and, more importantly, our souls so that at least those events in which humanity can be said to have played an instrumental role will not happen again?

Or has religion in all of its manifestations become so superfluous in our world today that its leaders, for fear of becoming entangled in the sticky, bureaucratic web of politics and secular affairs, must remain forever silent, relegated to the sidelines, thereby revealing its impotence for all to see? Or do they themselves become merely political tools of exploitation and oppression, forcing a religiosity on peoples unwilling and uninterested?

After much reflection, my response is still one of hope. Today and always, religion or, more explicitly, people of faith have not only a critical role to play in rebuilding the lives and spirits of the people of Los Angeles, Oklahoma City, Sarajevo, Jerusalem, Port-au-Prince, and wherever else chaos appears to have the upper hand; they have, more importantly, a responsibility to help influence the future of this nation and our world, global village that it has become, guiding our tortured and seemingly increasingly devastated homelands on the human journey toward truly becoming the City of God—a world where all people, regardless of race, class, gender, or faith can live in peace and solidarity with one another and we will study war no more.

This is my hope, grounded in my faith as a Catholic Christian and emerging from my ongoing struggle as an African American woman in a society and a Church which too often reflect the ills of that society. Through it all, I and many like me have been sustained and nurtured by a "wonder-working" God who empowers her people to do her will if they but have the courage to step out on faith.

There are many questions which can and must be raised on this issue, few, if any, of which can be fully answered here, but all of which we need to begin not only exploring but also acting on in order to shape the critical conversations which need to take place. However, I would like to use the City of Los Angeles and the "riot/rebellion" that took place there, as well as my own perspective as an African American Catholic womanist theologian, as the context for this essay and to raise critical questions: What can we, as a people of God and an increasingly diverse and pluralistic nation, learn from the events that have taken place in Los Angeles in the past few years? Is there any reason to hope for a transformation of our lives and world as a result?

Los Angeles, a city still recovering from the shocks of the 1992 disturbances, has subsequently been hit by repeated blows: devastating fires, a massive earthquake, and torrential rains, followed by mudslides which have swept away what was not already destroyed by the other events. Acts of God? Acts of nature? Acts of humankind? Is there fault to be laid at any particular doorstep, and, even if there is, does doing so help to heal or simply further destroy the spirit of this city and its people and thus the spirit of us all? Is L.A. a microcosm of the United States, increasingly divided by freeways on which the "haves" sweep blindly past the rotting and stagnant ghettos and barrios of the "have-nots" to their immaculate homes with all of the latest gadgets and toys? Were the events that took place after the Rodney King verdict a portent of things to come, as people of color—Asian, Latino, Native American, and Black—find themselves still unable to possess the so-called American Dream, which is increasingly beginning to look like a nightmare? What has happened to the promised "liberty and justice for all"? In our human attempts to become more like gods, intent upon our own private freedoms regardless of their impact upon others, have we, at the same time, unleashed forces of almost satanic evil?

Has humanity today gone beyond the mandate given it by God, misinterpreting God's grant of dominion over nature to subdue and control it for the benefit of all to mean a willful destruction of our mother earth, a willful refusal to accept that there may be limits upon where and what we can build, construct, pave over, and dig out, so that we are now truly reaping the bitter fruits of what we have sown in a nature seemingly gone wild and destructive, a wounded beast crying and lashing out mindlessly in its death throes, a death agony which, if it continues, will negatively affect us all, not just those unfortunate and invisible "others" out there?

Is it not long past time for us to be reminded of God's mandate "to walk justly and righteously in God's sight"; to remember that we are and always have been our brother's and sister's keeper; that we do have a responsibility to this once fruitful land of ours not only to give it time to heal from the ravages we have inflicted upon it, so that we and our children will be able to breathe freely in green places, to drink deeply of clean, clear, unpolluted water, but also to be mindful of those who are not here with us and their right to eat freely without the fear of having to fight each other for the last crumbs on the table that have been left for them?

Speaking as a Christian, is it not the responsibility of the Church to call us, the People of God who are, in its fullest understanding, the Church, to account; to call us back to a responsibility to love God *and neighbor,* the earth which sustains us as well as ourselves? John Paul II has consistently affirmed in his writings that human beings are made from love and for love. We were created by God's love in order to love each other and all of creation—a love which carries with it the responsibility to nurture and maintain rather than destroy. Love is an emotion which has been eroded in the twentieth century by anger, greed, envy, jealousy, spite, hatred, prejudice, and a narrow-minded parochialism which has destroyed our psyches and is well on its way to destroying our very souls. What cause is there for hope?

The Challenge of Hope

St. Augustine wrote centuries ago: "*Hope* has two beautiful daughters, *anger and courage*; anger at the way things are, and courage to work to make things other than they are."[1]

James Baldwin also wrote about hope arising from his own experiences as a gay Black man attempting to survive in a racist, homophobic society:

> Here we are, at the center of the arc, trapped in the gaudiest, most valuable, and most improbable wheel the world has ever seen. Everything now, we must assume, is in our hands; we have no right to assume otherwise. If we—and now I mean the relatively conscious whites and the relatively conscious blacks, who must, like lovers, insist on, or create the consciousness of the others—do not falter in our duty now, we may be able, handful that we are, to end the racial nightmare, and achieve our country, and change the history of the world. If we do not now dare everything, the fulfillment of that prophecy, recreated from the Bible in song by a slave, is upon us: God gave Noah the rainbow sign. No more water, the fire next time.[2]

The imagery of fire is an important one. Jesus said: I came to bring fire on this earth! Will that fire be cleansing and healing, or will it be destructive? Which choice will we make? Do we have the courage to release the fire of hope, which despite its anger, or precisely because of it, will lay the path for a fruitful and common journey for us all, or will we, by our denial, our apathy, our fears, enable the fires of destruction to sweep across this land leaving a scorched and bitter earth in its path?

Both Augustine and Baldwin, perhaps unwittingly, were invoking the wisdom and experience of African American women who not only understand but live that understanding of hope on a daily basis. African American women, as the bearers of many burdens, have also been, most importantly, the bearers of culture. It is as the givers of life and the teachers of the future that they have suckled their children with the passionate anger and courage which sustained the hope that always dwelled within them, despite and through it all.

Fannie Lou Hamer, the backbone, like most Black women, of her church, community and the Civil Rights Movement, was heard often to proclaim, "I am sick and tired of being sick and tired!" This did not stop her, however, from continuing in her efforts to educate and uplift her people. She was one of a long line of strong Black women who lived what it means to be womanist—to be bold, daring, audacious, and outrageous—and she lived it proudly. It is these women who have nurtured and sustained the Black community through all of its ups and downs over the past four hundred years.

Baldwin speaks of choices, and African American women, in community with their men (whether fathers, husbands, brothers, or sons) and their sisters (whether mothers, daughters, lovers, or friends), have consistently chosen the path toward a better future, if not for themselves, then for those coming after them. These choices must still be made today, but for many, the context in which they are made is being or has changed. To address these choices, we must look at the reality of the United States today, one which seriously challenges the hope that, as Christians, should always be a part of us. Yet, in challenge there is also the hope for transformation, for *metanoia*.

Whose Culture?

Following the Los Angeles uprising, Cornel West stated:

What happened in Los Angeles this past April was neither a race riot nor a class rebellion. Rather this monumental upheaval was a multiracial, trans-class, and largely male display of justified social rage. For all its ugly, xenophobic resentment, its air of adolescent carnival, and its downright barbaric behavior, it signified the sense of powerlessness in American society . . . What we witnessed in Los Angeles was the consequence of a lethal linkage of economic decline, cultural decay, and political lethargy in American life. Race was the visible catalyst, not the underlying cause.[3]

We in the United States have allowed ourselves to believe that all criticisms of our way of life, all questioning of our successes and failures, all dissent and violence can be laid at the door of race, particularly the clashing of Blacks and Whites. It is a trap we have fallen into which enables us to ignore or overlook issues of class and gender that are also tearing at the fabric of our society. At the same time, we refuse to engage in any intelligent or reasonable discourse on the issue of race at all, feeling that all that can be said and done has been.

The result, as West and others have noted, is that Blacks have become the "problem" people who are never satisfied no matter what is "done" for them. Little attention is given to the humanity behind this "problem," even less to innovative ways of seeking to resolve the "problem" by going beyond it to see the harsh reality of a people trapped by stereotype and false consciousness. The result of our lack of vision and unwillingness to look beyond the facade to the reality is that our inner cities have become filled with ghosts—the ghosts of a people from whom much that personifies a human being, in its fullest and deepest sense, has been taken.

It is the Black woman who

> survived the long middle passage from Africa to America, bringing with her many of the diverse characteristics of her African mothers . . . She gave her children love [and so today must we]; cooked for them (as we must); protected them, told them about life, about freedom, about survival, about loving, about pain, about joy and about Africa.[4]

And so must we continue to do so, for the children have lost touch with their past and are left searching, unguided and alone, for their futures:

> Our communities have become only "neighborhoods." The value images are gone. The teachers are gone. The counter-balancing forces are ineffective—there are no "elders," no priests, and so our children are suffering. They become enraged through disappointment at finding that what they have come from the spirit world to possess no longer exists. They turn on their parents, who have already abandoned them, and then they turn on themselves. Children of "hustlers" become "hustlers," and we are locked into despair.[5]

We are a spiritual people living in a profane society, and we are in danger of losing, if we have not already done so, that spirituality which has consistently enabled us, with the help of Jesus the Christ, to "make a way out of no way." We have become like "ghosts," depersonalized and depersonalizing in constant search of "respect" and willing to kill or be killed for it. Yet our children, ghosts who have no memory of a childhood, have no idea of what respect truly means or how it can be honestly earned.

As Black women, we must reassert that spirituality and thereby regain the respect we once had for all our people, especially for the elders. We must do this not just for ourselves, not just for our Black men, but for the sake of our children whose tears and cries call us out of ourselves to recreate that community of love we once had. As, historically, we have been the ones who were able to keep our families together and pass down the faith—a faith that was religious in more ways than are usually understood in our individualistic and consumer-oriented society, a faith which encompassed all of life, making all of life sacred and therefore to be cherished—today we must rekindle that faith, blowing on the sparks that still linger deep within us, fanning them into a flame which will consume the world, not with bloodshed, not with wrath, but with love—a love that surpasses all other forms of love; an agape love.[6]

The ghosts that exist, because their experiences cannot truly be called living, haunt our streets and our minds, flashing into focus for a few minutes in lurid newspaper headlines or bloody scenes on the evening news but quickly fading back into obscurity—leaving ghostly images of anger, seemingly mindless hatred and violence, a humanity gone wild—if it is even seen as human at all.

The Shadow of Race

This nation's historic obsession with race has led to the denial of race to the dominant group, White Americans, and the disappearance or scapegoating of other races that exist in this pluralistic nation upon which we pride ourselves. Only minorities—people of color—are seen in terms of race, and then only in terms of how they do or do not fit into the Black-White polarization which the dominant group has established. Thus, Latinos, who are increasingly moving into areas inhabited formerly or still by Blacks, are set up not as persons with whom Blacks share any commonalities—whether of oppression based on race and/or skin color, of poverty, of "foreign" (non-European) cultures, of colonization, of forced assimilation, or of denial of humanity—but as competitors fighting over the same small piece of the American Dream pie while the largest cut is left for others.

The L.A. riots took place in South Central L.A., nearly one-half of which is now Latino. Of those involved who were arrested, only 36 percent were Black; the majority were Latino, with a number of Asians and Whites thrown in for good measure. Yet the media persisted in depicting the disturbances as Blacks versus Whites, ignoring the fact that others were involved and that the businesses damaged or destroyed were not only White but also Black, Latino, and most importantly, Asian (Korean specifically). This is said not to get Blacks "off the hook" in any way but to expose today's racially driven reality.

Asians are seen as the "model" minority in our midst (a label they themselves neither have sought nor accept), in that after immigration, few go on welfare, few seek federal aid or assistance, and few, once they learn English, require special education classes or affirmative action programs. In fact, today Asians and Asian Americans are such a majority, especially in the California University system, that negative quotas have risen their ugly heads again.

Reality: The majority of businesses destroyed were in Koreatown. The memory of media shots depicting armed Koreans patrolling the roofs of their stores, guarding them against looting Blacks and Latinos, is still with us, but little or nothing was said about why they were forced into this situation or that Blacks and Latinos were often patrolling (off camera, of course) with them. Once again, a false duality has been set up, with Blacks as the problem and others, even their fellow people of color, allegedly finding it difficult, if not impossible, to work with them in any reasonable way.

Elaine Kim, an American of Korean ancestry, speaks painfully of the shock and anguish she felt during those days in 1992: "As someone whose social consciousness was shaped by the African American–led civil rights movement of the 1960's, I felt that I was watching our collective dreams for a just society disintegrating, cast aside as naive and irrelevant in the embattled 1990's." She continues:

> It was the courageous African American women and men of the 1960's who had redefined the meaning of "American," who had first suggested that a person like me could reject the false choice between being treated as a perpetual foreigner in my own birth place, on the one hand, and relinquishing my identity for someone else's ill-fitting and impossible Anglo American one on the other. Thanks to them, I began to discern how institutional racism works and why Korea was never mentioned in my world history text books. I was able to see how others besides Koreans had been swept aside by the dominant culture. My American education offered nothing about Chicanos and Latinos, and most of what I was taught about African and Native Americans was distorted to justify their oppression and vindicate their oppressors.[7]

Thus, Kim was horrified to hear and see Blacks and Latinos attacking Korean American merchants while other Asian Americans were disassociating themselves from Korean Americans. Then she began to realize what was happening, namely, the scapegoating of Korean Americans. Rather than being recognized as a people in their own right, they were merely an instrument, a weapon, if you will, in the ongoing, divisive Black-White struggle. Their identity and being were not what they deemed themselves to be but what others manipulated them into being.

Coming to a country, Kim notes, "where they believed their human rights would be protected by law," Koreans raised on American television were unprepared "for the black, brown, red and yellow America they encountered":

> They hadn't heard that there is no equal justice in the U.S. They had to learn (as all immigrants to this nation learn) about American racial hierarchies. They did not realize that, as immigrants of color, they

would never attain political voice or visibility but would instead be used to uphold the inequality and the racial hierarchy they had no part in creating.[8]

These lessons, if not understood before, were learned with a vengeance on April 29-30, 1992. Korean Americans had, Kim believes, "a baptism into what it really means for a Korean to 'become American' in the 1990's." This is her account:

When the Korean Americans in South Central and Koreatown dialed 911, nothing happened. When their stores and homes were being looted and burned to the ground, they were left completely alone for three horrifying days. How betrayed they must have felt by what they had believed was a democratic system that protects its people from violence. Those who trusted the government to protect them lost everything; those who took up arms after waiting for help for two days were able to defend themselves. It was as simple as that. What they had to learn was that, as in South Korea, protection in the U.S. is by and large for the rich and powerful. If there were a choice between Westwood and Koreatown, it is clear that Koreatown would have to be sacrificed.[9]

The lesson Korean Americans learned was a harsh one, but it was one learned long before them by their Black, brown, and red fellow Americans, and by American women of all races and ethnicities. In the greater stream of things, they simply did not count. It is a lesson which sears one's soul and calls into question the beliefs and dreams of peoples whose major crime is that they are "people of color" or women, and that, for the most part, they are poor.

Whose Faith/Whose Violence?

This rude awakening to the limitations placed on one because of class, gender, and race is a psychological assault on the human ego, which may survive it but only with significant damage done, as Langston Hughes realized:

What happens to a dream deferred?
Does it dry up
like a raisin in the sun?
Or fester like a sore—
And then run?
Does it stink like rotten meat?
Or crust and sugar over—
like a syrupy sweet?

Maybe it just sags
like a heavy load.

Or does it explode?[10]

Our nation and our world are becoming increasingly violent. The hopes and dreams of many have had to be deferred over and over again while a few seem to reap unjustly the rewards of others' hard work. Many see this rising violence as evidence of the action of God, as a sign of Armageddon, the coming of the end of the world. Others, however, see more human reasons behind it.

Robert McAfee Brown presents an interesting definition of both religion and violence that can be fruitful for ongoing dialogue and eventual action.[11] He first looks at two negative definitions of religion—one equates religion with metaphysics and leads to a dualistic approach to life and the secularization of religion, while the other concentrates on the "inward" God and leads away from God's involvement "in the social dimension of human life," thereby privatizing God and making religion into an individual, personal encounter and dialogue with God and a turning away from neighbor and society. How we see God, therefore, shapes our actions and interactions with others.

Brown provides a fuller understanding of religion as "the notion of a binding constraint from which we cannot escape, and to which we feel deeply committed."[12] Recognizing that this is in keeping with Paul Tillich's notion of "ultimate concern," he sees as the important emphasis the fact that "God, if he is truly God, must be found in the midst of everyday life."[13] Thus, the two great commandments set forth by Jesus to which all of humanity must adhere are "You shall love the Lord your God with all your heart, mind, soul, and strength" and "You shall love your neighbor as yourself." For how can you claim to love God whom you have not seen yet hate and despise your neighbor whom you see regularly? Fannie Lou Hamer put it succinctly: "There is no way I can hate someone and expect to see God."

These variant negative understandings of religion are old yet increasingly prevalent in the United States. The Great Commandment is even older, yet it is increasingly absent from societal debate. How many of us truly live out this mandate in our daily lives but instead find ourselves slipping and sliding into a relationship with God that allegedly nurtures us but does not, at the same time, prod us into taking a stand for others, especially those who are truly "other" because they are so unlike us—whether because of race, gender, class, ethnicity, or other factors that have no bearing on their actual humanity or God-createdness?

Stephen Carter voiced in *The Culture of Disbelief* what few are willing to acknowledge: "In our sensible zeal to keep religion from dominating our politics, we have created a political and legal culture that presses the religiously faithful to be other than themselves, to act publicly, and sometimes privately as well, as though their faith does not matter to them."[14] Today, the common belief seems too often to be that "rational, public-spirited people"[15] cannot take religion seriously. Engaging in discussions about one's "ultimate concern" is seen as undignified, if not downright embarrassing—best left to those with little education or ability to engage in serious public debate about issues that matter. Religious beliefs are seen as "arbitrary and unimportant," and quite often, it is those with religious beliefs who are the most hesitant about bringing them out into the glaring light of the public square. The result is that, for many, religious belief is seen as a somewhat amusing hobby to be dabbled in privately but certainly not something to be brought out into the light of day, at the risk of public exposure:

> We are one of the most religious nations on earth, in the sense that we have a deeply religious citizenry; but we are also perhaps the most zealous in guarding our public institutions against explicit religious influences. One result is that we often ask our citizens to split their public and private selves, telling them in effect that it is fine to be religious in private, but there is something askew when their private beliefs become the basis for public action.[16]

Yet should it not be the other way around? If we are to be whole human beings, how can we split off what is supposed to be an essential part of our being and relegate it to scheduled times and places while forcing it to lie low when we go about our daily lives? Is not this dichotomy part of the reason for the decline of values in our nation, for the seeming inability of our children to make conscientious decisions about right and wrong in their lives, and for the growing divisiveness in our nation—both in the halls of Congress and in the streets—released in outbursts of rudeness, lack of charity, selfishness, egotism, lack of humility, aggression, and violence on all sides—in short, for the lack of hope in too many people's lives? If we *are* religious, should that not be expressed in our lives in all ways?

One way to start is by clarifying what is meant by the word *violence*. Most think of violence in terms of an overt physical act of destruction—hitting, beating, stabbing, raping, shooting, and so on. But does this definition go far enough? No, it does not. Violence is a violation: "Whatever 'violates' another in the sense of infringing upon or disregarding or abusing or denying that other, whether physical harm is involved or not, can be understood as an act of violence. The basic overall definition of violence would then become *violation of personhood*,"[17] an attack on the very being of a person created, as all are, in the image and likeness of God. Violence is an assault on human dignity in whatever form it takes. This fuller definition forces us to recognize that "each person has unique worth," so much so that any "act that depersonalizes would be an act of violence since . . . it transforms a person into a thing."[18]

This "thingification" or "objectification" of a people is what both Cornel West and Elaine Kim were protesting. It is what makes ghosts of living, breathing children who have had no childhood. Depersonalizing a person—making him or her a thing unworthy of notice or consideration—can destroy in more critical ways than simply sticks or stones battering flesh can. The children's rhyme that most of us learned was wrong—names do hurt, because they steal our identities as human beings and make us things that can be manipulated according to the whims and wishes of the namer—it is a theft of one's very soul.

It is this form of violence which is too often overlooked, ignored, or belittled, because usually the dominant group is the one wielding its negative power. It is only when the "things" rise up in anger and frustration, or "act out" in other ways, that we speak of violence.

Dom Helder Camara of Brazil speaks of violence in terms of a spiral forcing us to see the growth or development that takes place over time in human society. He asserts that the basic form of violence is *injustice*—the hidden or covert violence which is the "subtle, institutionalized destruction of human possibilities that is around us all the time, but is often not apparent to those who are comfortably situated."[19] When injustice becomes too oppressive, it bursts forth as *revolt* directed "against the status quo, against those who feel that they have been denied power and justice and personhood."[20] This is the second level, the "multi-racial, trans-class, and largely male display of justified social rage" that Cornel West was referring to. The third level of violence arises in reaction to revolt; this is *repression* or, as it is often spoken of in the United States, law and order. For when "confronted with revolt, those who hold power put down the revolt by whatever repressive means are necessary to ensure that their power is not threatened."[21] While token concessions may be made, they are given only to defuse the situation and make those revolting feel that they have been successful in their revolt. Again, we can look at L.A., in 1992 and 1965, at the aftermath of the long, hot summers in which much was promised and little resulted, and within the Roman Catholic Church, at the struggle of people of color and of women to have their voices heard and their presence recognized and utilized in meaningful ways, as examples of this "spiralling" of violence. In some instances, physical acts did take place, in others none, but the violence in all three forms was and still is alive and present and damaging to both body and soul.

Revolution in Our Midst

Today, we are reaping the sad harvest of seeds sown long before us—seeds of injustice and repression which have led to increasing spirals of violence in our midst. And yet we often still do not understand—we still fail to interpret the "signs of the times" in such a way as to uncover the root causes of injustice and, thus, to help eliminate the spiral.

We are at a critical period today. There are choices, once again, to be made, toward an Apocalypse seemingly all too near and a nation increasingly divided along racial, ethnic, class, and gender lines, or toward a nation pluralistic in more than name alone, one which is the multicultural beacon of hope we have always claimed it to be. The choice should be easy, but because of our dis-ease with dealing religiously with political issues and our seeming inability to live up to Christ's mandate of love, we have made the choice much more difficult for ourselves and the generations that follow us.

This is our calling as Christian people today: to be the heroes and sheroes of our children, of whatever race, class, or gender they may be, to be the bearers of hope and the instillers of a faith that can move mountains in our young who see a world that has turned away from them in search of the false glitter of gold and glamour and fame and that urges them to engage in the same fruitless, deadening chase. We are specifically called, as women, to be mothers, a generation of women who, in Bernice Johnson Reagon's understanding, come together as community to "nurture itself and future generations":

> [Mothers, biological or otherwise,] were the heads of their communities, the keepers of the tradition. The lives of these women were defined by their culture, the needs of their communities, and the people they served. Their lives are available to us today because they accepted the responsibility when the opportunity was offered—when they were chosen. There is the element of transformation in all of their work. Building communities within societies that enslaved Africans, they and their people had to exist in, at least, dual realities. These women, however, became central to evolving the structures for resolving areas of conflict and maintaining, sometimes creating, an identity that was independent of a society organized to exploit natural resources, people, and land.[22]

As we did in the past, we must once again do in the present, women "mothering" and men "fathering" our children, our people, and our communities into new life and passing on that knowledge to others in our world. For we are attached to one another whether we like it or not. Violence, in all of its manifestations, is still violent. One form is no more legitimate than another. We are now reaping the harvest in the physical violence of increasing crime, escalating gang wars, and turf battles, that we sowed in seeds of psychic violence for so many, many years.

Neither the violence in our city streets nor that in our local, state, and federal legislatures can be condoned. The "problem" is not African Americans or Latinos or any other "Other" from whom we wish to disassociate ourselves. The problem is all of us.

We tend to see only the *acts* of violence yet remain blind to the states of violence in which millions are unemployed, dying, and being dehumanized. The Ecumenical Commission on Society, Development, and Peace (SODEPAX) clearly spells out the ramifications of structural violence:

> Violence can have structural forms built into apparently peaceful operations of society as well as overt physical expressions. The failure to provide educational opportunity, or the manipulations of sources of information, can do violence to those affected. The existence in a society of intellectual repression in any form is psychological violence. The condescension and subtle forms of discrimination with which age sometimes treats youth or men treat women, or one race or religious group may treat another, are a part of it. We live in a society in which the drive for security, self-esteem or power, and the failure to share responsibility and decision-making often do violence to other persons . . . Violence is therefore a condition of which all of us are guilty in some degree.[23]

Whose Justice?

It is because of the injustices of our society that the spiral of violence initially gets launched, and until and unless we get at the roots of injustice, we will be dealing in only a superficial way with the problem of violence. As Dom Helder Camara put it, "The only true answer to violence is to have the *courage* to face the injustices which constitute" the first level of violence.

Cornel West is correct in asserting,

> We must begin not with the problem of black people but with the flaws of American society [of which, I must add, our churches are too often a reflection]—flaws rooted in historic inequalities and longstanding cultural stereotypes . . . As long as black [or any other] people are viewed as a "them," the burden falls on "them" to do all the "cultural" and "moral" work necessary for healthy race relations . . . [thus implying] that only certain Americans can define what it means to be American—and the rest must simply "fit in."[24]

A Return to Love

We are today living and dying in a world without love—love in the deepest sense of the word, not sexual or erotic love, not benign feelings for others, but *agape*—the soul-stirring, gut-wrenching, active force that is at the basis, the very foundation, of our faith. We must find, in the words of Martin Luther King Jr., the "strength to love" not just those who are like us but especially those who are unlike us. St. John writes: "If anyone says, 'I love God,' and hates his brother, he is a liar; for he who does not love his brother whom he has seen, cannot love God whom he has not seen. And this commandment we have from him, that he who loves God should love his brother also" (1 John 4:20-21).

We do not know how to love others or to be loved by others or to love ourselves. We are afraid of love, afraid of the commitments and responsibilities that love brings with it, all the extra baggage that entangles and entwines. It is so much easier to see love as simply a force of nature, a passion quickly satisfied in the sexual act and then discarded along with the other person involved.

This loss of love can be seen throughout our nation; it is witnessed in "the eclipse of hope and absence of love of self and others, the breakdown of family and neighborhood bonds, the cold, brutal and senselessly random killings that take place on the streets of our cities."[25] But we must renounce this loss and attempt a return. And what better source for learning how to love ourselves and others once again than our religious institutions? In legal terms, we talk about a person bringing a legal action against someone as having standing to sue; in other words, that person has an interest to defend and injuries which need redressing. We who are Christian people and our co-religionists of other faiths have the standing, legally and spiritually, today to take a stand on the side of God's justice and righteousness.

Our failure to love others as ourselves *and* ourselves as well has led to a spiritual impoverishment that threatens the very structure of our church and society. It is time for us to look behind the exclusive definitions of White or Black or Latino or Asian or Native American, beyond the labels of conservative, moderate, or liberal, beyond male and female, to a new perspective which brings us together across the barriers of nation, race, class, and gender. It is time to clothe the "naked public square," not by resorting to pressure tactics on others who are not of our faith, not by denouncing those who may or may not believe in God as they choose, but by "defending the faith that is ours" (1 Peter 1:5), by clothing ourselves not with self-righteousness but with the love of God—to stand as defenders of the poor and hungry, those in prisons and on the streets, those naked and ill, those used in our society.

We must live our lives, both publicly and privately, in the same subversive manner that Jesus Christ led his. For our God *is* a God who takes sides, the side of those most in need, to bring "the mighty from their thrones / and [exalt] those of low degree" (Luke 1:52-53), as Mary proclaims in her song. He is a God who "preached good news to the poor" and release to those in chains, whether physical ones or those of the mind and soul. To subvert means to turn reality upside down, to look at it in another light, to confound those who believe they are the only source of truth by presenting another, more far-reaching and earth-shattering truth. Sojourner Truth knew well the meaning of a subversive faith, noting that "If the first woman

God ever made was strong enough to turn the world upside down all alone; together women ought to be able to turn it rightside up again."[26]

As Christians, we must become "extremists in love," following in the footsteps of Jesus and the long line of saints and martyrs who followed after him; following also that long line of strong, proud, and loving Black women who were able to "run on for a long time." Only in so doing will we recapture the spirit of the early church, which was "not merely a thermometer that recorded the ideas and principles of popular opinion; it was a thermostat that transformed the mores of society."[27] For as Martin Luther King Jr. correctly noted, "wherever the early Christians entered a town the power structure got disturbed and immediately sought to convict them for being 'disturbers of the peace' and 'outside agitators.' " But they went on with the conviction that they were "a colony of heaven" and had to obey God rather than man. They were small in number but big in commitment. They were too God-intoxicated to be "astronomically intimidated."[28]

It is not only possible but necessary for us to go and do likewise, to become drunk on the word of God and set out to right the wrongs that have been inflicted upon so many in our nation and in our church for all of the wrong reasons. This is the stance taken by strong, courageous, angry, hope-filled African American men and women down through the ages, who allowed no one to tell them who they were capable of being or becoming.

As womanists, we must continue to be the "voices that speak when others fear to," recognizing with Audre Lorde that "we were never meant to survive."[29] As a people, as a nation within a nation, African Americans were never truly "meant to survive." But that has never stopped us before, and we cannot allow it to now. Black women's existence is "a continuum, an invisible thread drawn through the women's stories to women readers and the men who will listen. Through their alternative mothering practice, these (Black women) writers construct residual herstory as emergent culture."[30]

We are the weavers of our future's tapestry, one woven from the living, breathing souls of Black women, men, and children in every walk of life, of every shade of skin from deep blue-black to palest peach-blushed tan, a tapestry woven from our common origin—Africa:

It is our task to gather the scattered threads of our history, in this land and throughout the diaspora, joining with our sisters everywhere, and make it whole again, returning our past to ourselves and, thereby, regaining the way to our futures for ourselves and posterity.

We are the teachers, acknowledging that: "If you educate a man, you educate an individual. If you educate a woman, you educate a nation." This is not said to put down men but to raise up both women and men. It is time we climbed out of the dichotomous, dualistic trap in which we have been held for far too long to reclaim the understanding, which formerly never needed stating, that the enrichment of one does not require the impoverishment of another; the uplifting of one does not require the degradation of another; that in order to survive we must "walk together, children and not grow weary." We cannot live if half of our wholistic selves have to be sacrificed so that the other might prosper—that is not a true or healthy prosperity—that is suicide.

It is time for black women to reclaim their voices, voices somehow silenced in a "culture that depended on her heroism for its survival." That voice has been silenced because women lacked the power, as the "disinherited," to recognize and claim their own power. Thus, the power of naming was left "in the hands of men—mostly white but some black."[31]

Black women are making a claim that they have the right and the responsibility in today's world to name their own experience and the experiences of their people, whatever they may be.

We have been nurtured and sustained by a spirituality which paved our way and softened the rough places just enough for us to continue. For, as an African people, we recognized the importance of and maintained our ties with the spiritual:

Spirituality is a rock to hang on to when the world is rushing out of control. It is the unseen force that gives you the courage to push when you'd much rather pull. It shows the way when it seems there is no way. It makes sense out of the nonsense and encourages you to have faith—help is just around the corner.

It is the balm that soothes and heals your inner wounds. With spirituality, you rest easy knowing that whatever ails you, enrages you, troubles you, or gets on your last nerve, this too shall pass. It's the map to inner peace on a road that never ends. And it ain't just about being deep.

Spirituality makes you leave the pity party. It lightens you up. All of a sudden, you find that you are laughing at yourself. And with others. Even when it hurts. Simply put, feeling the spirit brings you joy.

And as countless sisters who have gone before you and who are living it every day will testify, spirit is the salve needed to heal and transform.[32]

It is a time for us as a people to leave the "pity party"; to stop making excuses for ourselves and our children; to stop calling on others to do for us what we can do for ourselves. We must return to the strengths which reside deep within us and use them to challenge the status quo. It is time for us to walk out yet again on faith and proclaim our hope by having the courage to release a cleansing anger which transforms not only ourselves but our communities, our society, and even our world.

Women, Black women of the African Diaspora, remain the "heartbeat" of our African American communities, a status for which they are both exalted and maligned. We must use the strength of that status to be, once again, the bearers of culture and the birthers of the future to confound the minds of those who look down upon us and to "critique all human domination in light of Black women's experience" wherever that domination exists—in our homes, in our workplaces, in our communities, in our places of worship, and in our society as a whole.

Black women, in company with their Black men and their Black children, as family, have reason to hope. Ours is a hope firmly grounded in an incandescent love of self and community, a love threatened by today's "fatal attractions" but which persists regardless. We must pass on that love to those around us, teaching them how to love as well, across racial, sexual, ethnic, and class lines. We must love ourselves into life once again, thereby defeating the miasma of defeat and self-hate which pervades our once thriving communities. "We must love one another or die." We must be servants, not leaders; seek justice, not personal fame or fortune:

> In spiritual solidarity, Black women have the potential to be a community of faith that acts collectively to transform our world. When we heal the woundedness inside us, when we attend to the inner love-seeking love-starved child, we make ourselves ready to enter more fully into community. We can experience the totality of life because we have become fully life-affirming. Like our ancestors using our powers to the fullest, we share the secrets of healing and come to know sustained joy.[33]

We *must* take a stand—a stand against the principalities and powers of our day. It *must* be revolutionary—that is, going against the grain, against the complacency, against the status quo that fosters injustice; it must be nonviolent; and it must embody love.[34]

There is hope. When in doubt, we recall the experiences of African American women and men who were required to work from "can see" to "can't see," a people who were given no reason to hope at all. Yet, as King preached their experience, these same people, torn from family, friends, and all kinship ties, thrust into a foreign land amidst a foreign and hostile people, yet remade community within their midst and did even more. They took a question raised by the prophet Jeremiah and turned it into a proclamation of hope that could not then and cannot today be denied. They proclaimed to the world, in song—their deepest, most heartfelt form of theologizing—the reason for their hope:

> Sometimes I get discouraged
> And think my hope's in vain
> But then the Holy Spirit
> Revives my soul again

There is a Balm in Gilead
To make the wounded whole
There is a Balm in Gilead
to heal the sinsick soul.[35]

Their hope, my hope, our hope, as a people both African and American who are unafraid to tap into the strength found in our women as well as our men, is in the Lord. And with the Lord on our side, whom shall we fear?

Notes

1. Quoted in Robert McAfee Brown, *Religion and Violence*, 2d ed. (Philadelphia: Westminster Press, 1987), xxii.

2. James Baldwin, *The Fire Next Time* (New York: Dell Publishing, 1963), 141.

3. Cornel West, "Learning to Talk of Race," in *Reading Rodney King, Reading Urban Uprising,* ed. Robert Gooding-Williams (New York: Routledge, 1993), 255.

4. Gay Wilentz, *Binding Cultures: Black Women Writers in Africa and the Diaspora* (Bloomington and Indianapolis: Indiana University Press, 1992), 9-10.

5. "The Implications of African American Spirituality," in *African Culture: The Rhythms of Unity*, ed. Molefi Kete Asante and Kariamu Welsh Asante (Westport, Ct.: Greenwood Press, 1985), 228.

6. See Diana L. Hayes, *Hagar's Daughters: Womanist Ways of Being in the World* (Mahwah, N.J.: Paulist Press, 1995).

7. Quoted in Gooding-Williams, *Reading Rodney King*, 217.

8. Ibid., 218.

9. Ibid., 219.

10. Langston Hughes, "Harlem," *Selected Poems of Langston Hughes* (New York: Vintage Books, 1974), 268.

11. Robert McAfee Brown, *Religion and Violence*.

12. Ibid., 3.

13. Ibid., 5.

14. Stephen Carter, *The Culture of Disbelief: How American Law and Politics Trivialize Religious Devotion* (New York: Basic Books, 1993), 3.

15. Ibid., 6.

16. Ibid., 8

17. Brown, *Religion and Violence*, 7.

18. Ibid.

19. Quoted in ibid., 9.

20. Quoted in ibid., 10

21. Cornel West "Learning to Talk of Race," in Gooding-Williams, *Reading Rodney King*, 255.

22. Bernice Johnson Reagon, "African Diaspora Women: The Making of Cultural Workers," in *Women in Africa and the African Diaspora*, ed. Rosalyn Terborg-Penn, Sharon Harley, and Andrea Benton Rushing (Washington, D.C.: Howard University Press, 1987), 169.

23. SODEPAX, *Peace: The Desperate Imperative* (Geneva: Committee on Society, Development, and Peace, 1969), 13-14.

24. West, "Learning to Talk of Race," 256-57.

25. Ibid.

26. Sojourner Truth, from speech "Ain't I a Woman?" given in 1852 and reprinted in *Daughters of Africa: An International Anthology of Words and Writings by Women of African Descent from the Ancient Egyptian to the Present*, ed. Margaret Busby (New York: Pantheon Books, 1992), 38.

27. Martin Luther King Jr., "Letter from a Birmingham Jail," 300.

28. Ibid.

29. See Hayes, *Hagar's Daughters*, 46ff.

30. Ibid., 47-48.

31. Ibid., 48-49. Quotations in the final paragraph are from Henry Louis Gates Jr., ed., *Reading Black, Reading Feminist: A Critical Anthology* (New York: Penguin, 1990), 5.

32. Linda Villarosa, ed., *Body and Soul: The Black Woman's Guide to Physical Health and Emotional Well-Being* (New York: HarperPerennial, 1994), 396-97.

33. Delores Williams, *Sisters in the Wilderness* (Maryknoll, N.Y.: Orbis Books, 1993), 190.

34. Brown, *Religion and Violence*, 99.

35. "There Is a Balm in Gilead." This spiritual is listed variously in hymnbooks as being "traditional," "Afro-American," and "American." There is no date given.

3

Overcoming Susto

Restoring Your Soul

Rosita deAnn Mathews

The patient was a woman from Ecuador. At the psychiatrist's office she had exhibited symptoms of depression and psychosis. She had recently experienced a death in her family. Her uncle, who lived in her native Ecuador, had died suddenly. She had not been able to see or be with him. The news of his death had so overwhelmed her that she had to be hospitalized.

Another patient was a middle-aged White woman who also had a history of depression. Doctors had reworked her medications, and they stabilized her physically and mentally. Spiritually, though, she had feelings of guilt, anomie, and abandonment. Her psychiatrist requested that I, the Chaplain on the unit, discuss spiritual issues with her. In our interview time, I ascertained that the feeling she was experiencing was a result of a break in her relationship with God. This exacerbated her condition.

A Hispanic male in his twenties began to cry as we conversed about his hospitalization. His alcoholism had destroyed his family and his life. He was also feeling estranged from God. He was despairing. His tears revealed a hopelessness that he could overcome this disease and a sense of having lost himself in his alcoholism. He felt a stranger was living in his body.

When the *American Journal of Psychiatry* published guidelines that recommended that a patient's ethnic or cultural heritage be considered when making a diagnosis, it was confirming the experiences of many people who face the loss of hope. Though religious writing through the centuries has addressed such phenomena as the dark night of the soul and spiritual despair, it has been a recent occurrence for science and medicine to affirm what biblical and spiritual writers have long known: there is an unhappiness so deep and wrenching that it can affect not only our spiritual and psychological makeup but our physical selves as well. The despair from some precipitating event or loss can be so destructive to our well-being that it feels as if our souls have been injured or stolen away. The loss of soul is what the American Psychiatric Association has called this condition *susto*.[1]

Taken from Latin American culture, susto is a term that expresses deep despair. It is a folk explanation of an emotional and physical condition that medicine and psychiatry are recognizing as a legitimate and treatable malady. Susto occurs when persons feel their souls have departed from them. They may feel empty and abandoned. Susto, usually associated with the loss of a loved one, also occurs in relation to an event that is frightening. It is thought that the event makes the soul leave the body, resulting in unhappiness or even sickness.

Feeling disconnected from what gives us life can make us feel as if we have lost ourselves, our very essence. Losing your soul means you have lost your connection with God, others, and even yourself. Losing your soul means you feel alienated from a larger source of power within you. You may feel as if you are a stranger to the larger Being. Losing your soul means you may feel disconnected from life itself.

Other peoples also have culturally defined maladies. For instance, anorexia nervosa is common in European Americans but not African Americans. Japanese can suffer from a disorder named *taijin kyfusho*. This disorder afflicts people who are in fear of causing shame to others through some action they may do. Native Americans have many names for depression, including one translated as "heartbreak." When the heart is dying, because of the rupture of a close relationship, despair can result.[2] Yet the feeling of losing your soul can be a universal malady, particularly during times of grief, struggle, and loss. The threat of this occurring is part of the human experience, for if we love and care about ourselves, our loved ones, and our culture, we are in jeopardy of losing pieces of ourselves when we face disappointments around these objects.

Symptoms of susto may appear anytime after the precipitator has occurred. It can be days, months, or years after a fright is experienced, a major episode occurs, or a significant change in a social situation develops. Susto may result in troubled sleep, appetite loss, sadness, low self-worth, or even death.[3] It is usual to hear of those who have experienced the death of a loved one and then die themselves soon after, of what may be called a "broken heart."

When Susto Visits, Don't Give It a Chair

Heartbreak, or susto, is a real condition for some African Americans as well. The concept of losing one's soul or losing hope in oneself or in God is a predicament that many of us encounter and do battle with throughout our lives. It is not surprising that this is the case. There is a constant onslaught of situations that assault our character and our psyches as we live within the American culture. The repeated insults, omissions, and fears that bombard African Americans can result in a loss of self, or at least a diminishing of oneself. It takes place gradually as our psyches are exposed to these occurrences. It can depress our spirits, cause us to lose our faith, or cause us to lose ourselves and become something or someone else just to survive. We can experience susto and still function within the larger culture. This is the most deplorable manifestation of this illness; we will have lost ourselves, our uniqueness, our ethnicity, to survive.

Susto can happen when we are languishing between interesting projects. It can also happen when we are enmeshed in activity. Losing your soul is a symptom that something must change within us or around us. It is a signal while we travel on the track of our everyday life. Very often we miss the signal and derail in one way or another. This can happen when we do not care for our souls and our selves. When we make ourselves a low priority, we can find that our very essence is missing. Without care for ourselves, we can meet our goals, but we may find we have lost our souls in the process.

The persons in the preceding cases felt they had lost their souls, their very essence. Having lost their souls, they felt disconnected from themselves and from others. They were unable to function within their contexts. They were despairing. In our first case, the Ecuadorian woman was advised to have a wake for her lost uncle. She could not attend his funeral in Ecuador, so she could not grieve appropriately. Within a few meetings after this service, her symptoms had improved and she was back in life again. The second depressed patient was also able to experience relief from suffering. When I met with her and listened to her narrative, the story of how she perceived her illness, I advised her to write a letter to God. She wondered as to the effectiveness of this act until I told her that the Psalms were letters and songs written to God to express joy and pain. After hearing this, she could write poems to God in which she released some of her anxiety and feelings. She was soon discharged from the hospital. The young Hispanic man had a more difficult journey, because of the nature of alcoholism. It would take several more attempts for him to find his soul and claim victory over alcoholism.

The African American struggle is one of not just survival of body and mind but survival of soul as well. It is a persistent endeavor to maintain one's faith and thrive in a land that does not want to hear African American voices. If we African Americans do not voice our pain, we inhibit it and it becomes a destructive force within us. Moreover, "Black women's voices don't move through public arenas in the same way that black men's voices do."[4] Expressing your voice is a way to cleanse the soul.

Taking Care of Your Soul

In the Old Testament, soul was created by the "breath," or *ruah,* of God. *Nephesh* is translated as the "spirit," the animated being.[5] The New Testament refers to *soma* and *psyche*, body and soul. In contemporary psychology and pastoral care, the "soul" is recognizing a renaissance of sorts as its importance in healing and health is recognized.[6] New medical and psychological literature is confirming that one's soul, the spiritual and unique self that is part of each of us, is crucial in maintaining health and hope. The difficulty that many (but not all) African American women face in caretaking of the soul can be seen in the way we must live in the world. We must protect ourselves and exercise caution, yet balance that with adventure and risk. It is exhausting at times.

Much of the work we do in our spiritual lives is an effort to overcome spiritual injury. Spiritual injury occurs when a tenet of faith or understanding of God or oneself is trespassed. Spiritual injury occurs when the opinion one has of God is tarnished or challenged, or if questions are not answered when asked. When God is questioned or someone feels let down in not receiving an answer to a prayer, spiritual injury can occur. When it does occur, there can be susto, a loss of self, a loss of soul.

Racism can also lead to susto and spiritual injury. Countless racist acts are perpetrated against African Americans. More than only causing an injury to one's ego or self-esteem, spiritual injury can also diminish one's coupling with the Holy. Countering racism also requires an extra expenditure of energy each day that often makes us feel as if we are running just to stay even with others not facing racism. If we encounter the Holy in each moment, then how do we see the Holy when we are facing acts of oppression and omission? Kristal Zook asks, "How do we survive in a world that abhors us?"[7] Creating ourselves each day allows us to maintain our equilibrium.

I have encountered many instances of discriminatory treatment in everyday life. Northampton, Massachusetts, is a college town in the western part of the state. It is known for several colleges and universities in the area, which, one would assume, would lend itself to creating a more liberal and open atmosphere. A few years after arriving here, I was shopping one day at one of the major grocery stores. It was a pleasant summer afternoon. I took a small purse and a handful of coupons with me. As I walked through the store, I noticed that two young, White college-age men were following me through the store. I thought they were trying to steal my purse, so I alerted a store manager with whom I was friendly. She informed me that they were not thieves, they were store guards. It was obvious they thought I was a thief, so they were trailing me. I was livid. After pausing for a moment, I decided to confront the men myself. I stopped one of them in the feminine protection aisle. The presence of these "female" products instilled in me much power. I began confronting the security guard with the racism of his following the only Black person in the store when there were two hundred White people in the store, many of whom were women feeding their children from open containers of unpaid for food. He tried to calm and quiet me, but I refused to be compliant. What had for so long been a safe place had now become a war zone where I was the target and the enemy.

The next day I contacted the local National Association for the Advancement of Colored People (NAACP) branch to discuss the incident with them. We decided to speak with the management and ask for an apology. After the apology we would also insist on diversity training not only for the security but for the staff as a whole. After many delays and much local publicity, we held a meeting with store management from Boston. I had decided to let the NAACP attorney handle the discussions, but when I sat at the table and faced my accuser, my ire was stirred. I took the lead in the discussions. We had requested an apology that we received. The apology was, "We are sorry this happened, but you looked suspicious." It appeared that the moment I entered the store I was "suspicious."

"How many turkeys do you think I could have fitted into a purse the size of an 8 ½ by 11 notebook?"

"Well, you acted suspiciously from the time you entered."

"Can you list any suspicious acts I committed?"

There was no response. The meeting continued for about thirty minutes. There was no resolution other than that the apology would be in writing and the store would hold diversity training. The newspapers were contacted, and we ended the matter.

Something was stolen in this process. It was my belief that a middle-class, college-educated, African American Baptist minister could shop safely in a grocery store in a small town in the 1990's. Instead of my feeling safe, however, two twenty-year-old White males who could label me a criminal and trespass on my dignity accosted me. If there is no safe space in which to exist, how can we live? How do we nourish our souls?

I saw one of the store detectives several months later at another store of the same chain. I had not returned to the store where the incident occurred. When I saw him, rather than feeling victimized and defeated by the event, I felt empowered. I acted a little crazy. I started speaking very loudly to everyone who was around me, identifying the store detective and warning women not to make any suspicious moves. He quickly left. I had exposed his role and made him visible. This would happen every time I saw him, until he learned to stay out of my way when I was in the store. It took him a while, but he finally got it. It was the act of saying "no" to the affront that gave me power. Stopping the offense with a speedy and directed defense sets boundaries and helps us to regain our souls when they have been threatened.

Keeping Hope Alive

Moving to hope that things can improve among races is a motivator for disputing an incident when it occurs rather than ignoring it. Part of my method for dealing with racist acts, acts that can threaten to rob me of strength and joy, at least temporarily, is to bring the perpetrator to account, to make him or her confront the incident of which I disapprove. Another example occurred when I was purchasing a book with a picture of an African American woman on the front. The clerk, a White male, looked at the book and then at me and said,

"Is this you?"

"No, it is not. What makes you think I would be on the front of this book?"

"It looks like you."

"No, it doesn't." Finally I said, "Your statement was racist and I think you should apologize."

"I don't have to apologize for anything. The woman on the front of this book looks like you."

I finally left the store. The next day I called the manager and outlined the steps I would take if I did not receive a written apology from the clerk. I received it with the elements I wanted included.

When I received the letter, I went to the register where customers were waiting and stepped to the front of a long line. "I was in this store last week and was insulted by the sales clerk," I announced. "I asked the clerk to write a written apology. This is it."

By then everyone was quiet. After I read the letter I said, "I was insulted publicly, so the apology had to be public as well." Then I left the store.

These incidents are difficult to experience. If we do not respond to them and stop the attempts at humiliation and harassment, they will continue. If we ignore them, we are condoning them and encouraging their repetition. If we do choose to respond, then what have we done to ourselves? Have we lost energies or gained them? How many of these indignities have to occur before we lose our souls, our spirits?

When your spirit has been offended, challenged, ridiculed, overlooked, you can begin to lose your soul if it is not healed. Abuse not countered is devastating. When your community is attacked, it loses a piece of its soul. Responding to racism helps us to care for our souls.

We can choose different ways in which to respond when our souls are threatened. We can choose avoidance and make excuses for the acts others commit toward us. We can respond directly to acts. If our souls implore us to respond to an abuse or a slight and we do not do so, we are harming ourselves, our community, and our future. We do not have to respond in ways that close down the teaching moment or even the venting moment, but we must respond to purge our souls of the evil directed at us when we face efforts at nullification. This helps our souls to heal and helps us to regain our spirits. This is caring for the soul.[8] Caring for the soul is like caring for plants. You plant a seedling, fertilize it, water it, nourish the soil, give it sun, and watch it grow. No matter how well it is growing, when parasites and weeds appear to choke it, the plant will not grow further.

Similarly, when incidents happen which deplete our souls, we must rescue them. The act of interrupting racism when it occurs will force it to lose its power and velocity, and will empower us, for we are caring for our psyches, ourselves, our souls. We must care for our souls so they can survive and flourish. We care for our souls so they can care for us. How many of us would ignore a child in pain? None of us would. Yet we ignore our own pain when we do not care for our souls. As African American women, particularly those of us who live and work in circles where our heritage is not the norm, the efforts to live in a non–African American space is like trying to walk on the moon without a moon suit. You will float away or die of lack of oxygen unless you equip yourself properly. It is compulsory that we care for those places within us that are eroded away, bit by bit, by our moving within the larger culture.

Another reason we care for ourselves through these incidents is to perpetuate the ability to sustain hope. The ability to hope affects our physiology and can improve or deteriorate our physical selves. Hope can spring from within tragedy or stress where escape or "psychic refutation" is not possible.[9] Hope allows us to journey from the places where we are to the places where we can be despite mitigating factors that may oppress us. Hope helps us to believe in ourselves and in the presence of a powerful, acting, though sometimes silent, God. Hope can also be therapeutic when offered within a community of people who support us. Through the community, we can transform negative thinking to possibility thinking that reminds us of God's nearness even within darkness. Hope helps us live transexistentially—beyond the momentary suffering in the place of expectancy.

Perhaps there is no better biblical example of susto than that exhibited by Elijah (1 Kings 19). After completing a very taxing encounter with civil authorities concerning his religious convictions, Elijah finds that a death threat has been placed upon him. Running away to protect his life, he finally collapses under a broom tree. His exhaustion is so intense and his spirit so emptied that he prays to die. God intercedes with some basic life-renewing advice and actions. Food is prepared for him, and he is allowed to rest. Then he is told to go to Mount Horeb, where God's presence renews his spirit and he receives a new sense of purpose.

Soul Power

African American women need to design and build a theology that allows us to power up our souls and to counter the susto that crouches at the door of our hearts waiting for a moment of weakness. We need a theology that helps us to value and empower ourselves, not a theology that is destructive. By protecting our souls, we can then do what is most creative— art, poetry, writing, and my favorite, music. By not harboring the pain that comes from being devalued, by expressing it when and how it is appropriate, by acknowledging the sin of humanity that continues to allow people to exploit and abuse one another, by voicing a resounding "no" to a time and place in creation that seems to abhor African American women at times, we can begin to let our souls heal, rest, and come into their own. This is what womanist thought and thinking and acting must allow and encourage. If we are to reach hope from despair, if we are to be transformed from how the contemporary world attempts to oppress us, we must be empowered with a theology that gives us the tools to succeed and conquer.

Yet we do not ask for help. We do not confess the difficulties of isolation. We do not work through our own psychological and emotional issues. We lose support from each other because we feel we cannot trust each other. In the process, we isolate ourselves and lose one of our best defenses against meaninglessness and disconnection—one another. As professional African American women, we put ourselves in danger of losing our souls because we have lost our collective, united selves. Instead of being conquering African American women, we choose to protect our individual egos. We cannot do this. We must create and provide safe places for one another. We must be harbors of renewal and restoration, not places of battle and subterfuge. By treating each other as competitors rather than sisters and fellow sojourners, we may find that what we have won will not compare with what we have lost. We are always in jeopardy of winning the world but losing our souls.

We must acknowledge each other. By valuing and encouraging each other, we are countering what the larger society does when it tries to nullify and ignore us. When we affirm each other's contributions, then we are giving strength to each other. When we remain in a competitive strain with other African American women and withhold our support, then we are perpetuating what the larger society has always done to African American women. We silence each other rather than empower each other.

We must voice our stories to one another as well, for when we give voice to the pain and the triumphs, we strengthen ourselves and each other. When we give voice to the interactions that try our souls and hearts, we can categorize them, wrestle with them, and lasso them to make them tamer. We cannot eradicate these things all alone, but together we can begin to corral the racist acts, the devaluing acts, that cause us to lose ourselves and that try our souls.

Healing Ourselves—Healing Each Other

To find healing from susto or isolation, a place to begin may be to voice your story by sharing it with someone else. The power of the women's club movements in the early part of the century was that African American women gathered together. Today the gathering of African American professional women can be infused more with competition than with encouragement. For those of us who work in isolation away from our communities, the meeting together of women is more than just for social reasons; it is also for soul recreating. It is a time for us to offer support to each other.

We can affirm each other's accomplishments and struggles. We can pass on stories to each other.

Pastoral care professor Dr. Edward Wimberly suggests storytelling plays an important role in pastoral care.[10] Narrating one's experiences to an interested second party brings healing and may allow guidance from the listener. Solutions may be suggested, and resources may be made available. In the least, someone else can affirm that our experience is valid. They can also validate us and the feelings we experience around issues that may attempt to devalue us. If there is one area that African American women need to reclaim, it is this one of transmitting our stories, the narratives that make up our lives and the lives of our ancestors. Rather than sharing stories of our past and the present, we entomb them and suppress them. As the old song says, "We will tell the stories of how we've overcome."[11]

Unfortunately, our careers as ministers, academicians, and denominational leaders pit us against each other, at times, as competitors rather than supporters. We feel we cannot let down our guard and reveal ourselves to one another. We cannot confess to each other our fears. We cannot show need or weakness. Instead, we shore ourselves up against the vicissitudes and despair we face, keeping them to ourselves so we can seem successful.

However, if stories are spoken and heard without diminishment, the healing work can begin. Rather than respond critically, we can affirm the success of our sisters in making it through a situation. Then other sisters can help work through the myriad of responses that could have been valid. Having a safe place where African American women express their narrative without criticism and can receive support is invaluable. It is a gift we can give one another.

Envisioning the future is the result of this exercise, particularly affirming each other in the process. In a world that often does what it can to devalue our contributions, we must continue to value each other. As we sustain ourselves as African American women and recreate ourselves and our theology, it is imperative that we keep our stories sounded and sung, that we solidify our support, and that we keep our hearts and souls well nourished.

Can Hope Overcome Susto?

Hope is an essential element of psychological, social, emotional, and spiritual lives. Without hope, the anticipation of future events and possibilities is laden with negatives, diminishing what we can accomplish or realize. Hope points to fulfillment of one's efforts and dreams. Psychological hope enables us to grow and change, to face our demons or shortcomings, and gives us the power to overcome them. Hope imbues us with the power to realize our potentials. Social hope enables us to believe that we can fit into our communities despite our differences. Hope for our communities evolves from within people who believe they can change their environs and improve them. Hope emotionally gives us the strength to endure and to change ourselves and to believe that we are worthwhile.

Hope helps us to deal with losses related to the death of loved ones, our own aging, and the difficulties we face each day. Hope spiritually affirms our place in God's realm and on earth with our spiritual sisters and brothers. When these hopes are diminished or eradicated, the soul enters a spiritual or emotional darkness. This darkness can manifest itself as depression, anorexia, addiction, or suicide. When our hopes are stolen, our souls are lost. Susto overcomes us. Having hope that there will be justice and an end to discrimination is a hope that requires a large input of belief: "Where freedom is denied, hope is denied also; and where hope is denied, persons are being destroyed, for to be a person means to be constantly projecting oneself in hope toward goals in which personal being will find fuller expression and satisfaction."[12]

I have had a myriad of experiences attempting to survive in a world that does not welcome African American women. The ability to self-reconstruct is as important a reconstruction as the historical Reconstruction is in our country's history. Recreating fertile ground upon which to continue to cultivate ourselves when we face racial affronts restores our souls and saves us from susto.

As a Chaplain, this is the work I do with my patients—helping them discover fertile ground after a spiritual injury has infested their religious soil. Salvation, then, is a continuing and kinetic process. It takes place when we tend to the gardens of our souls when we face disbarment from humanity because of our race or our theology or even our call. Replenishing the soils of our souls, just as we would replenish our gardens, is how we maintain ourselves and move from potential despair to the joy of being ourselves. Hope gives us the strength of mind and spirit to persevere, to nurture ourselves, and to face the future with a frame of victory.

If African American women are to develop and promote a theological understanding of life as individuals and as sisters, we must include a construct that provides a foundation for establishing and maintaining hope when met by dismay or despair. Womanist theology, using a hermeneutic that views the world through the lens of African American women, can empower us and keep us thriving. This is the bridge we can travel from soullessness, or susto, and spiritual emptiness or injury to hope and meaning. Womanist theology offers us a place to see ourselves as God sees us and to love ourselves as She loves us. When we use the tools to deconstruct and reconstruct our theological reasoning and to infuse our faith, our souls can be saved repeatedly.

Instead of being captured by life's issues that attempt to suffocate us, we will have a platform from which to catapult ourselves toward our dreams. Then we will realize the possibility of transformation, for we will have found

God within us, instead of being overcome by the evil that tries to hold us ransom.

What Will It Profit a Woman If She Gains the Whole World but Loses Her Soul?

To save our souls, we must feed our spirits. We feed our spirits by tending to our needs spiritually, emotionally, psychologically, and culturally. Spiritually, we must allow for an infusion of new theological thought. We must feed our faith through music, good preaching, and congregational involvement, when possible. To feed ourselves emotionally, we can avail ourselves of the possibilities that emotional and psychological exploration affords. By entering the adventure of self-discovery through therapy, we can release what is within us that works against us and we can nurture what is within us that wants us to grow. Personal reconstruction places us within a framework of improving ourselves through confession, honest reflection, and spiritual and psychological growth. Corporately, we cannot omit the importance of assembling together as African American women.

One of the most nourishing experiences I have had was the opportunity to do an invocation for the visit of the Presidential Cabinet member Secretary of Veterans Affairs, Jesse Brown. The invocation I offered was a heartfelt one in which I prayed for our veterans, our country, and the secretary. When Secretary Brown began his speech, he stopped and turned to me. He stated that the prayer I had offered was one of the most stirring prayers he had ever heard. He later asked me for a copy of the prayer. A few months later, I received a call from his speechwriter asking me for help in writing a speech that Secretary Brown was to give for President Bill Clinton. It was a very high honor for me to have the opportunity to contribute to a speech given on behalf of our country's president.

As we journey through our lives, we must do all we can to save our souls by nourishing them, sharing ourselves and our essence with each other, and being beacons of faith as we take this adventure of life together. Then we can transform despair to hope and find our true salvation. Then we can set ourselves free from the despair that turns into susto and threatens our vitality and our lives. It will be then that we can begin to live every moment to its fullest.

Notes

1. American Psychiatric Association (APA) Staff, *Diagnostic and Statistical Manual of Mental Disorders: DSM-IV*, 4th ed. (Washington, D.C.: American Psychiatric Association, 1994), 848.

2. See Daniel Goleman, "Making Room on the Couch for Culture," *New York Times*, December 5, 1995.

3. APA Staff, *DSM-IV*, 849.

4. Kristal Zook, "A Manifesto of Sorts for a Black Feminist Movement," *New*

York Times Magazine, November 12, 1995, 86.

   5. See Rodney Hunter, ed., *Dictionary of Pastoral Care and Counseling* (Nashville: Abingdon Press, 1990), 1201.

   6. See Herbert Benson, *The Relaxation Response* (New York: Avon Books, 1976).

   7. Zook, "A Manifesto of Sorts," 86.

   8. See Thomas Moore, *Care of the Soul* (New York: HarperCollins, 1992), xvi.

   9. See Hunter, *Dictionary of Pastoral Care and Counseling*, 534.

   10. Edward P. Wimberly, *African American Pastoral Care* (Nashville: Abingdon Press), 20-21.

   11. Charles A. Tindley (1851-1933), "We'll Understand It Better By and By."

   12. John MacQuarrie, *Christian Hope* (New York: Seabury, 1978), 8-9.

4

Womanist Work and Public Policy

An Exploration of the Meaning of Black Women's Interaction with Political Institutions

Rosetta E. Ross

As early as the life of Sojourner Truth, it is evident that Black religious women activists have been participants in the public sphere at varying levels. Generally, their activity has been in behalf of African Americans, but it also has been holistic in its larger emphasis on attending to the needs of all marginalized persons. Because the everyday circumstances of Black women activists in history included conventional and institutional repression of Black people and repressive social perspectives about all women, these women's ordinary activities, which otherwise may have developed as easy, mundane tasks, became hard work. Relying on what they understood as God's provisions in their lives, the women demonstrated fidelity to God by routinely working hard and taking risks as they sought to change repressive traditions, institutions, and social conventions that generally hampered the well-being of African Americans. Responding to God in this way has been one historic form of Black religious women's activism that coincides with what I have elsewhere identified as "womanist work."[1]

Womanist religious writers variously explore this work as moral activity and as response to theological perceptions.[2] As moral activity, the endurance of this work as consistent practice deriving from character attributes is viewed as a transvaluation of the virtuous and as bold, persistent practice for the community. Theologically, womanist writers describe the response as practice undergirded by identification with Jesus' resurrection and validated through Jesus' attention to the least. The practice also is described theologically as propelled by belief in the need to radically obey God's direction of work and as faith that God makes the work possible.

While these perspectives appropriately describe the genesis and suste-

41

nance of some Black religious women's activity, it is also the case that transformation of public policy and political institutions has been a consistent
goal of this public work. Historically, the women sought to change material conditions of the persons for whom they practiced. Their efforts for
change sought not only to relieve suffering, but also to reproduce formal
and informal social structures that required or contributed to these oppressive material conditions. As efforts to change formal social structures,
the women's activity sought to engage public policy. This essay explores
the public policy implications of more contemporary "womanist work" in
civil rights activism, particularly that of Victoria Way DeLee. First, I present
voting rights and school desegregation work as civil rights practice to
change public policy and as activity with which Victoria Way DeLee's local
community work resonated. Next, I present particular instances of DeLee's
civil rights work as efforts to address specific policies. I then investigate
general policy implications of DeLee's work. In the final section, I make a
modest assertion about future directions for womanist work.

I

The modern civil rights movement focused on a number of ways that
persons, primarily African Americans, were denied two things: (a) full access to social goods and (b) the possibility of full social participation in
their local communities and in U.S. society.[3] While informal structures, mores, and ideological perspectives contributed significantly to the
marginalized conditions of African Americans, it was the formal structures
toward which some major efforts of the civil rights movement aimed. In
this regard, two pivotal civil rights endeavors may be viewed as seeking to
change the public policy and political institutions that undergirded exclusionary activity. These were voting rights activities and school desegregation work.

In Dorchester County, South Carolina, near the beginning of the civil
rights movement, Victoria Way DeLee participated in activities that led to
her full involvement with the civil rights movement. Responding to what
she felt was God calling her to "help those who can't help themselves,"[4]
DeLee worked as a civil rights leader for more than twenty-six years. She
was born in 1925 to Essie Way in the town of Ridgeville. Along with her four
siblings and her mother, Victoria lived with her grandmother, Lucretia Way,
on property of a local White farmer. Essie Way worked as a domestic for
local White households to support the family. Lucretia reared the children
and supplemented family income by taking in laundry and working as a
field hand. Before the children were old enough to work, Lucretia took
them to the fields and left them at the end of rows until her day was over. It
was during her youth that Victoria first experienced the desire to struggle
against racial repression. She was greatly affected by seeing her mother
and grandmother labor hard for as little as twenty-five cents per day. Remembering those times, Victoria says, "Well, really, we were treated like

slaves, because when the White people came in and said that you had to go to work, you had to work whether you wanted to or not . . . So when I was a little girl growing up, and I see how my grandmomma had to work, and my momma . . . being treated like that, I used to say, 'Well, one day I'm gonna fix it.' "[5]

DeLee began local community work by organizing a protest against the firing of a Black schoolteacher because she lived outside the county.[6] Eventually DeLee entered the flurry of activism that became the civil rights movement and during which she participated in an array of undertakings as she tried to improve life for Black people in Dorchester County, South Carolina. Her early work included organizing to improve education at her local school and protesting against discriminatory hiring practices and against closed access to public accommodations. As a participant in the civil rights movement, DeLee also engaged in those thrusts of civil rights work that sought to change public policy. Particularly significant were her voting rights and school desegregation efforts that corresponded with DeLee's goal of "fixing it" for persons in her immediate community.

II

DeLee's Voting Rights Work

DeLee began voting rights work in 1947 at age twenty-two after she obtained a voter registration certificate. Her pastor at St. John Baptist Church, R. B. Adams, "preached about civil rights" and urged his congregation to attempt registering to vote. When these exhortations caught their attention, DeLee and her husband, S. B., traveled fifteen miles by train to St. George, the Dorchester County Seat, to register. Because she had come without "permission," the registration agent told DeLee that he could not register her. She insisted that he would, and the two argued back and forth until DeLee, standing in front of the door and keeping one hand in her pocket as if she had a weapon, told the registrar that he would not leave the room if she were not given her "civil rights." The agent finally complied.[7]

Feeling empowered because of her own success, DeLee immediately began to pursue voter registration as the major vehicle by which she sought to make a difference. "I'll never forget that day!" she says. "That was a good feeling day. I felt so good that that man registered me!" As a result of realizing the possibility of this political activity making a difference, DeLee became tenacious in efforts to register other persons. "Then I went out, and I start talking to people," she recalls. "I start tellin' 'em 'bout my registration certificate. I come back to the church, and I get up in the church and tell the preacher how I get my registration certificate. And the preacher went to telling everybody how they must do like I done."[8]

Noting DeLee's leadership, Adams supported her work by introducing DeLee to South Carolina's National Association for the Advancement of Colored People (NAACP) Field Secretary, the late Reverend I. DeQuincey

Newman. Newman, who oversaw the NAACP's state registration drive, particularly promoted DeLee's activities. When NAACP activities began to be severely scrutinized and restricted in South Carolina and across the South,[9] DeLee continued her efforts by founding a local organization, the Dorchester County Voters' League. DeLee began the Voters' League by traveling around the county on Sundays, seeking permission from Black pastors to make appeals for participation by their congregations.[10] As she became more active in voting rights work, DeLee began to engage in those processes and institutions by which she might more fully affect African Americans' social participation opportunities. This included political party activity and the judicial system.

While political parties are not formal arms of the state, as a means by which persons can exercise voting rights they are public institutions. In this regard, DeLee's efforts to make party politics useful for voting rights activity coincided with voting rights public policy activity. Following voter registration successes,[11] Dorchester County African Americans sought to influence electoral results. Uncooperative poll workers encumbered this, however. In one instance, when illiterate and semiliterate African Americans sought assistance in voting, the "poll manager, claiming to be acting in accordance with instructions from the U.S. Attorney in Columbia (the state capital), refused to permit Negroes who had registered in 1965 to receive assistance in voting from anyone except the poll officials, all of whom were white." This was done although state law permitted assistance by a poll manager or by any precinct elector of one's choice who was standing nearby.[12]

Responding to such circumstances, DeLee led county African Americans in entering Democratic Party precinct activity. Assisted by the state NAACP and implemented through the Dorchester County Voters' League, Black residents began competing for offices in every voting precinct in the county. During one year, African Americans won almost every major county Democratic precinct office. As African Americans became officers who helped run polls during elections, they changed an institutional barrier to their equal participation in voting.[13]

DeLee's role as leader of efforts to engage the State Democratic Party involved challenging other efforts to exclude or restrict Black participation. In one instance during a 1966 Democratic Party precinct meeting in Ridgeville, ten local residents postponed calling the meeting to order so that "a large number of white persons, including families with their children" could be gathered to outnumber the African Americans present. Also, the precinct chairperson ruled African Americans out of order when they attempted to nominate persons for office. DeLee complained to the State Democratic Executive Committee, which told her she must first contest the precinct meeting at the county convention. DeLee brought the complaint to the county convention; however, this was unsuccessful. She then appealed to the state convention credentials committee. After a full hearing, the committee rejected the complaint and took no disciplinary action against the delegation.[14]

DeLee's experience of being excluded from various levels of the Democratic Party was like that of other African Americans in South Carolina.[15] This common experience led Black leaders, including DeLee, to form a new party. The letter calling persons together for an initial meeting to create a third party in South Carolina cited abuse and repression by the State Democratic Party and the anti–African American "full-slate" law[16] as reasons requiring their actions to ensure "meaningful enfranchisement for black people."[17] DeLee attended the organizational meeting and was elected the vice-president of the new United Citizens' Party (UCP).

According to UCP President John Harper, the party sought to "speak for the 'silent majority' of Blacks and poor Whites who are vitally concerned with issues of survival."[18] This philosophy of attending to the needs of these excluded persons coincided precisely with DeLee's goals. The Party immediately entered races for local office and, by November 1970, fielded candidates for governor and lieutenant governor.[19] After the death of South Carolina's First Congressional District representative, the UCP entered its second statewide race, unanimously nominating DeLee as its candidate.[20] In keeping with the UCP position and continuing her work with participation and social access issues, DeLee said her candidacy "would be aimed at 'the red, white and black man' " in the district, using her "real experience in Washington to help get something done for the poor."[21] "I know the things people need and I feel the truly underprivileged have never had a representative in Congress," she said.[22] Although DeLee lost the race for Congress, she won many precincts and upset the balance of power between Democrats and Republicans in three (including the largest) counties of the district.[23]

DeLee's interaction with courts in three cases particularly focused on policy goals related to voting rights. Seeking full benefits of voter registration gains and the Voting Rights Act, these three cases were all class action challenges of institutional barriers to meaningful enfranchisement.

DeLee was a lead plaintiff in a 1971 case that asserted that race, class, and gender were barriers to jury participation. This action, initiated against county jury commissioners, opposed the exclusion of African Americans and all women from the jury selection process.[24] Since the juror list should have originated from the pool of registered voters in Dorchester County, immediately subsequent to presentation of the complaint, James A. Bell, attorney for the jury commissioners, filed a motion to annul the current jury list and to constitute a new one.[25] This response prevented an injunction against the jury commissioners. Saying that establishment of the new jury list was an act of good faith, the district court refused to intervene. The response did enlarge the pool of persons selected for jury duty (DeLee and her husband were among the names drawn in the next two jury selections). However, having no assurance that exclusionary practices would cease, plaintiffs appealed the district court's decision.

Barriers to full political participation continued in spite of increased registration and voting, party participation, and election of Black persons. These barriers included the legacy of gerrymandered and disproportionately drawn voting districts. Seeking to expand previous progress and to resist restrictions of these barriers, DeLee joined seventeen other plaintiffs in a class action in behalf of Black citizens seeking to reapportion the State House of Representatives.[26] The case challenged districting and voting requirements for electing state representatives, principally contesting the use of county boundaries for deciding house districts. Further, the case opposed use of multiple-member districts and the full-slate requirement. Both diluted the voting strength of African Americans.

The U.S. District Court held that use of county boundaries and multiple-member districts did not harm African Americans as a class, but it struck down the full-slate law as inhibiting exercise of the right to vote.[27] Upon appeal, the U.S. Supreme Court reversed the District Court's decision and sent the case back to District Court. In what seems a bizarre turn of events, this Supreme Court action had no effect on South Carolina apportionment. The District Court recognized the "Supreme Court's reversal [as] an effective rejection of the present apportionment of the House." However, it did not act further, saying, "The absence of a remand with instructions leaves nothing before the district court and nothing for it to decide or declare."[28]

Such barriers to full social participation also existed at the county level. Again, DeLee participated in resisting these restrictions as lead plaintiff in a voting rights suit challenging the method of electing members to Dorchester County Council. In Dorchester County, seven council members were elected from two districts subdivided into seven areas, with four representatives elected from one district and three from the other. This manner of election yielded a higher percentage of council members from one district than was the percentage of the population in that district. Moreover, the higher percentage fell in the district where African Americans were less concentrated. In addition to the disproportionate representation, groupings in the subareas were organized to further dilute Black voting strength.[29]

Finding the arrangement discriminatory against Black citizens, on January 3, 1974, Circuit Judge Charles E. Simons Jr. enjoined further elections. Simons required the County Council to file a reapportionment plan by February 1, 1974,[30] and ordered the plan approved by the U.S. Attorney General. When the Civil Rights Division of the Attorney General's Office rejected the first reapportionment plan proposed by the Council, Simons maintained jurisdiction over the case, and in October 1974, he ordered a plan for single-member districts.

DeLee's School Desegregation Work

The major school desegregation activity in South Carolina began with the Clarendon County suit, one of the several decided in the 1954 *Brown* ruling. Although the Clarendon case was a part of *Brown*, it was at least fifteen years before any semblance of full school desegregation occurred across the state. After *Brown*, South Carolina continued and intensified efforts to resist integration. The next year, Governor George Bell Timmerman declared, "South Carolinians 'are determined to resist integration' of the races in the public schools . . . 'There shall be no compulsory racial mixing in our state.' "[31] Furthermore, South Carolina's delegation to the 1955 White House Conference on Education presented a report from the state saying, "Public schools will not be operated in South Carolina on a racially integrated basis."[32] The state's legislature appointed a special unit, the State School Committee of Segregation, headed by State Senator L. Marion Gresette, to ensure the continuation of segregation.[33] By 1960, the Committee of Segregation recommended, and the legislature approved, a statute "repealing specific requirements for segregation in South Carolina." The strategy of this legislation was to eliminate "a major point on which school integration suits [had] been brought into Federal Court."[34] Over the next five years, state officials took various other legislative actions to circumvent desegregation.

In 1964, the DeLees initiated desegregation activities in Dorchester County School District Three when Victoria and S. B. attempted to enroll two of their children at Ridgeville Elementary School. Other parents later joined the DeLees; however, school district officials repeatedly resisted these efforts by disqualifying some Black students from eligibility to attend the White schools or by allowing only a few students to be received at any given time. In early 1966, under a requirement by the U.S. Department of Health, Education, and Welfare, Dorchester County Three submitted an acceptable voluntary desegregation plan.[35] Dorchester's plan, like that of many other districts across the South, was called "freedom of choice." Placing the burden of desegregation on the Black community, the freedom of choice plan provided opportunities for parents to choose which schools in the district their children would attend. The effect was to dilute the possibility of desegregation. Fearing severe reprisals, most Black parents and children in Dorchester County (and in other counties across the state) took the physically, financially, and emotionally safer route of leaving things as they were. In response, DeLee, in behalf of her sons Van and Elijah, led the list of plaintiffs in a March 1966 suit seeking to completely desegregate the district's schools.[36] In addition to initiating the court action, DeLee continued to lead demonstrations, encouraged other parents to reject segregation, and frequently sought to meet with district superintendents and the school board.[37]

As DeLee and other African Americans continued to resist school segregation, they were joined by county Native Americans who then attended a third school system located geographically within Dorchester District Three.[38] While the district's 1966 approved desegregation plan asserted freedom of choice, when Native American parents sought to exercise choice, "those choices were uniformly denied even though the choices of Black children were uniformly granted."[39] When officials refused Native American enrollment by freedom of choice, DeLee organized "demonstrations against [their] having to attend [the] inadequate school." Following several days of protests, the district superintendent agreed to admit fifteen Native American children "on the basis that that number would not overcrowd the white school."[40] When the group sought an order requiring the district to admit all Native American children who chose to enter the White schools, presiding District Court Judge Robert Hemphill "stated several times his willingness to cite these [protesters] in contempt and to have a marshall sent down to arrest them."[41] Hemphill enjoined further demonstrations and issued an order upholding the superintendent's decision to admit only fifteen children. When it became clear that only a limited number of Native American children would be admitted, as leader of local desegregation activities, DeLee went with Native American parents to enroll fifteen children in Ridgeville Elementary School. Shortly after she arrived at the school, marshals arrested DeLee for disobeying the demonstration injunction. Judge Hemphill placed DeLee under a $10,000 bond and ordered her to show why she should not be held in contempt of court for failure to obey the injunction against demonstrations.[42]

DeLee and others continued desegregation work, however, and because it progressed so slowly, they also took their protests beyond the state. By 1969, only 10 percent of Black students attended White schools, and no White students attended Black schools in District Three.[43] That year, the U.S. Department of Health, Education, and Welfare set the fall as the deadline for full school desegregation. At the same time, news reports from the White House said school desegregation guidelines would be relaxed to give schools with special problems additional time.[44] Responding to these reports, South Carolina and Mississippi field workers for the American Friends Service Committee organized a multistate grassroots bus caravan to Washington to protest relaxation plans. Dissatisfied with desegregation progress in Dorchester County, DeLee joined the caravan. As a participant in this protest, she expressed her disappointment with the federal government's slowdown first to Jerris Leonard, Assistant Attorney General for Civil Rights, and later to Attorney General John Mitchell.[45] When she returned home, DeLee encountered threatening letters, phone calls, and other harassment as a result of news reports about her participation.[46] In spite of these and other consistent attempts by DeLee and others, schools in Dorchester County District Three were not completely desegregated until 1971.

III

Implications of DeLee's Practice for Public Policy

Throughout her civil rights endeavors, four interrelated points of view motivated DeLee's activism. These viewpoints—equality, membership, justice, and marginalization—are discernible in activities DeLee undertook and in statements reflecting her ideas about a good society. While I explicate them separately below, the views are combined in her work and suggest a particular perspective about forming and judging civil institutions and other social structures.

DeLee's perspective about equality asserts that all persons have equal value as members of the human community and, as such, deserve respect. For DeLee, an important element of exercising one's humanness and receiving respect relates to being able to make choices comparable to the ordinary choices made by others in the society. Exclusion from opportunity to exercise the franchise and from access to equitable educational resources denies such ordinary choices to some.

Coinciding with this view about human value is DeLee's standpoint about membership in society. DeLee presumed membership for those living in the society. Further, her presumptions about choice imply rights that appear to be specifically related to her ideas about human value. Two that are most apparent in her work include the right to fair treatment and the right to full social participation. Fair treatment for DeLee is relative to the ordinary possibilities experienced by others in the community or society. Her concern about the wages and work conditions of her mother and grandmother grew out of the incomparably better economic chances and life conditions of other persons in the same community. DeLee's school integration work for African American and Native American children related directly to substandard conditions of non-White facilities in the same geographic district.

Closely related to her fair treatment ideas is the assertion that full social participation options should be available to all members of society. DeLee's work to ensure the right to full social participation is evidenced both by efforts to help secure voting rights for those excluded in the county and by campaigns to register voters once technical enfranchisement was possible. DeLee further asserted ideas about full participation through attempts to stop intimidation of Black voters. Engaging the Democratic Party and the United Citizens' Party also reflects this perspective. When the Democratic Party failed to provide open opportunities to participate, DeLee helped found the UCP to provide an alternate vehicle for participation. Finally, the three class action cases all raised issues pertinent to full participation. One challenged exclusion of persons from participation as jurors, while the others sought to ensure meaningful participation through equitable opportunities for all persons to elect representatives.

Beginning early in her life and continuing throughout her civil rights work, DeLee seems to have been motivated by a personal sense of what she felt was just. This sense of justice was consistently asserted throughout her life's activity. This exhibited DeLee's position that unfair treatment and barriers to full social participation should be challenged. Possibly arising from the conditions into which she was born, DeLee's sense of justice seems substantially bound to judgments about conditions of the most marginalized in society. Reflecting her perspective about human value, DeLee consistently worked to ensure that the most marginalized should be heard, represented, and attended to. Her initiation of efforts with Native Americans to enter school desegregation activity demonstrates this position. In Dorchester County, Native Americans were relegated to a third, even more poorly facilitated school system, and geographically and economically they were more ostracized from the community than were many African Americans. DeLee asserted this during her Congressional race, saying her candidacy was significant to "the truly underprivileged [who] have never had a representative."[47]

Perhaps the preceding three viewpoints are best understood when correlated with DeLee's regard for the most marginalized. She says that even as a child her concern was for those whom she felt could not help themselves. In her adult life, DeLee maintained this concern. "There was so many people who couldn't git what they wanted," she says of the pre-movement period, "and they couldn't stand up for themselves. That's the people I wanted to do something about. So . . . that was in my mind to make some changes there." Moreover, DeLee asserts that intervening in such circumstances is a central message of Christian scripture. "The Bible tells us help them who can't help themselves," she says.[48] Apparently, she felt those farthest away from obtaining the goods and services of society are least likely to have significant opportunities to realize ordinary possibilities afforded to those living in the society.

Taken together, DeLee's perspectives about equality, membership, justice, and marginalization infer at least three specific implications for public institutions and public policy. First, these perspectives imply that it is the responsibility of those who are able, to make the goods (including and especially opportunities) of society available to those who are least likely to receive them. Second, an underlying tenet of her position suggests that if society's benefits are not available to those most marginalized, the policies governing social distribution and social opportunity are unjust. Finally, according to this view, the measure of public policy and public institutions as good is based on their benefit to those most marginalized from the center of the institutions and services governed by the policy.

IV

Victoria DeLee joined her contemporaries and predecessors in a tradition of work that made possible an array of social participation and access opportunities for formerly excluded persons. In spite of that work, however, large numbers of persons do not participate in the franchise and experience or perceive educational opportunities as of questionable value. If policy and institutional changes resulting from the tradition of work in which DeLee participated have played a role in moving the United States toward the goal of becoming a more just society, the challenge for continuing womanist work is to carry forward the accomplishments of this tradition. While the particular means of carrying forward this work will be various, perhaps it is necessary for some work of contemporary womanist activity to contend with the details of engaging in these altered public institutions and policies as translators. Through such work it may be possible not only to change the institutions and policies so that they become more responsive, but also to provide means by which the most marginalized may themselves participate in further altering and developing public policies and institutions.

Notes

1. Rosetta E. Ross, "Womanist Work: Civil Rights Activism, Self-Actualization, and the Transformation of Community Consciousness" (paper presented at annual meeting of the American Academy of Religion, New Orleans, Louisiana, November 20-23, 1990). I assert that much of Black women's "laborious, steadfast, tenacious activity is struggle against racist and other dehumanizing phenomena, and struggle for human-affirming structures and conditions. Occurring through satiation of desire, through responsible, in-charge being, and through audacious behavior, this is 'womanist work.' "

2. In ethics, see Katie G. Cannon, *Black Womanist Ethics* (Atlanta: Scholars Press, 1988). In sociology, see Cheryl Townsend Gilkes, "Going Up for the Oppressed: The Career Mobility of Black Women Community Workers," *Journal of Social Issues* 39 (Fall 1983): 115-139; " 'Liberated to Work like Dogs!': Labeling Black Women and Their Work," in *The Experience and Meaning of Work in Women's Lives*, ed. Hildreth Y. Grossman and Nia Lane Chester (Hillside, N.J.: Lawrence Erlbaum Associates, 1990); "The Role of Women in the Sanctified Church," *Journal of Religious Thought* 43 (Spring-Summer 1986): 24-41; and "Successful Rebellious Professionals: The Black Woman's Professional Identity and Community Commitment," *Psychology of Women Quarterly* 6 (Spring 1982): 289-311. In theology, see the work of Jacquelyn Grant, *White Women's Christ and Black Women's Jesus* (Atlanta: Scholars Press, 1989) for her discussion of Jesus; and Delores S. Williams, *Sisters in the Wilderness: The Challenge of Womanist God-Talk* (Maryknoll: Orbis Books, 1993) for her more theocentric discussion.

3. Social participation is here understood both as a social good and as a means by which social goods are defined. Therefore, social participation refers to participation in the execution of the array of formal processes by which economic and social structures of a society are determined and maintained. Economic and social structures, of course, are the primary means of governing a society and of defining social goods like prestige, power, class, opportunity, etc.

4. Victoria Way DeLee, interview by the author, August 8, 1992, Ridgeville, South Carolina.

5. DeLee, interview by the author, July 4, 1988, Ridgeville, South Carolina.

6. Ibid.; JohnEtta Cauthen, interview by the author, April 8, 1994, Charleston, South Carolina.

7. DeLee, interview by the author, July 4, 1988. S. B. was not able to register.

8. Ibid.

9. Aldon D. Morris, *The Origins of the Civil Rights Movement: Black Communities Organizing for Change* (New York: Free Press, 1984), 26; South Carolina Code of Laws, *Statutes at Large* (1956) #741, 1747, #920, 2182; "Propose Open NAACP Roll: Bill Would Require Group to File List," *The [South Carolina] State,* January 25, 1957.

10. County resident Roosevelt Geddis of Givhans says his initial knowledge of DeLee came through these appeals and meetings: "She started working, most a one-family drive, as far as I can remember. She started coming around to the churches and talking to some people about the civil rights. That's how I remember her . . . that's how she really got to be known to start with. Her plea was for the people of Dorchester County to get together and start . . . some sort of organization." Interview by the author, October 26, 1994.

11. Between 1956 and 1968, the percentage of registered African Americans increased from 7.2 to 33.5 percent of the total county registered voters. See "S.C. Voter Registration History: 1956 to 1979," in *Reports and Resolutions of South Carolina for Fiscal Year Ending 1979* (Columbia, S.C.: State Budget and Control Board), 447.

12. United States Commission on Civil Rights, *Political Participation* (Washington, D.C.: Government Printing Office, 1968), 72, 114.

13. DeLee, interview, July 4, 1988.

14. United States Commission on Civil Rights, *Political Participation,* 62-63.

15. Ibid., 61-64.

16. See Laughlin MacDonald, "An Aristocracy of Voters: The Disenfranchisement of Blacks in South Carolina," *South Carolina Law Review* 37 (Summer 1986): 557-582. Enacted in 1950, the South Carolina full-slate law invalidated all ballots on which persons voted for more or less than the number of seats open in a multimember district.

17. James E. Clyburn, Charleston, South Carolina, to Paul Mathias, Columbia, South Carolina, October 20, 1969, South Carolina Council on Human Relations Files, South Caroliniana Collection, University of South Carolina.

18. "Blacks May Support Write-In," *Charlotte Observer,* July 7, 1970, sec. A, p. 6; "Black-Oriented Party Head Vows to Dismantle System," *Charleston News and Courier,* September 5, 1970, sec. B, p. 12.

19. "Black-Oriented Party Head Vows to Dismantle System."

20. Robert G. Liming, "Mrs. DeLee Says 'Urged to Run,' " *The [South Carolina] State,* January 31, 1971, sec. D, p. 3; "Civil Rights Leader Gets UCP First District Nod," *Charleston News and Courier,* 31 January 1971, sec. D, p. 1.

21. Liming, "Mrs. DeLee Says 'Urged to Run.' "

22. "Civil Rights Leader Gets UCP First District Nod."

23. Margaret Berry Bethea, "Alienation and Third Parties: A Study of the United Citizens['] Party in South Carolina" (M.A. thesis: University of South Carolina, 1973), 22. Bethea writes: "Although it cannot be said with absolute accuracy that the absence of the UCP would have resulted in a Democratic victory in every county, an analysis of black majority precincts comparing votes cast in 1968 to votes cast in 1971 for the Democratic candidates will suggest that the UCP did" affect the Democratic Party's showing in the race.

24. *DeLee v. Patrick,* CA#71-581 (USDC S. Carolina 1971).

25. *DeLee v. Kizer,* CA#73-521 (USDC S. Carolina 1973).

26. *Stevenson v. West* Governor of the State of South Carolina, CA#72-45 (USDC S. Carolina 1972).

27. Ibid.

28. Ibid.; see Judge Clement F. Haynesworth Jr., Columbia, to Attorney Randall T. Bell and Attorney Matthew J. Perry, Columbia, July 5, 1973.

29. *DeLee v. Branton*, CA#73-902 (USDC S. Carolina 1973).

30. Ibid. Simons ordered that the next election be held on a county-wide, at-large basis.

31. Quoted in "Governor Says S.C. 'To Resist Integration,' " *Richmond News Leader*, November 4, 1955.

32. W. D. Workman Jr., "No Integrated Schools for S.C., Says Report to White House Meet," *Charlotte Observer*, November 17, 1955.

33. "Segregation Unit Head Keeps Mum," *Charlotte Observer*, December 4, 1959.

34. "Hollings Praises Assembly for Segregation Actions," *The State*, May 28, 1960. Also see "Two Attack S.C. Segregation Statute Change," *The State*, May 5, 1960.

35. Office of Education, U.S. Department of Health, Education, and Welfare, and U.S. Commission on Civil Rights, "Status of School Desegregation in Southern and Border States," an occasional report, March 1966, Southern Regional Council Files, Atlanta University Center Special Collections.

36. *DeLee v. Dorchester County School District Three*, CA#66-183 (USDC S. Carolina 1966).

37. Roosevelt Geddis, Ridgeville, to Richard Detreville, Dorchester, January 13, 1969, South Carolina Council on Human Relations Files, South Caroliniana Collection, University of South Carolina.

38. See *DeLee v. Dorchester County School District Three*, "Motion to Add Parties," December 11, 1967; DeLee, interview, July 4, 1988.

39. Mordecai Johnson, Florence, to Selected Persons with S.C. School Cases, October 8, 1969, South Carolina Council on Human Relations Files, South Caroliniana Collection, University of South Carolina.

40. Ibid.

41. Ibid.; Mordecai Johnson, interview; *DeLee v. School District Three*; Attorney Fred Moore, Charleston, to Paul Anthony, Atlanta, March 3, 1970, Southern Regional Council Files, Atlanta University Center Special Collections.

42. *DeLee v. School District Three*.

43. "Hemphill Raps 'Political Rumors,' " *Charleston News and Courier*, July 18, 1969, sec B, p. 6.

44. Matthew D. McCollum and Paul Matthias, South Carolina Commission on Human Relations, Columbia, S.C., telegram to President Richard Nixon, Washington, D.C., June 26, 1969, South Carolina Council on Human Relations Files, South Caroliniana Collection, University of South Carolina. *Charleston*.

45. Hayes Mizell, former field worker, American Friends Service Committee, interview by author, June 18, 1993, tape recording, New York, New York; "Mitchell Reassures Protesters," *The State*, July 2, 1969, sec. A, p. 1; "30 'Occupy' Attorney General's Office," *Washington Post*, July 2, 1969, sec. A, p. 4; "The Administration: Tenuous Balance," *Time*, July 11, 1969, 14-15; "Civil Rights: A Debt to Dixie," *Newsweek*, July 14, 1969, 23.

46. "NAACP Asks Protection for Woman," *The State*, November 25, 1969, sec. B, p. 4.

47. "Civil Rights Leader Gets UCP First District Nod."

48. DeLee, interview, August 8, 1992.

5

Christinah Nku

A Woman at the Center of Healing Her Nation

Linda E. Thomas

Ubuntu is a term used in the Black South African community to express what it means to be a full human being in the context of community. I initially heard of *ubuntu* when I visited South Africa in 1985, and I noted its frequent use during subsequent research trips in 1991, 1992, 1993, 1994, and 1996. In 1985, I experienced firsthand the turmoil in African townships in Johannesburg, Bloemfontein, Cape Town, and Durban that stemmed largely from the state of emergency imposed by the P. W. Botha regime. The meaning of *ubuntu* became clear to me as Black people's actions displayed a defiance against the brutal system of apartheid that violated them daily. Having experienced the effects of more than three centuries of tragic usurpation of structural power by whites, Black South Africans use the concept of *ubuntu* to claim their "peoplehood" despite the wilderness experience that began in 1652 with the arrival of Jan van Riebeeck and the Dutch East India Company.

Ubuntu also describes the central cultural values of African people. It denotes "the centrality of human beings in society."[1] I believe that *ubuntu* can be directly related to Alice Walker's womanist perspective that affirms commitment to community. For Walker, a womanist is "committed to the survival and wholeness of entire people, male and female."[2]

Since it is through women that the human community comes into existence and is sustained and maintained, it seems fitting to examine the life experiences of Black South African women in relation to the "wilderness" concept of womanist theologian Delores Williams. Williams argues that "wilderness" or "the wilderness experience" is a "symbolic term that represents a near-destruction situation in which God gives personal direction to the believer and thereby helps her make a way out of what she thought was no way."[3]

Generation after generation of Black South African women have known the reality of the wilderness as they and their communities lived under the death-dealing system of apartheid. Although South Africa held its first democratic elections in April 1994 and elected Nelson Mandela as the first Black president, apartheid lives on.[4] The core of apartheid, which was officially launched in 1948 but began as early as the original Dutch invasion of the Cape Colony, was separate and unequal development for people of African descent.[5] After apartheid was established in the White Dutch Reformed Church, the political architect of apartheid, Hendrik Verwoerd, vowed that Africans would be a servant class for the White minority. He accented this pledge in his statement about the education of Africans:

> Education must train and teach people in accordance to their opportunities in life, according to the sphere in which they live . . . The Bantu must be guided to serve his own community in all respects. There is not a place for him in the European community above the level of certain forms of labour.[6]

Unequal educational opportunities were one of the primary tools apartheid used to attack the minds and identity of Black South Africans. African children were not allowed to receive a sense of Black people's contribution to their country's history and culture. This unequal development adversely affected children's self-esteem and their ability to think of themselves in a positive sense. Economist Francis Wilson and anthropologist Mamphela Ramphele's research for the Carnegie Foundation further demonstrates the intentional underdevelopment of education for the Black majority. They write:

> There is the matter of sheer discrimination in the funding of education by the state . . . African pupils, each with a subsidy of R234 in 1983/84, received only one-seventh (14 per cent) of the subsidy of R1, 654 available for white pupils. These statistics understate the actual difference in subsidy to the two groups as virtually all white children of school-going age are at school whilst for black children, particularly in the rural areas, the proportion at school is well below the maximum.[7]

While education is one example of the deep structural effects of apartheid that continue to have implications in a post-apartheid South Africa, there are many others, including housing, unemployment, and medical care. Although these remnant apartheid structures affect the entire Black South African community, African women in particular daily bear the brunt of this unrelenting oppression. This is because African women must deal with the multiple categories of race, class, and gender that interact in a way that not only adds but multiplies the dangers of oppression. Sociologist

Cheryl Townsend Gilkes argues that African American women experience multiple jeopardies that permit them to see the dominant controlling system for what it is.[8] This is also true for Black South African women, and thus it follows that, in South Africa, African women are "the most abused by the process of apartheid and capitalism" and are at the "centre of the struggle for meaningful change."[9]

While issues about race have dominated political discourse in South Africa, many African women are aware of their class and gender oppression. A group of African women formed a collective and wrote a volume of essays entitled *Vukani Makhosikazi: South African Women Speak*. They argue:

> Although we locate the position of women within a class framework, in the book we draw out those factors which comprise their specific burden. These include the assumption of differing sexual roles in the family and male dominance in sexual relationships. As a result women shoulder responsibility for the household and children. Women are also drawn into the labour market at the lowest levels of employment—capital conveniently assumes that they are supplementary earners within the family.[10]

A principal form of employment for African women in South Africa is domestic work. In White households, we encounter the unequal race and class relations between White and African women. Sociologist Jacklyn Cock writes about these unequal relationships:

> In South Africa most white households employ servants. Poverty, labour controls and a lack of employment alternatives combine to "trap" many African women in domestic service. They are trapped in a condition of immobility within which they are subject to intense oppression. Such oppression is evident in their low wages and long working hours and in the demeaning treatment of them by the white women who are their employers. ("She does not see me as a woman. She looks down on me.") This oppression is expressed in many domestic servants' sense of being slaves, of leading wasted lives which they are powerless to change. ("I have been a slave all my life." "We are slaves in our own country.") Other Africans also experience their working lives as a form of slavery. This is because Africans in South Africa are one of the most regimented labour forces in the contemporary world.[11]

Cock goes on to argue that African women domestic workers experience "ultra-exploitation":

> As an occupational group domestic workers are subject to a level of "ultra-exploitation." They are denied a negotiated wage, reasonable

working hours, family and social life. They are also denied favourable working conditions, respectful treatment and any acknowledgement of the dignity of their labour, as well as specific legal protection and effective bargaining power.[12]

Many African women recognize the extreme burden placed upon them and their community. A group of African women who lived in Black townships surrounding Johannesburg wrote about domestic work:

> Domestic work is the main form of employment for African women. Domestic work and housework isolate women from each other, locking them into a daily experience of solitary suffering. These women have little chance to move out of these narrow confines and identify with other women. It is all the more difficult for them to identify with men. As domestic workers women may be completely separated from their men. As wives they may be dominated and maltreated in their own homes.[13]

In examining the full dimension of Black South African women's lives, oppression in its totality is a wilderness experience. As gendered persons, women are controlled by different men all their lives. Ramphele comments, "It is a control that stretches from the cradle to the grave. This system, which the legal provision of successive White governments has reinforced, confers the status of perpetual minor upon African women."[14]

Not only have African women been controlled by men throughout their lives, they are also controlled by "tradition" as manifested in various African cultures in South Africa. "Tradition" here means a reconstruction of history that creates a reality believed to be indisputable and that is employed to sanction particular actions advantageous to men.[15] Oppression by tradition further contributes to the wilderness experience of Black South African women. For example, bridewealth, known as *lobola* in South Africa, is an institution that is a "traditional" form of domination of women by men in many African cultures.[16] Bridewealth is an exchange of some sort of wealth that flows from the husband or his family to the wife's family. The practice is usual in societies with patrilineal descent groups. It serves to make marriage relationships acceptable to both spouses' families and signifies the transfer of rights over women and/or children. In sum, through bridewealth the reproductive power of women is harnessed. Reproductive power in this case is not limited to the procreative powers of women, but includes all actions by women that are for the maintenance and enhancement of their families and their communities. While bridewealth controls women, it simultaneously establishes the way males relate to each other individually and as a group. Money is usually substituted for cattle as the unit of exchange for women, but women are still expected to ritualistically eat *amaas* (sour milk) as a signal of their acceptance into their husbands' families. This ritual continues a symbolic link to the former use of cattle as the unit of exchange for women.[17]

Among Black South Africans it is understood that a woman marries into her husband's family, while men have few obligations to their wives' family beyond bridewealth and sporadic voluntary monetary contributions. Ramphele argues that tradition is "at the very basis of bringing women into a system of control that ensures the perpetuation of patriarchal family relations."[18] The custom, in some Black South African cultures, of giving a woman a new name at the time of marriage reinforces the expectation that she will contribute her reproductive skills to her husband's family and not to her own. This is another cultural feature that reinforces the control of women.

Tradition, as it relates to gender oppression of African women, is supported not only by men, but also by women. Since the male system, whether it is among White or African men, determines the degree to which women amass power in macro and micro systems, most women have internalized expected gender roles. Thus, among African women, mothers-in-law and sisters-in-law socialize newly wed women to the appropriate marital role. Mothers-in-law and sisters-in-law, who typically are older women, derive emotional and financial advantages through this tradition.[19]

Hierarchies of control by older African women are also present in the "king-maker" tradition that belongs to mothers-in-law.[20] Not only does this category signify the role of mothers in choosing acceptable brides for their sons, but the mothers also continue to claim power over their sons and daughters-in-law during marriage. Daughters-in-law are sometimes a threat to mothers who have received economic benefits from dedicated sons. Mothers-in-law realize that they will no longer be the sole recipients of their son's earnings, because he must also support his wife and children. If the issue of economic support is worked out, the relationships among all parties are not as strained. Because of macro-level capitalist apartheid structures that have severely disadvantaged all aspects of African women's lives, women compete with each other for the little money that African men earn. The apartheid and post-apartheid capitalist system's negative effect upon a monetarily bankrupt African community is another reason that Black South African women experience the wilderness.

The oppression of Black South African women is quite complex, and thus an integrated approach to their wilderness experience is necessary. Ramphele argues that

A recognition of gender as but one of the power differential demands an integrated analysis. The recognition of the different experiences of women is not enough. An attempt has to be made to understand how race, class, geographical location, age, etc. articulate with gender if we are to help formulate viable intervention strategies, which can speak to women and men under different circumstances ... This should not be seen as being blind to the risk inherent in this type of

integrated analysis. There are enormous risks inherent in this proposed approach.[21]

Ramphele's argument that an integrated analysis is a critical tool for understanding the complex lives of African women in South Africa sets a clear
vision for what needs to happen theoretically and empirically. To further
elucidate an integrated analysis and our understanding of the wilderness
experience of Black South African women as systematically produced in
macro systems that have denied them personhood by restricting their
educational opportunities, radically exploiting their services as domes-
tics, and trapping them in economic practices that disadvantage their status, we return to *ubuntu*. This word testifies to the tangible expression of
people being with each other in all conditions of life, so that individuals'
personhood is enhanced in the experience of community even in the midst
of the wilderness.

Mother Christinah Nku is a historical figure whose lifeworks embodied
the active engagement of *ubuntu*. We now turn to the herstory of Christinah
Nku, a woman who stepped outside the usual race, gender, and class roles
expected of African women. Nku founded St. John's Apostolic Faith Mission Church and in so doing set a course for the healing of a nation. I will
argue that she did so because of *ubuntu*, a commitment to the essence of
her community as worthy of full humanity even while the White minority
government was establishing the forces of apartheid.

Mother Nku founded her church because she had a dream and vision to
offer ministry to Africans based on John 5, the story of Jesus healing a
disabled man who sat for several years by the pool at Bethesda. The ministry of Nku's church brought healing to the broken and sick bodies of
thousands of Black people in South Africa. Throughout her ministry, Nku
walked through the wilderness of an emerging apartheid state to establish
an institution where poor Black South Africans created religious rituals
that helped them "to make a way out of no way."

Glimpses of the Life of Christinah Mokotuli Nku

In 1924, a Sotho-speaking African woman named Christinah Mokotuli
Nku had a dream in which she saw a large brick church with twelve doors
and heard a voice telling her to build a church for God. The voice told her
that her children would help to build the church and that her son John
would one day be the chief priest of all of the churches that emerged from
the original church with twelve doors. This dream gave Christinah Mokotuli
Nku the conviction to establish her own church, whose primary ministry
was for the healing of the sick.

Mokotuli, the daughter of Enock Lethamaha and Magdalene Serati, was
born in the Transvaal in 1894, baptized during her childhood, and given
the Christian name Christinah. She attended a primary school that Methodist missionaries opened. While schools for White children progressed

to standard 10, the highest level of education a Black child could achieve at the mission school was standard 3.[22] As an accelerated student, Christinah achieved the merit title "Royal Reader," which meant that she could read and write.

During her childhood, Christinah was quite different from her siblings. She spent most of her time praying and did not interact very much with children her age. In 1906, at the age of twelve, Christinah had her first vision, which she later recounted:

> I saw a tall man very black with bundles and bundles of money. He wanted to give me the money, but I refused—a voice called me. I looked up and someone unseen spoke and said "He is the Devil, you must not take his money." I saw one like an angel. He gave me a hymn book and asked me to sing.[23]

In 1914, Christinah had a dream in which she was told she would have children. In her sleep a voice said:

> Christinah, you will be married and have children. Your first child will be a boy. His name is Johannes or St. John. He will be powerful in God's work. The second will be a girl. Her name is Anna. The third a boy. His name is Obed.[24]

After she was married to Lazarus Mosioa Nku, the voice spoke again and refined its message about her children:

> I was then promised twins, but when I was left with two months before confinement, I was told, I am carrying a girl. Her name is Mary. After Mary there was a change again. A voice told me I was expecting a boy. His name is Joel, but just before confinement, I was told it is a girl. Her name is Jael Lydia. The sixth child will be a boy. His name is Joel. Joel will be a very red baby at birth. The seventh child will be a girl. Her name is Magdeline. The eighth will be a girl too and her name is Selena.[25]

Before the birth of every child, Nku heard from "a strange voice" which told her the future of each child. She, in turn, shared this information with her husband, who "believed because God had shown him strange things too."[26]

According to her family's records, early in 1918, Nku affiliated with the Apostolic Faith Mission Church, a White mission denomination with ties in the U.S. This affiliation began when she went to Father Elias Nkitsing of the Apostolic Faith Mission Church to receive prayer. While he prayed, Nku had a vision in which a ball of fire became seven stars. During the vision, everyone was inspired by the Holy Ghost and spoke in tongues.[27]

Her prayer relationship with Father Nkitsing continued over several years, and in time, she received prayers from his brother, Ishmael Nkitsing. In the same year, Nku began to pray for the sick. She said, "At this time I had also prayed for the sick and through God's mercy many were healed."[28] It was during the period when the Nkitsing brothers prayed with her that she had the vision of the church with twelve doors.

The Social Context and Ministry of Mother Christinah Nku

Mother Nku's life spanned more than nine decades. Therefore, from birth to old age she experienced the multilayered and complex history of the nation of her birth. Most important, as an African woman, she lived with the devastating effects of segregation administrated by local authorities in Johannesburg and of formal apartheid as executed by the Nationalists in 1948. Mother Nku's healing treatments were initially administered to people who lived in African townships on the Witwatersrand.[29] According to Eddie Koch, from 1913 to 1940, Black people who lived in townships on the Witwatersrand were proletariats from various social locations. Many were migrants who worked in mines and lived in single-sex hostels; others were "*amakumsha* or *abaphakathi*," people who lived betwixt and between; some lived on the margins because they did not have an economic base in rural areas or wage work; and, finally, some were forced to relinquish their land and establish life in the city.[30]

During and after World War I, the African population on the Witwatersrand soared, because the effects of the 1913 Land Act caused entire families to enter a proletarian status.[31] Manufacturing and commercial businesses such as the mining industry paid wages that were based on the subsistence needs of an individual worker. These industries refused to add capital to public housing for workers. Moreover, Africans were affected by the coalition between local capitalists and White workers who insisted on a policy of residential segregation that became public policy formulated by the Stallard Commission and enacted in the 1923 Urban Areas Act. This policy enshrined the White supremacist belief that "natives—men, women and children—should only be permitted within municipal areas in so far and for so long as the wants of the White population demand their presence."[32] While an act of the Supreme Court in 1926 made the 1923 Urban Areas Act void because alternative housing was not available for Africans, White landowners cashed in on this ruling by building shantytowns in the city and charging excessive rents.[33] White residents moved out of the areas occupied by Black renters, and "old 'fashionable' suburbs were transformed into highly crowded slumyard areas."[34] Slumyards grew all over Johannesburg and included areas such as Doornfontein, Vrededorp, and Prospect Township, all of which were close to the healing ministry of Mother Nku.

The wilderness that Black people experienced daily is highlighted in a report published by the Johannesburg "Joint Council of Europeans and Natives" in 1921. The wages paid by Johannesburg industry were woefully inadequate, as they were based on the "industrial male worker" who was not related to his family. The report claims that

> the native engaged in town work looks for quarters of his own and perhaps brings his family with him. Under these altered circumstances it is impossible for the wages received ... to meet the requirements of town dwellers.[35]

Children were forced to move to the city because of the extreme poverty in rural areas, but employment was not always available. This resulted in high unemployment and social deterioration in urban areas occupied by Africans. In 1924, J. D. Rheinhallt Jones, a liberal, wrote about the social situation of some African workers who "have become aged, crippled or otherwise incapacitated from earning a livelihood . . . The living conditions under which some of them exist and eke out a precarious living are deplorable."[36] Another report, written by the Director of Native Labour in 1937, indicated that 100,000 children, women, and men were unemployed on the Witwatersrand. In the same year, Councillor A. Immink reported that 93,000 people in the same area did not have the means to live decently, as "they live by their wits, sleep with their friends at night and are not included in the census."[37] The conditions of life, the squalor, lack of sanitation, high rents, and overcrowding produced a horrific situation for Africans. These factors also contributed to the genocide of Africans, as the infant mortality rate for Black children was double that of Whites for the period between 1923 and 1936.[38]

Mother Nku practiced her ministry in those areas where social and economic conditions were oppressive. Thousands of desolate and forlorn people gathered daily at her two-room Prospect Township home for prayer and healing services held at 5:00 A.M., 9:00 A.M., 3:00 P.M., and 7:00 P.M.[39]

Circumstances related to emergent apartheid policies forced Nku to move to her sister's home in Evaton, a peri-urban area on the Witwatersrand. Services were conducted there, and hundreds were healed through her prayers, among them a disabled woman named Mrs. Dinah Ratefane.[40] People also came from neighboring Black townships in VeVeeniging and Meyerton to participate in healing services at no cost. While Nku refused to take money from her patients, her supporters were concerned about the cost of feeding those who came for healing.[41] They felt that if she did not want to receive money, then converts should make a donation at the end of every month. Nku refused this suggestion, because she was convinced that God would provide money: "I refused this suggestion because God had shown me big white dishes full of silver. He promised he was going to give them to me, so I was waiting."[42]

In 1937, Mother Nku decided to collect one shilling from each person who came to her for healing to extend the church's ministry. As a result of this collection, seventy churches with exteriors painted blue and white were built throughout Southern Africa. In 1938, the government gave official recognition to St. John's Apostolic Faith Mission Church, an institution which patients and others who lived in surrounding townships called a hospital. The church created an admissions committee responsible for recording personal data for each individual who came for healing and was known far and wide as a place where people could be renewed and restored from the wounds of the wilderness generated from the effects of apartheid. People were revitalized through the therapeutic benefit of ritual and community.

If the vicious and inhuman White supremacist policies that formed the sociopolitical environment for Black life in South Africa constituted the context for Christinah Nku's life, and healing rituals the agency through which she willfully and vigorously gave witness to her profound religious faith and dedication to her community, then prophecy gave Nku a commitment to her life's work that reflected theological urgency and "oppositional engagement"[43] against the suffering of African people. Nku's singular focus in life was listening to messages from God. As a result, she was not a political activist in the usual sense of the term. She did not attend political meetings nor belong to a political party.[44] Nku believed herself to be an agent of God on earth. God told her what to do and she resolutely carried out her assignments. This life of pure devotion and unyielding attention to God led her to create healing rituals that liberated the oppressed to such an extent that they were empowered to believe that they were worthy of and entitled to food, shelter, and clothing. As the Union of South Africa became an apartheid state and the genocide of Black people became more overt, Nku's church grew rapidly, and congregations spread all over South Africa and its borders. As the church grew, Nku's ministry expanded through the establishment of schools for children and programs for youth and adults. People's lives were transformed, and this directly benefitted the community. Nku's ministry was subversive in that it functioned as a hidden transcript that was a response to systems that dominated the poor.[45] According to Ramphele, apartheid as a system "effect[ed] people's sense of well being along a continuum."[46] While there were a variety of responses to apartheid, the ministry of Nku was the medium through which poor people disempowered by a brutal state system "talked back."[47] The bodies of Black people afflicted with manifold illnesses undoubtedly rooted in the stressful social situation in which they lived were resurrected from the death-dealing system of racial discrimination through the healing rituals and the community that Mother Nku provided.

Prophetic Ministry

The prophecies of Nku symbolized her bonding with a deity who directed the course of history and intervened on behalf of the needy. When the prophecies were fulfilled, patients and church members were mesmerized by her power, spiritual centeredness, and fidelity to God. As a result, the numbers of people who came to the church increased. People who lived in an unpredictable world had someone in whom they could believe. That Nku was a mother to those who lived in a hostile environment is reflected by the testimony of her daughter Lydia August:

> She is a unique mother who will always be remembered by [the] millions and millions she through God's power . . . helped and healed from diverse diseases. She will always be thought of by the millions dedicated to the work she had founded. Our mother is a mother with a "thousand Teats" who had by the spiritual gifts fed millions.[48]

Nku's church provided a sense of personhood for its members. According to Frederick Klaits, personhood refers to the part of a person's identity that seeks to be in relationship with others.[49] The world of Nku and her followers was so unpredictable that a sustaining factor was the rhythmic pattern of prayer and healing services held four times a day, seven days a week. The services drew people to each other, as individuals stood before the congregation and asked God for what they needed (*isicelo*) and confessed (*ntlambulo*) what was going on in their lives in a fashion that resembles "testimony time" in Black churches in the United States. The only difference is that *isicelo* and *ntlambulo* are African rituals in which the speech that the person makes is directed to God in the hearing of the congregation. In other words, God is the gathered community.

During a St. John's service I attended in Guguletu Township in Cape Town in 1994, a pregnant woman asked God (*isicelo*) to protect the child that she carried:

> I was going all over the place looking for this church. I couldn't find this church. I come from the Transkei. I am asking God to help me to have children. Every time I get children, they pass away. Every time. I wish this one that I am carrying will survive. The child must survive. I ask people to pray for me to have this baby.[50]

After this ritual speech and enactment of sacred drama, each person in the congregation kneeled and said different prayers of the heart aloud in unison. The effect was a cacophony of ritual voices that surrounded this woman who had spoken to God. The spirit of the prayers made God's presence known to all who were present. This ritual, which enfolded this woman who dared to speak directly to God in the presence of others, dramatized "God with humanity" in sacred space that oppressive forces could not invade. This woman's person and the congregation's personhood were affirmed spiritually and emotionally. All who were present had a part of themselves nourished and transformed to "keep on keeping on" in spite of the wilderness.

While *isicelo* and *ntlambulo* take place at the beginning of worship, the service also includes scripture readings, hymns, preaching, and offerings. The last act of worship is the service of healing, in which water is blessed and people come forward to drink. After a person drinks holy water, ministers, evangelists, and prophets lay their hands, which have been washed in holy water, upon each person. Water is an element used throughout the world for cleansing and renewal. It is an essential part of all life forms. No living thing can exist without water; hence it is a powerful symbol through which the sacred is present. It is this powerful element, water, that is the center of St. John's ministry, as it is the agent used for healing. The healing rituals involve not only the consumption of water but also its use for bathing, vomiting, and enemas. These more elaborate healing treatments are administered twice a week by members who are specially trained. These ritual productions are the means by which people have a sense of power within themselves and within their community.

In addition to *isicelo*, *ntlambulo*, and healing rituals, St. John's provides social networks of support. For instance, Mother Nku prophesied that the church would have a marching band with colorful uniforms. In 1948, a church band was formed and blessed by the prophets. August observed that the band drew many young people to the church:

> Most young people join the church because of the band music they have heard and because of the attractive band uniform of blue and white. The uniform looks marvelous and very attractive.
>
> Because of the centre of attraction, our band has caused, we had a blessing in disguise because out of the many who came because of the music they heard and the band they saw and the band they admired, we have baptized hundreds of the young people joining and wanting to become band players. We have also produced ministers of religion from those with such godly gifts and [from those] who were spiritually seen to be ordained for the vocation by our leading prophetess in our church, mother Christinah Mokotuli Nku.[51]

In 1991, I had the honor of marching with a St. John's band in Khayamandi, a Black township in Stellenbosch. As we marched down the main street of the township to open a gala church festival, I noticed that people marched with their heads high and bodies moving beautifully to the beat of the drum. A sense of solidarity and pride was present, and an effusive energy flowed from one person to another as people who lived in the township came to their doors with a smile and waved at the band. It was a moment that spelled pride and transformation for the smallest child and the oldest adult who lifted their feet proudly and rhythmically walked down streets lined with little houses that reflected the handwriting of apartheid. Street signs erected at corners had the letters "NY," which stood for "Native Yard." In the midst of all the history of limiting structural forces and depravity, Black humanity from the grassroots marched with pride.

Uniforms have historically regimented Black life in South Africa and signal a person's status in society. Mother Nku's vision of St. John's members wearing blue-and-white uniforms was a counterhegemonic device that redefined the way that status was constituted for grassroots people. St. John's members wear blue-and-white uniforms to honor Mother Nku's vision of transformed life after baptism: "The uniform of blue and white was prophesied by mother Christinah Mokotuli Nku in 1936 . . . In 1937 a group of children were the first to use the church uniform at the church festival held in Evaton."[52] Personhood is affirmed as grassroots people wear uniforms that indicate a decision on their part to accept healing as part of their lives. Additionally, the uniform removes concern for the status consciousness that occurs in relationship to appropriate "church clothes."

A special ritual is conducted for persons who reach the point of wearing the uniform. The ritual includes sacred stylized movement by the minister who blesses the uniform before an initiate puts it on. In 1991, I attended several services in which new members were robed with their uniforms. All were highly celebratory services in which the uniform signaled transformation in the person's life and acceptance into a community that affirmed the personhood of grassroots people who are continually discounted by society. The rituals using uniforms symbolized *ubuntu*.

There were other concrete ways that the ministry of Nku exhibited attention to personhood. She established a school for children in Evaton during a period when poor Black children had little hope for an education supported by local municipalities. Mission churches usually arranged education for Black children. For instance, the African Methodist Episcopal Church established Wilberforce, an institution that was exclusively for the education of Black children. Nku's school was one of the first African Independent Church schools to be established. Lydia August recalls the role that her brother Obed played in establishing St. John's school:

> Obed played a very important part in the way that he pushed this one and only mission school to be officially registered, under the Education Department . . . other school[s] . . . were regarded as better . . . because they were not [founded by] the African Independent Churches but by churches that came from overseas.[53]

August also remembered her own vision to start a school:

> I had a vision to start a night school. Before I could go any farther with my thoughts, I was approached by the church to open up a night school . . . The idea of the night school was put before the church authorities and it was highly welcomed.[54]

In an interview I conducted with Lydia August on January 23, 1996, we discussed her mother's ministry. She reflected on the importance of the schools founded by St. John's, saying, "Our schools taught children the lessons of life for a difficult world. Our children were prepared for anything they encountered."

Personhood was also created for those associated with Nku's church through choirs. Like all groups that rely on the commitment of their members, church choirs were the vehicles for establishing group solidarity. Not only was this facilitated when the group came together for rehearsals, it was also augmented when the choir sang during worship services and in competitions with choirs from other churches. It was usual for choir members to sing during a morning worship service and then to have several commitments to sing at other church services on the same afternoon and evening. Thus, members of the choir sang and traveled together throughout the region to different churches and music festivals. Individuals with beautiful voices were affirmed as they performed solos.

Finally, personhood and group solidarity for grassroots people were produced when members of the church traveled to the denominational headquarters for triannual festivals. These festivals were the fulfillment of Nku's prophecy that three times a year members of various St. John's churches would gather at the "mother" church for fellowship. People traveled from all over southern Africa to participate in the festivals. Enduring friendships were established, and people looked forward to gathering at these multicultural and multilingual events. Services were held throughout the day and included an all-night vigil. Choirs from different churches were designated a particular time to sing, and communion was served in the evening to replicate the time of day that Jesus served the holy meal to the twelve disciples. The services were held over a four-day period to coincide with a weekend. On Sunday morning, many were baptized and robed as members. I attended several festivals over the course of my fieldwork and witnessed as many as two hundred people being baptized on a Sunday morning. The spirit of community exudes from people who travel to the festival from all over South Africa. All these rituals, which were prophesied by Mother Nku, have established personhood in very important ways. The prophecies of Mother Nku empowered people in her churches and in society.

Christinah Nku's Vision of *Ubuntu* for Black South Africans

Powerful spiritual forces inspire visions (God) in people's lives and are influenced by the sociopolitical situations in which persons find themselves. There are many examples of oppressed women responding to "the voice of God" to engage in liberating activities on behalf of their communities. Sojourner Truth, who lived many years a slave and many years a free woman, responded to the word of God to sojourn in the land and to preach for the liberation of Blacks and women in the antebellum and postbellum United States. Religious faith influenced Harriet Tubman, called the Moses of her people, to make many dangerous trips to win freedom for Black slaves as they boarded the Underground Railroad and crossed the border to Canada. Religious belief and commitment to community led Maria Stewart to give political speeches that called for the uplift of Black people during the Reconstruction period. It is no surprise, then, that Christinah Nku, being born in South Africa during the last decade of the nineteenth century and living into the twentieth century and having moral commitment and an *ubuntu* vision of community, would use religious symbols and rituals to bring relief to Black South Africans who suffered from various sicknesses that were the result of life lived under enforced deprivation.[55]

With the lives of Black South Africans so violently affected by the imposition of racial inferiority through the laws of the State, Nku's vision to establish a church where healing rituals were central captured the epitome of *ubuntu*, because African women and their communities needed a way to maintain the community's cultural memory and a means to proclaim an imaginative possibility for an affirming future. The rituals of healing, particularly as they were built upon John 5, were a means for the African community to claim autonomy through symbol systems that used both indigenous African and Christian elements. These creolized rituals were counterhegemonic devices that Africans used to signal their disdain for oppressive dominant power structures and to claim their own power. The rituals were the African community's way of turning the wilderness experience of apartheid into a positive struggle for self-determination.

Williams's category of "wilderness" describes poignantly the lives of Black South African women and their communities' negative economic experience of poverty and social displacement that resulted from apartheid. Healing rituals reflected the communities' positive encounter with God that provided hope for the future. Mother Nku's rituals provided a way for the church to hold African families together when the government systematically attempted to destroy African life at the core. It can easily be argued that the South African government policy of apartheid was genocidal for the African community. Mother Nku's church and its rituals of healing were a means to claim *ubuntu* and restore life for African people. The ministry of Christinah Nku placed an African woman at the center of the entire African community's history of victimization by apartheid policies. It also placed an African woman at the center of the healing of a nation, as the rituals represented a fierce survival struggle.

Conclusion

In this essay I have attempted to demonstrate how sociopolitical processes in the Black South African community and in the White South African apartheid community affected Black South African women's lives. We have seen how Black South Africans used the religion and rituals created by Christinah Nku to struggle with and change the detrimental qualities of some of those processes. We also have a sense of the experience of Black South African women and the complex multiple oppressions in their lives. The formation of a religious community and the creation of healing rituals by Christinah Nku restored life into African communities that, because of the effects of apartheid, had very little for which to hope in their lives. Apartheid's grip was so firm and so elaborately weaved into the formal and informal structures that African communities had very few choices about how to respond to their legalized oppression.[56] Religion and rituals that symbolically duplicated the chaos of the sociopolitical situation were part of the response of Mother Nku's African-initiated church, St. John's.[57] These rituals of St. John's and other African indigenous churches transformed the consciousness of many Black South Africans, so that apartheid ideology, which advanced self-loathing among Black South Africans, lost its grip on the minds of these members. Instead, those who participated in the rituals claimed a self affirmed by a mighty Spirit who was known through the present community living in the midst of apartheid and through the community of ancestors who had gone before them. The community thus claimed the individuals present and also its own identity as a group, a group that had a rich past and a positive continuing encounter with God, who was with them in the wilderness. While apartheid ideology had much negative impact on the consciousness of Black people, the healing rituals became counterhegemonic devices to confront the negative with claims to a great indigenous past that included God, Spirit, the ancestors, and historical knowledge about survival.

Christinah Nku's church and its rituals represent resistance strategies that belong to the "re/productive history"[58] in which the members of the church participated daily. Women's re/productive history involves far more than the birth process. According to Williams, it involves the ideas and works of Black women that they give to their communities for a positive quality of life.[59] Through the re/productive history that Nku created and passed on, we learn of the transformed lives of thousands of Black South Africans who continue to practice the rituals at St. John's congregations scattered all over southern Africa. The Nku re/production history restored a race of people confronted with the threat of genocide. Thus, we see Nku's "survival intelligence" revealed as a mode of "resistance, sustenance and resurrection from despair" created through ritual.[60] Indeed, Christinah Nku used her community's ancestral, spiritual, intellectual, and material resources to create a church to respond to destructive apartheid forces. This African-initiated church used the wilderness experience to restore life, proclaim hope, and promise a future for Black women, men, and children in South Africa. The promise has come to pass.

Notes

1. Mamphela Altetta Ramphele, "The Politics of Space: Life in the Migrant Labour Hostels of the Western Cape" (Ph.D. diss., Department of Social Anthropology, University of Cape Town, 1991), 86.

2. Alice Walker, *In Search of Our Mothers' Gardens* (New York: Harcourt Brace Jovanovich, 1983), xi.

3. Delores S. Williams, *Sisters in the Wilderness: The Challenge of Womanist God-Talk* (Maryknoll, N.Y.: Orbis, 1993), 108.

4. See "Apartheid Lives On" in the *New York Times*, 29 October 1994:19.

5. Other people of color, namely the so-called Coloured and Asians, were also

the target of separate and unequal development, but Black Africans were the most adversely affected by apartheid policies.

6. Quoted in Thomas G. Karis and Gail M. Gerhart, *Challenge and Violence, 1953-1964*, vol. 3 of *From Protest to Challenge: A Documentary History of African Politics in South Africa, 1882-1964*, ed. Thomas G. Karis and Gwendolen M. Carter (Stanford: Hoover Institution Press, 1977), 29.

7. Francis Wilson and Mamphela Ramphele, *Uprooting Poverty: The South African Challenge* (Cape Town: David Philip, 1989), 141-142.

8. Cheryl Townsend Gilkes, "The 'Loves' and 'Troubles' of African-American Women's Bodies," in *A Troubling in My Soul: Womanist Perspectives on Evil and Suffering*, ed. Emilie M. Townes (Maryknoll, N.Y.: Orbis, 1993), 235.

9. Jane Barrett, Aneene Dawber, Barbara Klugman, Ingrid Obery, Jennifer Shindler, and Joanne Yawitch, *Vukani Makhosikazi: South African Women Speak* (London: Catholic Institute of International Relations, 1985), v.

10. Ibid., 4.

11. Jacklyn Cock, *Maids and Madams* (London: Women's Press, 1989), 1.

12. Ibid.

13. Barrett et al., *Vukani Makhosikazi*, v.

14. Ramphele, "The Dynamics of Gender Politics in Hostels in Cape Town: Another Legacy of the South African Migrant Labour System," *Journal of Southern African Studies*, 15 (3) (1989): 400.

15. Ibid., 394.

16. Bridewealth and dowry are found in many societies and cultures around the world.

17. Ramphele, "The Dynamics of Gender Politics," 401.

18. Ibid.

19. Ibid.

20. Mamphela Ramphele, "Do Women Help Perpetuate Sexism? A Bird's Eye View from South Africa," *Africa Today* 37 (1) (1990): 16.

21. Ibid., 12-13.

22. Standard 3 is equivalent to grade 5 in U.S.A. schools. Standard 10 is equivalent to grade 12.

23. Quoted in Lydia August, "How St. John's Apostolic Faith Mission Came into Being," unpublished family records, Evaton, Transvaal, Republic of South Africa, n.d., 1

24. Ibid.

25. Ibid.

26. Ibid., 2.

27. Ibid.

28. Ibid.

29. The Witwatersrand is a geographic area in Johannesburg.

30. Eddie Koch, " 'Without Visible Means of Subsistence': Slumyard Culture in Johannesburg, 1918-1940," in *Town and Countryside in the Transvaal*, ed. Belinda Bozzoli (Johannesburg: Ravan Press, 1983), 151.

31. Ibid., 152.

32. Report of the Local Government (Stallard) Commission of Enquiry, TP 1, 1922, p. 241.

33. Koch, " 'Without Visible Means,' " 153.

34. Ibid., 154.

35. Johannesburg Joint Council of Europeans and Natives, Report of the Wages

Committee, 1921, p. 1.

36. J. D. Rheinhallt Jones, memorandum, "Home for Destitute Native Children," January 31, 1934.

37. *Star*, October 22, 1937.

38. See Ray E. Phillips, *The Bantu in the City: A Study of Cultural Adjustment on the Witwatersrand* (Lovedale: Lovedale Press, 1938), 110.

39. August, "How St. John's Apostolic Faith Mission Came into Being," 2.

40. Ibid., 3.

41. Ibid.

42. Ibid.

43. Clarice Martin, "Biblical Theodicy and Black Women's Spiritual Autobiography: 'The Miry Bog, the Desolate Pit, a New Song in My Mouth,' " in Townes, *A Troubling in My Soul*, 21, uses this term for Maria Stewart's biblical commitment and spiritual determination for African Americans to have racial equality in the nineteenth century.

44. While Mother Nku saw her role as a visionary totally committed to God's work and healing, her husband, Lazarus, and their daughter Lydia were members of the ANC and were extremely active in the resistance movement.

45. See James C. Scott, *Domination and the Arts of Resistance: Hidden Transcripts* (New Haven: Yale University Press, 1990), for a detailed cross-cultural presentation about subalterns' response to power and domination.

46. Mamphela Ramphele, personal communication, August 12, 1992.

47. See bell hooks's *Talking Back: Thinking Feminist, Thinking Black* (Boston: South End Press, 1988) for more detail about the ways that subordinates are empowered when they speak the truth to authority.

48. Lydia August, "A History of Mother Christinah Nku and St. John's Apostolic Faith Mission, 1980" TMs (photocopy), Johannesburg, Republic of South Africa, 1.

49. Frederick Klaits, "Children of the Flesh, Children of the Spirit: Reproducing Persons and Houses in Gaborone, Botswana," unpublished paper, 1994: 2 .

50. This and subsequent unattributed quotations are from interviews, field notes, and research diaries of fieldwork conducted by the author in the Republic of South Africa.

51. August, "A History of Mother Christinah Nku," 156.

52. Ibid., 157.

53. Ibid., 73.

54. Ibid., 106-107.

55. See Cock, *Maids and Madams*, 8, for examples of work patterns and poverty having adverse effects on health.

56. For a recent presentation on the various dimensions of apartheid, see Philip Bonner, Peter Delius, and Deborah Posel, *Apartheid's Genesis: 1935-1962* (Johannesburg: Ravan Press, 1993).

57. See Victor Turner, *Drums of Affliction: A Study of Religious Processes among Ndembu of Zambia* (Oxford: Clarendon Press, 1968) and *The Ritual Process: Structure and Anti-Structure* (Chicago: Aldine Publishing, 1969), for a theoretical orientation about the ways in which ritual symbolically reproduces adversity that people experience and alleviates it through dramatic enactment.

58. Williams, *Sisters in the Wilderness,* 153.

59. Ibid.

60. Ibid.,158.

6

Avoiding Asphyxiation

*A Womanist Perspective on Intrapersonal and
Interpersonal Transformation*

Teresa L. Fry Brown

*We need women who are so sure of their own social footing that they
need not fear leaning to lend a hand to a fallen or falling sister.*
                            Anna Julia Cooper, educator, 1892[1]

This quotation is as true today as it was more than one hundred years
ago when Sister Cooper outlined her vision for the empowerment of African American women. Based on my personal experience, I believe that the
person most likely to understand the needs and goals of Black women is
another Black woman. Over the past ten years, I have learned about
womanist theology and ethics and attended conferences at every opportunity to listen to sisters talk about their perspectives on womanist thought.
In the beginning these experiences invigorated me, and I could not wait to
get back home and discuss them with other African American women. As I
pulled together study sessions, seminars, and sermons for African American women at the church I served, I proclaimed the liberating power of
being a womanist. To my dismay, I was met with curious looks, head shak-
ing, and tongue-in-cheek comments and "Child, that's what happens when
they go to seminary. At least she ain't trying to be a feminist." I thought I
had a precious gift for my church sisters, yet I was met with closed hands
and heads. My academic elitism was showing. I had learned womanist language but forgot to translate it into the language of my sisters. I knew something and assumed other women needed to know it. Then I began to analyze why my sisters were seemingly slow to accept this "new" body of
information and why they did not want to be associated with being a
"womanist." Through informal inquiry and formal discussion groups, I

was told, "You keep talking about finding your own voice; we can't even breathe!" Transformation was not the primary consideration for these women—staying alive, gasping for air, making ends meet, raising children were.

In fifteen years as a speech/language pathologist, I taught people how to breathe deeply, effectively use their voices, articulate speech, and communicate with clarity. Although they may have entered therapy with speech problems, after a designated number of sessions I could see the change in their behavior, because others slowly understood who they were and what they needed to say. Even being able to take air into the lungs without coughing or sputtering, and breathing out without pain or misdirected air and sounds were measures of success.

As African American women, we have learned to breathe on stolen air, silently so that no one could detect our presence. We have attempted to inhale and then exhale to set our vocal folds in motion, only to stop because we were told we were too loud or that it was not time for us to speak. Some of us learned to breathe through someone else, like babies breathing through their mothers' umbilical connections. We were often tethered to a man or another power source who regulated where and when we could activate our respiratory system. Others of us found the strength to breathe on our own, only to be stifled because we found the air too heavy or polluted by barriers, acidic reactions, or pillows of doubt suffocating even gasps for air. During my thirteen years in ministry, Black women have related to me how difficult sustaining their breath flow is—whether in the home, church, community, office, or street; regardless of age, education, religion, income, size, or shape. Most understand the need for individual change, engagement of systemic evil, conversion from individual sins, strengthening their reserve, standing on the edge, and challenging oppression, but they need a discipline to articulate their beliefs, and vehicles to transform themselves and to aid their sisters and brothers in community transformation.

The central thesis of this essay is that in order for womanist thought to survive as a viable transformative agent in the lives of African American women, womanist scholars must develop methods of sharing womanist perspectives with our sisters who are not ensconced in the academy or as seminary-trained clergy. Additionally, the essay will provide a practical model for sharing womanist thought with "ordinary" African American women, families, churches, and community organizations. The model will focus on the transformative power of individual and small group discussions of African American women's social, theological, occupational, psychological, and health concerns; ethnographic studies of family members and friends who may have possessed womanist characteristics; and composition of womanist sermons and liturgical study groups. It will also review and discuss African American women's literature to avoid asphyxiation.

"Sister, Help Me Find the Oxygen"

Audre Lorde, in *Sister Outsider*, speaks of the danger of "tyrannies of silence"; of our needs to transform the silent spaces into action and for each person to establish her own voice; and of our individual responsibility to help ourselves and each other.[2] It is crucial for Black women to devise tools or ways to correct or obliterate oppressive systems, instruments that are innovative and consider or meet the needs and abilities of the entire community. In her provocative essay "The Master's Tools Will Never Dismantle the Master's House," Lorde challenges us with our responsibility for individual and collective transformation:

> Those of us who stand outside the circle of this society's definition of acceptable women; those of us who have been forged in the crucibles of differences—those of us who are poor, who are lesbians, who are Black, who are older—know that *survival is not an academic skill.*[3]

Academe teaches how to learn. Life experience teaches us how to survive. Sisters in the academy must remember those sisters who model survival every day and who stopped long enough to teach us how to act and live longer and better than they. Even in the presence of what we in the academy may classify as deference to men and "the man," these women find ways to insure that we can live and do more than they themselves will ever achieve in terms of education or income. Are womanist scholars in danger of "selective amnesia"? Wasn't womanist thought generated by analysis of the lives of "ordinary women" striving to be more than what others said they could become or could achieve? Higher education provided a technique for us to name their struggle in "acceptable academese," but their lives enable us to survive by naming our ability to "be the best you can" and "don't let nobody turn you around."

Lorde continues. Black women's implementation strategies particular to their culture and belief systems are essential to lasting, effective transformation. Billie Holiday sang "God Bless the Child That's Got His [Her] Own," and Lorde seems to say, "No one can save us but us" with our own specific, culturally devised methods:

> It is learning how to stand alone, unpopular and sometimes reviled, and how to make common cause with those others identified as outside the structures in order to define and seek a world in which we can all flourish. It is learning how to take our differences and make them strengths. *For the master's tools will never dismantle the master's house.*[4]

We must be cognizant and inform our sisters that beginning any procedure toward social change is seldom popular. They will lose the support of friends

and garner insults from enemies. Others will label and define them deroga-
torily. Whenever one steps out of a prescribed role, pain will follow. But
after the initial pain, a sense of relief similar to the cessation of a bad cold
will follow, and one can breathe freely—often for the first time in life. Freedom is contagious. If one is selfless enough to risk showing another how to
seek empowerment, how to take deep cleansing breaths rather than pant,
both are strengthened.

Our sisters are suffocating every day. They cannot find the air to begin
to speak. It is caught in their lungs, in their throat just below the vocal
folds. They feel it when fear wells up as they try to cry out for help. It
comes when they face the supervisor who harasses them or objectifies
them. They are asking for our help, and we dare not ignore them, even
when we no longer understand what it is like to be a laywoman in a male-
dominated denomination. We stand in the academy because those who
stay at home urged some of us to continue the struggle because they did
not have the energy to speak. They need to be "sistered" into individual
transformation and social change. "Sistering" can be accomplished only if
there are no value judgments based on age, belief, sexual orientation, economic standing, education, family status, geography, occupation, or any
other artificial barrier we seem to erect to establish "we-they" paradigms.

Womanist scholars are still in process, still defining themselves, still
broadening the idea. We need information from laywomen to deepen the
richness of the discipline. We will become a fad unless womanist thought
receives a constant infusion of reality and social relevance. Before one can
accept, one must know what one is required to accept. There needs to be
an explanation of the womanist definitions in "sisterspeak," or the vernacu-
lar of the day-to-day, in-the-trenches, ordinary sisters who provide supporting information and who are potential procreators of womanist beliefs.

Womanist consciousness, according to Elsa Barkley Brown, incorporates
racial, cultural, national, economic, and political considerations.[5] Womanists have a both/and worldview. There must be an intersection and an in-
terdependence of self/others, male/female, race/sex, community/family, and
Black/female to fully become womanist. The sisterhood of African American women leads to a self-sustaining, self-sufficient, and independent community that enables members to live their lives unhampered by manipula-
tions of the larger society. Womanist theologian Kelly Brown Douglas defines
womanism as Black women's resistance to the multidimensional oppression based on their experiences of being Black and female in the United
States.[6] As each individual discovers her own power, behavior changes. As
each takes control of self, breathes on her own, recognizes her personal
core beliefs, pushes the limits of comfort, and recognizes her own limits,
the transformation process begins.[7]

As womanist scholars use once silenced voices to espouse liberation,
we must be careful not to ignore the position and struggles of laywomen

who cannot find unrestricted air to even begin to inhale the first breaths of freedom. Advocating connections between African American women, scholars and communities of African American women, political activist Barbara Omolade presents a scathing challenge to those Black feminists and scholars who may have neglected or overlooked their sisters in the trenches:

> They forgot the griot-historians that came before them. They omitted the blood of their sister's abortions, their sister's lesbian lovers, the gelelapa wrapped women, the warriors who became "sick and tired of being sick and tired," the singers who shouted in church and the silent musings of dancers, teenagers and workers. They could not hear their own hearts and voices. The academy had successfully trained Black women against herself and her sisters.[8]

There are womanist scholars who are well aware of the day-to-day lives of their sisters. There are womanist scholars who are active in local churches, drawing strength from everyday, ordinary sisters. However, there are also scholars who have wrapped themselves in the robes of ivory-tower elitism and do not deal with Black women's daily reality unless one of our colleagues unceremoniously reminds us that we are still Black women in America.

Furthermore, womanist scholars must become more than special guest lecturers, token program participants, photo opportunities, or preachers at academic or women's conferences with brief, theoretically profound insights into the lives of Black women, or we will asphyxiate also. We must avoid the situations of the early civil rights workers who came to register persons to vote and then left them to deal with the entrenched, dangerous power and social structures alone. We must remember our inextricable link to our sisters and use "sisterspeak"—the articulated as well as the more often unspoken language of Black women—to share the empowering vision of womanist thought. When we see our sisters, we must remember whence we came and who broke down the doors that allow us to sit in book-lined offices and complain about the disparity in the system. We must use the voices we have found to articulate the needs of our sisters. When we are in conversation with our sisters, we must not speak at, over, under, or to them. We must speak *with* them and *hear* what they are saying, rather than assume that we know. Our social location has changed and our worldview is at a slightly different slant as privileged Black women in the academy. But we can be relevant, authentic bridges for our sisters who yearn to stop the madness and be free.

Black feminist Patricia Hill Collins's groundbreaking work *Black Feminist Thought* proposes that the key role of African American intellectuals is to ask the right questions, listen, hear, see, and fully accept Black women as they share "taken-for-granted knowledge" about their lives.[9] We must

analyze the social location, worldview, belief system, and resource availability of each sister we directly influence. We need to stick around, build
discussion groups, go one-on-one with our sisters, discuss the "whys" and
"hows" of womanist perspectives, and provide continual support as they
seek their own empowerment, their own air space. We must remember
that it has been ten short years since womanists began the process of avoiding asphyxiation, the struggle to breathe on our own. Womanists are still
learning how to articulate disappointments, needs, ideas, and definitions.
Womanists are currently finding ways to assist our brothers to accept the
fact that we are equally created humans. Womanists are at different levels,
depending on how long they have been in the academy or in ministry, or
have lived. Some have sonorous, audible, woman voices certain of themselves. Others still whisper through infant cries for attention. Womanist
scholars must patiently walk with our sisters and brothers to help facilitate their understanding of womanist pedagogy and must tolerantly answer challenges and questions. In the conversion process, we are all at
different levels. In like fashion, we must remain cognizant of the multiplicity of levels of acceptance and engagement of womanist principles by sisters in the academy and in communities.

"A Change, a Change Has Come Over Me"

*For one thing we can teach each other the differences in our experiences
rather than struggling all the time to say, "It's the same." We can ask each
other, "What's different about us?"*

Alice Childress, playwright[10]

Sociologist S. N. Eisenstadt's classic study on social change sets forth
fundamental elements of transformation.[11] All humans seek some form of
transformation. We each face the same general types of problems. The direction, level, conditions, degree, time, specialization, or differentiation of
problems is variable. The relative strength and composition of the collective determine the amount and type of change. "Innovating elites" are
change agents. They are able to offer vision and solutions to the problems.
These change agents, however, must be aware of the readiness for change,
possible rejection of or resistance to the proposed solution, and absence
of resources.

Intrapersonal transformation, conversion, or change is initially an individual response to a stimulus or situation. When one becomes "sick and
tired of being sick and tired," one has the choice of staying in the situation,
leaving, or working to effect change. One must realize there is a problem,
analyze the symptoms or issues, determine one's responsibility for remaining in the situation or for seeking change, assess internal and external resources to effect change, develop a plan of action and an implementation
strategy, decide on alternatives if there are hindrances to the initial plan,

modify the plan after initial data are collected and tested (exercising trial and error), live with the resultant metamorphosis, maintain the new situation, reassess, and share with or teach others the pitfalls and achievements of the transformative action.

Collective or interpersonal transformation occurs when we reach out to others in similar situations and collaborate. An Ethiopian proverb says, "When spiderwebs unite, they can tie up a lion." The African American saying "Each one teach one" means that combined efforts are most effective. We must establish our own way of being present with each other. Once we can freely breathe, we must take the oxygen mask and help apply it to our sisters so they can breathe too. Affirmation of self leads to affirmation of others. Our sisters in family, church, and community need a safe place to begin the tedious transformation process of hearing new thoughts, working through the pain of ingesting fresh air, and processing how womanist theology and ethics may grow in their lives.

As our sisters seek to avoid asphyxiation, attempt to speak, try to empty themselves of old tapes, old pains, old wounds, old stuff that blocks the pathway to liberation, womanist scholars must find ways to be relevant in the lives of sisters whose priority is survival. We must work together to overcome and change the oppressive stumbling blocks such as preconceived notions about "women's work and place," overdependence on others, not taking responsibility for our own transformation, mistrust and resentment of women in the academy or in the pulpit, and lack of knowledge about women of faith and spirit in history and home—famous and infamous, ordinary and extraordinary. Womanists should strive for a collaborative ministry. A nurturing, transformative "woman-space" must be provided for women to think, refresh, rest, and rejuvenate. This space must be free of the distractions of societal definitions of roles of women and of our need to be what someone else wants us to be.[12] It is hard to breathe when someone else is standing on your chest. Reaching the proper energy level for the liberation struggle is hard if you are tired, have paralysis of the vocal folds, or have a collapsed lung due to the weight of oppression.

The crucial point is to establish why change is necessary and what one is doing to be transformed. Transformation is relative and takes place at different paces for different people. In 1831, Maria Stewart wrote, "Sue for your rights and privileges. Know the reason you cannot attain them. Weary them with your importunities. You can but die if you make the attempt; and we shall certainly die if you do not."[13] The old saying is that "the more things change the more they remain the same." Maria Stewart advocated going to any length, even death, to change circumstances. One must decide for oneself how much one is willing to give up, to sacrifice for freedom. No one can determine that for us. Part of the rhetoric that separates womanist scholars and laywomen is that misappropriation of what it means to give up a part of one's life for the current liberation movement focus. Because a sister in the trenches is reluctant to give up her current life situation even if judged oppressive by the enlightened scholar does not mean that that sister does not want to be changed. Think of how long it took for those of us in our thirties or forties to accept our calls to preach with all the attendant baggage or to complete doctoral studies with all the political games? Did we begin the processes understanding the sacrifice and with eagerness to be beaten up by the system? In most cases we connected with a stronger sister, or at least a sister who was like-minded, who would say to us, "I got your back," and we believed her. Did every sister in the academy who started out touting a "womanist pedagogy" end up with the same fervor, or have some stepped away or back into the old self? Change means discomfort, and some of us are not strong enough to weather the storm alone or even with hundreds of others. As we demand change in systems and expect change in the lives of our sisters, we need to ask ourselves who is with that sister when she has to stand alone before her family, her ministerial board of examiners, her tenure committee, her dissertation defense committee, her pastor, or even her sisters who think that womanist thought is a fad that will pass as soon as its proponents are tired.

Learning from Our Sisters in the Trenches

Over the past thirteen years of ordained ministry, I have worked with social, civic, religious, and educational women's groups, attempting to develop a practical model for Black women's intrapersonal and interpersonal transformation and empowerment. My grandmother and other women in my life had begun the process and continued to support and encourage me. However, I still needed more information to sustain me as a Black woman seeking to serve the church and survive the academy. Through insightful lectures and motivating conversations with Katie Cannon, Jacquelyn Grant, and Cheryl Townsend Gilkes, I began to understand the genesis of womanist perspectives and the potential for personal growth and sharing with others. In recognition of the need for a new discipline to sustain my sisters in ministry and the church as we struggled to breathe freely in an aftershave-filled pulpit, I was led to initiate a practical model for Black women's transformation from a womanist perspective.

The components of this model were conceived, developed, modified, recorded, implemented, and eventually duplicated in other churches and cities. Any process of transformation must follow similar steps and honing in order for the program, concept, or idea to be effective and enduring. Change, whether individual or collective, does not come overnight.

This model was generated over the period of 1988-1994 with a core group of forty African American women, beginning at Shorter Community African Methodist Episcopal Church in Denver, Colorado. Membership and participants ranged from approximately five hundred to six hundred African American women from various organizations, individual interest groups, and churches in Denver. Sisters Working Encouraging Empowering Together (S.W.E.E.T.) was formed as a network for intentionally sharing womanist perspectives and undergirding Black women's efforts for spiritual and social liberation. S.W.E.E.T. was formed at a time when African American women were separated, fragmented, distrustful, defamatory, and competitive.

Membership was opened to any African American woman or woman of color who needed an opportunity for spiritual and social renewal, healing, sustenance, empowerment, and cooperation. There was also a group of about thirty African American men who regularly supported the group and attended seminars on relationships and community activities. The members ranged in age from five to seventy-eight years. Educational levels were from grade school to professional schools. Women were married, single, divorced, and widowed. They were heterosexual, lesbian, and bisexual.

The sisters were Baptist, Methodist, Catholic, Pentecostal, Muslim, Church of God in Christ, Episcopalian, and unchurched. Some had been incarcerated or on the way to jail, or knew someone there. There were Deltas, Alphas, Zetas, Sigmas, and Links sitting alongside Granny, MaDear, Mama, Big Momma, and Auntie. Each woman, whatever her status or station in life,brought similar concerns to the group. They felt stagnant, hemmed in, pushed down, limited and wanted to do more than survive. They each wanted to know how to really sing, "My soul looks back and wonders how I got over."

We began to develop annual seminars, inclusive sermons, intensive women-centered Bible studies, monthly workshops, relationship-building exercises, small group discussions, potluck dinners, informal and formal luncheons, community action projects, intergenerational mentoring groups, individual and group counseling sessions, guest speakers and in-group speakers, panel discussions, role-playing, ethnographies, health support groups, and African American women's literature study and discussion groups. Alice Walker's definition of *womanist* was used as the point of departure for each discussion. We targeted one section of the definition at each meeting to begin to share womanist perspectives with the group.[14]

Pedagogically, the model is deliberately inductive, teaching women to think for themselves and form their own paradigms while receiving support from and giving support to other women in the process of transformation. The viability of the model rests in each person being empowered to deconstruct oppressive paradigms, reconstruct liberating ones, and activate models that are most conducive to intrapersonal and interpersonal transformation. Conversations flowed from the requests of the sisters present. The coordinator was responsible for guiding discussions on particular issues. Delegation of leadership was the rule of the day. Everyone had a chance to lead, and all were encouraged to try new things and test their skills. Initially, meetings were held weekly, and, depending on agenda items, either on bimonthly or monthly Saturday mornings or Friday nights thereafter. Agreed meeting length was one and one half hours. If the discussion lasted longer, those who needed to leave did, and others remained until they felt the discussion was exhausted.

We began S.W.E.E.T. with one ground rule—"We will respect our sister's space, speech, issues, voice, pain, and sensitivities." There were no value judgments. Instead we replaced judgment with "I love you like you are," "I don't agree, but you have a right to your opinion," or "We're going to make it in spite of ourselves." We ran all meetings on a consensus basis. There was a coordinator but no elected officers. No dues were collected; each gave as she could whenever there was a need. We defined ourselves as a spiritual, universal sisterhood with no walls, barriers, or exclusions.

We pledged to "sister" each other into wholeness using "sisterspeak"— informal, no-pretense, at-home, dangling-participles, double-negative, tell-it-like-it-is, intense-body-language speech. There was no need to impress each other with credentials so we called everyone Sister ——, Girlfriend, or by first names, with the exceptions of our respected elder sisters, whom we called Mother —— or Miss ——.[15] The "mothers" of the group were the spiritual anchors of the group. Their presence added a sense of authenticity to the belief in the possibility of change. The model of their courageous living, sense of humor, and deep-seated faith helped us to continue to build when detractors—male and female—said there was no need for another women's group.

We treated teens and children with the same respect as others. They met in individual, age-appropriate groups or with the adults, depending on the subject matter of the day. While disagreements arose, especially over sensitive issues, everyone had to be heard. One sister would facilitate the discussion but could step out of the role and yield leadership to another person when she needed to contribute her thoughts.

Meetings began with sharing praise reports and requests for support. Women were not pressured to be a member of a church, but there was an understanding that the group was spiritually based. Each sister determined and articulated her own sense of spirituality. African American spirituality is the conscious awareness of God, self, and others in the total response to Black life and culture. It is an expressive style, a mode of contemplating God, a prayer life, and that which nourishes, strengthens, and sustains the whole person.[16] We coupled prayer, testimony, tears, laughter, or silence with embracing each other.

Sisters passed on their ideas of how to survive and thrive to each other and to younger women, and listened respectfully to the othermothers in the group. One opening exercise might be, "Who was the woman in your life who had the greatest impact on who you are today and why?" or "Where were you ten years ago, and how have you changed?" As each woman spoke, she also received affirmation of her situation or overcoming through a similar story repeated by another sister and embryonic sustenance from one who would become a sister.

The buds of extended families began when the discussion opened with, "What kind of sister are you?" "Who is your sister?" or "Do you need a sister?" Reassessment of the role of women in churches, ministry, or private quests for spirituality was initiated with questions such as, "Who is God?" "Who/what does your God look like?" "How do you name God?" or even, "Why do you go to church?" or "What is the most difficult part of attending church?" This usually evoked extensive discussion and usually reassessment of sisters' roles and responsibilities in churches or faith settings. This provided an opportunity to air opinions, to grieve the oppression relative to their experiences in churches, and to strategize ways to move the church structure to become more inclusive of women and to help other women identify church-centered discrimination and role stigmatization.

The majority of women had never questioned what women were required to wear or do, what positions in the church were traditionally assigned to women, what positions were closed to them, the language of sermons and songs that excluded women, and the instances when women were described as evil or weak by men and by some women in churches. We were at different levels of faith and different places in transformation. Old tapes about where women can stand, what is their appropriate manner of dress and carriage, and what they can do take a long time to wear out for some sisters. These discussions were generally initiated because the coordinator and four other members were pursuing ordained ministry, and questions were constantly presented regarding how we came to "decide to go against the men."

Releasing the Power Within

S.W.E.E.T. ventured into many areas based on the needs and desires of the membership and community. Through trial and error, components were added and subtracted. I will describe eight of the major components. One of the most powerful small group projects for understanding and cultivating womanist perspectives such as valuing self and gaining a sense of empowerment was ethnographies. Within the first part of Walker's definition of *womanist* is the phrase "wanting to know more and in greater depth than is considered 'good' for one." The ethnography activity required women to discover more about themselves by getting to know about where they came from and what family persons—grandmothers and othermothers—gave birth to them. We asked that each sister call, write, or visit the oldest living female family member and ask her about her life. Each woman chose her own questions based on what she wanted to know about spiritual, professional, familial, personal, or political aspects of the woman's life. Information that was to be considered included the following:

1. What was the historical context of the woman's life? the date and location of her birth?
2. Her life in a brief outline in ten-year increments: Family members? Schools? Best friend? Places she lived? Occupations?
3. The role of religion in her life: Spirituality or belief in God? Religious affiliation? Religious activities? Religion as a means of survival, empowerment, strength, oppression?

4. The most difficult period of her life? best part of life?
5. Her problem-solving strategies?
6. Her legacy: Typical/atypical? Compared to whom?
7. Was there a group of sisters, women, who helped her through her life?
8. What would she do differently or change about her life?
9. What did you learn about some of your own choices based on this woman's life?

Initially, some were hesitant to undertake the project but covenanted to do the best they could. Some were amazed at what the relative would not talk about, such as deaths, births, family members, or religion. Others unearthed a treasure right under their nose. One woman was inspired to finally answer a call to preach. She had been discouraged by several brothers and sisters but then discovered that there had already been two women in her family who had been preachers. Those without living female relatives called older friends and reestablished relationships. Some were sent mementos. Some were confronted with new, painful information about who they thought they were. A number of the older women voiced their pleasure that younger women took the time to find out about their "old, ordinary" lives. Some felt that they were not important enough for the questions and gave perfunctory answers.

A second component was a self-empowerment/living history project. It was a review of the lives of contemporary African American women leaders in various fields and in history who had exemplified the behavior or social consciousness necessary for intrapersonal transformation. The section of Walker's *womanist* definition focal to this exercise was "appreciates and prefers women's culture, women's emotional flexibility, and women's strength." Each member selected a biography or autobiography, then agreed to form a study group with six other women and report back to the larger group answering the same type of questions used in the ethnographic exercise. The lives of Anna Julia Cooper, Fannie Lou Hamer, Mary McLeod Bethune, Ella Baker, Jo Anne Robinson, Maria Stewart, Daisy Bates, Nannie Helen Burroughs, Jarena Lee, Amanda Berry Smith, Leontyne Kelly, Shirley Chisholm, and Barbara Jordan were a few of the women selected, along with any other woman who caught a sister's interest. Finally, the lives of the older relative/friend, the extraordinary woman, and the S.W.E.E.T. sisters were compared and contrasted in terms of location, situation, coping mechanisms, prejudices, and goals as a source of transformation. The following questions fostered intergenerational transfer of wisdom and empowerment:

1. What can be learned from the lives of African American women?
2. What values or moral wisdom is passed down through their writing or words?
3. What life-changing choices did they face?

4. How did they forge new or different paths for themselves, their families, or other sisters?
5. Did they accept, reject, assimilate, or change their situations?
6. What is your legacy for African American women and children?

Again sisters shared the information and perspectives with the larger group and began to associate their problem solving as historical or ordinary women with their own contemporary dilemmas and choices. This model was also useful in interaction between juvenile and adolescent members and adults. Daughters/Little sisters became more aware of their mothers'/othermothers' lives, and mothers/othermothers learned about the ambitions and concerns of the daughters/little sisters.

"Blest Be the Tie That Binds"

Another facet of womanist thought is "committed to the survival and wholeness of entire people, male and female." Given the sociological reports and media attention to the disintegration of the family, the group requested meetings on how to transform and save their families. Robert Staples argues that the assimilation of dominant society values has had a significant impact on the Black family. Since 1960, there has been a quest among Blacks for personal freedom and job mobility. Other cultural values have supplanted traditional child rearing in the name of "fitting in."[17] The African family value system incorporated respect, responsibility, restraint, reverence, and reciprocity.[18] Before this assimilationist period, parents, church, and community taught children that all persons were interconnected. There were no orphans, and everyone belonged to someone, whether informally or innately. We taught children to respect themselves and others. Each person was to be responsible for her own behavior. Restraint meant that the "I-must-have-anything-I-want-now" attitude was monitored. One understood that overindulgence was a sin. We revered elders and children. Reciprocity meant, "Do unto others as you would have them do unto you," not "before they do it to you."

A third component of S.W.E.E.T. was the "Back to the Kitchen Table" program. It was held on Saturday mornings for six-week sessions. Families discussed ways of reinstituting these values and other biblically based ways of being in community. Activities such as crafts, films, music, exercise, and Bible study were cultivated around a sit-down potluck breakfast. Each week a different family grouping was responsible for the food. The average attendance on Saturday mornings was seventy-five.

Survey information helped determine that Saturday morning was generally the only time all family members were together. These extended family breakfasts served two purposes—to share food and to share information. After the two hours, families went off to their various individual tasks. Issues of sexuality, parenting, domestic violence, suicide, education, relationship building, health, and job preparedness were discussed with

S.W.E.E.T. members using their expertise, invited guests, and films. Family was defined as blood relatives, relatives by marriage, friends, or "fictive" kin.[19] No one was left out because of marital status. Teens often volunteered to care for younger children so sisters and brothers could converse about particular topics without distraction.

An intergenerational mentoring program, "It Takes an Entire Village to Raise a Child," grew out of this component. It was set up beginning with a foster grandparents/grandchildren program pairing elders with young people who either did not have grandparents or wanted to help an elder. The elder, usually female, became the advisor to the younger person, and the younger person shopped, wrote letters, cleaned houses, cooked, or provided transportation for the elder, depending on the age of each person. The often city-raised younger person experienced the Mother Wit of the elder. Mother Wit is commonsense advice, communal sayings, or proverbs. Mother Wit is belief based on experience and time-honored proof. It instills in the younger person survival strategies and community behavior guidelines. It teaches us how to live in the world and understand who we are and can be. Time commitment was two hours per week.

We instituted the fourth component to fill a major void in the lives of most S.W.E.E.T. members. Many were professional women who had little contact with other African American women during the week and felt "in this mess all by myself." Due to Denver's demographics and the dispersement of the African American population, the majority of women saw each other at church or at some social setting but had not intentionally sought out friendships with other African American women. We started sister-to-sister mentoring with an occupational/talent mentoring program accomplished through "talent sheets." Members wrote down their profession, a talent they wished to share, what they wanted to learn or needed help with, and a pledge to commit one hour per week. The sheets were placed on a board, and they selected the person whom they could either learn from or teach for that commitment period. They could change every two weeks to another person.

In the "Sister/Girlfriend—I Got Your Back" activity, women were asked to choose someone they did not know and find out as much information as possible in five minutes. Then they introduced their new sister. Later they committed to call each other once a week for prayer, advice, networking, child care, tutoring—whatever the two of them needed. They decided their own time commitments and length of agreement. This nucleus usually joined other dyads, and the network was strengthened. In some cases, women who had disliked each other based on hearsay found common bonds to build a relationship.

"I Know in Whom I Have Believed"

The S.W.E.E.T. experience and model compel me to push Alice Walker's definition of *womanist* in a more theocentric direction. I would add "believes in Somebody bigger than you and me" or "possesses a radical faith in a higher power" to the established *womanist* definition as the basis for a fifth S.W.E.E.T. component. Churched and unchurched Black women carry deep-seated spiritual beliefs. Through conversations, counseling sessions, interviews, and analysis of women's roles in worship services, I have concluded that the majority of Black women are "recovering" Christians. They have a love/hate relationship with the church and with their own spirituality. They love God but strive to recover from the addictive nature of church-related oppression. It is difficult for some to stay away from church, even when they know that they might be carried away battered and bruised. This is where Walker's *womanist* definition "Loves the Spirit" is helpful. This love often supersedes human persecution. These Christian women's faith in God appears senseless to many who observe their social status, their relegation to cooking and singing, their being barred from pulpits and castigated as the source of sin in the world. Many women say, "I'm not going to church for men; I'm going because I love the Lord." They generally find ways of reading themselves into the text, "widening the tent" so that others can come inside, and maintaining a "holding-on-and-won't-let-go-of-my-faith" theology. Inclusion of a definitive faith element in the definition of *womanist* would draw more laywomen to the concept. I am asked, "Where is God in all of this?" and I can point out the "Loves the Spirit" language, but the sisters seem to need a definite articulation of a living God consciousness. The worship, study, service, and love of one's particular image of God are vital to the struggle and survival of Black women.

The Bible is central to the faith of African Americans. Black biblical hermeneutics is the quest for identity as God's believing, unified people. Interpretation of the Black experience, scriptures, and other data about one's culture is a part of one's pride and identity.[20] For Black women, formation of a biblical interpretation and understanding of oneself in relationship with God has been at best an uphill climb. Having to sit through countless sermons, Bible studies, male-led women's conferences, and prayers that ignore the presence or contribution of women is another method of suffocation.

Bible studies or sacred text studies led by womanists, or any religiously oriented seminars are crucial vehicles for planting seeds of change. Women appear to be more open in these settings, because they may have been excluded or beaten up in the regular worship service. The need to be released from a stifling lifestyle may be signified in a study of Psalm 69:

> Save me, O God,
>> for the waters have come up to my neck.
>> I sink in the miry depths, where there is no foothold.
> I have come into the deep waters;
>> the floods engulf me.
> I am worn out calling for help;

my throat is parched.
My eyes fail,
   looking for my God . . .
The Lord hears the needy
   and does not despise his captive people. (vv. 1-3, 33, NIV)

The Psalmist faces drowning but believes that God is able to save. Holding on to one's faith in the midst of the fatigue of treading water is the lot of many Black women. Bible studies may include assignments wherein the sisters trace family trees, locate women in the text, study the origin of the household codes, imagine the lives of women in the biblical world and compare and contrast them to contemporary situations, or provide a reinterpretation of the text that is inclusive of all class members.

Lyrics in traditional and contemporary gospel music are also rich topics for dialogue on womanist theology and ethics. In the 1950s and 1960s, Black women wrote, arranged, sang, directed, and recorded gospel music, in many cases as an alternative ministry to preaching.[21] We asked that sisters bring in their favorite song with research on the songwriter's life. Questions ranged from, "What do you think she was thinking about when she wrote the song?" to, "What did you learn about her belief in God?" to, "Why do you identify with this song?" The same process was followed for secular music—blues, soul, rock, instrumental and rap music—with the focus being on the emotions evident in the lyrics and in the way a song is sung or played. Finding the hope in each song was essential to the process. If hope was not evident, then the discussion would center on what would have to take place for the songwriter to heal given her status.

Designing liturgies was a challenge for all ages. At first, there was a belief that "that's the way we've always done it" and there is no way it can change. Initially, we asked that each member compose a service as part of their favorite holiday or liturgical event. We provided models of standard services in members' particular denominations. We asked that the sisters insert language changes, sounds, art, music, dance, silence, visual aids—whatever they wanted. The next process was for them to consider how they would change or modify the regular Sunday morning worship to be more inclusive of women. Finally, we asked that they pull together the type of worship they always wanted. They handed all the services in, and five were selected. The creators of those services selected other women to help them run through the entire worship. Some sisters took their ideas to their churches, and at least three were used in regular worship services. Most changes were in language and in the insertion of congregational singing to build community, rather than solos with choirs described as "star" vehicles.

Finally, in terms of spirituality, women in S.W.E.E.T. were encouraged to ask the church hierarchy questions about the role of women in the church. We paired those who feared male authority with a sister who could "stand boldly before the throne." The number of sisters who feared the pastor or the "leaders" was staggering. These same women ran businesses, supervised hundreds, taught school, raised children alone, yet felt out of place talking to men in the church. Through lengthy discussion, the group began to hash out the reasons for the fear and possibilities for resolution. The deification of the pastor and the "sanctity of the pulpit" as the place where God dwelled and only preachers (men) could stand because God was a man, were addressed through the belief in "the priesthood of all believers." The assurance that one should not question God led to the story of Jesus in the garden and on the cross. Tapping the professional survival skills of each woman and transferring them to the encounters with male leadership were difficult because of years of learning that women are to just obey with no questions asked. Most of the women had remained in their churches due to their upbringing or family affiliation. Being called "strong Black women" who kept the church going was almost a compliment for some sisters. Others opted to engage the oppression by becoming more vocal in business meetings, absenting themselves from services with restrictions about women, or withdrawing financial support for programs that overlooked the presence of women.

In the United States, the controversy over women in the pulpit is almost two hundred years old in many denominations. The struggle for the right to preach centers around biblical authority and male-female power distribution dynamics.[22] Black preachers are called to preach a gospel of liberation, but the question is, "Liberation for whom?" Faced too long with charges that women are to "keep silent in church," that they "defile the pulpit," or that they should "speak" rather than "preach," some women formed an auxiliary group called Sisters in the Spirit in 1992. This composed a sixth component. The members of this group were S.W.E.E.T. members who were also women in ministry. This became a support group for a group often labeled as "audacious and courageous." The sisters met at different homes for informal Saturday late lunches to laugh, cry, commiserate about the status of women in ministry, discuss sermon styles and plans, develop ways to cope with and confront those brothers who denied them access to ministry, and just to listen to music or sing. Sometimes we discussed serious books. Sometimes fashion tips were applicable. Most times the members just needed a safe place to bleed, to heal, to gain strength, or to be still. There was a covenant that whatever we said or did would be kept within the group. There was also a concerted effort for all to attend a worship service when a sister was on the program or preaching thereby showing solidarity or strength in numbers, even in a telephone call of prayer if one could not attend. Additionally, there was a pledge to avoid falling into the "old boys'" model of one-upsmanship. Each member reminded the others about the possibility of the oppressed becoming the oppressor. We called each other on those issues that would eventually prove detrimental and cheered each other in victory.

Womanist preachers must develop their own hermeneutic and delivery style. They are not in competition with men and should preach in their own voices. Womanist preachers theologize with their social location at the forefront. They, too, must preach as specialized instruments of God, not as clones of men. They must be both pastoral and prophetic. They must soothe the soul and incite the mind. Text selection is Spirit-led, not socially dictated. Care must be given so that the sermon does not become a place of either political correctness or political acquiescence. Balance is essential. Black women preachers must decide where or whether they will preach if the belief of a pastor has blocked the pulpit. One must wrestle with the questions, "Who called me to preach?" "Where is holy ground?" and, ultimately, "Is the message of liberation and wholeness that this community of faith needs to hear less important than where it is preached?"

Homileticians are to subsume personal agendas and preach an uncompromising, transformative gospel based on the biblical text. For Black women preachers, digging deep in texts for stories of women is an empowering search. Available research includes *Just a Sister Away* by Renita Weems.[23] We must transmit sermons about women of faith continually, not just on Women's Day. There is now a segregation of women preachers for special women's issue days. This is a subtle reinforcement of the idea that women may teach other women but not men. In order for the biblical texts on women to reach the brothers, they must be incorporated into each preaching event, whatever the gender of the preacher. If the task of the preacher is to preach the "whole counsel of God," then all of God's people must be addressed utilizing texts throughout the Bible.[24] Empowerment begins in the hearing about and identification of oneself in the text. The hearer must be able to see self in the living Word of God. Conversion or change of behavior evolves from a sense of surety that there is hope and space for entering into a different circumstance of life.

Inclusive language should broaden the riches and imagery of the sermon. The preacher must choose language, illustrations, images, metaphors, and content responsibly. Above all, she must be relevant and authentic, never contrived. The womanist preacher must understand her own faith system, image of God, and how to "speak the truth in love." Badgering, manipulation, misplaced anger, and resentment are not viable options for the preaching moment. Changes in language are an individual decision. If one is still working through concepts and language, other sisters should accept the time needed for individual change or modification.

Because the preaching ministry is one of the most revered ministries in Black church worship, womanists can influence innumerable sisters and brothers in the trenches, whether praying, singing, testifying, or preaching the major sermon. Pairing discussions with the community about womanist thought with an anticipated sermon undergirds the theology and ethics of the preacher. Black women must share the entire Bible with the congregation, warts and all, including male-dominated texts, and "bad" and faithful women's stories. They can also, however, in their own voice, interpret the text from a womanist worldview, finding points of connection with all members of the congregation.

When You Love Yourself

Self-concept, competition with other women, starving oneself to try to look like the cover girls in *Vogue* or *Essence*, stagnant jobs, continuing unhealthy relationships, worshiping like a marionette, and failure to obtain timely medical examinations were at the top of the list when S.W.E.E.T. members first met. "Loving and Caring for Yourself" was a seventh component of the S.W.E.E.T. model. Seminars and support groups such as the Hysterectomy Group, the Breast Cancer Survivors Group, the Divorcée Group, the New Christian Group, the Single Mothers Group, and the Workout Group were all subsections of the larger sisterhood. Members of the sisterhood were the "experts" for seminars. Using our own people was an assent to their abilities. We each realized that we often overlook the people right before us. This also provided additional insight into who our sisters were.

Health specialists (doctors, nurses, psychologists, herbalists, and mental health professionals) addressed the now clichéd "self-esteem" problem. They talked about care of Black women's bodies, diet, and exercise.[25] There was a Walking Group, a Bicycling Group, and a Funk Aerobics Group. A volleyball and a basketball team did not fare as well. One member provided workshops on AIDS and Black Women, and information on screening. Breast self-examination instruction and mammography screenings were available. Stress management and financial planning were also popular. Cooking clinics and dietary alternatives were regularly requested.

We often repeated panels on learning to affirm yourself and your sister. One-on-one and small group counseling to rid ourselves of the "strong Black woman" complex was done for self-preservation and enabled us to throw off destructive behaviors and nurture ourselves. Relationship workshops with role-playing, panel discussions, open forums, and films were done for women only and with men invited annually. Heated discussions on sexuality, particularly between conservative sisters and lesbian sisters, eventually led to slow bridge building. When the organization was branded "lesbian" because of open membership and awareness that there were some lesbian members, the group voted to affirm the sisters' right to be whoever they were. S.W.E.E.T. weathered the storm together, deferred any further discussion on the matter, and threw up a shield of protection around their sisters. These projects, exercises, and focus groups are not the only answer to helping laywomen understand womanist perspectives, but they are a starting point. There is room for development and specific foci based on the context of the sisterhood.

Group members accomplished hearing voices of African American women through literary study groups, leading to an eighth component that permeated the entire paradigm. Although the women were generally well read, many had not read women's literature. Self-concept, competition with other women, adverse relationships with men, feelings of inadequacy, being shut out of corporate promotions, day-to-day battles with racism, classism, or sexism, fear of failure, and a thirst for deeper spiritual presence in their lives compelled the women to seek answers through literature. Literary groups selected books from a reading list, and several different groups read books and compared the content, identified the characters, analyzed the characters' lives, their relationships with men and women, and their methods of change. In the literary groups, the womanist definition was used as a tool of analysis. The women in the groups decided for themselves if the protagonists were womanists or not. The most popular books were *Waiting to Exhale* by Terry McMillan, *The Color Purple* by Alice Walker, *Their Eyes Were Watching God* by Zora Neale Hurston, *The Women of Brewster Place* by Gloria Naylor, *Song of Solomon* by Toni Morrison, and *Ugly Ways* by Tina Ansa. African American women's poetry and short stories were also used in poetry and tea sessions or in dinner and short story sessions. Examination of art, commercials, films, television programming, and plays, such as *for colored girls who have considered suicide/when the rainbow is enuf* by Ntozake Shange, was done in small groups or on a "Sister's Night Out." Regardless of the component addressed, the voices of Black women in fiction, nonfiction, biography, medicine, education, finance, health, or relationship books or films were the center points of the discussion.

Throughout the history of the group, the focus was on self-determination, self-control, and self-love for each sister and on life-affirming solidarity of the entire group. These were basic ingredients of intrapersonal and interpersonal transformation. The sisters shielded each other as the first deep-breathing sisters helped the others learn to breathe on their own. A phenomenal sister writes:

> Each of us has the right and the responsibility to assess the roads which lie ahead, and those over which we have travelled, and if the future road looms ominous or unpromising, then we need to gather our resolve and, carrying only the necessary baggage, step off that road into another direction. If the new choice is also unpalatable, without embarrassment, we must be ready to change that as well.[26]

Maya Angelou sums up the preparation for intrapersonal and interpersonal transformation. We each must choose to reach out for what is rightfully our space and place in this world. The road may be rough, we may retread a part of it for a while, we may be trailblazers, we may be the one who tries to keep the road open. We can take only a limited amount of stuff with us, for our travel will be severely impeded. There is also room for rest. If it is too hard, step off, sit for respite, reevaluate the plan. Remember that the plan did not succeed, and you did not fail. Mother Wit teaches us that "nothing beats a failure but a try."

Womanist scholars have a wealth of knowledge just around the corner of the academy—perhaps in sisters who are walking around emptying trash cans. Stop and ask these sisters what they think about womanist thought. Work with the definition. Remember the layers of tradition that must be blown away. Useable segments must be kept and reinforced. We must discard destructive, restrictive segments. Listen to what the sisters might add to the perspective. Hear what does not make sense to them. If womanists seek to avoid both being esoteric and holding meetings to impress ourselves with the profundity of our perspectives, then we must sit at the feet of our elders. We must also hear the inquiries of our little sisters whose zeal for life must not be snuffed out early in their careers. We must attend to the self-conceptions of Black girls whose self-image begins to change around age eleven. Often they begin to hate their appearance, hate their skin color, hate their hair, hate their bodies, and hate their inability to have a boyfriend before puberty begins to turn their hormones upside down. Consider for just a moment where they get the idea that they are ugly and worthless or that they need to change their appearance surgically or artificially. Womanists need to extend the dialogue from grade school to those sisters entering the academy. The conversation on womanist definition and perspectives must extend also to the nursing homes so that valuable pearls of wisdom are not lost on the lips of our mothers. We have to talk with our sisters who are not middle class, who are not well educated, who live where we might feel uncomfortable walking. If womanists seek to be a breath of fresh air in the academy, they must exhale the stale air of academic discourse from time to time and "sisterspeak."

Once we implement a continuing process of "sistering" each other, then we will be in a better position to help sisters in the "real world" avoid asphyxiation. We can help them find the energy to breathe in suffocating circumstances where they have few alternatives. They can begin to breathe on their own when they learn how to breathe properly and have a good support system around them. Then and only then can they inhale deeply and exhale slowly. When we remember that "we are our sisters' keepers" and that we must dialogue with our brothers too, womanists will begin the steps toward lasting viability.

Notes

1. Anna Julia Cooper, *A Voice from the South by a Colored Woman from the South* (Xenia, Ohio: Aldine Printing House, 1892), 32-33.

2. Audre Lorde, *Sister Outsider* (Trumansburg, N.Y.: The Crossing Press, 1984), 40-112.

3. Ibid., 112.

4. Ibid.

5. Elsa Barkley Brown, "Womanist Consciousness: Maggie Lena Walker and the Independent Order of St. Luke," *Signs* 14 (1989): 610-633.

6. Kelly Brown Douglas, "God Is as Christ Does: Toward a Womanist Theology," *Journal of Religious Thought* 46.1 (1989): 7-17. See also Douglas, *The Black Christ* (Maryknoll, N.Y.: Orbis, 1994), 104-116.

7. See Julia Boyd, *In the Company of My Sisters: Black Women and Self-Esteem* (New York: Dutton, 1993), 4, 134-139.

8. Barbara Omolade, *The Rising Song of African American Women* (New York: Routledge, 1994), 109.

9. Patricia Hill Collins, *Black Feminist Thought: Knowledge, Consciousness, and the Politics of Empowerment* (New York: Routledge, 1990), 30, 98.

10. Quoted in Diane J. Johnson, ed., *Proud Sisters: The Wisdom and Wit of African American Women* (White Plains, N.Y.: Peter Pauper Press, 1995), 51.

11. S. N. Eisenstadt, "Social Change, Differentiation, and Evolution," *American Sociological Review* 29.3 (1964): 375-386.

12. Jill Briscoe, Laurie Katz McIntyre, and Beth Seversen, *Designing Effective Women's Ministries* (Grand Rapids: Zondervan, 1995), provide a basic outline for ministry with laywomen and ways in which church-based networks may provide avenues for women's spiritual empowerment. See also Barbara King, *Transform Your Life* (Marina Del Rey, Calif.: DeVorss and Company, 1989).

13. Quoted in Marilyn Richardson, ed., *Maria W. Stewart, America's First Black Woman Political Writer* (Bloomington: Indiana University Press, 1987), 38.

14. Alice Walker, *In Search of Our Mothers' Gardens: Womanist Prose* (San Diego: Harcourt, Brace, Jovanovich, 1983), xi-xxii. Subsequent references to Walker's definition of *womanist* are also from this source.

15. See Cheryl Townsend Gilkes, "Role of Church and Community Mothers: Ambivalent American Sexism or Fragmented Familyhood?" *Journal of Feminist Studies in Religion* 2 (Spring 1986): 41-59. Gilkes argues the importance of elder women as the guardians of the oral tradition and cultural mores. She writes that churched and unchurched Black women tell of the purpose, meaning, and importance of sociocultural events and serve as the connective tissue of the community and culture.

16. See Celestine Cepress, ed., *Sister Thea Bowman, Shooting Star* (Winona, Minnesota: Saint Mary's Press), 17-125.

17. Robert Staples, "The Family," in *The Black Family: Essays and Studies*, 3rd ed. (Belmont, Calif.: Wadsworth Publishing, 1986), 145-148.

18. See Wallace C. Smith, *The Church in the Life of the Black Family* (Valley Forge: Judson Press, 1985), 13-42.

19. Fictive kin are those persons who are not related by either blood or marriage but function in the understood capacity of a brother, sister, mother, father, or other family member. Fictive kin are evident in most African American church "families" and in instances where one's blood relatives are living in other parts of the country.

20. See Stephen Breck Reid, *Experience and Tradition: A Primer in Black Biblical Hermeneutics* (Nashville: Abingdon, 1990), 15-16.

21. See J. Wendell Mapson, *The Ministry of Music in the Black Church* (Valley Forge: Judson Press, 1984).

22. See Barbara Brown Zikmund, "The Struggle for the Right to Preach," in

Women and Religion in America, vol. 1, ed. Rosemary Radford Ruether and Rosemary Skinner Keller (New York: Harper and Row, 1981), 193-241.

23. Renita J. Weems, *Just a Sister Away: A Womanist Vision of Women's Relationships in the Bible* (San Diego: LuraMedia, 1988).

24. See Olin Moyd, *The Sacred Art: Preaching and Theology in the African American Tradition* (Valley Forge: Judson Press, 1995), 49-98.

25. See Boyd, *In the Company of My Sisters*. Boyd, an African American psychotherapist, defines *self-esteem* as the core of personal beliefs that we develop about ourselves over the years. It is based on information directed at us individually and collectively.

26. Maya Angelou, *Wouldn't Take Nothing for My Journey Now* (New York: Random House, 1993), 22-24.

PART II

COMMITTED TO SURVIVAL
AND WHOLENESS
OF ENTIRE PEOPLE

7

Straight Talk, Plain Talk

Womanist Words about Salvation in a Social Context

Delores S. Williams

Womanists not only concern ourselves about the liberation of women, we also struggle along with Black men and children for the liberation, survival and positive quality of life for our entire oppressed Black community. We count Black civil rights experiences as community-building efforts we engage in along with Black men and children. Thus, when we talk and write out of Black civil rights/community-building experiences, we are talking and writing out of shared community struggles that are very much women's experience. Historian Elsa Barkley Brown makes a similar point when she chides feminists for not wanting to include Black women's civil rights experience with Black men in the definitions of women's experience.[1]

This essay derives from a sense of shared experience with reference to Black civil rights/community building. Inasmuch as Black people's physical and spiritual survival is now threatened and attacked by White supremacist groups and persons in the United States, many African Americans (female and male) hope for the full *resurrection* of the Black civil rights movement—a resurrection of the joint activity and collective power of all the splintered groups working in the Black community for the survival and quality of life of Black people. This essay is also a response to accusations I have heard time and again when I have addressed audiences in the Black church. Congregants have said that Black academics are excellent in their analyses of events and culture, but they do not offer any suggestions about "the strategies Black people can use to get out of this mess of White oppression," as one woman in a Baptist church identified the problem to me. "They don't suggest practical strategies that can be used in the church and community by ordinary people like me," she said.

I think an important strategy is to teach the history of the Black civil rights movement in Black churches, in the homes of Black people and in

Black tutorial centers on a permanent basis. That is why I speak of the resurrection of the civil rights movement. Far too many Black children (and adults) are unaware of this history. In order to survive and thrive today, children (and Black communities) desperately need the strategies the movement has created over time. Like Attorney Derrick Bell, I believe that

> The civil rights movement is . . . more than the totality of the judicial decisions, the anti-discrimination laws, and the changes in racial relationships reflected in those legal milestones. The movement is a spiritual manifestation of the continuing faith of a people who have never truly gained their rights in a nation committed by its basic law to the freedom of all.[2]

Womanists and Black male liberation theologians can make a special contribution to this resurrection. They can provide ideas about salvation in a social context for Black Christians who want to understand how Black people can be saved *in the material world*. Womanists and Black male liberation theologians can speak encouraging words about salvation to many young Black people who long ago gave up on the promise of heaven and a better "life" after death. Instead, they struggle for survival, meaning and a supportive quality of life in this world. Today Black people seek salvation for the African American communities whose major institution—the Black church—is threatened in some areas of the country with destruction by members of White hate groups.[3] This current history of destruction is especially painful for Black Americans because it is reminiscent of the years after the Civil War in the United States in the nineteenth century when Reconstruction ended. At that time Black people were severely harassed by White people. Black people's property was burned and destroyed by White people. Many Black men and women were lynched. The local and federal law agencies provided very little or no support for these harassed Black people and communities.

I contend that the need for social salvation then and now presents a necessary and serious challenge to all Black Christians.[4] It prods them to leave heaven and "otherworldly" pursuits to the business and judgment of God. There is only the material world in which to work out a plan of salvation for Black people and the Black community. However, I assume Black churches can still function as historic public sites where plans are made to help bring social salvation to the Black church and to the Black community; but the church must have a theological understanding of itself that promotes and urges participation in action for the sake of salvation in this world. The Black church must lose the notion of itself mired in a "heavenly salvation" having no counterpart in the daily world where Black people live.

That being the case, I direct this writing to Black Christian laypersons. I do not use the vocabulary of academic theology taught in seminaries and universities. Instead I communicate in straight talk, plain talk, using an English vocabulary associated with everyday life in the United States. I provide a discussion of "Black common sense" in order to arrive at an understanding of what salvation should involve in a context where Black people are struggling daily to survive the onslaught of White hate groups. I define "Black common sense" as the collective knowledge, wisdom and action Black people have used as they have tried to survive, to develop a productive quality of life and to be liberated from oppressive social, religious, political, economic and legal systems.[5] It is based on what Harry V. Richardson describes as "the accumulated experiential wisdom of centuries of observant living" in a racist society.[6] I assume that "Black common sense," as defined in this essay, has been operative among African Americans since their enslavement began on the North American shores.

Thus, the task of this essay is threefold. First, I support my claim that the spiritual and physical survival of Black Americans in the United States is seriously threatened by the activity of White supremacist persons and groups. Second, I provide a discussion of what it means to use Black common sense in order to arrive at an understanding of social salvation. Finally, I suggest a theological understanding of the Black Christian church that supports the quest for social salvation.

Before I proceed with these tasks, some prefatory comments are in order. The reader may assume that I intend to discourage the connection between ideas about salvation and Christian ideas about God. Such is not the case. My intention is to support faith, not destroy it, as I focus upon the atrocities challenging Black Christian people to rethink and reformulate their notions of what it takes to be saved in the material world. However, I cannot deny that I am urging Black Christians to use the Black common sense they have gained in relation to White racist people and structures to *re-view* (i.e., re-see and re-examine) what they have been taught to believe about salvation in a religious context. I am urging Black communities to reflect upon the adage that an unexamined faith, like an unexamined life, is not worth living. Unexamined faith leads a people to be unconscious instruments of their own oppression and the oppression of others.

An examined faith is a critical way of seeing that shows those things in a belief system that are life-threatening and life-taking. An examined faith inspires people to discard beliefs, images and symbols that have the potential to support scapegoating and destruction. This essay assumes that by examining faith in light of the death threats facing their communities, Black people get closer to God, not farther away. They draw nearer to a God who slave ancestors believed led them out of bondage in nineteenth-century America, a God of anger, justice and mercy. They draw nearer to a God who never mandated the acceptance of "peace at any cost" in the struggle for freedom, survival and a productive quality of life. An examined faith discards any religion and any God who commands Black people to sit idly contemplating love of their oppressors while they (Black people) are threatened and destroyed by those who hate them. Peace alone is of no value. Peace and justice connect in an examined faith.

Now to the tasks of this essay.

Black Survival Threatened by White Hate Groups

The core of Black Christian spiritual life, the center of Black society—i.e., the Black church—is now under attack in more than nine states by members of White supremacist groups. The Center for Democratic Renewal (CDR) in Atlanta, Georgia, issued a report on June 10, 1996, entitled "Black Church Burnings in the South." It describes the situation this way:

> Today, CDR's records show that 80 mostly rural, historically Black and multiracial churches have been firebombed, burned or vandalized since January 1990. Of that number, 28 have occurred since January 1996, at a rate of what appears to be about one per week. CDR's data show that generally, the attacks occur between the hours of 12 midnight and 7:00 a.m., and in most cases, firebombs or other types of accelerants were used to destroy the structures. Of those persons arrested and/or prosecuted for destruction to African American houses of worship, the majority have been White males between the ages of 14 and 45. Most travel in groups ranging from two to five, and many come from middle class suburban families. Our data also shows that since 1990 at least 13 of these arsons took place in January, around the Martin Luther King holiday.[7]

According to the CDR report, thirty-two White males "have been arrested and/or prosecuted in connection with the bombings, burnings and vandalism of Black churches/lodges in the South." There have been twenty-three convictions. Individuals who have been convicted are responsible "for firebombing and/or vandalizing more than one house of worship."[8]

However, local and federal officials have often harassed the Black church victims, accusing them of starting the fire in their own churches. Testifying before Congress on May 21, 1996, the Reverend Algie Jarrett claimed that "a federal agent, when investigating the burning of the Mount Calvary Church of God in Bolivar, Tennessee, showed up at the high school of a seventeen-year-old student, harshly questioning and interrogating her. She felt that the investigator was trying to get her to say something that was not true." CDR reports that "While investigating the arson of the Inner City Baptist Church in Knoxville, Tennessee, federal authorities have polygraphed pastors, fingerprinted church members, shown up unannounced at job sites and homes, and implied that church members burned their own church."[9] Many reports of this kind have been made by members of the Black churches.

Then there are church fires that received very little investigation by the local or federal officials. According to CDR, these "burned out churches provoked so little interest, that only a cursory investigation has taken place, if any at all. Church members are left wondering why so little has been done when their spiritual homes have been destroyed."[10] The following extensive quotation deserves visibility, because it shows clearly the combination of White hate and the negligence of local and federal officials:

> On March 8 & 9, 1995 during the early morning hours, the interior structure of the Hammond Grove Baptist Church in Aiken, South Carolina was almost destroyed by vandals, causing nearly $20,000 worth of damage. Two young White males, 14 and 15 years of age, left a path of destruction that included racist graffiti of every hate-filled phrase imaginable—"Kill Niggers, Satan Rules, White Aryan race"—plus the drawing of a noose with the word "nigger" pointing to the inside. Despite widespread local coverage and the evidence that this was a racially motivated act, never once did members of this church receive as much as a phone call from state or federal authorities. It is believed that these young men may have connections to a White supremacist group that reportedly organized on the local school campus. The church is located in a majority White community.[11]

Though White supremacist motivation is involved in these attacks upon Black churches, there may also be economic factors. Some of the churches have occupied the same location for many years. The sites were originally rural, but towns and communities are expanding and growing up around some of these churches. Thus, the church property is now very valuable. "Some church members feel that the arsons are a deliberate attempt to frighten the church families into moving from the land and selling off their heritage."[12] However, in another report on church arsons, CDR concludes that "White supremacist ideology is the driving force behind the hate rhetoric and the use of violence to threaten and intimidate. The attacks on Black churches are acts of domestic terrorism and must be placed within the context of White supremacy."[13]

There is evidence to support CDR's conclusion. In Prattsville, Alabama, in 1992, swastikas, racial slurs and satanic symbols were burned into the walls and pews of a Black church. In 1993, the Knights of the KKK put a warning on the door of a Five Points, Georgia, church whose membership includes Blacks. In southeastern Arkansas in 1992, two White men burned three Black churches because they wanted to "get" African Americans. The men pleaded guilty to one count of violating Title 18 United States Code, Section 371, conspiracy. They were sentenced to thirty-seven months. The firebombing that destroyed two Black churches in Columbia, Tennessee, in 1995 was done by three White men who reportedly attacked the churches because "they wanted to teach Blacks a lesson" after one of the men discovered that his daughter was involved in an interracial relationship. Three young White males in Clarksville, Tennessee, were convicted in federal court for firebombing two homes of Black families as well as the Benevolent Lodge. The White men, between the ages of fifteen and eighteen, claimed that they were members of a group they identified as the Aryan Faction.

White supremacists have also threatened, attacked and killed Black individuals.[14] Thus the following information from the CDR report:

- When the Mount Zion A.M.E. Church in Greeleyville, South Carolina, was burned, the persons charged with the crime attended a preliminary hearing where they claimed involvement in the Christian Knights of the Ku Klux Klan. After the hearing, a terroristic threat was made to the pastor. Someone approached him outside the courthouse building saying, "I'm going to get you, nigger." The same threat was reportedly made a second time under different circumstances.
- Immediately following the burning of the Inner City Church in Knoxville, Tennessee, on January 8, 1996, pastors from the church, along with their family members, began to receive threatening phone calls at their homes. During one such incident the caller reportedly threatened, "Your wife is going to leave home one day and not come back." Although each incident was forwarded to federal authorities, family members received no response. "They acted as if it just didn't matter," stated one pastor.
- After a series of violent attacks in Alabama on homeless African American men, in April 1992 a Black homeless man was murdered in Birmingham by four skinhead members of the Aryan National Front and the Confederate Hammerskins.
- In Mobile, Alabama, on March 31, 1990, Darren Jessie, a young Black man who was dating a White woman, was shot to death while sitting in his car outside a grocery store. A second victim was paralyzed. A White man was convicted and sentenced to life without parole.
- In Little Rock, Arkansas, in March 1993, a Black woman was raped by two White men who claimed they liked to kill Black people.
- In Chatham County, Georgia, the son of a Ku Klux Klan leader was indicted in 1993 for spray painting "KKK" and "Move or else" on the pickup truck of a Black family living in an all-White neighborhood. A picture of the Georgia flag was painted on the truck window.
- A Black couple seeking to buy a house in Austell, Georgia, a suburb of Atlanta, were dissuaded when the house was vandalized with red "KKK" symbols and "Nigger go home."
- In St. John the Baptist Parish, Louisiana, in July 1991, a Black youth was murdered by a white teenager who wanted the thrill of killing a Black person.
- In 1993 in New Orleans, Louisiana, the only person of color in a group of youths, a Black college student, was struck and dragged by a car occupied by White men who yelled racial slurs at the student. Also in New Orleans, Chad Sullivan, sixteen, was accused of shooting a fifty-nine-

year-old Black woman. Sullivan had White supremacist and satanic slogans tattooed on his body and on the walls of his apartment.

- In Forest, Mississippi, in May 1990, the father of the Confederate Knights chaplain fired shots into a car occupied by five Black men. About sixty Klansmen attended a rally on the chaplain's property on May 19, 1990.
- Fliers praising Blacks for killing each other were distributed in Jackson, Mississippi, in November 1991.
- Skinhead soldiers from Fort Bragg in North Carolina killed a Black couple, execution style, who were walking down the street in Fayetteville. The skinhead soldiers had determined earlier that they would go "hunt" some Blacks.
- In August 1993 in Virginia, a Black couple's car was destroyed by fire and they were sent a death threat by a White supremacist group who identified themselves as the Virginia Aryan Chapter. The racist group claimed responsibility for the arson.

Many more incidents have been reported about threats and attacks upon Black people by White supremacist persons and groups. Cross burnings have been numerous. Alabama, Georgia, Louisiana, Mississippi, South Carolina, Tennessee and Virginia are among the southern states where cross burnings have happened. These escalating threats and attacks upon the spiritual and physical lives of Black people are no doubt connected with the proliferation of White supremacist organizations. For instance, there are 19 known White supremacist groups operating in Alabama, 7 in Arkansas, 19 in Georgia, 12 in Louisiana, 12 in Mississippi, 29 in North Carolina, 11 in South Carolina, 20 in Tennessee and 14 in Virginia. Added together, the White supremacist groups in these nine southern states total 143. There may be still others working in more subtle ways throughout the United States in order to avoid visibility.

This essay does not intend to suggest that all the threats and violence done to Blacks out of White supremacist motivation is done in the U.S. South. In most areas of the United States, White supremacist groups and individuals are operating. Attacks upon Black people are also escalating in the northern U.S. In spring 1996 in the Hamptons (Long Island, New York), a young Black man coming out of a restaurant with a White woman was viciously beaten by White men, one of whom was a New York City policeman. In the spring of 1996, in another northern location, a Black woman who had lived peacefully in a White neighborhood for twenty-seven years was shocked to witness a cross burning in her yard. On June 18, 1996, New York newscasters reported that on June 17, members of the Mt. Sinai Seventh-Day Adventist Church in Queens, New York, discovered the initials "KKK" burned into the lawn of their church. Also, the "KKK" initials and swastikas had been printed on the church's large sign outside the building. On June 20, 1996, the C-Span 2 television channel broadcasted the Congressional Black Caucus's hearings on the church burnings. A congressman from Chicago reported that a cross had been burned at a home in Chicago. He also referred to the burning in Chicago of five upscale homes owned by Black people in integrated neighborhoods. (At the same hearing it was reported that, in some parts of the South, the graves of Black civil rights workers are being desecrated.)

In many areas of the country, members of White hate groups have become police officers. Often White supremacist ideology is manifested in police relations to Black communities. A case in point is the shooting of an unarmed Black teenager, Aswon Keshawn Watson, by police officers in Brooklyn, New York, on June 13, 1996. A newspaper local to the Brooklyn community reported that the Black youth was walking toward his car. A White policeman was reported to have yelled, " 'You're dead, nigger' and told him [the Black youth] to put his hands up. As he [the youth] did, they [the policemen] just started shooting." Police riddled the young Black man's body with "as many as 17 shots."[15] Witnesses claimed this was an execution. There was no cause for the policemen to fire even one shot.

The reason for cataloging all this abuse to Black people is to demonstrate that in the United States at this moment, attempts by White supremacists to destroy the spirits and lives of African Americans have reached epidemic proportions. On June 15, 1996, I received word that another Black church in the South had been burned earlier in the week. On June 17, I learned that two more Black churches in Mississippi had been burned at the same time. One of them was a historic church well over one hundred years old. On June 25, I learned that another church had burned in the night. Atrocities continue to accumulate against Black people in the United States. Some very young White people also seem determined to do injury to Black folks. A thirteen-year-old White girl was reported to be involved in one of the church burnings. New York newscasters reported in June of 1996 that a group of young White people had prepared to shoot every Black person who entered Disney World in Florida.

Today, African Americans must save their lives, churches, homes and communities. But even as they contemplate salvation, some wonder if White hate groups are trying to incite Black people to retaliate with violence so that White supremacist persons in the U.S. armed forces and the local police forces will have an excuse to destroy Black people and Black communities. Will the media stop reporting the crimes that members of White hate groups inflict upon Black people, thereby giving the false impression that the attacks have stopped?

For more than three hundred years, African Americans have been trying to save their lives, spirits, property and community from the violent onslaught of White hate. No strategy had proven to be permanently effective. White supremacist consciousness has irrupted in violent acts against Black people and Black communities over and over again. Though Martin Luther King Jr. appealed to the "moral conscience" of the nation in the 1960's Black civil rights struggle and though some legislative gains were made by African Americans, White hate groups did not disappear. They shrank from major visibility only to return in various places in the late '70's and '80's. In the 1990's they are present in full array: organized, strong, numerous, proliferating and apparently determined to carry out genocide against Black people.[16] The small legislative gains made as the result of the 1960's civil rights movement have all but disappeared.

Several questions now face African Americans. How do they organize locally and nationally to save their churches, homes, communities and lives from destruction by White supremacist persons and groups (now named domestic terrorists in some quarters)? What can African American Christians do "in-house" to prepare community consciousness and action for social salvation and self-defense? What kind of theological understanding of itself does the Black church need to support the salvation of its people in the world?

Reflecting upon the "in-house" question in relation to Black common sense will yield a response to the first and second of these questions. The final task of this essay is to discuss the latter question.

Using "Black Common Sense"

Earlier, I defined "Black common sense" as the collective knowledge, wisdom and action Black people used as they tried to survive, to develop a productive quality of life and to be liberated from oppressive social, political, economic and legal systems. At least three "in-house" strategies need to be implemented in order to retrieve and perpetuate this collective knowledge, wisdom and action.[17]

The Initial In-House Strategy

The first strategy is to reactivate and sustain memory of the activity of Black heroes (like Malcolm X) and sheroes (like Angela Davis) whose actions and words have shown the community how the dominating White Western culture has been organized historically to oppress Black people. The strategy of reactivating this memory will show the *masses* of Black people that assimilation into White Western society has never been possible for them. As long as White hate of Black continues and manifests itself in the virulent racism that has existed in the West for hundreds of years, Black people will live in tension with White people. As long as the capitalist economic order in the United States promotes the idea that the African American community and African American individuals are the bases upon which every non-Black (and often immigrant) group can build its route to financial stability, Black people will remain economic "footstools" in America. They will not have equal access to the financial resources the country provides for its citizens to achieve financial stability and to accumulate wealth.

The solidification of oppressive White power—traditionally following several years after bursts of Black civil rights activity—has finally shown Black people the futility of the goal of integration into White society. Many Black people once believed integration would pave the way for our full assimilation into the rights and privileges a democratic society is supposed to afford. Martin Luther King Jr.'s dream of the time when little White children and little Black children would sit down together in equality has proved to be only wishful thinking. White-controlled educational and economic systems, racist politicians and White supremacist groups have done everything in their power to thwart Black people's realization of the full rights, privileges and entitlements the U.S. Constitution promises. Attorney Patricia J. Williams aptly describes the current tactics by which Blacks are excluded:

> No longer are state troops used to block entry to schools and other public institutions—segregation's strong arm, states' rights, has found a new home in an economic gestalt that has simply privatized everything. Whites have moved into the suburbs and politicians have withdrawn funds from Black to White areas in unsubtle redistricting plans. No longer is the law expressly discriminatory (as to race and ethnicity at any rate; this is not yet the case in terms of sexual orientation)—yet the phenomenon of laissez-faire exclusion has resulted in as complete a pattern of economic and residential segregation as has ever existed in this country.[18]

Along with the politicians' redistricting methods and the privatization processes that neutralize the legislative and economic gains of the Black civil rights movements, the violence of White hate groups against Blacks arouses fear in Blacks. This fear can generate inertia among African Americans who know that, in the past, law officers have sided with White perpetrators. More often than not, African Americans suffered a harsh penalty for lodging a complaint or for exercising self-defense.

In order to experience social salvation, African Americans need to commit to memory and pass along from generation to generation *specific* wisdom and knowledge. The deposits of African American folklore communicate some of this special wisdom and knowledge that subsequent Black history has borne out. Case in point is the story of Sis Goose who, threatened by Brer Fox, takes the problem to court. But when she gets there, she discovers the judge is a fox; all members of the jury are foxes; the attorneys are also foxes. The moral, according to the lore, is that "if the judge, the jury, the attorneys are all foxes," there will be no justice for a "poor goose."[19] As an analog, this story emphasizes what experience has taught Black people in the United States: when all the judges, juries and attorneys are White, very little justice happens for Black folk. Case in point, among many others: the Rodney King case in California a few years ago, in which an all-White jury acquitted the policemen who savagely beat King. Only mass-protest demonstrations and federal intervention caused some small semblance of justice to happen for King. For generations, the custom in the southern U.S. was that White people accused of lynching, raping and maiming Black people were acquitted by all-White juries and judges.

This suggests that since the law often fails Black people, and since the police forces are often populated by White police officers who hate Black people and carelessly murder and maim Black youth at will, the Black community must devise ways of saving its people. Across the country, too many young Black men and women have been murdered by police. The case of the racist White policemen's murder of the Brooklyn, New York, youth in June of 1996 (described earlier) is one example among many that have occurred over time. In the United States, memory of Black civil rights history must be reactivated in order to lift up those brave heroes and sheroes whose collective action shows Black people strategies that can be used to avoid destruction and subservience to White domination.

Black people can obtain and have obtained some rights through the work of organizations powered with long-term impact, like the NAACP (the National Association for the Advancement of Colored People), SCLC (the Southern Christian Leadership Conference) and the Center for Democratic Renewal in Atlanta, Georgia. Since the early twentieth century, the NAACP has worked through the U.S. courts to change laws and challenge oppressive traditions denying the rights of Black Americans that are promised to all citizens by the U.S. Constitution. Remarkable Black heroes and sheroes who pioneered this organization were W. E. B. Du Bois, Walter White, Modjeska Monteith Simkins, Thurgood Marshall and many others. However, there are often attempts in the culture to present this organization in a negative manner. Black children (and adults) must be trained to recognize the attempts, channeled through popular culture, to discredit organizations like the NAACP that have worked for many decades to obtain rights for Black people through the courts. One such recent attempt to discredit the NAACP occurred in the motion picture *A Time to Kill*. The NAACP was represented as trying to sacrifice a Black family's survival needs for the sake of achieving a legal goal that would deliver a message to the nation about the affirmation of Black people's rights under the law in the South. The Black star of the picture, Samuel Jackson, was presented with the choice of selecting the NAACP lawyer as his defense agent or retaining the Southern White male lawyer he had from the beginning. The Black star chose the White male lawyer. The point here is that the "NAACP scenes" in the movie were not necessary for the plot to unfold. We must ask why viewers were encouraged to believe that the NAACP did not have the best interests of the Black family at heart but that southern White legal agents did. We must regard these scenes as propaganda pieces meant to convey the message that some Southern White law officials are more concerned about Black family life than are organizations like the NAACP. Our history with racism in the United States has *not* corroborated this southern White legal concern for Black life.

In addition to the NAACP, there are other long-term organizations working tirelessly for Black people's well-being. Through the dedicated work of Coretta Scott King, the widow of Martin Luther King Jr., the activities of King and the SCLC have been documented and preserved. She has built a fine research center, the Martin Luther King Center in Atlanta, Georgia. Then there is the Center for Democratic Renewal in Atlanta. It keeps track of the White supremacist groups designed to threaten and destroy the lives and property of Black people. It too is powered for longevity.

African Americans also need the work of organizations powered with short-term impact, powered more for a particular time than for a long term. Organizations like CORE (the Congress of Racial Equality) and SNCC (the Student Nonviolent Coordinating Committee) served the community well during the 1960's Black rebellion. Whether powered for long-term or short-term, these groups need *African Americans to provide full financial support and man/woman power so that Black people can have the major voice in determining the agenda of the groups.*

Black Americans have obtained some justice through mass-protest demonstrations accompanied by boycotting White-owned businesses. Three of these marches on Washington, D.C., stand out in American history: the march on Washington in the early twentieth century led by A. Phillips Randolph (and the sleeping-car porters); the "renewed" march on Washington featuring Martin Luther King Jr. in the period of Black resistance history now referred to as "the 1960's"; and the latest march on Washington, in October 1995, named "the million man march" led by Muslim Minister Louis Farrakhan in collaboration with several Christian ministers, among them the Reverends Hycel Taylor, Jesse Jackson, and Johnny Youngblood.

In some quarters of the community, the million man march has been challenged. Black women identified it as sexist because Black women were told not to come. The questions I heard Black women raise are these: Was this march in behalf of the liberation and well-being of all Black Americans—women and children as well as Black men? Or was it the biggest public demonstration of patriarchy in our time? If one of the goals of the march was for Black men to atone to Black women for their sexism, desertion of children and abuse of women, why did men have to go to Washington, D.C., to do this; why was it not done in the local communities where Black women live? How could men atone to women without women being present to respond? When the voices of women are silenced in the struggle by the men in the struggle, is that not blatant sexism? Since Black Christian church membership is 70 to 80 percent female, how could Christian ministers support a march that discriminated against the majority of the church membership? In its exclusion of women and its lack of serious attention to Black women's issues, did this march actually support the reemergence of White male supremacy? Did it support the current backlash against the meager liberation gains Black women have realized in the last few years? Did this march demonstrate that White males and Black males are bonded on the issue of the subservience of women to men? If so, do

Black men, in this bonding, help White men maintain White racist oppression of Black people?[20]

In addition to mass-protest demonstrations to obtain justice, Black people have attempted to form new political parties, like the Black Panther Party, and to challenge the racist practices of the traditional political parties in the United States. An example of this challenge is the Mississippi Freedom Democratic Party (MFDP), established in 1964 and led by Fannie Lou Hamer. Its goal was to challenge the racist practices and policies of the (White) Mississippi Democratic Party. Initially, it sought a working relationship with the Democratic Party in Mississippi. But when it was "excluded from participation in the state party procedure the MFDP held its own state convention and selected sixty-eight delegates to send to Atlantic City" to the national Democratic Party convention, where Lyndon Johnson was to be nominated for president of the United States.[21] Regardless of Fannie Lou Hamer's dynamic speech; regardless of the freedom songs sung at the convention; regardless of the continuous reappearance of the MFDP on the main floor of the convention after it had been expelled from the floor; regardless of the support Hamer and the MFDP received from other delegates, the sixty-eight delegates from MFDP lost their challenge to the national Democratic Party. There was no total rejection of the (White) Democratic Party representatives from Mississippi. Instead, the national convention indicated that three representatives from the Mississippi Democratic Party would be seated on the convention floor. All three representatives chosen were from the White Democratic Party of Mississippi.

Not devoted to reforming the existing political parties in the United States, the Black Panther Party was autonomous. Its work extended beyond mere political activity. Members of the party nurtured community life as they started and supported food programs to feed children who came to school hungry and as they organized child-care groups to service working parents. They also worked in the area of proper health care for the community. To date, political party formation is the most undeveloped area of the justice-seeking activity of Black Americans. Inasmuch as the FBI and other agencies went far in dismantling and/or neutralizing the power of the Black Panther Party, African Americans may be reticent to become engaged in the kind of work it takes to establish and assure the longevity of a third political party in the United States.

To make sure that this justice-seeking wisdom and knowledge of Black common sense is passed along to each generation, the Black community and Black churches must organize for this purpose. In the churches, Sunday schools should provide materials and resources that teach this wisdom and this knowledge to children from an early age. Through a variety of stories recounting the history, children at every level in Sunday school should be constantly urged to remember that their ancestors have provided "blueprints" for self-defense, for legal pursuit and for effective political organization.

In the committee structure of every African American church, there should be a permanent "demonstration and boycott committee." This committee should meet regularly to plan demonstrations, boycotts and other pressure tactics at the local level in order to secure economic, legal and social justice for Black people. These committees should come together across denominational lines in order to plan and help each other activate their plans. Another function of the demonstration and boycott committees should be constantly working to build alliances with non-Black groups that want to help support economic, legal and racial justice for African Americans. If every African American church in the United States had one of these committees, there could be an annual, national meeting of demonstration and boycott committees. Black people could identify national and international issues negatively affecting the freedom and well-being of Black people. Then collective action could be designed. In order for these committees to work effectively on both the local and the national levels, they should be constantly communicating with each other. Some of this communicating can be done on the computer. (We must work to impress every Black household with the value of computer education. Every home should be provided with a computer so that Black people can have access to the information highways that the new technological age is constructing. Without extensive computer knowledge, Black people can slip back into slavery. Though they may not reexperience chattel slavery, there are other kinds that can be just as deadly.)

"Black Common Sense" and the Second In-House Strategy

The second "in-house" strategy needed to activate Black common sense and to work toward social salvation is the development of Black community consciousness and actions that continuously transform "can't do" into "can do." This technique emphasizes and promotes the work of getting beyond the obstacles that oppressive systems put in the way of Black people.

Moving from "can't do" to "can do" means fostering and disseminating in the community the kind of ideology it takes to move Black people away from "can't do." It means prodding Black people's memory about Black individuals and groups in the community who have modeled and do model the movement to "can do." One such group emerged in the context of the 1960's Black rebellion. That group was Deacons for Defense. Emerging from the church, these deacons transformed "We can't defend ourselves" to "We can and will protect our families, our people and our property." While they never advocated aggression, they were not slow to protect Black families and communities.

Deacons for Defense now needs to be revived and institutionalized as a permanent structure in the community organized for self-defense. From an early age, African American children, female and male, should begin to go through an educational process acquainting them with the reasons for and function of this group and other groups committed to the defense of Black people and Black communities. The survival of the people—women, men and children—depends upon keeping the "can do" ideas and groups alive. Were Deacons for Defense active today, the burning of Black churches could not have been done so easily and so extensively. With regard to the longevity of the African American community, there is an urgent need for constant and vigilant action in order to prevent the physical and cultural genocide constantly threatening Black people in Western culture.[22]

Transforming "can't do" to "can do" means educating Black people about the *kind* of political, religious, economic and social alliances with other groups beyond the Black community that will support Black advancement. It means discovering the groups to which Blacks can connect in order to get free of the "can't do" economic bind that the ruling-class power structure uses to hold Black people in a subservient position. But Blacks are not to believe that economic prowess will save them from genocide. The example of another group of people is instructive here. Strong, viable economics did not save the Jews from the genocidal fascism of Nazi Germany. Too much anti-Semitism, too many generations of negative stereotyping of Jews, too many pogroms had happened in Europe. Hate of the Jew was ingrained in the consciousness of too many European people; therefore, very few non-Jews cared what happened to the Jews. When some Jews boarded a ship fleeing Nazi Germany, they sailed into many non-European ports (including the United States) seeking asylum. No country would accept these Jews. They returned to Germany and were no doubt put in concentration camps, where many of them, more likely than not, suffered extinction.

Neither will Black economic power erase White hate of Black. Too much anti-Black sentiment in America, too much stereotyping of Black people, too many White supremacist assaults upon Black people have happened in the United States. Hate and distrust of Black people are encoded in the national consciousness of America. African Americans must constantly organize to save Black people and communities.

Nevertheless, strong economic foundations are needed to support the Black movement from "can't do" to "can do." There are many ways this foundation can be built by Black people in the church and in the community. In the educational function of the church, Black congregants can be taught how the banking system works in the United States and how to use it effectively. With this kind of information available to congregations, they can see the benefit of Black churches organizing for the ecumenical effort of many Black churches banking at the same bank, so that Black people would be able to demand that the bank invest in Black communities.

There are other ways the church can be instrumental in helping Black people develop strong and supportive economics for the Black community. It can reconceive itself not only as a religious center but also as a marketplace, as an economic enabler and as an educational center. As marketplace, the churches—again in an ecumenical effort—would support "market days" on the church premises *for Black people to sell to each other* vegetables, foodstuffs and other commodities. In an ecumenical endeavor, some churches could put their financial resources together and purchase farms that produce the vegetables and foodstuffs sold on market days. Black people in the church and community without jobs could be taught to form collectives that operate the farms. (Then Black people could own and operate the vegetable and fruit markets in the Black communities.) At some point, the collective could take over the ownership of the farm. Of course, one of the educational functions of the church would be to put people and groups in touch with resources that provide the kind of training needed for this endeavor. Churches and mosques and other religious groups in the community could come together to plan for this kind of activity. A single church or a single mosque or a single group cannot do it alone. In their economic, political and social planning, Black people must cross denominational and religious boundaries so that collective action can be engaged to save Black people and their communities.

There is not enough space in this essay to provide a full "blueprint" for actualizing this idea. But enough is written here to suggest that Black churches, because they can have access to monies from banks and foundations, can serve as economic enablers for their parishioners. An economic enabler obtains financial resources and then, through a plan of "provide and pay back," makes these resources available to people in the church and community who want to go into business. Of course, the business pays the church back, and the pay back money is used to repay financial sources and to help other Black people start businesses.

There are some Black churches already modeling roles similar to that of economic enabler. Abyssinian Baptist in Harlem, New York, pastored by the Reverend Doctor Calvin Butts, was the founding agent for the Abyssinian Development Corporation, now an independent concern. Initially this corporation worked to develop low-income housing for Black people. Now it has extended its function to provide resources that help Black people go into business. In Detroit, Michigan, the Hartford Memorial Baptist Church, pastored by the Reverend Doctor Charles Gilchrist Adams, is a major economic enabler in the Black community there. Allen Memorial A.M.E. Church in Queens, New York, under the leadership of the Reverend Congressman Floyd Flake, has provided services in that area. There may be other churches serving as economic enablers about which I do not know. The point here is that the enabler role of the Black churches should be much more expansive, with churches cooperating with each other, merging their efforts in order to boost the economic capability of the Black communities and their residents. One of the important features of the enabler role is its connection with African American tradition. It resembles an old African American custom that apparently drifted out of Black consciousness in the twentieth century. This role revives memory of the "mutual aid consciousness" that ex-slaves actualized into mutual aid societies through which they helped each other.

Along with the church, secular institutions in the Black community can also contribute to the emphasis upon moving from "can't do" to "can do." Beauty shops and barber shops are institutions in the Black community. They are places where information is exchanged, where people get to know each other, where values are expressed and debated. In each barber shop and beauty shop there could be a community bulletin board alerting citizens about jobs, career possibilities, vocational realities, certain "how-to" information and any other news about economic life in the United States and world that might be of use to African Americans. These bulletin boards could also provide referral lists for people who need services—whether medical, clerical or related to a particular craft, like carpentry.

It is in the education of children that the church can be most helpful. African Americans have learned, after years of trying, that the public schools are not going to teach Black children the things they need to know about Black history in this country and in the world. Neither are the public schools providing the kind of instruction children need to become mathematicians, scientists, doctors, nurses and other professionals. Classes are too large. The equipment is often outdated in many of the schools African American children attend. Academic content is not interesting or relevant enough to hold children's attention. Some children cause serious discipline problems. Pedagogy gets waylaid, and teachers become exhausted trying to deal with the discipline problems causing havoc in the classroom. There is no consistent and substantial relationship between the students' homes and the school that would allow the teacher to call on the parents for regular help. Teachers do not know enough about a student's home life to determine what is affecting the child's academic performance. As a result of these conditions, Black children are not learning to read, write, spell and do arithmetic at a high level. Parents unfamiliar with higher education are not encouraged to start early preparing children for college.

It is obvious that the African American community must take over the education of Black children. The church, the mosque, other groups and the homes will either work together for the education of children, or the Black community will continue to lose its generations to drug culture and other vice contexts. Churches, mosques and other public locations could be sites where tutoring centers are opened and administered by retired schoolteachers and other adults who want to be involved in teaching. The salaries for these teachers and helpers would come from affordable fees parents would pay and from other revenues provided by religious and secular organizations in the community and beyond. Some of this education should be designed to start children at an early age learning about economics; about how to plan, open and operate a business; about how to use the banking system to their advantage; about cooperating with each other to promote mutual progress. A few of our Black churches are already involved in the education of children on a daily basis. They provide instruction through the elementary levels. Bridge Street A.M.E. Church in Brooklyn, New York, pastored by Reverend Fred Lucas, is involved in this kind of education, as is Covenant Baptist in Washington, D.C., pastored by the Reverend Doctor Dennis Wiley. Allen Memorial A.M.E. Church, pastored by the Reverend Congressman Floyd Flake, also provides school for children.

In addition to regular schools and tutoring centers, there is a need for "Saturday programs" in the community to provide enrichment education. These programs would function to impress children with the idea that they are always to engage in "extracurricular" intellectual and physical activity that stimulates their imagination and enriches their lives from childhood throughout adulthood. Enrichment programs expose African American children to Black arts and artists, to art of other cultures, to travel in historic areas in the United States and beyond. These programs introduce children to positive entertainment experiences both in the community and beyond it.

All of these suggestions about "in-house" things Black people can do to save themselves and their communities are not easy to put into practice. They require organization of the church and community. They require a "self-help," "teamwork," "beyond-denominationalism" psychology on the part of preachers, parishioners, community leaders and other citizens. Implementing the "in-house" strategies requires reeducating the Black church population so that it understands and accepts the importance of the socio-politico-econo-educational function of the church—so that it understands this function is just as important for Black people's salvation as are the religious functions of the church.

Those in the church and outside the church need to be reminded of the past *working connection* between the Black church, family, school and mutual aid societies. This connection saved Black people from utter despair and destruction, especially after the failure of the Reconstruction following the Civil War. Today this working connection is needed, but it must yield positive, productive, educational, economic and political results for children and adults. If Black children and adults are to be saved in this world, Black consciousness must move beyond the provincial boundaries of denominationalism and beyond the boundaries imposed by biblical literalism. The communities must work together for the *common good* of all. Black people will not be saved in isolated patterns of individualism wherein a person concerns himself or herself only with his or her personal survival and quality of life formation, and wherein churches concern themselves only with life within their individual walls. No one person, no one church, no one mosque can save the Black communities. The crises and problems facing Black people in the world today are too vast and too complex for individual ministry. Black people must either work together or go down together. The late James Baldwin was correct years ago when he said that if they come for the masses of Black people in the daylight, they will come in the night for the few who think they have "made it" in dominant and dominating White Western cultures.

"Black Common Sense" and the Third In-House Strategy

This third strategy encourages constructive critical thinking and careful planning, rather than emotional reaction to issues affecting Black people's quality of life. In far too many of our Black churches, the leadership encourages emotionalism at the expense of constructive critical thinking—that is, critical thinking that will enhance survival and will lead people to challenge oppressive structures in church and society. In far too many churches and other Black religious bodies, members are not encouraged to question sermons or to critique decisions and practices of preachers and bishops. Emotionalism in the church ignores corruption. Its only goal is to allow Black people to experience a catharsis of their pain.

The more successful the preacher is at pushing the right "emotional buttons," the more dependent the church people (mostly women) are upon him or her for this exorcism that helps them to bear rather than oppose the oppression they experience daily. Hence, many of the church people (mostly women) hesitate to do anything that will interfere with the "exorcism skill" exercised by the preacher. Like flies caught in a spider's web, they become victims of oppressive machinations in the church. They become instruments of their own oppression and the oppression of female ministers. Women depending upon exorcism obey the preacher, and some preachers encourage women to avoid the kind of critical thinking that would hold leadership accountable for its moral posture in the church and community. Today the salvation of Black people and Black communities depends upon challenging corrupt and egotistical patterns of leadership in church and society—patterns that prevent constructive critical thinking and positive action against oppression in the church and community.

Black women (the majority membership in the African American churches) are advised to examine the African American denominational churches' models of leadership. In this process, they can review the moral grounding of that leadership to determine if it supports the survival, liberation and productive quality of life for the Black community, female and male. Then women must examine the power dynamics operative in the African American denominational churches and in other Black religious bodies in order to determine if they (the power dynamics) imitate the oppressive White-power dynamics operative in the societies where Black communities are situated. This means that the relations existing between males and females in the church must be assessed. If these relations are patriarchal and paternalistic, they must be routed out. Too often, Black patriarchal structures relate to Black females in the same way that White racist structures relate to Black people. Thus, as it functions in the United

States, Black patriarchy oppresses, devalues and destroys Black women in the same way that White racism oppresses and destroys Black people. (Black men often seem to be guided by the patriarchal prescription "Do unto Black women as White racist systems have done unto you.")

While there are many honest, hardworking, upstanding ministers in Black churches struggling to achieve liberation and a better quality of life for Black people, there are too many Black preachers caught up in male-ego posturing dedicated primarily to accumulating power, privilege and prestige for themselves and for males exclusively. Thus, Black women, who are the majority in the Black church and who provide the money to support the church, must work together across denominational lines in order to engage the constructive, critical thinking that will help the church contribute productively to the lives of Black children and their parents. Emotionalism will not save Black people.

It is important to understand what I do and do not mean by emotionalism. By emotionalism I mean those hysterical, reactive responses that bring neither reason nor resolution to an issue. Emotionalism allows a person or group to "vent" rather than to vision and to plan. (Certainly we feel better after we release our rage through spontaneous emotional reaction, but that does not solve our problems.) Black people must ask these questions: Does the church advocate the kind of critical thinking that helps us, on a daily basis, to design and to provide activities working toward alleviating our oppression? Does the church foster activity that strengthens our economic resources? Is the church's programmatic goal to organize the community for survival, liberation and a positive, productive quality of life? Emotionalism does not require planning or imagination. Longevity, economic progress and freedom do.

By emotionalism I do not mean the joyful noise made in the Black church as members praise and thank the God who supported them in their many trials and tribulations. Emotionalism does not refer to the wonderful gospel music that helps the spirit express itself in the church. Emotionalism is not the well-organized, inspiring and energetic sermons that some of the preachers deliver. Emotionalism does not refer to testimonies, praise services and praise songs through which parishioners establish connection and community. It is not the invigorating joy that Black people experience and express as the Spirit moves in the worship service. All of these activities involve more than screaming. They are a celebration of God's grace sourced by a complex of daily life experiences and encounters with God. They are sourced by interpretation of those experiences and encounters in relation to the community's history, traditions and faith. Emotionalism, by contrast, is sourced only by feeling rather than also by constructive critical thought. It is an end in itself. It promotes the idea that the only purpose of the church's liturgy is to excite women to scream rather than to think. Emotionalism is often manipulated into being by the preacher's way of relating to some Black women's need to vent their stored-up pain.

Contrary to emotionalism, constructive critical thinking creates responses reflecting a balanced blend of reason, imagination and emotion. It broadens the mind's vision so that women see oppression emerging from sources within the Black community as well as from beyond the community. It inspires female parishioners to demand that the church's liturgy and its major leadership and decision-making roles reflect Black women's presence. It raises the church's consciousness to women's experience as a vital and empowering force in the church and community. Unlike emotionalism, constructive critical thinking helps the church see, appreciate and actively acknowledge Black women's history in what historian Darlene Clark Hine describes as "making community." "Making community" is "the process of creating religious, educational, health-care, philanthropic, political and familial institutions and professional organizations that [have] enabled our people to survive."[23] Without a doubt, Black women have been the main force keeping the Black church alive.

Now it is time for Black women to reflect constructively upon their place and work in the church. Their thinking is constructive when it holds leadership accountable for its moral posture in the church and community. Female critical thinking is constructive when it does not degenerate into trite gossip or into what the old Black folks called "back-biting." Rather, it builds healthy community. It yields discourse and action that relieve the church of provincial denominational politics supporting patriarchy and prohibiting joint economic planning by different churches and various communities.

Taken together, Black common sense and the three "in-house" strategies described here provide suggestions for ways that African American imagination, intelligence, ingenuity and resources can be used to save Black families, homes, churches and communities. Reviving past and proven civil rights strategies, moving Black consciousness beyond "can't do" to "can do" and encouraging constructive critical thinking in church and community inspire Black people to believe in their capacity to act effectively in history in their own behalf. This kind of faith strengthens hope and yields the courage people need to stand guard against those who threaten, assault, burn and destroy Black property. This kind of faith, hope and courage affirms what Sandra Jackson-Opoku describes as calling "forth the 'imperishable' power of the ancestors who live on eternally through the generations."[24] This calling forth helps Black people map a journey to salvation in the here and now. It provides memory rooted in a history of kin who forged a path for Black people through the wilderness of the African Diaspora in the United States.

The Quest for Social Salvation

With the twenty-first century approaching, Black people must extend the road of freedom for the future generations of African Americans, male, female and child. The signs of the times must be seen clearly with regard to Blacks, and these signs must be communicated to the people. An urgent need for strategies of social salvation is determined by what this essay and the Afro-centric Presbyterian document "Is This New Wine?" diagnose as "the crisis of survival facing African Americans today." Like the drafters of this document, I suggest that Black Christians "must be concerned with the welfare of [our] children and communities as the first priority rather than the denominational politics of trying to be heard by others as a primary concern. That is common sense."[25] (Read "heard by others" as heard by oppressive White and Black denominational structures.)

While I am not suggesting that the reference to common sense in the Presbyterian document coincides with the definition of Black common sense I have provided, I do agree with the drafters that African American Christians have, for generations, believed in salvation through Jesus Christ. Referring to God and Jesus interchangeably, they have understood the gospel (or good news) to be Jesus' power to deliver the oppressed, Jesus' power to provide healing sustenance and to guide humankind toward a positive quality of life.

This faith is part of the special knowledge constituting Black common sense. African Americans have confessed it in spiritual songs, claiming, "My God delivered Daniel and why not every man?" In gospel songs with such lines as, "We don't believe God brought us this far to leave us," they have expressed faith in God's ability to sustain life. In testimonies in the churches, Black people have declared God helped them make a way out of no way, thereby confessing faith in God's participation in quality-of-life formation. Black ancestors have passed along this kind of belief to subsequent generations.

It is no wonder that a theology of liberation has been birthed by Black American theologians and that a theology with emphasis upon survival and quality of life has been spawned by some Black Christian women naming their theological movement "womanist." However, these theologies lose some of their power when the Black church does not support the people's quest for salvation on earth. In its theological understanding of itself, the Black church must encourage action in behalf of Black people's freedom and well-being in this world. A new theological understanding of the Black church is needed, but this understanding should also be relevant to the Christian church universal.

Because Black churches, communities and people have been assaulted time and again by White violence, the Black church is called upon to confess a self-understanding that provides additional marks of the Christian church universal. Along with the original distinguishing marks of apostolicity, catholicity, unity and holiness, the church needs to add another mark, namely, opposition to all forms of violence against humans, nature, the environment and the land.

These marks are not only the church's "badge of identity," they also suggest what the mission of the church is supposed to be. The church is to bear witness to the world that it is built upon a tradition of dedicated female and male disciples supporting each other in the work of hastening the kingdom of God on earth—the kingdom mandated by God to serve *all* humanity, the world and land with justice, care, love and peace. There cannot be justice, nor care, nor peace nor love in the church when people and communities are beaten, burned and violated. To ask violated persons and communities to forgive their abusers without these abusers making reparations is to deny the justice God demands of the church. When justice, care, love and peace are absent, the church is not the church of Jesus Christ. It is merely an empty house without humanity, without divinity. Lacking justice, care, love and peace, this empty house becomes a domicile where evil dwells with impunity.

The catholicity of the church cannot mean that its mission is to proselytize the entire earth or to standardize a common theological interpretation of the gospel for all Christian communities. Catholicity suggests that the universal mission of the church should be to encourage every congregation to critically examine Christian sacred texts and to deconstruct theological traditions, liturgical practices and ecclesiastical policies that violate and sacralize violence of any kind against humans, against the environment, against the land. In its universal message, the church must be in agreement that violence comes in many forms—in physical, economic, sexual and gender manifestations. With this understanding of catholicity, the church builds a united foundation of action to support the alleviation of suffering in the various Christian communities and in the world; it takes actions against those people and groups in the Christian church that contribute to suffering in the world. Through this action, the Christian church realizes the holiness of its mission, that is, to reflect the life of the Spirit quickening the body and soul for liberating action in the world.

There can be no holiness, no unity and no catholicity of the Christian church until it identifies itself in active opposition to all forms of violence against humans (female and male), against nature (including nonhuman animals), against the environment and against the land. The church universal must not default on its mission to show the world that it affirms and advocates for the survival, liberation and positive quality of life for oppressed people and communities. When the church ignores the violence Black people suffer from White people, the violence women suffer from men, the violence the land suffers from human greed and exploitation, it loses its power in the world and forfeits its right to be identified as the church of Jesus Christ. The mission of the Christian church is continuously to act unequivocally and authoritatively against the abuse and violation that inflict people with physical bruises, emotional scars and spiritual shame.

Without confronting the fragmentation, fractures and wounds in the church and world that are caused by violence, the church cannot be the body of Christ. Without working toward a time *on the earth* when swords become plowshares because humankind has lost its thirst for violence, the church (universal or local) cannot be the welcome table God intended it to be. Without a viable commitment to help stop the violence Whites do to Blacks, men do to women, economically powerful people do to poor people, the Christian church loses its marks of apostolicity, catholicity, unity and holiness. If it does not add the additional mark of opposition to all forms of violence against humans, nature, the environment and the land, the Christian church becomes an empty symbol—perhaps full of sound, but signifying nothing of God. If the church does not participate in the work of bringing social salvation to the suffering and violated ones, it has no mission to speak of. It has no life in Christ.

Notes

1. Elsa Barkley Brown, "Womanist Consciousness: Maggie Lena Walker and the Independent Order of Saint Luke," in *Black Women in America*, Micheline R. Malson et al., eds. (Chicago: University of Chicago Press, 1988), 174.

2. Derrick Bell, *And We Are Not Saved* (New York: Basic Books, 1987), ix.

3. In this essay, "White supremacist groups," "White hate groups" and "White hate" are used interchangeably.

4. In this essay, "salvation in a social context" and "social salvation" are used interchangeably. In the final section of the essay, I merely use the word "salvation" when I discuss ideas about salvation deriving from Black Christian contexts. Perhaps my terminology in these two contexts suggests a separation of the sacred and the secular which most African American scholars deny. While I will not argue that issue one way or the other at this point, I do think the Americanization and Christianization of the Negro caused this separation in some areas of Black religious life.

5. This Black meaning of "common sense" differs from the ideas Thomas Paine expressed in his popular booklet *Common Sense,* which appeared in America in January 1776, during the Revolutionary War period. Paine, addressing a colony involved in disengaging itself from British rule and authority, makes a distinction between society and government, showing why government is necessary and why the type of government he suggests is preferable for the colonies to adopt apart from British rule. See Howard Fast, ed., *The Selected Work of Tom Paine and Citizen Tom Paine* (New York: Modern Library, 1945).

6. Harry V. Richardson, *Dark Salvation* (Garden City, New York: Anchor Press, 1976), 19.

7. Center for Democratic Renewal, "Report of Six Month Preliminary Investigation: Black Church Burnings in the South" (Atlanta), June 10, 1996, 1. This center is one of the most reliable in the country for keeping track of the number and activities of White hate groups directing their violence against Black people.

8. Ibid., 8

9. Ibid., 10.

10. Ibid., 12.

11. Ibid.

12. Ibid., 14.

13. Center for Democratic Renewal, "Black Church Burnings in the South Re-

search Report: Hate Groups and Hate Crimes in Nine Southern States" (Atlanta, 1996), 18.

14. The following catalog of incidents against Black individuals comes from the CDR report entitled "Black Church Burnings in the South Research Report: Hate Groups and Hate Crimes in Nine Southern States," 1-9.

15. "Teen Riddled by Police Gunfire," *Daily Challenge*, weekend edition, June 14-16, 1996.

16. In her book *Memoir of a Race Traitor* (Boston: South End Press, 1993), 5, Mab Segrest corroborates this lack of public appearance of the Ku Klux Klan. She writes, "It was a rainy Saturday on November 3, 1979. . . . The Ku Klux Klan, the 112-year-old terror organization indigenous to the American South, was on the march again after a decade or so of relative quiet."

17. By "in-house" I mean realities indigenous to the African American community.

18. Patricia J. Williams, *The Rooster's Egg* (Cambridge: Harvard University Press, 1995), 25. For an enlightening study of the effects of residential segregation upon Black people, also see Douglas S. Massey and Nancy A. Denton, *American Apartheid* (Cambridge: Harvard University Press, 1993).

19. The story of Sis Goose appears in Langston Hughes and Arna Bontemps, eds., *The Book of Negro Folklore* (New York: Dodd, Mead & Company, 1958).

20. Inasmuch as I actually attended the million man march, I now support some of these questions, because I have seen some negative (sexist) effects of the march in various African American communities and churches. But the march itself was an inspiring event in which Black male spirituality abounded. Because Black men in large numbers do not attend the Black church, we do not often get exposed to the outpouring of male spirituality. Those of us women who attended the march were treated royally by the men. Quite a number of women attended—especially single mothers with their young sons.

21. See Mamie E. Locke, "Is This America? Fannie Lou Hamer and the Mississippi Freedom Democratic Party," in Darlene Clark Hine, ed., *Black Women in United States History*, vol. 16 (New York: Carlson Publishing, 1990), 27-37.

22. I use "genocide" here in the sense expressed by Raphael Lemkin, who coined the term and whose definition influenced the definition of genocide provided in Article 2 of the Genocide Convention adopted by the United Nations on December 9, 1948. Lemkin described genocide as attacks upon a people's "political and social institutions, culture, language, national feelings, religion, and the economic existence of the group." The UN definition added, "deliberately inflicting on the group conditions of life calculated to bring about its physical destruction in whole or in part." For a discussion of Lemkin's definition as well as the UN definition, see Frank Chalk and Kurt Jonassohn, *The History and Sociology of Genocide* (New Haven: Yale University Press, 1990). For a discussion of genocide as it relates to Black Americans, see Delores S. Williams, *Sisters in the Wilderness: The Challenge of Womanist God-Talk* (Maryknoll, New York: Orbis Books, 1993), 130-136.

23. Darlene Clark Hine, *Hine Sight: Black Women and the Re-Construction of American History* (Brooklyn, New York: Carlson Publishing, 1994), xxii.

24. Sandra Jackson-Opoku, "Ancestors: In Praise of the Imperishable," in D. Soyini Madison, ed., *The Woman That I Am* (New York: St. Martin's Press, 1994), 7.

25. "Is This New Wine?" A paper for discussion among African American Presbyterians presented by Presbyterians for Prayer, Study and Action, April 1993; unpublished and not for distribution.

8

The Strength of My Life

Karen Baker-Fletcher

The Lord is my light and my salvation.
The Lord is my light and my salvation.
The Lord is my light and my salvation.
Whom shall I fear?
Whom shall I fear?
Whom shall I fear?
The Lord is the Strength of my Life.
Whom shall I fear?

—a spiritual popular in Black churches

Womanist theology, being contextual theology, commences by considering the revelation of God in the lives of Black folk historically and in the present, particularly in the lives of ordinary women of African descent. It may take the form of a Christian theology, Islamic theology, or nonorganized religiosity and spirituality. Womanist theology asks, "Who has God been in the lives of Black women historically and today?" My focus here is on the experience of God in the lives of African American women. My own immediate tradition is Christianity, so I write as a Christian womanist theologian. But for me, to be Christian is very broadly understood.

Within Christianity, let alone the spectrum of organized religions and of nonorganized spirituality, God has *many* names. Yet God is unnameable. That which we traditionally call God in Black Western culture is not limited to churches, but has to do with everyday belief and practice in day-to-day life situations. It is something one carries within always and is not limited to a place one visits Sunday mornings and weekday evenings. Shug Avery suggests in Alice Walker's *The Color Purple* that God is not something one finds in church, it is something people bring in with them. I would add that when people bring God with them to church, it is possible to find

God in church *if* one is able to love the people as well as God. Moreover, I would depart a bit from Shug's angle of vision to add that if God is everywhere, one can find God in church even when no one else is there—whether that God is found within oneself or appears to be revealed from who knows where in the midst of prayer and meditation. Ultimately, however, faith must emerge from something deeper and more ancient than denominational churches, which are fallible human institutions comprised of people of limited knowledge and understanding in relation to God. One must be grounded in the source that the churches claim to represent, the divine ground of all creation, of all that is and all that will be—God Godself.

Christian churches and the God-talk that emerges out of them are sources of both liberation and oppression for women. I am very aware of both phenomena in my life and in the lives of others. Since women tend to be outsiders in terms of leadership in the very churches and other organized religious institutions that they hold together as subordinate insiders, I am aware of myself as both insider and outsider, supporter and critic. Because of this dual experience of oppression and liberation, the Church is not my only or even my primary source of spiritual strength except in some ideal, utopian sense. Black churches, like any human institutions, are places of celebration and struggle, healing and pain.

As Delores Williams points out in her groundbreaking work *Sisters in the Wilderness*, it is necessary to make a distinction between the Black Church and Black churches.[1] By Black churches she has in mind the everyday practices, beliefs, ritual, music, and art of local denominational churches. By the Black Church she has in mind a larger sense of what Black churches sometimes claim to be about, struggle to become, and in certain moments actually embody. Her focus and mine is on God-talk that promotes survival and wholeness for entire communities, male and female. Because the churches are complex systems of liberation *and* oppression for Black women, ultimately it is God, not churches, who is the strength of one's life. God transcends the evils of patriarchy and oppression wherever they exist.

The song in the epigraph, "The Lord Is My Light and My Salvation," derived from Psalm 27, is a popular one in contemporary Black churches. Womanist hope is found in that which is greater and stronger than any evil. Such hope transcends fear, creating visions of promise and resources for survival, for resistance against evil, for liberation, and for healing. "The Lord" refers to God, which from a womanist perspective is Spirit. For womanists, "God is Spirit and those who worship God worship God in spirit and in truth" (Jn. 4: 23). God as Spirit is the light, salvation, and strength of one's life. With such inner spiritual affirmation, sustenance, and empowerment, one need not fear the vicissitudes of life nor those who bear ill will against oneself, family, or community.

Psalm 27, from which the spiritual "The Lord Is My Light" is derived, is a First Testament text, written thousands of years prior to the life of Jesus.

In traditional Black churches where this song is popular, however, "Lord" refers to God and Jesus. Among many Black Christian women, there is a tendency to conflate God (Creator), Jesus, and Holy Spirit during the ordinary, everyday, eloquent prayers heard in homes, churches, and gatherings. Sharp lines are not always drawn among the three persons of the trinity. God is Spirit. Jesus is Spirit and human. The Spirit is the all-encompassing, inclusive force in which God/Creator, Jesus, and all of creation are inextricably enwombed. Igbo African theologian Okechukwu Ogbonnaya has explained that from an Igbo perspective, the nature of God most fundamentally is Spirit. Spirit, he explains, is like the amniotic fluids—the waters of the womb—that encompass a child before it is born and accompany it, flowing out with it, as it makes its way into the world as we know it. It surrounds the *chi* and forms the first environment out of which it is born. Among the Igbo, the third person of the trinity is referred to not simply as the Holy Spirit, as in Western tradition, but as Holy Mother. In this worldview, Jesus has a mother *and* a father, as does all that lives. Without the Holy Mother, the Spirit, life, and creativity could not exist.[2]

Jesus is the human embodiment of Spirit. "Lord" in the aforementioned spiritual may refer to God, Jesus, the Spirit, or all three. Since God and Jesus, for Black women, are experienced as Spirit, the song likely refers to the entire trinity or community of God. While the reference to "Lord" in the song is somewhat problematic in an era when we question hierarchical models of reality, what is significant about the song is the faith in a Spirit of Light, Salvation, and Strength. These appellations for God/Jesus are sung in mantra-like repetition.

While women and men evidence the power of creation within our bodies and participate in God's creative activity, the stuff out of which we are made, its cycles, development, and organization, is not really of our own making, regardless of how much we may take events of conception, gestation, and birth for granted. We think we have so many answers, but where the power of life really comes from remains a mystery. Even when modern technology enters in to create babies through in vitro fertilization, it is dependent on that which already exists, which was previously created by the mysterious source and strength of Life itself. Technology and our own acts function at best as secondary sources in the creative process. There is something greater than ourselves that surrounds us, embraces us, encompasses us, gives us life, and interconnects us within a web of creation and creative activity that is beyond our understanding. It precedes us and survives us.

Alice Walker emphasizes in her definition of "womanist" that a womanist "*loves* the Spirit."[3] In traditional Black churches, Black women rejoice in being touched by or moved by the Spirit. God is beseeched in opening prayer to send the Holy Spirit to bless the service, the pastor, the speaker, the congregation. A good church service is one where one can really feel the Spirit. The Spirit is a healing, reviving source of positive power that gives new insight, courage, endurance, and meaning in the midst of the trials and tribulations of life. Through being touched by the Spirit, Black women proclaim that God provides vision for new resources of survival. There is so much love of the Spirit in Black churches that caution to "discern the spirits" is advice well given. For example, sometimes women claim to be able to remain in abusive relationships because the power of God as Spirit enables them to do so. Sometimes the pastor or deacon who is so deeply moved by the Spirit during church service returns home to beat his wife. More Christians are learning to ask: Is this really the will of God? How do we discern when a religious experience is truly an experience of the Spirit and a revelation of God? Who is God? What is the Spirit? How do we know when revelation has truly occurred? How do we know when we have read God's message to us correctly? How clear is our vision? Do we have a darkened eye that needs to be restored?

Womanist theologians have described God as a God of liberation, a God of survival, and a God of resistance against evil. Delores Williams, building on the language of traditional Black church cultures, has carefully demonstrated that for Black women, God "makes a way out of no way."[4] Jacquelyn Grant, building on other aspects of Black women's experience and the work of James Cone and feminist liberation theologians, has suggested that God is a God of liberation and survival. She has emphasized that if God is a God of liberation, God's liberating activity is "holistic, concerned with the well-being and survival of men *and* women."[5] The poet Ntozake Shange, author of *for colored girls who have considered suicide / when the rainbow is enuf,* is known for the last section of her famous choreopoem that asserts "i found God in myself & i loved her / i loved her fiercely."[6]

For Alice Walker, whose work is foundational for womanist theology, Creation itself is where we find the sacred, the Spirit, which includes the self. Historically, many Black women have seen God as "deliverer" who lifts one "out of the miry clay."[7] Anna Julia Cooper in the early twentieth century referred to God as "a singing something." And Lucie Campbell, whose hymns have become part of Black folk tradition across church denominations, refers to God as "something within me."[8] There are many names for God in Black women's culture that emerge from a diversity of experiences of the nature of God that, when taken together, provide a deep, rich spiritual heritage. But what is striking is the theme of finding God as Spirit within. Shange's poem, while initially striking and jarring to many, is in keeping with Black women's Christian and other spiritual traditions. It simply reminds all that God is the strength of life. This strength and life is with and within Black women and all of creation.

Renita Weems, in *I Asked for Intimacy*, points out that many Black women in churches argue that to call God "she" "sounds funny."[9] Many women find Shange's emphasis on finding God in oneself a stumbling block. We are not accustomed to thinking of ourselves as being created in God's image really, which means we have difficulty imaging God as female. But if we are to love our God with all our hearts and all our mind and all our strength and all our soul and our neighbor *as ourself*, how can we love God or neighbor if we do not love ourselves? If God does not identify with Black women, what kind of God is that? If we take the first account of the creation of human being in chapter 2 of Genesis, we find the creation of Adamah, which means simply "earth creature." We are creatures of the earth. "Male and female" created God them, explains chapter 1 of Genesis.

If we, male and female, are created in God's image, then it is possible to image God as male and female. In fact this often happens in certain prayers and songs in traditional Black worship where God is "my mother, my father, my brother, and my sister." There is something within Black culture that recognizes the wholistic nature of God, which identifies with humanity in its fullness as male *and* female. Such recognition resonates with the first creation account of humanity in Genesis and with both traditional and Christian African religious understandings of the nature of God. Such understanding must be lifted up without shame. To be ashamed of it is to be ashamed of the fullness of God and of ourselves as women created in the likeness of God. Surely if we are created in the likeness of God, we can love ourselves as we are scripturally challenged to do. If that likeness of God is within us, surely we can find God in ourselves, realizing empowerment and our full potential as we learn to love God and ourselves. Such love is the first order of business before we can go on to love others, beginning with our own daughters to whom we pass on the unholy, unsacred habit of low self-esteem if we do not love ourselves. We cannot claim to love life as a whole without loving our own lives.

Lucie Campbell's hymn "Something within Me" is a fine traditional hymn in Black churches that reminds singers and listeners alike of the power of God as Spirit within the souls of those who walk in faith with a God in whose likeness they are created. "There is something within I cannot explain," the hymn goes. Shange's "i found God in myself & i loved her / i loved her fiercely" is a contemporary way of describing the spiritual experience of finding something within that reveals that "the rainbow is enough." Her choreopoem goes beyond Christian understandings of spirituality to speak in broad terms. However, it is a poem that both Christian and non-Christian Black women can relate to. For Christian Black women, the rainbow has long been a symbol of God's covenant with humankind and with creation. For Shange, the rainbow similarly symbolizes a covenant with life rather than a contract with death. Colored girls do not have to consider suicide when the rainbow is enough. We are called away from choices in our lives that are ultimately self-destructive, and we are called to a covenant with the source of life itself. Anna Cooper referred to this as "a singing something" that can be traced back to the Creator. Even in the face of the evil of sociopolitical domination, it rises up and cannot be squelched. For Cooper, humankind is not only created in the physical image of God but also echoes something of God's voice, word, and speech. This suggests a prophetic element in human nature. For Cooper, this *singing some-thing within* rises up in the face of domination. She saw such prophetic speech in various social movements around the world—India and Russia, for example, as well as the French Revolution and Haiti's revolt against French slavery and colonial rule.[10]

Favored hymns among Black Christian women refer to *feeling* God, Jesus, the Spirit *within the heart.* God is embodied in humankind in Black Chris-tian women's concepts of God. Moreover, if we look beyond Christian Black women to womanist author Alice Walker, God is not only within the human heart but within all of creation. Walker's character Shug in *The Color Purple* explains that her first connection to God was a tree, a rock, or a flower, then later people. In her transformed state from feeling like a motherless child, which she was, to being a courageous survivor, she exclaims that if someone cuts a branch from a tree, she feels that her own arm bleeds.[11] God is not only within herself but in nature and the entire cosmos.

There is an African folktale that says God is on one's back. One cannot see God, but one needn't build ladders to the heavens to find God. God is perpetually present, always immanent. Even as God transcends particular human situations, God is present in our everyday lives, and infinite possi-bilities for healing and wholeness are in our midst. For womanists, God is neither simply that ultimate ground of being by which we are grasped in moments of mystical experience nor some ultimate point of reference whom we come to understand primarily by reason. It is in our human bodies, souls, and minds in our everyday lives that we *experience and reason* about the sacred. Such everyday experience of and thought about the sacred enables humankind with powers of sustenance to *practice* survival, heal-ing, and liberation in the midst of oppression, injustice, and the multitudi-nous vicissitudes of life. While there are many names for God among Afri-can American women, there is a common strand that appears, imaging God as empowering, sustaining, life-giving, strengthening, delivering bod-ies and souls from the pit of death, whether such death is imposed from outside by oppressive forces or from within by self-destructive, suicidal tendencies.

Psalm 27 speaks of eschatological hope and promise in God as the strength of life who sustains not only oneself, but the universe. In the end, it is this God that will prevail. For womanists, eschatology does not have to do with the "last things" or "end time" in any far-off, abstract, otherworldly sense. Rather, eschatological hope and envisionment have to do with the daily, moment-by-moment business of living. The reign of God's strength for life is an ever-present reality. The hereafter is in the here and now. We live into it in our everyday acts. The *life* that the spiritual refers to is key. That God is the strength of one's life indicates God's presence in human history. Not only is God present, but God's presence has a specific quality to it. God has a saving, strengthening presence in human life and, one might add, in keeping with the Psalms' frequent references to the earth, in the life of all creation. This also has eschatological ramifications, since God as the strength of life is not only in and with creation, but also transcends it. God as the strength of life is the power of life. Given such power, whom should one fear? Ultimately, that which threatens life is limited, in contrast to the very strength of life. That which is the very strength of life transforms fear into faith, salvation, and hope.

The Reign of God

For Christians, the promise of God's Kingdom or reign stands at the center of personal and social salvation. For those who explore the meaning of Christian scriptures for families, communities, and societies, the promise of God's Kingdom involves more than individual salvation—it involves social salvation. Eschatology—the study of "the last things" or "the fullness of time"—is concerned with the realization of God's reign on earth as in heaven. Jesus' most powerful saying for many Americans has been "The Kingdom of God is at hand." The Kingdom of God was at the heart of the Christian message for nineteenth-century American reformers across racial lines, who were committed to realizing salvation in the social sphere as well as the personal sphere. Walter Rauschenbusch, in his *Theology for the Social Gospel*, places it at the center of Christian faith and theology. The significance of Jesus for Rauschenbusch was his role in ushering in the Kingdom of God and transforming not only the world but also God's feeling for the world so that God suffered with it. The calling of the church, in his view, was to follow Jesus' example by preaching a Gospel that ameliorated society.[12] Although *A Theology for the Social Gospel* was published in 1917, it was a systematic exposition of ideas and beliefs that had characterized Social Gospel thought in nineteenth-century and early-twentieth-century America.

While Rauschenbusch, Washington Gladden, and Lyman Abbott are among the names most often cited in discussions on Social Gospel theology, Ronald White points out that there were numerous African American Social Gospel leaders: Francis Grimké, W. E. B. Du Bois, Ida B. Wells, and Anna Julia Cooper.[13] James Washington further observes that Black Americans were among the progenitors of Social Gospel thought and movement.[14] The distinctive contribution they provided the movement was criticism of racism as well as classism. For Anna Cooper and Ida B. Wells-Barnett, equal rights for women were of concern as well. At the heart of such theological thought was an interpretation of the Gospel of Jesus as promising not only individual salvation but also social salvation—a moral transformation of entire societies.

While the eschatological visions of thinkers like Walter Rauschenbusch, W. E. B. Du Bois, and Anna Cooper were anthropocentric, today theologians must ponder the meaning of the reign of God not only for humanity but for all of creation. It has to do with the fulfillment of God's vision for the entire cosmos. All of creation is redeemed—delivered from evil, oppressive, and corrupting forces—and brought into healing and wholeness by that which is the strength of life and transforms fear of evil into faith and hope.

Eschatology involves the transformation of society and all creation with it from what it is to what it ought to be according to God's vision for the world. As Psalm 27 and the spiritual "The Lord Is My Light" indicate, such transformation does not necessarily mean that evildoers are transformed into doers of good. Rather, regardless of the presence of evil doers in human existence, believers are transformed by the empowering strength of God so that they no longer live in fear. One then has the capacity for the kind of womanist audaciousness and courageousness that Alice Walker refers to in *In Search of Our Mothers' Gardens*.[15] Such courageousness is evidenced in the history of African American women freedom fighters like Harriet Tubman, Sojourner Truth, members of the Black women's club movement of the late nineteenth century, and women's organizations in Black churches. Given such courage, there is hope not only for personal transformation in the life of the believer but also for social transformation as believers press on with the strength of God for the amelioration of society.

Black women and men can transform present existence by actively remembering and practicing the prophetic, generative wisdom of the ancestors, particularly the greatest of our ancestors: Jesus. Such transformative activity is salvific, communal, and, for Christian womanists, based in the God of Jethro, Moses, Zipporah, and Jesus. For womanists, as for so many African American women and men historically, the words "the Kingdom of God is at hand" have profound meaning for how we live our lives on a daily basis in our present existence. The "hereafter" is not so far off. As Anna Julia Cooper put it, it is close enough that we must "live into it."

Womanist theology considers the location of eternity. Is it in those sacred and profane places called heaven and hell in traditional Christian thought? If so, the question of the location of eternity remains unanswered. Where are heaven and hell? Where is the reign of God? Are there places of salvation and damnation beyond this earth? Black liberation theologians like James Cone and J. Deotis Roberts emphasize that African Americans historically have been concerned about heaven and hell on earth. However, there certainly have been African Americans who ascribed to a "sweet-by-and-by" concept of salvation, as echoed by Celie in Alice Walker's *The Color Purple* and in James Baldwin's *Go Tell It on the Mountain*. These authors present the problem of unhealthy images of a life beyond this present one that encourages the oppressed to accept their oppression. In such worldviews, religion becomes Marx's "opiate" that seduces exploited workers into apathy about their exploitation.

Beyond the concrete symbolizations of heaven and hell in Black liberation and Social Gospel theologies or the ethereal, utterly transcendent symbolizations of heaven in sweet-by-and-by religious belief are worldviews based in traditional African and Native American belief systems. In these latter worldviews, the afterlife is transcendent and immanent. It is yet and not yet, much as Christians have traditionally described the reign of God. Not only is it yet and not yet; it is past and it is present. The "hereafter," or eternity, is not only in the future but also in the past. It includes the ancestors and those who will be future ancestors. It is indeed a fullness of time in which past, present, and future coexist and are held together. The world of the Spirit is ever present. God is Spirit, the resurrected Jesus is Spirit, the Holy Spirit is Spirit, we human beings are flesh and spirit, and all of creation is matter and spirit. We humans, along with the rest of creation, belong to Spirit itself. We are within it and it is within us. Interrelated with that which is beyond time, we participate in all times and no time in this time from moment to moment. I will say more about this later. First I want to reflect on the understanding of heaven and hell as concrete locations in the thought of Anna Julia Cooper's Black feminist Social Gospel theology, because it is in keeping with a very strong strand of eschatological understandings in African American history since the nineteenth century. It is older than Black liberation theology and, like other Black Social Gospel theological perspectives of her era, forms part of the cultural and religious soil from which it emerges.

Living into Eternity

While I was growing up, one of my grandfather Taylor Baker Sr.'s favorite preachments was that "Heaven and Hell is right here on this earth." He had different ways of coming around to this climactic statement at different times, but that was always the crux of his theological teaching. Sometimes it was a Sunday sermon that sparked this regular sermon. Other times it was a Jehovah's Witness who had come by to talk about the last days that fired him up to remind the entire family that heaven and hell were not in some far-off place. We were all taught that it is what we do in this life that determines whether we live in heaven or in hell. Grandpa Baker (Baker Taylor Sr.) is not a preacher or pastor of a church. He is a barber. But anyone who knows anything about neighborhood barbers in Black culture knows they are pretty close to being preachers and ministers in their own right. They hear a lot, see a lot, think a lot, and gain quite a bit of wisdom that they pass on. Moreover, Grandpa was a trustee in the church and involved in the church's leadership. He has had experience in years of church service and work in the community. Like James Cone, he is a product of the African Methodist Episcopal (A.M.E.). church. While he became United Methodist later on in life, it is the independence of the A.M.E. Church, a Black independent church, that he cites as an example of Black spiritual and social empowerment.

Later, at Harvard, reading the Black liberation theology of James Cone and the Black christology of Albert Cleage, I found that Grandpa Baker was preaching the theology of a multitude of Black Americans. A decade later, by the time I completed my doctoral studies, I learned that certain Black

Americans had always believed and taught that heaven and hell are right here on this earth. The teaching I had grown up with on a daily basis and the preachments I still hear when I go back home are rooted in a historical tradition in Black religious thought. Historical figures like Frederick Douglass, Sojourner Truth, Francis Grimké, Anna Julia Cooper, Fannie Lou Hamer, and Martin Luther King Jr. believed in a God, embodied in Jesus, who ushered in the reign of God on earth. They envisioned this reign of God as a reign of justice, social equality, and spiritual and political freedom. James Cone's symbolization of the reign of God on earth is not at all the fad some of his critics have held it to be. To the contrary, such a concrete understanding of the reign of God on earth echoes the historical understandings of certain ancestors. Anna Cooper insisted on a concrete understanding of the reign of God in a poem entitled "The Answer":

> God—is not afar!
> The simple may know:
> The Hereafter is here;
> Eternity is now.
> And myself am Heaven or Hell.[16]

For Cooper, eternity, the hereafter, heaven, and hell were not outside human history and existence. They were present in persons and in the moral choices they made. Heaven and hell were actual moral states of existence. Whether one lives into heaven or into hell depends on whether one works in harmony with Jesus' Gospel message of equality and freedom. For Cooper, this Gospel message of freedom and equality was like a germ or seed that Jesus the Nazarene planted in the soil of civilization. It is the responsibility of the Church to lead humankind into a fuller realization of the Gospel within civilization. By "civilization" Cooper had in mind the moral development of humankind in the social sphere as well as in personal lives. In her view, existence beyond this one is real and "culturable": "Yes, I believe there is existence beyond our present experience; that that existence is conscious and culturable; and that there is a noble work here and now in helping men live *into* it."[17]

We live into the hereafter. We cannot sit idly with folded hands, hoping for entry into a better life. We are not called to say, like Walker's Celie before her redemption in *The Color Purple*, "This life soon be over. Heaven last always."[18] Like Cooper and the awakened Celie, we are called to arise from whatever slumber seduces us to inaction and to act with God, who is on the side of justice.[19] Existence beyond our present experience is not some dream-like state. It is conscious. It is not otherworldly. It is in this life, and we human beings participate in making it a present reality and shaping it. Empowered by the delivering, freeing, healing, and redeeming Gospel message of Jesus of Nazareth, we effect the positive possibilities of future existence by our moral actions in the here and now. The promises of heavenly well-being and abundant life require our ethical transformation in the present. The gain from believing in an existence beyond present existence is concrete and social.

Cooper's understanding of the "hereafter" involved development of the here and now by the present generation for the next generation. Far from Lutheran in her eschatological understanding, she argued for faith that works, moving humankind onward and into the hereafter. To help humankind live into the best possibilities for its development "is a noble" work, as she describes it. Such belief, she argues, was central to Jesus' message and ministry:

> Jesus believed in the infinite possibilities of an individual soul. His faith was a triumphant realization of the eternal development of the best in man—an optimistic vision of the human aptitude for endless expansion and perfectibility. This truth placed a sublime valuation on each individual sentiency—a value magnified infinitely by reason of its moral destiny. He could not lay hold of this truth and let pass an opportunity to lift men into nobler living and firmer building. He could not lay hold of this truth and allow his own benevolence to be narrowed and distorted by the trickeries of circumstance or the colorings of prejudices.[20]

Cooper's understanding of Jesus' teachings on salvation emphasizes the perfection of individual human souls and a positive valuation of "each individual sentiency." The destiny of each soul was immortal. Given such positive valuation of the sublimeness of every soul, Jesus refused to participate in color or caste prejudice. He extended the promise of salvation to humankind across circumstances of race, color, class, gender, or nationality. Infinite possibilities for developing the best in men and women were promised to the human race, not exclusively to a White race, Black race, Red race, or Brown race.

While she emphasized the development of individual souls, Cooper was ever the social activist. She placed responsibility for the well-being of the entire society on individuals working together for its betterment. It was the Church's role to be a leader in this work, although she was well aware that historically it was full of members who "trampled the Gospel" rather than worked toward its fulfillment. In spite of its own human imperfections, it was still the Church's calling to work with God in fulfilling God's vision of freedom and equality. The amelioration or improvement of society was the responsibility of Christ's Church—all of those who believed in Jesus' altruism and in God's message of freedom embodied in the life, words, and ministry of Jesus. It required working in harmony with God's message of freedom and equality, the germ of the Gospel planted in the soil of human culture by Jesus Christ. Jesus, in Cooper's view, was at the forefront of the movement toward human fulfillment. She described Jesus as leading civilization forward in the way a mother leads her toddling child:

The quiet face of the Nazarene is ever seen a little way ahead, never too far to come down to touch the life of the lowest in days the darkest, yet ever leading onward, still onward, the tottering childish feet of our strangely boastful civilization.[21]

There was not one "idea," "principle of action," or "progressive social force," she argued, "but was already mutely foreshadowed, or directly enjoined in that simple tale of a meek and lowly life."[22] Cooper's representation of Jesus in relation to eschatology speaks to the ministerial empowerment of Black women in two respects. First, her imagery of Jesus is parallel to her imagery of Black womanhood and motherhood. Just as Black mothers are vital elements in the regeneration of a particular race, Jesus is the vital element in the regeneration of civilization universally. In this respect, not only does Cooper sacralize Jesus as the Christ, but she also sacralizes Black women's bodies, hands, and hearts. The fulfillment of God's vision of freedom and equality for humanity is embodied in the work of Black women, as far as the particular salvation of Black communities is concerned, and in Jesus, as far as salvation of the larger human civilization is concerned. Second, it is the life of Jesus, not his death, that is most important for Cooper. Present generations have hope for the future because of the legacy Jesus the Nazarene left in the past. This legacy is still unfolding. It is in everyday living that Black women and humankind in general ought to place its energies, not in prospects of death. This life is good, valuable, and worth living.[23] Hope is not only in the future. Hope is in the present and in history as each moment lived in faith moves from future time to present time and past time.

Jesus as a Symbol of Life, Strength, and Hope

Historically for Black Christian women, the embodiment of God as Spirit is evident in the saving, liberating, and healing activity of Jesus Christ in the lives of Black women, men, and children. Jesus embodies God, who is Spirit and who provides empowerment for resistance. As Delores Williams eloquently observes, Jesus assured salvation by a life of resistance and by the survival strategies he used to help others survive the death of identity. Eschewing a christology that glorifies the cross, she argues that "the spirit of God in Jesus came to show humans life—to show redemption through a perfect *ministerial* vision of right relations between body (individual and community), mind (of humans and of tradition), and spirit." Because the cross for Williams is an image of defilement—human sinfulness—to glorify it is to glorify suffering and render exploitation sacred. To ask Black women to glorify the suffering of Jesus and to focus on the sacredness of their own suffering is to render their exploitation sacred.[24] Williams implies that the effect of such christology is to encourage Black women to accept their suffering, often phrased by preachers as, "Bear the cross God has given you." This is a lesson, Williams argues, that Black women do not need to learn. They have already learned it too well. Black women, she suggests, are already expert cross-bearers and do not need those who could help empower them to encourage them to glorify the miry pits in which they struggle. Jacquelyn Grant similarly points out that Black women since at least the modern era have mastered endless lessons in suffering servanthood. This symbolization of Jesus, she contends, has become a symbolization of bondage.[25]

What both authors demonstrate is that however well-intentioned ministers who glorify suffering and servanthood may be, the effects of such ministry is detrimental. It effectively supports suffering, oppression, and exploitation. It is disempowering. Williams's emphasis on the ministerial, life-affirming, and sustaining vision of the Spirit of God in Jesus points to a fuller promise of redemption, deliverance, and salvation. On Sunday mornings, some of the most resounding shouts to Jesus I have heard are to Jesus "my deliverer!" The testimonies that receive some of the most heartfelt responses are those that witness to the healing, saving, and delivering power of Jesus. While preachers may preach at length about the power of the cross, it is the daily healing, delivering, saving power of Jesus that one hears about from congregational testimonies.

While Williams's criticism of the glorification of the cross reveals an urgent problem for Black women's faith understanding, the cross holds much meaning for many Black Christian women. Williams does not deny this, contending that Black women should neither forget the cross nor glorify it. If the cross should not be forgotten, it still must hold some significance. Indeed, just as praises rise to Jesus for providing healing and delivering power on Sunday mornings in traditional Black churches, many testimonies also give thanks to "Jesus Christ my Savior, who died for me that I might live." Abundant life is associated not only with Jesus' ministry during his life but also with his death on the cross. One of the most popular communion hymns during the serving of the bread and wine is, "I know it was the blood / I know it was the blood / I know it was the blood for me. / One day when I was lost / he died upon the cross. / I know it was the blood for me." What are womanists to make of such imagery of the atonement, which is unlikely to disappear from Black church services? It seems important to examine it critically. But how might one constructively reenvision it?

Sharon Welch, a White feminist theologian, also criticizes symbolizations of Christ that emphasize Jesus' suffering on the cross as indicating a call to sacrifice for all who follow Jesus. She rejects Western Christian obsessions with suffering and sacrifice, whether voluntary or coerced. So many women, she observes, have withstood domestic abuse in the name of Christian discipleship because of the poor counsel of ministers who liken spousal abuse to Jesus' suffering on the cross. Welch suggests another angle of vision on the meaning of suffering that moves toward a positive reaffirmation of faith, hope, and promise for healing in present existence.

Building on the life and writings of Black thinkers who have fought for freedom and justice in the United States, she suggests that the persecution and violence suffered by those who resist evil and injustice are the result of an *ethic of risk*.[26]

In this interpretation, the assassination of a Martin King or the crucifixion of Jesus Christ is part of the risk involved in actively struggling for social justice. But such risk involves hope. While there is a possibility of death and temporary failure, there is also a possibility for deliverance, healing, and liberation. Resisting the powers of systemic injustice that may result in persecution or assassination is based in faith and hope, not in a fatalistic vision of death and sacrifice. The will and desire of those who engage in an ethic of risk are a will and desire not for death but for abundant life in the immediate future. Williams's preachment that Jesus came for life, not for death is central to a theology that is consistent with a Gospel message of healing, deliverance, survival, and wholeness. Moreover, it is consistent with Jesus' ministry of resistance against evil and his empowerment of others to participate in this ministry. The cross must not be forgotten because persecution is a real consequence of standing up for what is true and morally right. The cross must not be glorified because it was a tool of oppression, much like the automatic rifle that assassinated Martin Luther King Jr., or like the trees with lynch-ropes from which hung the strange fruit of thousands of Black bodies in the segregated South. This particular interpretation of Jesus is consistent with the symbolization of Jesus in the Book of John, who "came that they might have life and have it abundantly" (Jn. 10:10). We see this image of Jesus in the life of Sojourner Truth, whose experience of Jesus gave her hope for her own freedom, the freedom of her children, and the freedom of an entire people, hope that delivers communities from powers of oppression. We see this image of Jesus in the writings of Anna Julia Cooper, who describes Jesus the Nazarene as ever present, leading civilization onward into broader lived principles of freedom and equality.

The Fullness of Time, the End of Time

As I have mentioned, there are at least three strands of thought among African Americans regarding the intersection of present life with the reign of God. One strand, represented by Cooper and James Cone, emphasizes a concrete understanding of the reign of God. Another, criticized by writers like Alice Walker and James Baldwin, points to fulfillment in a life beyond present, concrete existence. Certain traditional African cosmologies, such as Bantu Muntu cosmology or Gullah understandings of West African cosmologies in North America, suggest a both-and understanding of a life beyond present existence as we know it that holds past, present, and future times together within a spiritual reality that is both immanent and transcendent. In Walker's novel *The Color Purple,* the weakness of Celie's early faith in an existence beyond her present oppressive condition was that it was thoroughly otherworldly. She accepted beatings and verbal abuse as her lot in life with the hope and expectation that she would find happiness in a new, heavenly world after she died. Traditional African spirituality is wholistic in its understanding of time in relation to Spirit. Eternity is in the past, not simply in the future. It is also in the present, since the present becomes the past and the future becomes the present. As Nana Peazant reminds her son Eli in Julie Dash's acclaimed film *Daughters of the Dust,*[27] the womb and the ancestors are one. Such spirituality moves beyond debates about the location of God's reign, which have been characteristic of Black dialogue since the Harlem Renaissance, to insist on a both-and perspective. It affirms both concrete and "otherworldly" concepts of the world of the Spirit. The world of the Spirit and the reign of God as Spirit is everywhere at all times. It transcends time and space. It is in time and space. And it is with time and space.

For womanists and for Black women historically, hope and salvation have not been a matter of interpreting what it means to "be grasped by the ultimate ground of being" as if God were outside the self, nor of rationally constructing a theology in relation to an ultimate point of reference that provides adequate orientation for life. Rather, theological reflection involves interpreting what it means to experience connection with God as Spirit within creation—in sky, trees, water, land, birds, family, friends, humanity, one's own self and body—and gaining wisdom from such experience to practice harmonious living with that which is on the side of life. Nineteenth-century evangelist Zilpha Elaw, for example, describes her sanctification experience as one in which she seems to hear God rustling in the tops of the mulberry trees and feels herself moving beyond the trees to find herself caught up in the disc of the sun. Whether she is in body or out of body, she does not know. She experiences herself as part of the cosmos and as transcending it at the same time, her spirit merging with Spirit in nature. Once she experienced a vision and assurance from Jesus in a barn as she was singing and milking a cow. She describes the cow as bowing to recognize the liberating, "heavenly appearance" of her savior.[28] The *Narrative of Sojourner Truth* and a multiplicity of slave narratives refer to finding God in hush arbors, out in the wilderness.[29]

Today, womanist theology *presupposes* the presence of the sacred in creation—in all of life. For Walker, God and creation are so deeply interrelated that Creation becomes a metaphor for God. Most Christian womanists have not gone that far. I understand God as creativity itself, with creation playing a role in God's creative activity. While God and creation are within each other, they are not the same thing. Both Walker's understanding and my own, however, are based on traditional African cosmological understandings of the sacredness of all life and of God's being and becoming as moving dynamically in all of life. God is the strength or power of life. Such an understanding of God and creation moves beyond a humanocentric emphasis to a more integrative understanding of theology, culture, and nature.

The task for a womanist theology of survival, liberation, and wholeness is to address the existential *and* essential brokenness of all of creation in a wholistic manner, ministering to body, mind, spirit, and the material. An adequate theology is one that remembers God who is the strength of *all* life, who keeps humankind in harmony with the sacred in our everyday work and works for the healing and wholeness of creation. The words of Nana Peazant, a matriarchal character in Julie Dash's film *Daughters of the Dust*, about a Gullah African American family in the Georgia–South Carolina Sea Islands, refer to spiritual memory within that is ancient, belonging to ancestors and descendants:

> Those in this grave, like those who're across the sea, they're with us. They're all the same. The ancestors and the womb are one. Call on your ancestors . . . Let them guide you . . . There's a thought . . . a recollection . . . something somebody remembers. We carry these memories inside of us. Do you believe that hundreds and hundreds of Africans brought here on this other side would forget everything they once knew? We don't know where the recollections come from. Sometimes we dream them. But we carry these memories inside of us . . . I'm trying to teach you how to touch your own spirit. I'm fighting for my life, Eli, and I'm fighting for yours.[30]

Nana Peazant's words are grounded in an African worldview in which God, Being-Itself, is in all of creation. There is great continuity between past, present, and future. Eternity transcends and coexists with all of these. The ancestors, or "old souls," like the saints of the Christian faith, carry wisdom from the past that has meaning for the present and must be remembered to sustain present life.[31] Life continues beyond the temporal world we are all a part of, but this does not mean we can be irresponsible in the here and now. The memories we are called to carry of those who have gone before us remind us of who we are and whose we are. We are children of Dust and Spirit, earth creatures who carry within us the strengthening breath of life, Spirit itself. Those who have lived in the past continue to live in spirit. To touch one's own spirit is to be connected with the past, present, and future. It is to be connected to the creative, life-giving source of all that is. In addressing various crises in the lives of Black women, men, and children today, it is important to consider the ways in which we become disconnected from our own spirits and thereby disconnected from Spirit, the source and womb of life itself. There is a tendency to forget that there is something greater than our individual selves or communities within the very midst of us that can transform fear into hope, ignorance into the light of wisdom and knowledge, weakness into strength, and brokenness into salvation.

We are the descendants of a people who know what it means to belong to the life-giving source of the universe. We may have many names for God. We may not always agree on who God is or how to describe God. Indeed, what an ambitious task it is to name the unnameable. For this reason, in the Hebrew tradition God is simply called "Ha Shim," which means "The Name." This name is a name above, beneath, beyond, and within all the great names we can conceive of for God, the very source of our lives and of our power to name. What we know best about this unnameable, unseen God is the ways in which it has functioned, acted, and moved in our various communities, histories, and individual lives.

Notes

1. Delores Williams, *Sisters in the Wilderness* (Maryknoll, NY: Orbis Books, 1993), 204-228.

2. Okechukwu Ogbonnaya, *On Communitarian Divinity: An African Interpretation of the Trinity* (New York: Paragon House, 1995), 12-31, 55-62, 72, and 80-86; and notes from a lecture by Ogbonnaya, "On Communitarian Divinity," for Garth and Karen Baker-Fletcher's course "Pan African Theology and Moral Philosophy" at Claremont School of Theology, Claremont, CA, Fall 1994.

3. Alice Walker, *In Search of Our Mothers' Gardens: Womanist Prose* (New York: Harcourt Brace Jovanovich, 1983), xii.

4. Williams, *Sisters in the Wilderness*, 6.

5. Jacquelyn Grant, *White Women's Christ and Black Women's Jesus* (Atlanta: Scholars Press, 1989), 1-7 and 195-222; and "Black Theology and the Black Woman," in *Black Theology: A Documentary History, 1966-1979*, ed. James H. Cone and Gayraud Wilmore (Maryknoll, NY: Orbis Books, 1979), 418-433. See also Grant, "Subjectification as a Requirement for Christological Construction," in *Lift Every Voice: Constructing Theologies from the Underside*, ed. Susan Brooks Thistlethwaite and Mary Potter Engel (New York: Harper & Row, 1990), 201-214.

6. Ntozake Shange, *for colored girls who have considered suicide / when the rainbow is enuf: a choreopoem* (New York: Macmillian, 1977), 63.

7. See Clarice Martin, "Biblical Theodicy and Black Women's Spiritual Autobiography: 'The Miry Bog, the Desolate Pit, a New Song in My Mouth,'" in *A Troubling in My Soul: Womanist Perspectives on Evil and Suffering*, ed. Emilie M. Townes (Maryknoll, NY: Orbis Books, 1993), 21-31.

8. See Jualynne E. Dodson and Cheryl Townsend Gilkes, "'Something Within': Social Change and Collective Endurance in the Sacred World of Black Christian Women," in *Women and Religion in America*, vol. 3, *1890-1968*, ed. Rosemary Radford Ruether and Rosemary Skinner Keller (New York: Harper & Row, 1986), 11-12 .

9. Renita J. Weems, *I Asked for Intimacy: Stories of Blessings, Betrayals, and Birthings* (San Diego: LuraMedia, 1993), 25.

10. See Karen Baker-Fletcher, *A Singing Something: Womanist Reflections on Anna Julia Cooper* (New York: Crossroad, 1994), 27-85. See also Anna Cooper, *A Voice from the South*, ed. Mary Helen Washington, Schomburg Library of Nineteenth-Century Black Women Writers (1892; New York: Oxford University Press, 1988), 168, and Cooper, "Equality of Races and the Democratic Movement," privately printed pamphlet, Washington, D.C., 1945, 4-5.

11. Alice Walker, *The Color Purple* (New York: Harcourt Brace Jovanovich, 1992),167.

12. See Walter Rauschenbusch, *A Theology for the Social Gospel* (New York: Macmillan, 1917; Nashville: Abingdon Press, 1981).

13. Ronald C. White Jr., *Liberty and Justice for All: Racial Reform and the Social Gospel, 1877-1925* (San Francisco: Harper & Row, 1990), xvi-xxiv, 107-113, 118-119, and 136-140. The entire text examines Black Social Gospel leadership and its extended influence in the twentieth century, as evident in the life of Martin Luther King Jr. The weakness of the volume is that while it mentions women like Ida B. Wells-Barnett, it does not provide very extensive discussion of her role or the roles of numerous other church women and members of the Black women's club period who played a vital role in addressing sexism *and* racism as Social Gospel concerns. Yet the book is important in its examination of the Social Gospel movement as a cross-racial movement.

14. James Washington, lecture at Harvard University, Cambridge, MA, September-October 1994.

15. Walker, *In Search of Our Mothers' Gardens*, xi-xii.

16. Anna Julia Cooper, "The Answer," in the Anna Julia Cooper Papers, Box 23-4, Moorland-Spingarn Research Center, New York, NY.

17. Cooper, "The Gain from a Belief," in *A Voice from the South*, 303.

18. Walker, *The Color Purple*, 39.

19. See Marcia Y. Riggs, *Awake, Arise and Act! A Womanist Call for Black Liberation* (Cleveland: Pilgrim Press, 1994), for a discussion of the important motto of the Black women's club movement in America which serves as the title for her book.

20. Cooper, "The Gain from a Belief," in *A Voice from the South*, 298.

21. Cooper, "Womanhood a Vital Element in the Regeneration and Progress of a Race," in *A Voice from the South*, 23-24.

22. Ibid., 28.

23. See Baker-Fletcher, *A Singing Something*, 68-97.

24. See Williams, *Sisters in the Wilderness*, 164-166.

25. Jacquelyn Grant, "The Sin of Servanthood," in Townes, *A Troubling in My Soul*, 199-218.

26. Sharon D. Welch, *A Feminist Ethic of Risk* (Minneapolis: Fortress Press, 1990).

27. Julie Dash, *Daughters of the Dust* (New York: Kino International, 1991).

28. Quoted in William L. Andrews, ed., *Sisters of the Spirit* (Bloomington: Indiana University Press, 1986), 57. See also Karen Baker-Fletcher, "Voice, Vision and Spirit: Black Preaching Women in Nineteenth-Century America," in *Sisters Struggling in the Spirit*, ed. Nantawan Boonprasat Lewis et al. (Louisville, KY: Women's Ministries Program Area, National Ministries Division, Presbyterian Church U.S.A., 1994), 31-42.

29. Margaret Washington, ed., *Narrative of Sojourner Truth* (New York: Vintage Classics, 1993), xxii-xxix and 43-55. This reprint of Olive Gilbert's 1850 *Narrative of Sojourner Truth* has an introduction that is attentive to both the African and New York Dutch foundations of Truth's spirituality, as well as informative appendices.

30. Julie Dash, *Daughters of the Dust: The Making of an African American Woman's Film* (New York: New Press, 1992), 94-96.

31. Ibid., 97.

9

Justified, Sanctified, and Redeemed

Blessed Expectation in Black Women's Blues and Gospels

Cheryl A. Kirk-Duggan

Prelude: Call to Worship

Justified, sanctified, and redeemed—what joys do these portend? African-American women live, compose, and sing spirituals, hymns, Gospels, and Blues. Sometimes they sing because they're happy; sometimes they sing because they're free; sometimes they sing from plain ol' misery. Black women sing what they experience. Their songs, born of an African milieu, are tempered by the pain of evil, racism, and subjugation; and their songs reflect the joy, blessedness, and beauty of spirituality and survival. Black music, including Gospel and Blues, the younger sisters of the spirituals and work songs, offers responses to life. Black Gospels and Blues emerged when creative Black women and men blended their consciousness, visions, interpretative grasps of the Bible, glimmers of God's grace, hopes for freedom and equality, and contemporary life experiences into a melodic potpourri of song.

I explore a message of hope, salvation, and transformation embodied within certain Gospels and Blues created and/or performed by African-American women. This scenario (1) contextualizes Black women as signifiers and gives working definitions of Blues music, hope, salvation, and transformation; (2) gives a brief biography, surveys the repertoire, messages, and performances of Blues singers, composers, and arrangers Ma Rainey, Alberta Hunter, and Tracy Chapman; (3) defines Gospel music and presents a synopsis of the lives, music, and performances of Gospel composers, singers, and arrangers Lucie Campbell, Roberta Martin, and Shirley Caesar; (4) reviews the life, music, and performances of songstress Aretha Franklin; and (5) summarizes and critiques the views of hope, sal-

140

vation, and transformation expressed in selected works of these Blues and Gospel singers, in concert with tenets of womanist theory.

Hymn of Praise: Black Women Signifiers

Black women signify as they wear and celebrate the garments of self-expression. No system could silence Black women's signifying—the revising and renaming of their realities. These magnificent creatures of ebony, chocolate, and cocoa butter give utterances of exultation and excitement, pleasure and pain, love and life, anxiety and anger, relief and reverence for God. With the onset of slavery, sounds of Black women's daily life in the African Mother Land became mere echoes of the near, yet remote, past, when the waves of the Atlantic rocked slave ships during the Middle Passage, the denigrating journey toward institutionalized slavery that brought African women to our shores. The stench of death and nausea, the near starvation, and the angst of hopelessness did not kill the spirits of African women. Not the intentional separation of peoples with similar language and culture, nor the dehumanization of bodies packed like sardines, nor the loss of home and country, nor the fear of what was to come silenced Black female signifiers. From the beginning of civilization to the present day, these same women signified, or renamed and revised. Black women engage in renaming and revising. This renaming and revising expresses double-voicing in complex ways typified in Black music, *particularly* the Blues and Gospel songs, which are liturgical, evangelical, erotic, and experiential litanies.

Prayers for the People: Preaching Blueswomen

The color *blue* signifies serenity, peace, space, work, calm, and royalty; it tends to unify, spiritually relaxes, and effects godly grandeur and greatness; it also symbolizes coolness, even cold. The "Blues," ethnographically derived from "Blue Devils" (an Anglo-American usage in the late eighteenth century for despondency or depression, a coldness and absence of serenity), developed as a song form at the turn of the twentieth century. These empathetic, attitudinal, cosmological, responsorial psalms signify African-American life experience beyond but not isolated from the Black Church.[1] This experience, rooted in West African musical heritage, metamorphosed via slavery, the Emancipation, the ex-slaves' mastery of English, minstrelsy, World War I, 1920s events (the Harlem Renaissance, the Depression, the Great Migration encouraged by *the Chicago Defender*), the end of the Church's hold on African-Americans' leisure time, and the music business, as Africans took on the consciousness of being *American Negroes*—a permanent part in, without being privy to all the rights of, American culture, given the essential nonhumanity that dictated a slave's and sharecropper's life and the impact of this imposed culture.[2] Blues evolved from spirituals, work songs, cries, hollers, and ballads, through an improvisational, unaccompanied, musical speech, to a twelve-bar Blues vocal melody based on a five-tone scale with three-line stanzas and instrumental accompaniment.[3] These paradoxical entities express the torment and tribulations of African-American life and articulate a toughness that liberates, inspires, and rejuvenates. As such, the Blues becomes a metaphor for these existential and ontological realities as well as the personification of the powers that instigate those pathologies which lead to illness, addictions, and human demise midst a politics of poverty, an omnipresent force in rural and urban African-American communities.[4] Blues music is a therapy for the souls and angst of Black folk.

Singing the Blues, with their plaintive poignancy, functions as a therapeutic impetus that may be a cathartic, psychological relief and has a communicative and evocative tenet that is mood-creating and mood-matching.[5] Functionally, one "feels" the Blues: "feeling" is an essential element of effective Blues singing, and vice versa. These psychosociological elements occur in three categories: country rural, or archaic Blues; city or classic Blues; and urban Blues. *Country Blues*, the earliest form, began throughout the South, especially in the Mississippi Delta. These Blues characteristically had nonstandard forms and spoken introductions and endings, and usually involved a male solo singer with an unamplified guitar accompaniment. Later, accompaniment included string and/or jug bands. *City or classic Blues*, dominated by female singers, had a standard form with regular beginnings and endings and instrumental accompaniment of up to seven pieces. City or classic Blues drew from country Blues, Black minstrel shows, vaudeville, folk Blues, and popular song styles. Mamie Smith, the first artist who recorded Blues commercially, was a classic Blues singer. The onset of the Depression and shifting audience aesthetic sensibilities caused the demise of city Blues. The third phase, *contemporary or urban Blues*, from the '40s and later, involved the addition of saxophones, electric guitars, and basses, with written, arranged music, but without the country musical instruments, such as harmonicas.[6] The sociohistorical development of the country, classic, and urban Blues patterns the subject matter and performance style of the Blues, particularly the locale of the sacred and the secular within the Blues. Scholars classify the Blues into (1) "Devil's music," that is, irreligious and atheistic; (2) religious and theological; and (3) neither demonic nor theological, but the articulation of social and existential concerns.

Blues scholars Paul Oliver, Paul Garon, and Giles Oakley claim that Blues is "the Devil's music," that is, that the language, ethos, and morality of the Blues are demonic and evil.[7] Theologian James H. Cone argues that Blues are artistic, responsorial, "secular spirituals"—functional, worldly songs that express the core of daily African-American experience. These songs unmask the chaos and difficulties Black people meet with fortitude when they try to deal with White Christian categories midst oppression; consequently, Blues people do not reject God but ignore God by embracing the joys and sorrows of life—from love and sex, mules and boll weevils, to destitution and survival. Secularity defines the focus on the immediacy and the affirmation of all physical expressions of the Black soul; spirituality defines quest for an existential and ontological truth about the African-American experience.[8] Jon Michael Spencer, theomusicologist and Blues scholar, takes great exception to the irreligious and demonic theory, agrees with Cone, and argues that for those who *have lived with* the Blues, the Blues have a meaning rife with mythologies about evil, folk theologies about evil, and theodicies that reconcile the incongruity of historical evil with a good God. The move of the Blues from its southern, spiritual home to the urban North resulted in a shift from the country Blues experience of mythology, theology, and theodicy to a diminished religious capacity, because of the rupture and displacement of the country-to-city diaspora.[9] Theologian and ethicist Thomas Poole contends that the lyrical Blues forms are neither the Devil's music nor theological, although the music deals with evil and has some theological insight. He contends the Blues provide an avenue for examining an African-American existential milieu; the meaning of life and death; one's sense of guilt and remorse; the adequacy of religion; and a celebratory, defiant survival that occurs prior to salvation and liberation.[10]

I contend that the Blues, as signification, personification, and metaphor—in multiple levels and valences—recreate and respond to the many facets of African-American life. The Blues express double-voicing: multiple messages that signify—echo, reflect, mirror, repeat, revise, and respond to life in various ways. Black Women's signifying is part of the sociomusical infrastructure of Black language systems and embraces the rhythm of Black life itself. The beautiful and the brusque shape these women's creative utterances as they signify via word and song, in praise and in protest, about their existential life rhythms. These secular and spiritual melodies, by definition, are neither implicitly evil nor atheistic, since they come from a people who are neither evil nor atheistic, a people rooted in an African holistic heritage intimately related to many deities. The Blues enable Blues people to reckon with realities: life, death, sex, humor, sickness, transportation, movement, nature, suffering, humiliation, liberation, and survival. Blues provide affirmation in the face of the absurdity of oppression. Given the historical impact of the Black church in Black communities, Blues people were aware of and therefore in dialogue with concerns that were the concerns of the Church: life, liberation, and love. Realism, irony, and humor allowed Blues people to critique religious hypocrisy or to offer parallel options. The Blues did not and do not happen in a vacuum. The fluidity and oppression of Black society mean that the same tune and similar phrases may be part of a Blues and a sacred song. While the evolution of the Blues may not be as systematic as Spencer's work implies, and while his stimulating exegesis of the Blues god is highly theoretical, his analysis that the theologies of the Blues engage in dialectical tension with Christianity wherein Blues people borrow from "religious folklore" of the South has great credence in numerous extant recordings.[11] In sum, the Blues offer a rich vehicle to explore the possibilities of hope, salvation, and transformation toward somebodiness.

"Hope" refers to an imaginative vision toward overcoming a state of reality, an expectation of the good via God's gracious gift of liberation. Hope moves one from despair to change amid history. For the Church, the foundation of hope lies in an intimate relationship with God grounded in the overcoming of sin and death symbolized in the cross and resurrection. "Salvation" pertains to holistic health, freeing oneself, and liberation; to being delivered from evil, oppression, and dehumanization. In Christianity, salvation concerns the process of atonement, becoming "at-one" with God through Christ Jesus, as God turns "human will back to the divine orientation for which it was intended."[12] "Transformation" concerns being remade toward ultimate potential and fullness of life. Transformation means overcoming obstacles to a new way of being which allows one self-actualization, celebrates creation's beauty and the process of owning and affirming one's inner beauty, transcends denial, sees the interconnectedness of all life, and moves from daring to dream toward authentic existence. To explore the Blues as a vehicle for investigating hope, salvation, and transformation, we will examine the lives of three Blues women, beginning with the premier signifying diva, Ma Rainey, the "Mother of Blues."

> Rushing headlong
> into new silence . . .
> of a cherished dream
>
> . . . .
>
> No reckoning allowed
> save the marvelous arithmetics
> of distance[13]

Ma Rainey, (Gertrude Malissa Pridgett Rainey [1886-1939]) signified a "marvelous arithmetics of distance" in the era of classic or city Blues, when the most popular Blues singers were the women of the 1920s. During this time, also known as the Harlem Renaissance, many Black intellectuals and trained artists despised the "low-life" Blues, but the Black masses identified with the Blues. Classic Blues women rendered songs about deep emotional issues, poverty, and oppression, especially the oppressive contradictions of 1920s American democracy in the United States. John W. Work III, composer and folk song collector, says that classic Blues were secular songs about daily life; classic Blueswomen were disillusioned, had little hope, and interpreted daily life into their own "intimate inconvenience."[14] Disillusionment bolstered the artistry and truth-telling in their songs. In 1902, Rainey first heard the Blues, and she began to specialize in singing these songs of signified misery, a response, through moans and tones, to specific life events which makes life bearable again. Rainey linked older rural Blues to classic city Blues as she worked with numerous great musicians, including Louis Armstrong, Joe Smith, and Bessie Smith. Thomas A. Dorsey, the father of Gospel music, was Rainey's arranger, pianist, and band director.

Born in Georgia, Rainey debuted in a revue at fourteen. Rainey, a complex yet obscure person, married Will "Pa" Rainey in 1904, and the two became a song and dance team.[15] Her fame increased as the Blues gained in popularity, and she toured with various revues and entertainment organizations, such as Tolliver's Circus and Musical Extravaganza and the Rabbit Foot Minstrels. Bedecked with diamond tiaras, necklaces and earrings made of gold pieces, rings, and bracelets, Rainey danced and did comedy, novelty, ballads, and topical songs. Rainey, also known as Madame Gertrude, was both a comic big mama and a sex symbol. She participated in tent performances despite segregationist oppression; her variety shows included her telling vulgar jokes about craving young men, followed by her singing, often ending with "See, See Rider," a showstopper:[16] Rainey knew how to work an audience. She worked with local jazz bands, did stage work, and was a recording artist in New York and Chicago. This even-tempered, big-hearted woman was sexually involved with men and women and sang about the troubles of lonely, violent women, inequality, private hardships, lynching, and chain gangs—balanced with comedy. Rainey became a national recording star in 1923 with a recording contract from Paramount Record Company, continued doing independent acts, and toured with the Theater Owners' Booking Agency.[17] Rainey toured until 1935, then returned to the South, the place of her home and her heart. She bought and operated two theaters near Columbus, Georgia, until her death, around Christmas 1939. Her recordings remind us of who she was. For example, Rainey acknowledged the human need for frailty, the need to feel special, and the wrong of spousal abuse, and she blamed human troubles on the Blues:

> You can have my money . . .
> But for God sake,
> Leave my man alone
> 'Cause I'm just jealous, jealous, jealous
> I'm just jealous, tired, and mean.[18]
>
> It's raining out here
> And things ain't working right;
> I'm going home, I know I got to fight.
> If you hit me tonight,
> Let me tell you what I'm going to do
> I'm going to take you to court
> And tell the Judge on you . . .

I'm tired of this life
That's why I brought him to you.[19]

I'm so sad and worried
Got no time to spread the news;
Won't blame it on my troubles
Can't blame it on the blues . . .
Can't blame my daddy . . . my mother . . .
Can't blame nobody,
Not my lover, my husband,
Must blame it on the Blues.[20]

Rainey's poetic style, apparent in ninety-two extant recordings, divides into two large categories: songs about love, especially love gone wrong, and commentaries on life from a humorous, scatological, semipornographic, or cynical slant. The subject matter of her songs reflects the general Black female experience, not a psychological or biographical profile of Rainey herself.[21] Some of her songs reflect the lyrical feel, stock phrases, images, and melodies of country Blues. Her popular Blues made private pain public. Her rough, heavy contralto voice was full of energy and conviction, life and vigor. This artist excelled onstage, making life onstage real for her audience. Her forceful style integrated African-American entertainment and folk Blues, affected by minstrelsy and vaudeville, synthesizing Black folk Blues and Black entertainment.[22] As a classic Blues woman, Rainey ignored traditional key events in women's lives, like children, family relations, and motherhood, and focused on essential truths about African-American life experiences of oppression, pain, poverty, humor, survival, and love—notably violence and sexuality. Sandra Lieb writes:

> It is now a common assumption of the women's liberation movement that female depression is actually a state of anger turned against the self. Blues about love performed and written by Black women in the twenties contain a similar sense of fury toward Black men . . . internalized as depression in the most passive songs, but becom[ing] murderous rage in the most active songs . . .
>
> Perhaps the best way to understand the love songs is to see them as reactions to the central fact of women's Blues: men mistreat the women who love them . . . ignoring her, exploiting her sexually, taking her money, beating her, being unfaithful, or abandoning her for no good reason or (worst of all) for another woman. The woman's response to such mistreatment forms Ma Rainey's great theme: a Black, sensual song cycle about depression, and about a woman's anger which is directed both against herself and against others.[23]

Ma Rainey's performed music provides an aesthetic and social commentary on Black life, especially 1920s female life experience. Rainey gives women, especially those wronged in love, permission, passively or actively, to name the demons, to personify, to identify their angst, and to experience and respond to that angst in a variety of ways. Her other, lighthearted or cynical song categories involved comedy, parody, self-mockery, and songs of oppression that lead to suspicion and fear or philosophical reflection, all dealing with the tough realities of life.[24] Ma Rainey, a new female Black entertainment symbol, was "a *mama*, an authority generative, nurturant, yet sexual, who combined eros and homeliness, sex appeal and self-mockery, pathos and humor; the mythopoetic establisher of tradition, a Black culture-heroine."[25]

An energetic, two-career musician and former nurse, a contemporary of Ma Rainey who was so enamored of America that she did seven USO tours, was Alberta Hunter.

> I, too, sing America.
> I am the darker brother.
> They send me to eat in the kitchen
> When company comes;
> But I laugh,
> And I eat well,
> And grow strong.
> . . . .
> Besides, they'll see how beautiful I am
> And be ashamed—
> I, too, am America.[26]

Alberta Hunter (1895-1984), best described by "I, Too," her favorite Langston Hughes poem, was an international Blues/jazz/cabaret singer, songwriter, recording artist, chanteuse, Broadway star, entertainer, humanitarian, and nurse par excellence. Born in Memphis, Hunter was dubbed "Lady Hunter," "ragtime songbird deluxe," "prima donna of Blues singers," "the Songbird of the West," one of "great, great presence," "dusty songstress," "Apostle of Gaiety," "Hospital Mommy," a "rare gem," and the "Sapphire of Blues," a captivating persona with a lyrical voice.[27] Hunter moved from a life of poverty, discrimination, and little formal education to become a renowned preacher of Blues songs throughout the world. An optimist and survivor, Hunter did not let racism hinder her self-esteem, although the sexism of childhood molestations caused her to fear or resent most men. She left Memphis for Chicago, while still in her teens,[28] with great determination to become a singer. Willing to work hard, she peeled potatoes and washed dishes. She started singing at Dago Frank's, a bordello, for pennies, and was nurtured by the women who worked there. She later moved her mother to Chicago and continued to work at her singing and songwriting.

Hunter advanced to more elite clubs and made money by singing new works of other composers. She continued to soar, claiming that the Blues were not evil but were stories from one's soul, even though Blues broke social conventions by allowing singers, notably women, to talk about loneliness, frustrations, sex, and infidelity.[29] Early on, Hunter became friends with Eubie Blake, Love Austin, Harry Watkins, and Paul Robeson, forming friendships that lasted fifty to sixty years. Even with her associations, however, Hunter remained a loner and continued to pursue her own solo career. Alberta was friends with Lil and Louis Armstrong and later married Willard Townsend. Independent Alberta thought a man could be a status symbol but was not interested in intimacy with her husband, because she was a lesbian and a most private person; she loved Willard as a special friend but went on entertaining at cabarets and had no desire to be a stay-at-home wife.[30] Alberta worked in both Chicago and New York clubs and cut her first record for Black Swan Records in 1921. Her first song to become a hit, "Down Hearted Blues," was also recorded by Bessie Smith:

> My man mistreated me, and he throwed me from his door;
> My man mistreated me, and he throwed me from his door;
> But the Good Book say, you got to reap just what you sow.
> I got the world in a jug, & the trouble right here in my hands,
> I got the world in a jug, & the trouble right here in my hands;
> And if you want me sweet papa,
> You got to come under my command.
>
> I ain't never loved but three men in my life,
> I ain't never loved but three men in my life;
> But my father, and my brother,
> And a man that wrecked my life;
> Lord it may be a week, and it may be a month or two
> Lord it may be a week, and it may be a month or two;
> All the things you're doing to me sho's coming home to you.
>
> Lord I walk the floor, wring my hands and cry,
> Lord I walk the floor, wring my hands and cry;
> Have the down hearted Blues
> And I couldn't be satisfied.[31]

In 1927, Hunter went to Europe, allegedly for a vacation but actually to further her career, knowing that her African-American friends such as Roland Hayes, Florence Mills, and Marion Anderson were having success abroad and often had European benefactors. Hunter used travel as a substitute for the formal education she did not have. She wrote letters that were published in Black American newspapers as travelogues, including a recurring column in the *Afro-American* called "Alberta Hunter's Little Notebook."[32] She sang with various combinations of piano, horns, reeds, guitar, strings, and light percussion. After her first stint in Europe in 1929, Hunter found that her sophistication and her fluent French were not enough to thwart rampant racism. Not bitter, however, Hunter encouraged Black entertainers to perform in the South in the early 1940s, and groomed others for greatness. Hunter quit her singing career in 1956.[33]

In 1955 and 1956, Hunter did volunteer work at the Joint Diseases Hospital in Harlem, passed the city's elementary school equivalency exam, and persuaded the director of the YWCA nursing program to push her age back and admit her to the LPN program. At the capping ceremony, Hunter sang her own song, "I Want to Thank You, Lord." Hunter finished her internship and went to work at the Goldwater Hospital at age sixty-two. She was a gracious, kind, loving, and sympathetic attendant to mostly elderly and chronically ill patients for the next twenty years. During these years, she lived a spartan, anonymous life but was a benefactor to many.[34] After her mandatory retirement at eighty-two, Hunter was "rediscovered" and opened at the Cookery in Greenwich Village in October, 1977. She was an immediate sensation.

With mystery, innate elegance, and style, Hunter wowed her contemporary audience. She sang about truth, and she sang about love. Jazz, Blues, ballads, and show tunes were her sermons as she preached. She told children to get in touch with their parents; she was everybody's grandmother. The "Apostle of Gaiety" sang her thoughts and advice in English, German, French, and Danish. Hunter claimed that the Blues were like the spirit to a minister, and one would sing the Blues because of past hurt.[35] The Blues were not a few ordinary worries, or wanting things one could maybe do without: "Blues is when you're hungry and you don't have money to buy food. Or you can't pay your rent at the end of the month. Blues is when you disappoint somebody else."[36] For Hunter, the Blues were a language of love. She was continuously interviewed and feted on national television; appeared in numerous clubs and jazz festivals; was on the soundtrack for the film *Remember My Name*; was the toast of Brazil; was honored by the city of Memphis; and sang at the White House for President Jimmy and Rosalynn Carter. She inspired thousands not to give up, as she championed the human spirit. When Hunter, aged eighty-nine, died quietly and unexpectedly at her apartment in October 1984, she wanted "no funeral, no flowers, and above all no exhibition even for the most loving friends . . . If I have been help to any living being, let them think of that the day they hear I am dead. A-men."[37]

Another private woman, with a distinctive personality, dreadlocks, and casual appearance, is Blues-folk artist Tracy Chapman.

> sing a Black girl's song
> bring her out
> to know herself
> to know you
> but sing her rhythms

carin'/struggle/hard times
sing her song of life . . .[38]

Tracy Chapman (1964 -   ), a Blues-folk singer and songwriter like Rainey
and Hunter before her, sings many a Black girl's song, and helps make personal and social issues public. Many of these issues concern self-esteem,
self-actualization, and dignity midst political relevance of the self, which
seeks to achieve power over the self and shapes one's identity.[39] Chapman
gained a following while pursuing a bachelor of arts degree in anthropology at Tufts University, where she graduated in 1986 cum laude. Her folk-
influenced, gimmick-free style soars via her husky, powerful alto voice,[40]
which is influenced by rock, reggae, and Latin elements but also signifies
in the preaching Blues tradition. Chapman lives, sings, and talks about a
revolution:

> Don't you know, they're talkin' about a revolution;
> It sounds like a whisper
> Don't you know, they're talkin' about a revolution;
> It sounds like a whisper
>
> While they're standing in the welfare lines
> Crying at the doorsteps of those armies of salvation
> Wasting time in the unemployment lines
> Sitting around waiting for a promotion.
>
> Poor people gonna rise up
> And get their share
> Poor people gonna rise up
> And take what's theirs.
>
> Don't you know; You better run, run, run . . .
> Oh I said you better, run, run, run . . .
>
> Finally the tables are starting to turn
> Talkin' 'bout a revolution.[41]

Chapman, accompanying herself with acoustic guitar, combines traits
from all eras, from the country to urban periods, including rhythm and
Blues. Thus, like country Blues, she sings solo with guitar (even though
she is female and uses an amplified guitar); like city Blues, she has a sophisticated overtone to her earthy performance; and like urban Blues, she
uses amplification. Chapman sings about love, fidelity, self-actualization,
freedom, revolution, conflict, ecology, racism, spirituality, theology, time,
life and death, dehumanization, women's issues, and everyday personal
struggles contextualized by social constraints and oppression. She creates

an intimacy that "like a blanket of fog, envelop[s] the audience with a plea-surable authority. And the audience love[s] it."[42] Her nonstandard music videos have a "raw desperation in her bluesy voice, and her shy-yet-tough demeanor enable[s] her performance[s]"[43] to be moving and powerful. Chapman's shyness and comfortableness with intimate settings perhaps explains her preference for the coffeehouse milieu and to make a living by making music but not to be a superstar. Chapman has already won numer-ous awards, domestic and international. She also played at Wembley Sta-dium in England for the Nelson Mandela Birthday Tribute.[44]

Given the ties between Thomas A. Dorsey and Ma Rainey, and Dorsey's development of the Gospel music tradition, when taking a broad look at African-American religious and cultural history, the relationship between Blues and Gospel becomes apparent. Just what is Black Gospel music?

Scripture Reading: Pronouncing the Gospel

Black Gospel music, a product and symbol of African-American religion like the Blues, was shaped by the sociocultural environment of the Great Migration. These songs come out of a Black aesthetic that reflects a his-tory, ritual, and social interaction of a collective Black ethnic, holistic, cul-tural identity.[45] Black Gospel song developed in northern urban, revival, and evangelistic settings. Building on their southern roots, church singers created a music that blended Blues tunes and sacred texts in the early 1930s. The various melodic, harmonic, and rhythmic configurations in the Gospel song revealed a personal experience, either in solo or choral Gos-pel Blues.[46] Up to the 1960s, the Sanctified or Holy Rollers and a few Free Will and Primitive Baptist churches nurtured this music. The Church sees the proper context for Gospel music as the Church. The evolution of Gos-pel music, however, has produced a sacred style by singers who sing ei-ther for church people or in church settings, and secular Gospel performed in nightclubs, jazz clubs, and other more secular venues. The meaning of the songs became predicated on place and audience. The 1969 success of Edwin Hawkins's arrangement of "Oh, Happy Day," not only made Gospel music a "hit" but also created a wide acceptance of message songs, songs with a text that counsel or comment on society (avoiding the words *heaven, Jesus,* or *God*) but that depend musically on the Gospel style and sound. These songs are a midpoint between Gospel music, both typology and pianistic style, and soul music.[47]

This type of song involves texts about the trinitarian God, blessings, sorrows, difficulties, praises, joys, and laments. The piano style involves chords and syncopation. Gospel began to make a large impact after being adopted by National Baptist Convention soloists. Gospel music, first no-tated and published by Thomas A. Dorsey, has five basic styles: (1) a cappella male songs; (2) quartet groups; (3) female Gospel groups; (4) the chorus or choir of combined male and female voices; and (5) congregational Gospel songs, or those songs adapted by each congregation from written and oral sources, usually performed during testimony and tarrying services in Black holiness churches, with solo Gospel singers who may or may not have choral backup. Gospel singing styles involve four distinctive elements: (1) melodic and rhythmic timbre, (2) range, (3) text interpolation, and (4) improvisation. Timbre, or tone quality, focuses on a strained, full-throated, authoritative sound, with or without amplification. Along with the Gospel timbre, singers must have an even, fast vibrato and agility. A wide range from earthy, low, moanful tones to high tenor and soprano with falsetto sounds is also a "must" for a beautiful Gospel voice. Interpolation involves an ability to use ornamentation, to play with the notes, bend, slur, scoop, slide, skillfully use textual repetition, and create emotional climaxes through sound. In contemporary Gospel, instrumental music with a variety of forms, from verse-chorus and theme and variation to Blues structures, strophic, and call-and-response forms, is integral.[48] A Gospel singer must be able to improvise, to ad-lib words, interject responses to a choral call, and vocally do obbligatos and scales interspersed with high notes. These various stylistic techniques are the tools that Gospel composers, singers, and arrangers use to signify in Gospel music. A preeminent leader in this genre is Lucie Eddie Campbell Williams.

> If when you give the best of your service,
> Telling the world that the Savior is come;
> Be not dismayed when friends don't believe you;
> He understands; He'll say, "Well done."[49]

Lucie Eddie Campbell Williams (1885-1963) was the first woman Gospel composer. Campbell served on the committee that chose the music for the monumental 1921 collection: *The Gospel Pearls*. Basically self-taught, she studied music and earned a bachelor of arts degree at Rust College in Holly Springs, Mississippi. With her organizing ability and leadership, Campbell was instrumental in shaping the music of the National Baptist Convention (the largest body of African-American Christians) during her professional career from 1919 to 1962.[50] Campbell wrote the songs and shaped the singing and performance style of the new pioneers of Gospel music, including the lined hymn style, where one recites the text in an oratorical fashion and then the congregation sings them in time and in tune. Campbell, with strong melodic gifts, liked the classical tradition and songs that stressed a slow pace, especially the Gospel ballad, in which one could signify about sorrow and joy. Her early hymns involved original songs and arrangements of spirituals. She also wrote jubilee songs which had a moderately fast, steady tempo, responsorial call and response, and some syncopation. A key contribution was her Gospel waltz, which stressed three beats in the bass with a contrasting melody in the treble, and which became a standardized form by the 1950s.[51]

Born in Mississippi to former slaves, Campbell lived through a period that recognized the aesthetics and originality of the spirituals and saw the end of minstrelsy, the beginnings of ragtime, the emergence of the Blues as a genre, the beginning of jazz, the impact of African-Americans on Broadway, and the Great Migration to urban areas like Chicago that ushered in the modern Gospel music era. Black church people enjoyed her music because it expressed the Black experience, and because of her vivid use of biblical narrative imagery to minister and offer coherence to her life and the life of the Black community. A modest, pampered persona who glorified her womanhood, and a committed educator and evangelist for Jesus Christ, Campbell also had a fiery temper and temperament. Major conflicts between Campbell and Black Baptist church administration and protocol twice resulted in Campbell's being "churched," wherein the right hand of fellowship is withdrawn, that is, one is excommunicated. These painful events led to two of her most inspiring songs, "He'll Understand and Say Well Done" and "Just to Behold His Face." The song "Something Within" developed when Campbell witnessed a destitute singer refusing to sing Blues because there was "something within." Campbell also signified by teaching American history and English for more than fifty years at the B. T. Washington High School in Memphis, Tennessee.[52] Married at age seventy-five, Campbell died in Nashville in 1963.

Another signifying, pioneering Gospel singer and composer was Roberta Martin.

> God is still on the throne
> within your bosom you have the phone
> where e're you walk you're not walking alone
> Remember God is still on the throne.[53]

Roberta Martin (1907-1969), committed to Christian hope and love, signified as she introduced and developed the classical Gospel choral sound that created the model sound of the community-based church Gospel choir. Martin excelled as composer, singer, pianist, arranger, and group and choral organizer, and she founded and operated her own Gospel music publishing house in Chicago. She combined the "moan" from her Arkansas Baptist childhood with the Dorsey bounce, a bit of semiclassical expression, and the sanctified churches' syncopation to help forge the classic Gospel music sound. The Roberta Martin sound embraced a collective resonance, a vocal sheen, and a professional and spiritual integrity that, according to Gospel announcer and promoter Joe Bostic, was righteous, rich, and restful. Martin combined female high soprano, second soprano, alto, male first and second tenor, and baritone to create a mellow, smooth, harmonic, rich sound. She composed about 70 songs and published and arranged 280 Gospel songs.[54] She arranged many songs for James Cleveland, Alex Bradford, Lucy Matthews, Jessye Dixon, and Myrtle Jackson. Through performances and selling sheet music, Martin reached thousands. She made the music come alive in a way that the printed score alone could not. During the 1940s and 1950s, the Roberta Martin Singers did singing evangelizing with the masses in their travels throughout the United States and Europe, with dignity and integrity, calling all to love, hope, and Christian discipleship.[55] The message was packaged in a merging of West African and Western European traditions.

Martin combined the African melody, rhythm, and ensemble with European order, form, and harmony to produce her classic Gospel sound, especially the use of scales, tension and release in each song, the development of the Gospel cadence formula, and the introduction of substitution chords to end a song. Horace Boyer, Gospel music scholar, claims Martin's pianistic style held the "nuances of a Horowitz, the inventions of an Ellington, and the power of an Erroll Garner, all the while playing 'straight from the church.' "[56] Those who sang with Martin, selected for their individual style, applauded her giving spirit, her unique abilities and approach to Gospel music, and her commitment to ministry. Martin's music targeted the listener's heart, mind, soul, hands, and feet. That same commitment shaped her roles in marriage and motherhood. Sources disagree as to her wealth, but Martin left the world a richer place. Gospel scholar Tony Heilbut notes that the sound Martin helped create is everywhere, from rock music's resiliency and symphonies to detergent commercials.[57] At her death in 1969, fifty thousand Chicagoans went to Mount Pisgah Baptist Church to say "thank you."

A dynamic songstress and minister who also writes and preaches Gospel is Pastor Shirley Caesar.

> This joy I have, the world didn't give it to me; . . .
> The world didn't give it, the world didn't give it to me.
> This love I have, the world didn't give it to me; . . .
> The world didn't give it, the world didn't give it to me.
>
> There are many things in this life that we have,
> That people can take from us. . . .
> The holy ghost that I have, the world didn't give it to me . . .
> The world didn't give it, the world didn't give it to me . . .
> Who gave it to me?
> Nobody but Jesus.[58]

Shirley Caesar (1938–), a native of Durham, North Carolina, signifies as a contemporary Gospel singer, pastor, evangelist, civic leader, and businesswoman, an educated, saved soulster filled with the spirit, a marionette for Jesus. Gifted with great muscular control, Caesar dances, shouts, moves, preaches, and inspires. She is full of energy and spunk. She steps quickly in her two-inch heels between boardroom, pulpit, and concert stage as a concerned citizen and minister who focuses on the needy as opposed to the greedy. A Durham City Councilwoman from 1987 to 1991, Caesar spends about twenty-five hours a week at the Shirley Caesar Outreach Ministry (funded by 50 percent of her earnings) out of her concern that the economic boom in the North Carolina Research Triangle area will not displace people and that she is obedient to God's message "Feed my sheep." Consequently, her ministry focuses on emergency food, funds for utilities and rent, clothing, and shelter for the destitute and needy—to give a hand, not a handout.[59] Caesar, one of twelve children, once intimately knew that need.

Her father, a Gospel quartet singer with the Just Come Four, died when she was twelve, and she was left with an invalid mother. Caesar joined forces with Leroy Johnson, an evangelist gospel preacher in the 1950s, in a traveling and television ministry and joined the Caravans in 1958 with lead coloratura Albertina Walker; Inez Andrews, the "High Priestess of Gospel"; and Sarah McKissich, Gospel ballad singer. By 1961, she both found her own style and turned the Apollo Theatre out singing "Hallelujah Tis Done" in the African-American folk preacher style, that is, the song and sermonette style actualized by Mother Willie Mae Ford Smith and perfected by Edna Gallmon Cooke, which became Caesar's trademark. Her style grew with using blue notes and slurs, and achieving rhythmic effects by repeating consonants and using intense nasality, and high or very low "yeahs" with the heavy breathing of an old country preacher.[60] In 1966, Shirley left the Caravans and moved into the genre of "mother" songs and "house-rocking" songs.

Caesar's "Don't Drive Your Mama Away" (1969), a song-sermonette, tells a story of a mother and two sons, which ends with the rescue of the mother by the wayward son. "No Charge," the story of a small child who submits a bill to his mother for his chores and receives in response a list of all she has done for him at no charge, was also a hit. Her "house-rocking" songs involve a fast or medium tempo and her top range, ornamentation, and improvisations as she runs and shouts for Jesus. Her "running for Jesus" involves performing more than 150 concerts a year, including Caravan reunion concerts, and serving as pastor of the Mount Calvary Word of Faith Church in Raleigh, North Carolina. Previously, she copastored in Winston-Salem with her husband, Bishop Harold I. Williams. Caesar's greatness has been recognized by academics and the music and entertainment industries.

Known both as the "First Lady" and "Queen of Gospel," her honors include five Grammy Awards and six Dove Awards for Gospel. Caesar has also performed at the White House for President George Bush. One of her current passions is to use song, nurturing, teaching, and talking, to be a preacher and reacher for youth:

"I come from a long line of poor folk, and I told the Lord God if [God] helped me to pull up and out of the ghetto, I would reach back and help

pull others up and out. . . . God has given me a ministry of help." . . .
[Though] she still sometimes feels discouragement at the enormity of
her undertaking, Sister Caesar not surprisingly, falls back on Scripture for strength and hope. . . . "I'm a pastor, but I'll always be just a
down-to-earth singer serving an up-to-date God."[61]

Another singer who signifies, preaches, and serves an up-to-date God
with her Gospel and also wails and moans through the Blues is songstress
Aretha Franklin.

> What you want; Baby I got;
> What you need, you know I got it
> All I'm asking, is for a little respect when you come home . . .
> I ain't gonna do you wrong; while you gone
> I ain't gonna do you wrong; cause I don't want to; . . .
>
> . . . .
>
> R-E-S-P-E-C-T, find out what it means to me
> R-E-S-P-E-C-T, take care, TCB.[62]

Aretha Franklin (1942-), born in Memphis and raised in Detroit, was
crowned "Queen of Soul" in 1967, when *Billboard*, *Cashbox*, and *Record World*
proclaimed her the year's top female vocalist. She signifies through Gospels, rhythm and blues, soul, and popular music. Along with the mothering
and musical influence of Mahalia Jackson, Dinah Washington, and Clara
Ward, she received the musical inspiration of James Cleveland, B. B. King,
Dorothy Donegan, Arthur Prysock, Lou Rawls, and Sam Cooke. These
family friends helped shape and nurture Franklin's talents. She traveled with her father's revival and sang in a Gospel quartet led by James
Cleveland, who coached her in singing and piano playing. She had four
children during her teens. According to her biographer Mark Bego,
Franklin's teenage victimization fixed the pattern for bad relationships
with the men in her life.[63] After birthing her children, Franklin became
fascinated by the Blues and wanted to go to New York to pursue a popular music career.

Franklin melds Gospel, Blues, popular tunes, and jazz into her own style
and chooses her own material. Franklin's use of her powerful, robust, expressive alto voice that has tremendous flexibility, color, dexterity, and
volume has won her more than ten Grammies and numerous television
appearances, videos, and awards from the music industry. She has been
equally generous with others. Though her success has been marred by
failed marriages and the suffering and subsequent death of her father in a
home burglary, Franklin continues to sing and preach her songs in performances always shaped by her Gospel roots. In 1986, Michigan named
Franklin's voice one of the state's natural resources, and Wayne State University gave her an honorary doctorate in 1991. With more than thirty years

of soulful signifying, Franklin is to contemporary pop and soul what Ella Fitzgerald is to jazz. Certainly, "Lady Soul" commands R-E-S-P-E-C-T.

Sermonic Reflection: Hope, Salvation, Transformation

Rainey, Hunter, Chapman, Campbell, Martin, Caesar, and Franklin have signified and continue to signify through Blues and Gospels. This study has focused on their biographies, their stories. This step is critical for womanist reflection that, by definition, uses many sources, like social, anthropological, and theological materials, to engage in dialogue, celebrate liturgy, be pedagogical, and commit to using female imagery to unmask and transcend oppression due to race, class, and gender. Womanist reflection celebrates these powerful women with diverse, difficult, and amazing life experiences, filled with talents, goals, visions, personas, relationships, spirituality, and theologies. What, if anything, does *justified* (saved), *sanctified* (perfected in hope), and *redeemed* (transformed) mean in selected works of these seven songsters?

Ma Rainey sings songs about love and life. She minces no words as she describes the blues, misery, infidelity, alcoholism, hysteria, revenge, illness, prison, death, murder, finding a man, education, migration, and natural disasters, along with singing songs of female aggression and unconventional sexuality. In Rainey's classic "Downhearted Blues," she tells about the reality and pain of a bad relationship but argues that (1) it is hard to love someone who does not love you; (2) she will get a good man next time; (3) the Good Book says you must reap what you sow; and (4) she has a choice of who is a part of her world. She does not settle for being a victim, but owns up to her own responsibility. In this song and others, Rainey brings hope through her use of irony, comedy, and double entendre. One experiences hope and salvation through living life to its fullest and through self-actualization as a Black woman, especially sexually. She makes private matters public and sometimes entertains sexually controversial issues. Her form of unmasking becomes therapeutic, as one must examine those issues previously kept hidden. Sometimes her songs are reflective and mainly social commentary. Sometimes the songs espouse sound ethical choices; other times the "reap what you sow" theodicy allows redress. In still other instances, "the Blues" become the scapegoat for all manner of social and interpersonal ills. Her songs become transforming as she (1) talks about reality—violence and sex, suffering and poverty, hope and humor—the first step for overcoming any obstacle; (2) omits more traditional roles often used to oppress women; and (3) sings about strength, fortitude, and endurance, the qualities needed for survival and for fueling change. Her "love" songs reflect that one has choices: to suffer passively, be catatonic, be a victim; to get in touch with one's anger; to change one's depressed state by thinking, by having an aggressive catharsis, by getting drunk; to take action through making a geographical move, reclaiming one's man, taking refuge with family; to confront one's betrayer; or, when abandoned by a man, to appeal to God for salvation from starvation and to no longer focus on a man for economic support. Her comic and cynical songs, where humor may be in the context rather than the content, use parody to talk about topics from sore feet, self-mockery, and fatalism to having fun singing and dancing. Ultimately, most of Rainey's female characters want to experience transformation, and her lyrics provide choices.

Alberta Hunter also offers her listeners choices. Hunter's choices deal with relationships and with one's own vision of life. By "Always" being there for friends, she celebrates the importance of relationship. Forever an optimist, she also talks about reality and the possibility of overcoming; when her "Handy Man Ain't Handy No More," or when he will "pawn his Bible to get Amtrak fare," she knows that trouble cannot last always. Through struggle, she will see a brighter day. In her "Now I'm Satisfied," she maintains hope through prayers, tears, and searching, which then allows her to hear the voice of salvation, giving her a grand and glorious feeling, since the Lord is always by her side. Salvation involves the call to be accountable and to ask the Lord for forgiveness, for God tries to warn one through the sign of the rainbow. Heaven, the social location of salvation, is free and comes with everlasting life for the faithful. Salvation may come through that "second handed man of hers" and, therefore, does not preclude one from a full life experience of sorrow and joy. She calls for dancing at the "Darktown Strutter's Ball" to the "Jellyroll [sexual technique and genitals] Blues"; all is not carefree, however, because "Nobody knows you when you're down and out." One must live for today and deal with the consequences, without the control of others. This quest for freedom and self-reliance can be viewed as a basis both for hopeful living and for experiencing transformation. Sometimes bad luck and trouble may arise, but change through good luck is bound to come one's way; other times one can act through singing a new tune.

Tracy Chapman often sees opportunity and possibility in sociopolitical and geographical terms. She frames hope through movement and action, as "Matters of the Heart." One can envision newness through a revolution, by daring to go "Across the Lines" in a "Fast Car" and by asking hard questions and facing hard realities: Why do babies starve in a world with abundant food? Is love worth the sacrifices one makes? How does one deal with alcoholism? How can we sleep when from behind the wall the cries of spousal abuse result in a silence that chills the soul, when we meet with an ambulance and police apathy? A reality check precedes salvation and liberation, often self-actualized. Salvation involves loving oneself today, not waiting until morning, a new day, or until the loss is too great. Sometimes liberation comes through an exodus, so if "She's Got Her Ticket," it is time to leave the hatred, corruption, and greed that leave one with nothing, no chances. Salvation is personal and social; thus society is responsible for the accessibility of guns and drugs that anesthetize and remove young men or us from our reality. Salvation calls for social equity, an appreciation of nature, and the love for others. Transformation occurs when society and individuals see and own up to reality and dream about the possibilities to have patience and trust and to experience pain and memories, "If These Are the Things" of which dreams are made. Transformation requires that we hold each other and open our arms to each other, for these are "Matters of the Heart."

Lucie Campbell signifies about matters of the heart in light of her relationship with Christ Jesus. Campbell, a keen observer of life, knows hope because Jesus knows how much one can bear and understands, which allows people to understand life's chaos and confusion in time. The possibility of overcoming personal or social mistakes can happen because Jesus promises never to leave one alone and provides leadership; life is sweet when one follows the "Footprints of Jesus." This leadership allows one to praise and honor God as gracious redeemer, master, and friend, and to be a soldier in God's army. Knowing whom to praise and honor begins the experience of salvation. Salvation and liberation are freedom from thirst, loneliness, betrayal, being misunderstood, and wrongdoing. That kind of freedom pushes one daily to want to be with Jesus, "Just to Behold His Face." Jesus is both a historic figure and "Something Within." Something within helps to change and transform one's life situation and personal attitudes. When the Light of Jesus shines on a person, that person can let his or her own light shine. Light transforms darkness, transforms the self.

Roberta Martin lets her light shine through creating a sound and body of songs that invite people to "Try Jesus." Martin's songs express hope through consolation and reassurance: no matter the magnitude of personal burdens, sorrows, weariness, or sin, Jesus satisfies. One has blessed assurance in the Savior. The good news is that when in trouble, when others fail, "God Is Still on the Throne." In this hope, one finds salvation because those who labor and are heavy laden can come to Jesus. One knows salvation and holistic health by going to the supreme physician, the one who never loses a case, for "God Specializes." God dispenses a type of freedom that effects healing, illumination, and empowerment. Regardless of the depths of disease, God's remedies transcend need, neglect, and harassment. The knowledge of that transcendence opens the door to transformation. Transformation occurs on a daily basis through God's many glimmers of grace. "Only a Look at Jesus" personifies a move toward peace, comfort, and safe completion of a journey. One can overcome denial and all other obstacles, because God's "Grace" is sufficient. Because "There Is No Failure in God," ultimately those who trust God never fail.

Shirley Caesar also preaches and teaches a gospel about a never-failing God. Caesar talks about hope on a daily basis, for one can only live life "One Day at a Time." If the Lord teaches one to live one day at a time, there is always possibility and a sense of renewal. The reality of hope also implies that possibility always exists, because there is nothing people do that can earn what God gives. The fact that people often fall short reiterates one's inability to obtain God's goodness; thus, one needs Jesus. Human shortcomings make salvation an ongoing and dynamic process. One may have to find one's way to Jesus, who then helps one see the light. The experience of the gift of salvation becomes the call to "Reach Out and Touch" someone else. Because "Jesus Is a Friend," one can get up off one's sickbed and be upon one's feet. Salvation involves asking, "Lord Let Your Spirit Fall on Me" for empowerment through a Pentecostal blessing. Salvation and liberation involve working on personal relationships, knowing that the Lord is ever present. Just as the "Eye [Is] on the Sparrow," the Lord is with humanity. The beginning of transformation is knowing that people need God to walk in front of them, to empower and guide them. Although powers and principalities come against people, like they did against Jesus, "Sunday's on the Way," the possibility for resurrection time, changing time. Having a little talk with Jesus the source, the energizer, the eternal love serves as a catalyst for minuscule or cataclysmic movement. Change requires one to accept God's love, encourage and honor others, and, "Be Careful of the Stones You Throw." One not only experiences self-actualization in the Lord, but one can then help others know authentic existence.

Aretha Franklin testifies to that kind of relationship with God in "One Lord, One Faith, One Baptism." Steeped in Gospels, Franklin remains hopeful because "One Lord" is the author and finisher of her faith. These songs not only praise God but also talk about a person's relationship with God, proclaiming good news, glad tidings. Hope is present because "Jesus Hears Every Prayer," and that "God Is Able" is symbolized by rainbows. Rainbows do not expect that people do not have hard times. One may have "Trouble in Mind." If the blues overcome an individual, he or she may lose his or her mind or at least will have to leave the troubled environs. Nevertheless, the sun will shine someday. In bad relationships, Franklin would rather drink "Muddy Water" before she sees her baby with another woman. The realization that she cannot trust that man opens the possibility for a newness, the newness born of freedom. Salvation portends a divine and a human process. This liberation means to "Walk in the Light," to dance, sing, and shout about "Oh, Happy Day." Liberation for Franklin means a cornucopia of choices: to be alone, to have company, to say yes, no, or maybe, because she is in the presence of "Dr. Feelgood" and delights to "Walk on Higher Ground." Feeling good allows one to know when "I've Been in the Storm Too Long" and to demand R-E-S-P-E-C-T. One must be in tune with God and with self. Being in tune with reality supports an experience of transformation. Transformation means that one can "Never Grow Old" in the revealed newness of life in Christ, moment to moment.

Invitation and Benediction: Come Listen, Go Tell It!

From Rainey to Franklin, these dynamic women preach and teach about all facets of life. Some are anthropological, moving from an earthy, humanistic, sensual, practical perspective that exposes the school of hard knocks.

Some champion a love of *eros, filia,* and *agape* shared with an implicit or explicit God, self, and society. The *eros* celebrates sexuality in a biblical and a profane manner. *Filia* allows one to maintain healthy relationships and to be conscious and supportive of one's neighbor. *Agape* invites one to be Jesus and to be of Jesus to self and others however one may be. In sum, the hope is that one lives a responsible life and is not a victim of the self or of another—that one embraces life with a hopeful imagination and with laughter. Salvation is the gift of freedom from alienation, destruction, evil, apathy, betrayal, denial, and self-imposed limitations. Transformation involves imagining a personal and societal metamorphosis that allows humanity to "go where no one has ever gone before," without self-destruction. Gospels and Blues, sociopolitical vehicles, can raise human consciousness and accountability.

Many of these songs embody an evolving eschatology wherein one does not defer life until after death. One experiences life to the fullest (sometimes responsibly, other times not) and thus envisions heaven as either intimacy with God or peace with self now. From a Christian perspective, the expectations after death are for a heightened experience of what already is.

In 1990s womanist language, these artists call everyone to (1) be real; (2) name the oppressions (e.g., spousal and child abuse, AIDS, apathy) and work to transcend them; (3) celebrate ourselves, our gifts, and each other; (4) recognize the Blues and deal with them; (5) recognize the Gospel message and live by it; and (6) live life and do your job with integrity. Bad things happen, but one does not have to go around creating them. Thus, an individual, created in God's image, can live in hope and anticipation. One is justified and saved to be loved: doing love better and living life rightly. One is redeemed and freed toward greatness and community.

On behalf of these preaching, singing women, I extend an invitation to listen to their words, meditations, the music. Go in peace and celebration. A-men.

Black Women's Gospels and Blues: An Eclectic Discography

	Singer	Disc	Reference
Blues	Tracy Chapman	*Tracy Chapman* Elektra Entertainment, 1988	CD: Elektra 9 60774-2
		Crossroads Elektra Entertainment, 1989	CD: Elektra 9 60888-2
		Matters of the Heart Elektra Entertainment, 1992	CD: Elektra 9 61215-2
	Alberta Hunter	*The Copulatin' Blues* *Compact Disc:* *You Can't Tell the* *Difference after Dark* Jass Records, 1967	CD: Jass J-CD-1

		Amtrak Blues CBS, 1980	CD: CK 36430
		The Legendary Alberta Hunter DRG Records, 1981	CD: CDSL 5195
		Chicago: The Living Legends Riverside Records, 1984	CD: OBCCD 510-2 (RLP 9418)
		Young Alberta Hunter: The '20s and the '30s Jass Records, 1988	CD: Jass J-CD-6
	Ma Rainey	*AC/DC Blues: Prove It on Me Blues,* Stash Records, 1972	LP: ST 106
		Street Walking Blues: Hustlin' Blues Stash Records, 1979	LP: ST 117
		Them Dirty Blues: Sissy Blues [Side E] Jass Records, 1985	LP: Jass Box 1
		News and the Blues: Telling It Like It Is: Memphis Minnie CBS, 1990	CD: CK 46217
		Ma Rainey Milestone, 1992	CD: MCD-47021-2
		Ma Rainey: The Complete 1928 Sessions Document Records, 1993	CD: DOCD 5156
Gospel	Roberta Martin	*The Great Gospel Women: What a Friend* Shanachie, 1993	CD: Shanachie 6004
	Shirley Caesar	*Sailin'* Word/Epic, 1984	CD: EK-48800
		First Lady HOB Records, 1992	CD: HBD-3515
		Shirley Caesar's Treasures HOB Records, 1992	CD: HOB-3501
		Why Me Lord HOB Records, 1992	CD: HBD-3510
Songstress	Aretha Franklin	*I Never Loved a Man the Way I Loved You* Atlantic, 1967	CD: Atlantic 8139-2
		Aretha: The First 12 Sides CBS, 1972	CD: CK 31953
		Aretha Sings the Blues CBS, 1985	CD: CK 40105

		One Lord, One Faith, One Baptism Arista, 1987	CD: A2CD 8497
Composers and Arrangers	Lucie E. Campbell	*African American Gospel: The Pioneering Composers:* Something Within, He'll Understand and Say Well Done, Touch Me, Lord Jesus, Smithsonian/Folkways Recordings: Wade in the Water Series III, 1994	CD: SF40074
	Roberta Martin	*African American Gospel: The Pioneering Composers:* God Is Still on the Throne, Smithsonian/Folkways Recordings: Wade in the Water Series III, 1994	CD: SF40074

Notes

1. No single identifiable entity called the "Black Church" exists; this institution is a multiform, diverse institution labeled such because the membership and leadership are presently and have always been predominately Black. The sociohistorical, dogmatic differences between African-American sects have always been adjuvant to the unifying force engendered by a common ethnicity and a shared oppression.

2. See LeRoi Jones (Amiri Baraka), *Blues People: The Negro Experience in White America and the Music That Developed from It* (New York: Morrow, 1963), x, 3, 7, 50-51, 59, 63.

3. See Sandra R. Lieb, *Mother of the Blues: A Study of Ma Rainey* (Amherst: University of Massachusetts Press, 1981), 4.

4. See Daphne Duval Harrison, "Wild Women Don't Have the Blues," *Living Blues Magazine* 79 (March/April 1988): 25-26, 27, 29.

5. See Harriet J. Ottenheimer, "Catharsis, Communication, an Evocation: Alternative Views of the Sociopsychological Functions of Blues Singing," *Ethnomusicology* 23 (1979): 75-86.

6. See Eileen Southern, *The Music of Black Americans: A History* (New York: Norton, 1971), 332-36, 339. Mamie Smith recorded her song "Crazy Blues" on the Okeh Recording Company label and sold more than seventy-five hundred recordings per week. Within two years, companies were selling more than 5 million "race records" to African-Americans. A Black-owned recording company was born in 1921: Harry Pace's Phonograph Corporation, later renamed the Black Swan Phonograph Company. Pace finally found a company, New York Recording Laboratory Company, in Port Washington, Wisconsin, to press his records. Pace made a good effort and lasted for about two years, when the invention of the radio threatened to put all recording companies into bankruptcy.

7. See Paul Oliver, *Blues Fell This Morning: Meaning in the Blues*, 2d ed. (Cambridge: Cambridge University Press, 1990); Paul Garon, *Blues and the Poetic Spirit*

164   CHERYL A. KIRK-DUGGAN

(1975; New York: Da Capo, 1979); and Giles Oakley, *The Devil's Music: A History of the Blues* (New York: Taplinger, 1977).

8. James H. Cone, *The Spirituals and the Blues: An Interpretation* (New York: Seabury Press, 1972), 108-17.

9. Jon Michael Spencer, *Blues and Evil* (Knoxville: University of Tennessee Press, 1993), xii-xxvi, 100.

10. Thomas G. Poole, "Theological, Moral and Existential Themes in the Blues" (paper presented to the Society of Christian Ethics, Washington, D.C., January 6, 1995), 3, 21.

11. See Spencer, *Blues and Evil*, 36, 71-75, 86-89, 94-98.

12. Marjorie Hewitt Suchocki, "God, Sexism, and Transformation," in *Reconstructing Christian Theology*, ed. Rebecca S. Chopp and Mark Lewis Taylor (Minneapolis: Fortress Press, 1994), 29.

13. Audre Lorde, "Smelling the Wind," in *The Marvelous Arithmetics of Distance: Poems, 1987-1992* (New York: Norton, 1993), 3.

14. Quoted in Philip McGuire, "Black Music Critics and the Classic Blues Singers," *Black Perspective in Music* 14 (1986): 105, 107.

15. See Lieb, *Mother of the Blues*, 4. White minstrelsy appeared in the 1840s; Black minstrelsy was developing by 1855 and was standard fare by the 1870s. The Black minstrel entrepreneurs and owners of the 1860s became usurped by richer, more influential White entrepreneurs in the 1870s.

16. Ibid., 8-13.

17. Ibid., 18-21, 26-37; and Hettie Jones, *Big Star Fallin' Mama: Five Women in Black Music* (New York: Viking Press, 1974), 25-39. The Black Patti and, later, the Black Swan labels involved Black stockholders, artists, and employees. The latter produced opera, Blues, rags, and comedy, and merged with Paramount in 1924. Paramount, first appearing in 1917 along with Columbia and Okeh, dominated the race market. The Theater Owners' Booking Agency (T.O.B.A.) was a major southern and midwestern theater circuit geared toward African-American vaudeville entertainment, managed by an interracial, negligent group of theater owners. Its entertainment included comedy, drama, vaudeville, dancing, singing, and circus acts. T.O.B.A. began as early as 1907 and began to decline about 1927.

18. Ma Rainey, "Jealous-Hearted Blues," *Ma Rainey*, Milestone, MCD-47021-2, 1992.

19. Ma Rainey, "Hustlin' Blues," *Ma Rainey: The Complete 1928 Sessions in Chronological Order*, Document Records, DOCD-5156, 1993.

20. Ibid., "Blame It on the Blues."

21. Lieb, *Mother of the Blues*, 49-55.

22. Ibid., 58-79.

23. Ibid., 82-83.

24. Ibid., 85-128, 130-64.

25. Ibid., 170.

26. Langston Hughes, "I, Too," in *Selected Poems of Langston Hughes* (New York: Vintage Books, 1975), 275.

27. See Frank C. Taylor with Gerald C. Cook, *Alberta Hunter: A Celebration in Blues* (New York: McGraw-Hill, 1987), 44, 56, 61, 124, 134, 153, 205, 252. "Hospital Mommy" was the name children used for Hunter when she did more than one thousand hours of volunteer work at the Joint Diseases Hospital in Harlem.

28. Several accounts of Hunter's life claim she left for Chicago when she was

only eleven. Taylor and Cook state that she traveled on a child's train pass but place the date as 1911, which would make Hunter sixteen. Other passages in the same biography imply that she was a mere child, which is why she could not sing in clubs early on without getting owners in trouble for having a minor on the premises.

29. Ibid., 12, 14, 28, 35-37.

30. Ibid., 36, 42.

31. Alberta Hunter, "Down Hearted Blues," *Young Alberta Hunter: The '20s and '30s* (1939), JASS J-CD-6, 1988.

32. Taylor and Cook, *Alberta Hunter*, 152-58.

33. Ibid., 54-57, 68, 88, 100, 104, 164-75, 181, 190-95, 198-203; Sheldon Harris, "Obituaries: Alberta Hunter," *Living Blues: A Journal of the African-American Blues Tradition* 64 (1984): 68; and The Christian Methodist Episcopal church was the denomination of her childhood, in Memphis.

34. Taylor and Cook, *Alberta Hunter*, 204-32.

35. Harris, "Obituaries," 69.

36. Alberta Hunter, quoted in Taylor and Cook, *Alberta Hunter*, 263.

37. Ibid., 282.

38. ntozake shange, *for colored girls who have considered suicide / when the rainbow is enuf: a choreopoem* (New York: Macmillan, 1977), dust jacket notes.

39. See Ray Pratt, "The Politics of Authenticity to Popular Music," *Popular Music and Society* 10 (1986): 57-59.

40. See *Who's Who in African-Americans*, 1994-95, 261; and Nelson George, "New Kids in Town: Chapman, Living Color," *Billboard* 100 (April 9, 1988): 22.

41. Tracy Chapman, "Talkin' 'bout a Revolution," *Tracy Chapman,* Elecktra 9-60774-2, 1988.

42. Jean Rosenbluth, "Tracy Chapman," *Billboard* 100 (May 26, 1988): 5.

43. John Bream, "Tracy Chapman; Gil-Scott-Heron; Spirit." *Billboard* 103 (March 9, 1991): 9.

44. *Who's Who in African-Americans*, 261.

45. See Mellonee Victoria Burnim, "The Black Gospel Music Tradition: Symbol of Ethnicity" (Ph.D. diss., Indiana University, 1980), 1-3, 6, 9, 192-97. This musical tradition transcends age, denominational, and geographic boundaries; comprises social and ritual interaction within the United States; has a multifaceted ideology, aesthetic, and behavior; has a uniform yet contrasting individual and collective system; has diverse functions; and encompasses sacred and secular musical forms and nonmusical forms of expression.

46. See Southern, *Music of Black Americans*, 401-2; and Michael Harris, *The Rise of Gospel Blues: The Music of Thomas Andrew Dorsey in the Urban Church* (New York: Oxford University Press, 1992), xvii, 100, 209.

47. See Horace Clarence Boyer, "Contemporary Gospel Music," *Black Perspective in Music* 7 (1979): 5-6, 10.

48. See ibid., 22-28; and William Thomas Dargan, "Congregational Gospel Songs in a Black Holiness Church: A Music and Textual Analysis" (Ph.D. diss., Wesleyan University, 1983), 6-9.

49. Lucie E. Campbell, *He'll Understand; He'll Say, "Well Done,"* EMI Music, 1933, 1950, 1978.

50. The National Baptist Convention of the USA was formed in 1895 in a merger of the Baptist Foreign Mission Convention (founded 1880), the American Baptist

Convention (1886), and the Baptist National Educational Convention (1893). In 1915, the National Baptist Convention of the USA split over the ownership of the Publishing Board. The parent organization became incorporated, and the National Baptist Publishing Board (NBPB) and the Home Mission Board withdrew to become the National Baptist Convention of America (unincorporated) until a split in 1988 resulted in the National Missionary Baptist Convention of America and the National Baptist Convention of America, Inc.

51. See Horace Clarence Boyer, "Lucie E. Campbell: Composer for the National Baptist Convention," 81-85, 95, 102-3; and Luvenia George, "Lucie E. Campbell: Her Nurturing and Expansion of Gospel Music in the National Baptist Convention," 114, in *We'll Understand It Better By and By*, Wade in the Water Series, ed. Bernice Johnson Reagon (Washington: Smithsonian Institution Press, 1992).

52. See George, "Lucie E. Campbell," 113, 115, 118-19; and Charles Walker, "Lucie E. Campbell Williams: A Cultural Biography," in *We'll Understand It Better By and By*, 126-32, 138.

53. Roberta Martin, "God Is Still on the Throne" (Chicago: Roberta Martin Studio of Music, 1959).

54. See Pearl Williams-Jones, "Roberta Martin: Spirit of an Era," 255-58; and Pearl Williams-Jones and Bernice Johnson Reagon, eds., "Conversations: Roberta Martin Singers Roundtable," in 296, *We'll Understand It Better By and By*.

55. Pearl Williams-Jones, "Roberta Martin," 266, 271.

56. Horace Clarence Boyer, "Roberta Martin: Innovator of Modern Gospel Music," in *We'll Understand It Better By and By*, 275-76, 280, 283-86.

57. See Williams-Jones and Reagon, "Conversations," 290, 293-94, 295, 304; and Tony Heilbut, *The Gospel Sound: Good News and Bad Times* (New York: Anchor Books/Doubleday, 1975), ix-x.

58. Shirley Caesar, "The World Didn't Give It to Me," *Treasures*, HOB Records, HBD-3501, 1992.

59. See Heilbut, *Gospel Sound*, 238; "Shirley Caesar: Putting the Gospel Truth into Politics," *Ebony* (December 1988): 66-67, 70; and Horace Clarence Boyer, "Shirley Caesar," in *Black Women in America: A Historical Encyclopedia*, ed. Darlene Hine, Elsa Brown, and Rosalyn Terbory-Penn (Indianapolis: Indiana University Press, 1993), 214.

60. See Boyer, "Shirley Caesar," 215; and Heilbut, *Gospel Sound*, 240-41.

61. Promotional materials, Shirley Caesar Outreach Ministries, Durham, N.C., Summer 1995.

62. Aretha Franklin, "Respect," *I Never Loved a Man, the Way I Love You*, Atlantic 8139-2, 1967.

63. See Heilbut, *Gospel Sound*, 275-76; Virginia Wilson Wallace, "Profile: Aretha Franklin, Queen of Soul," in *Epic Lives: One Hundred Black Women Who Made a Difference*, ed. Jessie Carney Smith (Detroit: Visible Ink Press, 1993), 183-84; and Jones, *Big Star Fallin' Mama*, 122, 124; Mark Bego, *Aretha Franklin: The Queen of Soul* (New York: St. Martin's Press, 1989).

10

Woman at the Well

Mahalia Jackson and the Inner and Outer Spiritual Transformation

Mozella G. Mitchell

Jules Schwerin, in his impressionistic biography of Mahalia Jackson, *Got to Tell It: Mahalia Jackson, Queen of Gospel*, describes his work as not a formal biography as such, but one about Mahalia's voice, where she took it, and where it took her. He elaborates on his personal impressions and reactions to the events of her life as she related them to him, blended with his later observations (both "gentle and critical").[1] He has performed an excellent task in examining and relating Mahalia's life from his own and many other perspectives. Yet amid all the facts, information, descriptions, insights, and impressions the author presents, Mahalia remains an enigma to him and to most of those whom he consults. Near the end of his absorbing portrayals of her in the book, one sees in the concluding reflection a probing concern but a surface understanding in relation to the true Mahalia Jackson:

> She wrestled with the two Mahalias she had become: The powerful public one with fits of anger, ruthless, unthinking; the other, lonely in the condominium, hours on the phone with her second husband, even though they were divorced; and when John[2] was there to help her maintain the apartments and cook soul food for her, she complained of nightmares, would come looking for him at night, way in the far side of the huge apartment, and they talk about the good old days: his boyhood, the beginnings—when he slept between her and Ike[3]—the days of music and struggle for recognition.[4]

Although Schwerin here gives an impression, borne out by the preceding analytical materials of the book, it is clear to anyone who probes deeper

167

into Mahalia's life, heritage, music, singing style, and spirituality that his views remain surface to the genuine Mahalia.

To get at the deeper Mahalia, one might consider the term used by Anna Julia Cooper in 1925, "a *Singing* Something," to describe the voice of God in every human being, "a divine spark," an "urge-cell," especially in its cry against injustice.[5] In my opinion, Mahalia Jackson literally becomes the "singing something" and exhibits the spiritual quality within herself: "This *Singing* Something, the progressive movement toward freedom and equality in human beings, rises against the evil of domination."[6] It is clear to me that what Mahalia Jackson was grappling with in her progressively complicated life and career was very similar to, and in many ways the same as, what Karen Baker-Fletcher interprets as Cooper's meaning of the "*Singing* Something." Baker-Fletcher asserts,

> For Cooper, freedom and equality, universal birthrights, are something that sings within the human soul. This "*Singing* Something" is directly traceable to the Creator. For Cooper, humankind's creation in the likeness of God is more than merely imagistic. It is vocal. It is musical. It is auditory. She was interested in the sound, the words, the composition of God's voice. It is in song, in voice, that humankind is created in the image of God, or better, in the sound of God.[7]

Lest I go too far too soon with this interpretation, which I will make much clearer further on, let me assert that Mahalia Jackson was not theologically astute and intellectually refined, as were Anna Julia Cooper and Karen Baker-Fletcher, both of whom attained doctoral degrees in their fields of study. Therefore, Mahalia would not have expressed her own self-understanding in the same terminology. Consequently, I do not intend to pursue this imagery and phraseology extensively. I choose, rather, to see and interpret Mahalia in the songs and music through which she understands and expresses herself. The song "Jesus Met the Woman at the Well" is representative of her own spiritual experience of salvation and conversion and of how she lived her life and developed spiritually throughout her personal and career life. One must probe the interconnectedness of the many aspects of her life to better understand the uniqueness and individuality of one of the greatest musical and spiritual personages of the twentieth century.

While Mahalia Jackson was an individual with all the needs, desires, aspirations, hopes, ambitions, and many other characteristics that make one human, along with unique endowments, gifts, reactions, responses, developments, and history—she was and is also an institution. She is an embodiment—a spiritual and physical one—of a people, a nation, a society. While many biographical presentations and reflections on her have emphasized the individual and unique side of her, none has dealt with the deep spiritual character and development of this Black woman who moved profoundly both the country and the world with the genuine and unique quality and style of her singing, and with her personhood. This can be done only through an analysis and interpretation of the music she sang as it grew out of and reflected what she was undergoing in various periods of her life. In listening perceptively and attentively to the many recordings of gospels, spirituals, hymns, folk songs, and a few popular songs, one cannot help discerning that various stages of a life story, a spiritual and social journey, unfold there.

One can gather from both the historical facts of her life and the soul-pourings of her songs that Mahalia started early in life with intense spiritual yearnings and encounters that continued all her life. One senses, in both, her soul struggles, fears, crises, needs, disappointments, spiritual hunger, and pleas to God to come to her aid. One also senses the levels of spiritual growth and commitment. There are high spiritual times and low spiritual times, and there are the pulls of so many social, religious, political, personal, and commercial forces on her life that her life in her Lord is constantly undergoing tests and trials.

Also discernible is that, although the music reflects her spiritual experiences and encounters, no one particular tradition or system structured Mahalia's religious life. It was obviously private and personal, unreflective of any special, orderly discipline. By all accounts of her life story, she was a Baptist who grew up in the church. As a girl in New Orleans, her place of birth, she says,

> I used to spend all my spare time at the Baptist church. If you helped scrub it out, they might let you help ring the big bell for the early morning service. On Saturday nights they showed silent movies in the church community hall. There were services there every evening and in those days people thought as much of the evening prayer service as they did the Sunday service so there was always lots going on for children to watch. Sinners who sat in the back would come forward to be prayed over by the preacher and be saved . . . In those days, once you were baptized, you were looked after properly by the church. You were under the eye of the missionaries of the church, who kept track of whether you attended church and prayer meetings and led a Christian life.[8]

This was part of the external regimen of disciplinary practices that may or may not have affected Mahalia's inner religious realities and development.

When she moved to Chicago, working as a laborer in her late teens, the Baptist church was still the focus of her religious and social life:

> The Greater Salem Baptist Church became my second home. I got to be real friendly with the Johnson family, and when I came back from my wash jobs on the North Side on the elevated at night, I would get

off at the stop near the church and visit. I went to church socials and picnics and excursions on the lake steamers.[9]

Still, church activities of the external social and religious nature filled Mahalia's life. On her own at such a young age (her mother had died when she was five years old, and her preacher father had sent her to live with her aunt, while he himself married again and started a new family),[10] Mahalia showed no signs of having received inner spiritual guidance and training other than through her own efforts. In other words, with little formal religious training and no spiritual guru as such to render support and guidance in inner spiritual development, she was left to her own prayer life and musical/spiritual lifestyle for sustenance.

Mahalia drew much spiritual enrichment, however, from the practices that she witnessed in her experiences of the Sanctified church that was next door to her home in New Orleans:

I know now that a great influence in my life was the Sanctified or Holiness Churches we had in the South. I was always a Baptist, but there was a Sanctified church right next door to our house in New Orleans. These people had no choir and no organ. They used the drum, the cymbal, the tambourine, and the steel triangle. Everybody in there sang and they clapped and stomped their feet and sang with their whole bodies. They had a beat, a powerful beat, a rhythm we held on to from slavery days, and their music was so strong and expressive it used to bring tears to my eyes.[11]

Clearly, Mahalia experienced God and Jesus Christ freely through church services and programs, through her own freely designed private devotions and experiences, and through the powerful religious music of her African American heritage through which she was able to gain genuine religious meaning and understanding and to express herself in its words and rhythm. This is why singing gospel music and the manner in which she sang it became vital to her. Although she used the blues, jazz, and swing styles of her New Orleans background, she never sang the blues, and she was known often to say that when you get through singing the blues you still have the blues, but the gospels give you a joy. She was adamant about this from a deep spiritual conviction:

I'll never give up my gospel songs for the blues. Blues are the songs of despair, but gospel songs are the songs of hope. When you sing them you are delivered of your burden. You have a feeling that there is a cure for what's wrong. It always gives me a joy to sing gospel songs. I get to singing and feel better right away. I tell people that the person who sings only the blues is like someone in a deep pit yelling for help.[12]

Singing the gospel was also a means of salvation and spiritual commitment for herself and a means of bringing the saving message and event to others for their own spiritual transformation. Therefore, she was given primarily to singing gospel rather than religious hymns, anthems, or Black spirituals. She also liked singing in the congregation rather than in the choir in the Baptist church: "All around me I could hear the foot-tapping and hand-clapping . . . I liked it much better than being up in the choir singing the anthem. I liked to sing the songs which testify to the glory of the Lord."[13] She felt that European hymns were just not her people's music,[14] and the spirituals were not the salvation songs to move her deeply.

Her deep commitment to sing gospels was confirmed in a spiritual experience in Chicago in 1934 involving her grandfather:

> Another reason I was so strongly drawn to gospel music was that I had a feeling by this time deep down inside me that it was what God wanted me to do. I'd felt closer than ever to God ever since he'd heard my prayers about grandfather Paul during that long week in the hot summer of 1934.[15]

Her grandfather was visiting Chicago from New Orleans. At her urging, he had gone to the recording studio to take a picture of Mahalia before returning to the South. Having collapsed with a stroke in the studio, he lay in the hospital near death, giving everyone a great fear and alarm. Accepting the blame for his predicament, Mahalia went into an empty hospital room and fell on her knees, asking God for forgiveness and begging for her grandfather's life. Promising to make her life as pure as she could and vowing to give up all "worldly" enticements, such as jazz and big-time entertainment, she saw the answer to her prayers. "For nine days while the doctors worked over my grandfather, I made the same vow to God over and over again. The Lord heard me and suddenly Grandfather began to get better. He walked out of the hospital well and strong and lived on down South for some years afterward."[16] This was her conviction from the experience: "I feel God heard me and wanted me to devote my life to his songs and that is why he suffered my prayers to be answered—so that nothing would distract me from being a gospel singer."[17]

Such was to become a hallmark of her singing/religious life that prompted this remark in her autobiography: "I've been singing now for almost forty years and most of the time I've been singing for my supper as well as for the Lord."[18]

Hers was a religious works mentality that, although her spirituality and religious development reached higher plains of pure joy and ecstasy in the enjoyment of God's presence and goodness, as any mystic's does, never fully left her Afro-centric religious understanding. Religious piety remained a part of her spiritual experience. So, considering herself always as serving God and Jesus through reaching as wide an audience as possible with the gospel message of her song, as well as in some of her social outreach efforts, Mahalia felt intense closeness and communion with her Lord and experienced the divine pull on her life. This too comes through in her singing. This is why her whole body would inevitably be involved in the performance, and why she rejected church criticisms of her style and body language, such as hand clapping and stomping, which the church claimed was undignified and brought jazz into the church. Her response to one preacher who spoke out in the pulpit against her style was,

> I got right up, too. I told him I was born to sing gospel music. Nobody had to teach me. I was serving God. I told him I had been reading the Bible every day most of my life and there was a Psalm that said: "Oh, clap you hands, all ye people! Shout unto the Lord with the voice of a trumpet!"[19]

Again, a parallel is evident here with Anna Julia Cooper's "*Singing* Something" concept. With this "*Singing* Something" within the human soul that is part of the being of God, one gives full vent to it throughout the human body:

> The entire body is engaged in voice: the lungs, the diaphragm, the voice box (the very breath of a human being, which is often symbolically equated with spirit). Also the head, the arms, the face, hands, legs, lips, tongue, and ears participate in the practice of vocal expression, whether in conversation, public speech, or song. Voice engages the whole person: the body, the mind, and feelings. Cooper's metaphor of a "*Singing* Something" points to the sacredness of human being as energy and force that moves the body to action.[20]

It is interesting that this highly educated Black woman (Cooper) had not abandoned the African spirituality of divine possession, which was also exhibited in Mahalia, who had not the sophistication of learning that Cooper possessed.

Nowhere is it evident that Mahalia Jackson was adequately exposed to a spiritual adviser of the caliber, say, of a Howard Thurman to whom she could go frequently for support and encouragement, understanding and comforting, and consoling dialogue on personal spiritual matters. If her occasional visits with Martin Luther King Jr. and his wife, Coretta, served such a purpose, sources I have encountered do not reveal it.[21] Neither of her two husbands was her spiritual equal to the point where she could experience satisfying spiritual companionship with him.[22] So her spiritual journey appears to have been completely a personal and private one, with Jesus alone, to whom she poured out her soul in song.

Being a Black woman, and a career one at that (especially at the beginning of her career, when her consciousness had not been raised generally concerning civil and human rights, rights of women, etc.), Mahalia had a tough and rugged journey, of which she chose to remain in complete control—except for her dependence on her Lord. She had learned early in life not to trust anyone but herself, and she followed this training to the full, even to the point of not accepting checks but only cash for her performances and never using a manager or agency but rather personally controlling her engagements and business affairs. All of this made for difficulties and sometimes extreme hardships.[23] Jules Schwerin, Mahalia's biographer, who is Jewish, cites his experiences of spending many days with her in Chicago and New Orleans as she relived her personal history of Blackness for a film venture of his. He knew she was testing him, and he became acutely aware of her shrewdness in dealing with people. He declares, "Unschooled and lacking alleged sophistication according to the standards of white society, she had fierce instincts, dead right, and exquisite insight about everything that had to do with her career, talent, and the circumstances of being a black woman."[24]

Mahalia fought many battles almost alone in her public career life, such as the racism encountered in her television appearances and concerts, especially through the South, from Virginia to Florida; the commercializing of the gospel music she sang as a divine mission and for soul salvation;[25] and her struggles with the television and recording businesses to retain the genuineness of her music.[26] Benjamin Hooks, former Executive Director of the National Association for the Advancement of Colored People, was closely associated with Mahalia and entered into a multi-million-dollar restaurant business with her. Having accompanied her on some of her concert tours, he described Mahalia to Jules Schwerin as a woman who had been "battered and mistreated" and who had known the "negative treatment women in America had come to expect," with the added and dubious distinction of being a Black woman:[27]

> "She had been hoodwinked, defrauded, and beaten out of money. She'd give concerts, you know, and at the close of it not get paid her money. She got to the place where she'd refuse to sing the second half of the program until she'd gotten the money due her *in hand*, in cash or cashier's check . . . and I remember her on so many nights she'd take that big roll of money from the promoter and stuff it right down into her bra. And then she'd sweep out onto the stage and sing like a mockingbird! Yes, she wasn't ever going to get hoodwinked again."[28]

In so many ways, Mahalia's character and personality seem to fit Delores Williams's "survival/quality of life" description of Black individuals, families, and communities. She defines this as their attempts to arrive at "well-being through the use of, search for and/or creation of supportive spiritual, economic, political, legal or educational resources . . ., well-being indicating a peaceful, balanced, upright, spiritual existence." Williams asserts also, "In the context of much Black American religious faith, survival struggle and quality of life struggle are inseparable and are associated with God's presence with the community."[29]

Mahalia fits well the type of woman that Alice Walker describes as "womanist," a Black woman who, in wanting to know and do more than "what is good" for her, displays "outrageous, audacious, or *willful* behavior," one who is "responsible, in charge, serious."[30] She was to the gospel music and recording world similar to what Zora Neale Hurston had been to the literary/professional writing world. Fierce and defiant, Mahalia did what no woman in her day was "supposed" to do. She stepped out of her "place," was self-directed and Spirit-led, and accepted the headship of no man to guide her career. Near the end of her first marriage, to Isaac Hockenhull (who tried to direct her singing into channels he saw as "respectable"), Mahalia acknowledged that she had inevitably yielded to the spiritual voice within, the "*Singing* Something," at the expense of losing a marriage partner:

> A man doesn't want his wife running all over the country, even if it's for the Lord—but I couldn't stop doing it. When you have something deep inside of you, when you're torn apart by it, when you've got to express what's inside of you for the world, nothing can stop you—and I guess that's the way it was with me.[31]

The accounts of Mahalia's life deal very little, if at all, with the inner spiritual character that comes through in her songs, her recordings, and her performances. Rather, they analyze and interpret the external facts of her life and career—her development from a poor, little-educated, southern Black girl into a world-renowned gospel singer who commanded the audiences of presidents and kings. However, Mahalia had a prayer life that she constantly resorted to in her social/commercial/spiritual journey. Teresa of Avila referred to her own prayer life and spiritual development as "the interior castle," but Mahalia, in the language of her people, used "the upper room" to reflect hers. Howard Thurman used such terms as the "inward journey" and the "inward sea," among others, to depict his spiritual quest. Mahalia was not as theologically sophisticated and articulate as Thurman, who in his many books expressed the meanings derived from his lifelong spiritual journey and stated that he never put forward any view that he had not tried and tested in his own experience. However, one may say of Mahalia that she rarely, if ever, sang a gospel song that she had not inwardly experienced or could identify with on one level or another of her own spiritual quest. We can now look briefly at some evidences of this fact.

As her spirited renditions of "Jesus Met the Woman at the Well" reveal, Mahalia identified with that woman and with her experiences with Jesus. Mahalia too was a woman at the well. She had been to the well, tasted the "living water," and was a continuous drinker there as well as a frequent runner into the city to spread the message of a joyful encounter.

I am convinced that Mahalia's singing performances, whether in church, onstage, or in the recording studio, were a salvation, a cleansing, purifying ritual involving herself, God, Jesus, and the audience. Some ritual benefits coming through the song performances that affected all involved were praise and adoration; confession; repentance; thanksgiving; submission; testimony to divine goodness, care, and concern; hope; joy; victory; and celebration. One notices that she was "in the Spirit" or Spirit-possessed even as one listens to recordings that depict her spiritual discernments and expressiveness on her more than forty-four-year journey. She was a gospel preacher in her songs, and the world was her parish. This is evidenced in such *gospel appeals* as "Come to Jesus" (1953), "Do You Know Him?" (1950), "Put Your Hand into the Hand of God" (date unknown), and "Didn't It Rain?" (1954). Early in her recording career, beginning in 1937 with Decca Records, there were *songs expressive of personal and racial trials and of pleas to and reliance on God*: "God's Gonna Separate the Wheat from the Tares," "Oh, My Lord," "Keep Me Every Day," and "God Shall Wipe All Tears Away" (all in 1937).[32] When Mahalia launched her nine-year recording career with Apollo Records in 1946, she began with *plain-time songs* to God about trials, enemies, and tiredness of labor, such as "I Want to Rest (on My Jesus' Breast)" (1946), "I'm Going to Tell God (All about How They've Been Treating Me)" (1946), and "Even Me" ("Lord I Hear of Showers of Blessings Thou Art Scattering Full and Free, Let Some Drops Now Fall on Me," 1947).

There is a definite spiritual progression in the recordings from 1946 to 1947, for in 1947 the movement is away from plaintiveness and self-pity to experiencing God's love and friendship with Jesus. "Move On Up a Little Higher" leads the 1947 list, and others expressive of this movement include "I Have a Friend (in Jesus)," "(I'm Gonna) Dig a Little Deeper in God's Love," "Tired (but I Can't Stop Now)," "Amazing Grace," and "Since the Fire Started Burning in My Soul" (all in 1947).[33] The progressive spiritual movement in these early stages of Mahalia's singing and recording career are indicative of the steady progression throughout her professional life.

Other songs in this development include songs showing evidence of her having been with God in her prayer life and experience, such as songs *indicating self-surrender*: "I Can Put My Trust in Jesus" (1949), "Prayer Changes Things" (1949), "I Gave Up Everything to Follow Him" (1950), and "In the Upper Room" (1952).[34] Another progression is indicated in her *songs of God's care and concern*: "He Is My Light" (1952), "His Eye Is on the Sparrow" (1951), "Said He Would (Calm the Raging Sea)" (1952),[35] "My God Is Real" (1958), "Jesus Met the Woman at the Well" (1954), "God Is So Good" (1956), and "The Love of God" (a nine-minute testimonial done in Hollywood in 1961 and on Columbia Records).[36]

There are *songs showing deep spiritual moments of alienation and longing for Jesus*, like "Jesus" (date unknown), "Out of the Depths (of My Soul I

Cried Jesus)" (date unknown), and "Run All the Way," which was really one of her "covenantal" songs, recorded on Apollo Records in 1954 after a serious illness during her first European concert tour in 1952. Here she was pleading with God to use her and allow her to continue the mission on which she was certain He had sent her.[37] There are also *songs of high spiritual moments of attainment and victory,* such as "I'm on My Way (to Canaan Land)" (1954), "Walk in Jerusalem" (1953), and "How I Got Over," first recorded on Apollo in 1951.[38] However, the most powerful rendition of the latter song was done in a live performance in Sweden in 1961, captured on Columbia Records. Leslie Gourse says of that performance,

> "How I Got Over" is Mahalia at her most pure and pristine, with a piano and an organ, in a live performance in Sweden. When she sings "mmmm," she implies the wordless spirit. The inspired audience called out to her. Her powerful rhythmically charged clapping is clearly audible, as she wonders how she ever got through all her troubles, then thanks God for his "old time religion," for giving her vision, and for being so good to her.[39]

In conclusion, Mahalia stuck predominantly and immovably to gospels because of the personal spiritual growth they provide. Gospels, in contrast to spirituals or hymns, reflect the personal trials, testimonies, and direct conversations with God and Jesus of the songwriter and singer (and, by extension, of the whole suffering, struggling people, of course). Through them she could experience her own personal growth and spiritual encounters while also getting the gospel message of salvation out to her audiences. So, through her singing, she was experiencing the conversion process continually from one level to another, as Thurman's creative encounter describes, and she was convinced that through her gospel performance, similar spiritual transformations were taking place in her audiences.

Notes

1. Jules Schwerin, *Got to Tell It: Mahalia Jackson, Queen of Gospel* (New York: Oxford University Press, 1992), 1.

2. John Sellers, Mahalia Jackson's godson.

3. Isaac Hockenhull, Mahalia's first husband.

4. Schwerin, *Got to Tell It,* 186-87.

5. See Karen Baker-Fletcher, *A Singing Something: Womanist Reflections on Anna Julia Cooper* (New York: Crossroad, 1994), 16. See also Baker-Fletcher's "Soprano Obligato," in *A Troubling in My Soul: Womanist Perspectives on Evil and Suffering,* ed. Emilie M. Townes (Maryknoll, N.Y.: Orbis Books, 1993), 174, 183.

6. Baker-Fletcher, "Soprano Obligato," 174.

7. Ibid., 183.

8. Mahalia Jackson, with Evan McCleod Wylie, *Movin' On Up* (New York: Hawthorn Books, 1966), 31-32.

9. Ibid., 50.

10. Schwerin, *Got to Tell It*, 21-22.

11. Jackson and Wylie, *Movin' On Up*, 32-33.

12. Ibid., 72.

13. Ibid., 32.

14. Ibid., 63.

15. Ibid., 66-67.

16. Ibid., 67-68. Both in her songs and in her living, Mahalia was constantly making such pleas and commitments to God, which may be referred to as little "covenants." And though some may consider such actions as not of a higher, more elevated spiritual plane, some scholars and interpreters see them as basic to African and African American spirituality on every level. Seeing the communal character of African spirituality, Peter Paris states, "In traditional African religions, evil is thought to have its origin in human wrongdoing, which in turn causes some form of imbalance to occur between the human community and the realm of spirit." Moreover, he declares, "Whenever they were faced with suffering of any kind, traditional African peoples became preoccupied with the quest for relief: a two-directional search that centered on God as the agent of relief and on themselves and others as the cause of their misfortune" (Peter J. Paris, *The Spirituality of African Peoples: The Search for a Common Moral Discourse* [Minneapolis: Fortress Press, 1995], 45). With Mahalia, this was a natural response that grew out of her African background without her having done a sophisticated analysis and interpretation of the African religious sources of her actions.

17. Jackson and Wylie, *Movin' On Up*, 68.

18. Ibid., 11.

19. Ibid., 12.

20. Baker-Fletcher, "Soprano Obligato," 183.

21. Mahalia was frequently a guest in the home of Martin Luther King Jr. and his wife, Coretta Scott King, and "shared their fears of a political nightmare to come." She listened to the dialogues of King, Ralph Abernathy, and other ministers and allied her singing art to the movement as a weapon for change (Schwerin, *Got to Tell It*, 131-32). But nowhere have I found that King in any way mentored her spiritually, although she may have gotten some spiritual nourishment from their close friendship as it developed in his and other Southern Christian Leadership Conference ministers' frequent visits to her home in Chicago (Jackson and Wylie, *Movin' On Up*, 125, 128).

22. Isaac Hockenhull, Mahalia's first husband (whom she married in 1938), was an educated and refined chemist who could not keep a job in those years of extreme segregation and discrimination. Aside from his gambler's lifestyle, he had little appreciation for Mahalia's gospel-singing ministry and tried to push her into singing secular music. Though he treasured her voice and promoted her work as a singer, their disagreements over her type of singing and her commitments, among other things, led to many word battles and their eventual divorce (Schwerin, *Got to Tell It*, 41, 42, 43, 45, 47-48). This marriage lasted only about three years. Mahalia was married a second time, to Sigmund "Minters" Galloway, a long-time friend and widower, in 1964 (Jackson and Wylie, *Movin' On Up*, 206-12). Schwerin says of this marriage that, though Minters served her career briefly and played his flute at numerous recording dates, the mood of the marriage was contentious from the start. His antagonism in trying to manage and direct her career she found intru-

sive and unacceptable. Mahalia was also averse to his drinking habit. They were finally divorced in 1967 (Schwerin, *Got to Tell It*, 159-60).

23. Mahalia records her experiences with a Mr. Brown in Philadelphia and Newark who tried to exploit her and take part of her earnings for a concert he had scheduled without her permission. She stood her ground even before the court when he tried to force her hand (Jackson and Wylie, *Movin' On Up*, 81-86).

24. Schwerin, *Got to Tell It*, 72.

25. Jackson and Wylie, *Movin' On Up*, 95-97, 108-10.

26. Schwerin, *Got to Tell It*, 83-84, 103-7, 109-10.

27. Ibid., 165.

28. Benjamin Hooks, quoted in ibid., 165-66.

29. Delores S. Williams, *Sisters in the Wilderness: The Challenge of Womanist God-Talk* (Maryknoll, N.Y.: Orbis Books, 1993), 246n and 5-6.

30. Alice Walker, *In Search of Our Mothers' Gardens: Womanist Prose* (New York: Harcourt Brace, 1983), xi.

31. Jackson and Wylie, *Movin' On Up*, 78.

32. Horace Clarence Boyer, program notes for *Mahalia Jackson: The World's Greatest Gospel Singer*, Sony Music Entertainment, 1992.

33. Schwerin, *Got to Tell It*, 191-92.

34. Ibid., 192-93.

35. Ibid., 193.

36. Program notes for *Mahalia Jackson: Gospels, Spirituals, and Hymns*, Sony Music Entertainment, 1991, 4.

37. Jackson and Wylie, *Movin' On Up*, 94.

38. Schwerin, *Got to Tell It*, 193.

39. Leslie Gourse, program notes to *The Essence of Mahalia Jackson*, Sony Music Entertainment, 1994.

11

"The Doctor Ain't Taking No Sticks"

Race and Medicine in the African American Community

Emilie M. Townes

what is it about the day of the Lord
 that captures our imagination
 that challenges our souls
 that calls us up
  into a hope
  a wish
  a challenge
  a ministry
what is it about the day of the creator
 that prompts us to take cover
 to deny we hear a voice
  calling
  insisting
  that we move beyond our todays
   into better, richer, fuller
    more faithful tomorrows
what is it about the day of God
 that we begin to see who we are
 how we are
 what we are
 and realize
  that our worship is full, but incomplete
  our mission is strong, but lacks power
  our caring is deep, but needs more compassion
that great day of Joel's people
 in which sons and daughters prophesy
 in which the old dream dreams

and the young see visions
in which the spirit is poured out
    so that all this can happen
that great day only comes *after* the locusts
        after the trumpet of lament has blown in Zion
        it comes *after* the day of darkness and gloom
        after the fire has devoured in front and the flame burns behind
        after the war horses and rumbling chariots
        after the invading army that makes the peoples' faces grow pale
            that scales the wall
            that keeps its own course, not swerving
                not jostling
            that climbs through the windows of the houses like a thief
        after the earth quakes and the thunder and the sun
            and moon are darkened
            and the stars withdraw their shining
the great day comes after the people of the land
    have been reduced to trembling
and the great and powerful army comes
    like none before it and none after it
and it devours everything
    they are relentless
    they are devastating

Setting the Scriptural Context

these people do not start out happy
    they are in full lament
    they are being more than whiny, cranky Israelites
    they are in trouble
no, Joel doesn't condemn Judah for its injustice
    or its vile behavior
Joel doesn't mention Judah's departure from God's standards
    like the other prophets
    (someone once said, well he did only have *three* chapters, he didn't
        have time to "say more")
we know that all this is true
but Joel has lament on his mind
    and he sees the problem differently
        the problem is not what Judah has done or not done
            he knows all that
        the problem is the inhumanity and evil of others toward the people
            of Israel
Joel's is a plea to God to come to the aid of those who trust in God
    no matter what trials and tribulations they face

no matter what the adversity is—this time
a lament, for Joel, is about repentance
   Joel tells the folk to *turn* to God
   to turn to God for assistance in meeting these bugs
      this drought
      that army
      those signs from heaven
turn to God
   for this is the God of the covenant
   this is the God who cares and controls the full sweep of time and space
   this is the God who upholds justice
   this is the God whose actions are designed to make God's own self
      known to us
turn to God for salvation and hope
   for if you are in big trouble, says Joel
      if you've got any faith at all
   it is God you must turn to
it's only then that we can talk about sons and daughters prophesying
   and dreams and visions and the spirit
this is the rending of the heart
   this is the pouring out of the spirit in our lives
   when we immerse ourselves
      in turning again and again to God
      when we open ourselves up to God's promise
what is important is the content of faith
for it is only after the people enter honest lament
   through a faith that leads them to hope
   that God's answer is: grace
it is only after the people enter into
   genuine assembly
   genuine weeping
   genuine sorrow
that God answers with a divine yes
this is when the day of the Lord comes
   this is when we can truly prophesy as a church
   this is when we have dreams that move us beyond where we are and
      how we are
   this is when we have a vision worth sharing as a church
this is when we can gather and celebrate ministry
   that seeks to be faithful
and responds to God's call: return to me with all your heart
   by saying i am willing to try to be a prophet, a dreamer, a visionary
Joel gives us moving, powerful language
   we know this passage
   we are captured by the power of

> i will pour out my spirit on all flesh; your sons and
> your daughters shall prophesy, your old ones shall
> dream dreams, and your young ones shall see vi-
> sions. even on the male and female slaves, in those
> days, i will pour out my spirit

but Joel does not give us this passage
    without stipulations
    it comes only after the people have been brought low by the injustices
        and evil of others
        and they *choose* to turn to God with all their hearts
the call to give up our certainty
    give up our comfort zone
    give up our structures and plans
    is before us
then we can claim the hope found in Joel's words
    then we can meet the challenges of God's grace
for in the Hebrew Bible
    laments mark the *beginning* of the healing process
and people need and want to be healed
if we learn anything from Joel
    it is to know that the healing of brokenness and injustice
        the healing of social sin and degradation
        the healing of spiritual doubts and fears
begins with an unrestrained lament
    one that starts from our toenails and is a shout by the time it gets
        to the ends of the strands of our hair
it's a lament of faith
    to the God of faith
that we need help
    that we can't do this ministry alone
    we can't witness to the world in isolation
    we can't fight off the hordes of wickedness and hatred with a big stick
    we can't do this by ourselves anymore, Lord
    we need some help
        no, we need some *divine* help

Claus Westermann maintains that there is no worship observance in ancient Israel better known to us today than the rite of lament.[1] Joel gives us a communal lament. In the Hebrew Bible, the communal lament is used by and/or on behalf of a community to express complaint, sorrow, and grief over impending doom that could be physical or cultural. It could also be a tragedy or a series of calamities that have already happened. But the appeal is always to God for deliverance.[2]

Joel urges Judah to plead publicly for Yahweh's help, but it is seen not as an act of penitence, but as a plea for assistance.[3] As one moves through Joel, one sees the crisis not as a punishment for disobedience, but as a deeply distressing reality that Judah longs to correct (1:5-14). The only way to get there is to repent. There is an urgent flavor of repentance in Joel. It must be more than a set of external rites, it must be a matter of the heart—for the God who judges sin is the God of compassion and mercy.

But repentance no more controls God than do the magic incantations of pagan priests. And Joel is clear that neither rites nor sincere contrition automatically guarantees the result (2:14). Rather, Joel tells Judah to blow the trumpet and begin a genuine lament that involves the whole community, not just those of privilege or the dispossessed. And, as with other laments, an oracle of salvation answers the prayer of the people (2:18-27). The day of the Lord begins with the reminder that God's spirit is poured out on *all* flesh.

It is the vision of Joel that encourages me to focus on a tragic consequence of an inadequate health care system that we all endure, on its particular impact on the lives of African Americans, and on the mission and ministry of the church in light of these factors. Black folk may be the focus, but these are issues that affect us all. That is why I believe that *communal* lament can help us best get at the complexities of these issues. Lament enables us and even requires us to acknowledge and to experience our suffering.

Suffering that moves us to pain that can be named and then addressed is, in a word, formful.[4] By extension, it has a deep moral character that helps the discipline of social ethics do its work. For a communal lament happens *in community,* and this corporate experience of calling for healing makes suffering bearable and manageable *in* the community. When we grieve, when we lament, we acknowledge and live the experience rather than try to hold it away from us out of some misguided notion of being objective or strong. *We hurt*; something is fractured, if not broken. A foul spirit lives in us and among us. We are living in structures of evil and wickedness that make us ill. We must name them as such and seek to repent—not out of form—but from the heart. It is only then that we can begin to heal.

Setting the Social Context

As compelling as the words of Joel are for us today, social ethics draws on scripture as only one of the groundings for doing its work. Social ethics considers social structures, processes, and communities—especially those that are large and complex. It also looks at socially shared patterns of moral judgments and behavior. Primarily, a social ethicist asks the questions of how we all belong together under God and what our responsibilities are for one another because of this soul-deep relationship with the divine. Some of the questions that the social ethicist asks again and again are, "Why?"

"How?" "What are we to do?" "How are we to respond?" "What have we created?" "What are we called to create?" "What leads to freedom?" and "Are we on the path to salvation?"

The discipline of social ethics pays close attention to social contexts and how they shape and direct our sense of a moral self and of moral action—in other words, our moralities. The social context influences the perspectives and incentives of the individuals acting within it. The challenge is to explore issues of individual and collective moral responsibility and right action. Therefore, social ethicists consider what policies and practices institutions should follow, not only how individuals should behave within the framework of existing policies and practices.

For this chapter, I will consider the structures of health and health care in the United States. I do so with the words of Joel as a major guide for me, the words of a communal lament that says there *is* hope for this world. The lives of us all deserve affordable and excellent health care. Perhaps by focusing on the lives of African Americans, we can get some clues for us all.

Health and health care do not take place in a vacuum. In 1990, Black folks were 12 percent of the U.S. population of 25.8 million people. However, media coverage presents a much higher profile of African Americans than is proportional. Some of these images are positive, some negative. On the one hand, we have successful African American journalists, actors, musicians, athletes, and talk show hosts. On the other hand, we also have a steady diet of criminals, Black poverty, drugs, homelessness, and violence given to us by the media. These images become problematic, given that a 1990 Gallup Poll revealed that the average American thinks that America is 32 percent Black, 21 percent Hispanic, and 18 percent Jewish. The figures were 8 percent Hispanic and less than 3 percent Jewish.[5]

The incongruity of these figures with the lives of so many African Americans (and the stereotypes, images, and attitudes they entail) moves us beyond the ironic to the burlesque. The U.S. Black infant mortality rate is 17.7 deaths per 1,000 births, compared with 8.2 deaths for White babies.[6] African American babies born to college-educated mothers have an 80 percent higher risk of dying in their first year than do White babies born to college-educated mothers. Poverty, poor diet, health care, and housing make survival problematic for many Black infants. A 1993 U.N. Children's Fund report notes that among industrialized nations, "the United States has by far the highest percentage of children living in poverty: 20 percent, which represents a 21 percent increase since 1970."[7]

African American children are nearly three times as likely to be poor as White children. In 1993, 46 percent of Black children were living in poverty, compared with 17 percent of White children. Sixty-three percent of African American youth grow up in single-parent homes, compared with 30 percent for all U.S. families.[8] The problem is *not* that the home is single-parent, the problem is that in today's economy, one-income families (unless they are television characters) increase the chances that children will be poor. Too often these children may drop out of school and end up in foster care, group homes, and juvenile justice facilities. However, let me stress the "may" in my previous sentence. *All* Black children from single-parent homes will not end up on drugs, in gangs, as dropouts, and on welfare. Many single-parent children survive and thrive among African Americans. Yet it is troubling that the United Nations ranked Black folks number 31—about the same as some two-thirds-world nations—in its quality-of-life index, while White Americans were number 1.[9]

Homicide is the leading cause of death for African American males between the ages of sixteen and twenty-four. The life expectancy rate for Black men is 64.6 years, compared to 73.8 for Black women, 72.9 for White men, and 79.6 for White women.[10]

These figures take place in a larger social arena where obtaining mortgages and business loans is more difficult for African American families. Blacks face steering in real estate, insurance and job discrimination, higher unemployment, and underemployment. Affirmative action, an idea we have never seriously tried in this nation, is under attack and, for far too many African Americans, threatens to reduce their chances to get into college and their possibilities for a job that will have a sustenance income.

All this is not good for our health.

These facts may be true, but they represent only one part of African American health and life. As Farai Chideya points out in her book *Don't Believe the Hype: Fighting Cultural Misinformation about African-Americans*, "There are many more Black accountants than there are Black athletes, many more young Black men in college than in prison, vastly more self-supporting African-American mothers than ones on welfare."[11] In 1992, 47 percent of Black families were headed by married couples, 46 percent were female-headed, and 7 percent were male-headed. For Whites, the figures were 82 percent, 14 percent, and 4 percent, respectively.[12] In 1992, 68 percent of Blacks aged twenty-five and over had a high school diploma. This contrasts with 51 percent in 1980. In 1992, 12 percent of Blacks and 22 percent of Whites had at least a bachelors' degree. This compares with the 1980 figures that were 8 and 18 percent, respectively.[13]

Blacks have made gains and suffered losses when it comes to income. The Black upper class has been rising, and the Black middle class has remained stable, but many in the working class have become poor. In short, we are a much more stratified community than we have been in the past when it comes to economics. We are not solely a community of the poor, nor do our numbers represent the majority of those who are poor in this country. We are, in short, a much more complex people than either the media or the perceptions of many would have us all think.

The Problem of Race and Medicine

These are only pieces to a much larger puzzle that African Americans bring to the health care debate. We live in a less-than-adequate health care delivery system in the United States. Thirty-seven million Americans do not have any health insurance. African Americans are a disproportionate number in this figure, and less wealth and jobs with few or no benefits are chief factors.

The stereotypes about health and health care problems in the Black community abound. First, there is the myth that drugs are a Black, inner-city problem. The reality is that although drug use is higher in inner-city neighborhoods than in wealthier ones, when one looks at the geography of the entire country, the National Institute on Drug Abuse found that African Americans account for just 12 percent of users, while Whites account for 70 percent.[14] Better predictors of drug use than race are socioeconomics and neighborhood type. Poverty, despair, and drug use *are* natural dance partners. Regardless of race, unemployed people are more than twice as likely to be current drug users. Twenty-eight percent of unemployed Blacks and 23 percent of unemployed Whites use drugs. The homeless are the heaviest drug and alcohol users. These facts prompt the National Institute on Drug Abuse to state that "race/ethnicity [is] not a significant determinant" of drug use.[15]

A second myth about drugs is that crack is a "Black" drug that is running rampant in the African American community. Socioeconomics comes into play as a more important factor than race with this myth as well. A study in the *Journal of the American Medical Association* found that crack use does not depend strongly on race-specific factors.[16] In fact, Blacks and Whites from similar neighborhoods are equally likely to smoke crack. The major thing to keep in mind is that due to the economics of our country, Blacks are more likely to live in a drug-infested neighborhood than Whites. However, the 1988 National Household Survey on Drug Abuse showed that the vast majority—more than 97 percent—of African Americans had never smoked crack.[17]

All this is not to deny the reality of the devastation of drugs on Black life in the United States. My aim is to put drug use into a much more realistic and attackable light. Too much of the rhetoric from pulpit to podium has painted the impact of drugs on Black life as a near-hopeless devastation. We can attack this problem, for all is not lost. But we must move beyond rhetorical flourishes to meaningful, church-based mission programs that reach out into communities hit hard by drug use and abuse.

There are other health issues. According to the *New England Journal of Medicine*, Black patients tend to receive less intensive hospital services and are less likely to be satisfied with the care they receive than are White patients with similar health insurance coverage.[18] We have much ground to make up when it comes to health care for African Americans.

Let me return again to infant mortality. The good news is that Black infants now have a better chance of surviving to their first birthday than at any time in our history in this country. The troubling news is that it is getting worse in relation to White infant mortality rates. In 1950, Black infants were 1.6 times as likely as Whites to die. In 1988, Black infants were 2.1 times more likely as Whites to die.[19] Poverty is not a dominating factor, as with the statistics for drug use and abuse. Black middle-class families suffer higher mortality rates than White middle-class families. The factors of this are "a lifetime of shoddy medical care, lack of prenatal care and—most telling—the chronic stress of being Black in America."[20]

Black heart patients get less advanced treatment than do Whites in our nation. A study of heart treatment in veterans' hospitals, where the patients' finances have less influence on the statistics, has made clear that the problem is race. White patients were consistently more likely to receive advanced surgery for certain heart conditions.[21] The likelihood is that in situations where doctors have more choices among types of treatments, African Americans get less advanced treatment than do Whites.[22]

Another troubling area is that Blacks are more likely to suffer kidney failure but less likely to get a transplant than are Whites. Also, environmental racism takes a heavy toll. Sixty percent of the total Black population lives in communities with one or more uncontrolled toxic waste sites.

Black men have the highest cancer rates in the nation. Black women have a rate higher than White women but lower than White men. AIDS is the eighth leading cause of death in the country and has a calamitous home in the Black community. Thirty-three percent more Blacks suffer adult-onset diabetes and are twice as likely to die of it as Whites.[23]

Heart disease is the leading killer of Black men and women and the leading killer nationwide. Black men have the highest incidence of heart disease; the rate for Black women is much higher than that for White women and almost as high as the rate for White men. Blacks are 33 percent more likely than Whites to have high blood pressure.[24] This is a condition that can lead to kidney disease, stroke, heart failure, and blindness.

The Doctor Ain't Taking No Sticks

To make all these matters worse, we live in the after-effects of the Tuskegee experiment, which began in the 1930s and which has caused bad blood between the African American community and the medical establishment. The events in Macon County, Alabama, are a microcosm of what can happen when an economically depressed Black community encounters health care. The Great Depression had a devastating impact on the county. In the 1930s, most of the residents lived below the poverty level, and as recently as 1970, one-third lived in homes with no indoor plumbing. The typical house was a shack with a dirt floor, no screens, little furniture, a few rags for bedding, and a privy only when underbrush was nearby. Drinking water came from an uncovered, shallow well that was often unprotected from direct surface drainage.[25]

There were fifteen White and one Black private physicians in the county during the early 1930s. Tuskegee Institute had five physicians, and the area where the government conducted the syphilis control work had five more. However, their services did not have much impact on the health of Blacks in the rural areas. Most blacks went "from cradle to grave deprived of proper medical care."[26] One elderly Black resident, speaking in 1932, paints a disturbing picture of what health care was like for these folks:

> I ain't had a Dr. but once in my life and that was 'bout 15 yrs. ago . . .
> The Dr. ain't taking sticks, you know; if you go to him, you better have
> money and if he comes to you, you better have it. So you see that
> makes a po' man do without a Dr. when he really needs him.[27]

The Tuskegee Syphilis Study conducted by the U.S. Public Health Service (PHS), involved four hundred southern Black men for forty years—from 1932 to 1972. The Public Health Service did not tell these men that they had syphilis, and they did not treat them, so that researchers could discover the "natural history" of the disease. The end point of the study was death, at which time the researchers autopsied the men to see what havoc the disease had wrought on their internal organs.

Medical officials told the men that they were being treated for "bad blood," a southern euphemism for a whole range of illnesses. Medical personnel never warned them that they could pass the disease to their sex partners or to their unborn children.

The experiment began with the best of intentions. Julius Rosenwald, the longtime president of Sears Roebuck and Company, set up a foundation, which as one of its projects began to fund syphilis testing and treatment projects in several southern rural Black areas in 1929. One control project began in Macon County, Alabama, where federal epidemiologists discovered that the infection rate was from 35 to 40 percent. The study had just begun when the Depression struck and money became tight. With financial support gone, the Public Health Service decided that the best way to attract more money for the program was to continue it as a study of untreated syphilis. They reasoned that poor, uneducated, isolated rural Alabamians would not have access to treatment. However, if the study showed how devastating the condition was for rural poor Blacks, then more money might be forthcoming.

A trusted Black nurse from the community was hired to keep track of the men, and the Public Health Service enlisted the cooperation of the nearby Black-run teaching hospital at Tuskegee Institute, where the men were examined annually to chart the progress of the disease. The men received free medical care, transportation, and burial stipends. PHS officials reasoned that because the standard treatment for syphilis, mercury and arsenic, was so potent that it sometimes killed, it was not awful to withhold a treatment that might be as deadly as the disease. This line of argument could be held with some measure of a clear conscience until the introduction of penicillin during World War II. It was not until 1972, when a PHS whistle-blower leaked the story to the media, that this gruesome "experiment" stopped. From the refinement of penicillin in 1941 until the study's forced demise in 1972, researchers actively prevented the men from receiving penicillin. This meant colluding with local physicians and health departments to keep the drug from the men.

There are myriad things that make this "experiment" appalling. For me, the fact that the experiment was not a secret study, but one about which there had been many reports in medical journals and open discussions in conferences at professional meetings over the years makes it more than a bit disturbing. One PHS official told reporters that more than a dozen articles had appeared in some of the nation's best medical journals during the time period of the study. These articles described the basic procedures of the study to a combined readership of more than one hundred thousand physicians. The official went on to state that the PHS had not acted alone. The study was a cooperative effort of the Alabama State Department of Health, the Tuskegee Institute, the Tuskegee Medical Society, and the Macon County Health Department. The numerous defenses that justified the study compound the plague of locusts. One doctor who served as director of the Division of Venereal Disease between 1943 and 1948 declared, "There was nothing in the experiment that was unethical or unscientific."[28] From the PHS to the Center for Disease Control (CDC), officials justified the study and the withholding of penicillin as medically justifiable. CDC spokespeople consistently presented the Tuskegee Study as a medical matter involving *clinical* decision that may or may not have been valid.

The issue of ethics took a back seat. The decision to withhold treatment was the immoral foundation of this experiment. It is only if one approaches the study from the view that treatment would be withheld that one can find little moral crisis when a new and improved form of treatment was developed.

From the justifications of the PHS and the CDC to the indignation of the press, public, and many in the medical community, one thing that was not a part of the debate when the story broke in 1972 was the scientific merits of the experiment. Many physicians defended the study, pointing out that there had been only one study dealing with the effects of untreated syphilis before the Tuskegee Study. One physician from Vanderbilt University's School of Medicine pointed not only to this, but also to the argument that penicillin would not have benefitted the men. However, this doctor went one step further and asserted that *the men* were responsible for the illnesses and deaths they sustained from syphilis. He held *them* responsible for not seeking treatment for a disease that went unnamed for them. The Hippocratic oath to prevent harm and heal the sick whenever possible was not a part of his argument.

To Heal the Wounded Spirit

We live in a time when Medicare fraud is roughly $17 billion. This is more than the federal government's bill for providing cash welfare assistance to poor families with children. We live in a time that demands a communal lament. The realities and some of the history of what health care has been for Black folks in our country are our contemporary locusts. Moreover, in the words of Joel,

> What the cutting locust left,
> the swarming locust has eaten.
> What the swarming locust left,
> the hopping locust has eaten,
> and what the hopping locust left,
> the destroying locust has eaten. (1:4, NRSV)

It is time we blow the trumpet in our contemporary Zion and sanctify a fast. It will take all of us, peoples of color and White, male and female, young and old, to carry out a communal lament. For only a lament that comes from all of us can address the complexities of health and health care in our lives and the peculiar way in which this affects the African American community.

Some good things that we would like to see happen are beyond our belief. We may hope for them, but we tinge our hope with skepticism. We seriously doubt the possibility of the very things we most want. We find ways to sell ourselves short, to deem others less than, to give up on living a life of justice and mercy—because, after all, *we are only human*. For all that we dream about, we find ourselves content to live out the weary drama of the nightmare—to accept the isness of our lives as the ought and to find ways to short-circuit the hope found in possibilities in and daring to reach beyond what we ever thought ourselves capable of. We lose sight of the fact that our lives may be the only chapter of scripture somebody reads. We forget or neglect that the miracle of God working in us is that God takes our brokenness, the threads of our lives, and weaves masterpieces—if we dare to let God.

We say, both overtly and covertly, that true justice and equality will never be a part of the fabric of living in our lifetimes; that we will always have the poor with us; that some of us can access adequate, if not superordinate, health care while others rely on a health delivery system overburdened with the sheer force of numbers and the acuteness of illnesses it must treat; that some of us are just destined to be wealthy and successful, and others of us will naturally fall by the wayside into despair and hopelessness.

We are afraid to live our hopes. We look at struggle as a sign of discord and turmoil, rather than realizing that our faith demands from us *seasons* of struggle and *moments* of glory. When we finally reach those places where we are close to attaining some measure of our best dreams—our moment of glory for ourselves and the world around us—we begin to get nervous, we begin to look around, we start looking over our shoulder, and we cannot *believe* that this moment is close at hand.

Hope that is birthed from lament is a strange thing, and each of us has suffered a loss of hope from time to time. We feel that what we wanted to happen was simply beyond the believable. We are not unlike the disciples after the resurrection. They were a people whose hopes had been crucified by the very nails that pinned Jesus to the cross. There was no confidence left in them; the future they longed for had seemed to die with Christ. They had depended on him to bring about the fulfillment of the promise of God. With Christ dead, they had nothing to look forward to. Their hopes had been misplaced, and emptiness was all that remained; but the rumors began to come—he lived, some saw him, and the hopes that were dying began to live again.

We must take our own dying hopes and breathe new life into them as we look at the worlds so many African Americans endure—regardless. What a paradox we place ourselves in when we hope and yet are afraid to hope. Hope is powerful. It enables us to press onward when we feel like giving up. It enables us to draw strength from the future to live in a discouraging present. It makes it possible for us to see the world not only as it is, but also as it can be. Hope can move us to new places and turn us into new persons.

Yet for all the possibilities in hope that bode well for us, we all know that hope is dangerous. It not only gives us strength, but also makes us vulnerable. Sometimes the causes we support and the vision we have prove to be unworthy of our support, and the vision of the future we long for fades from our eyes—a cold and desolate wind blows in our hearts. Yes, the chill of despair is doubly cold for those who have had their hearts warmed by hope. Hope can create new opportunities for pain and disappointment. It is undeniable that countless hopes have been short-lived and undependable. All of us are mindful of the tight circle in which our lives are lived. We know all the ways by which life closes in, stultifies, frightens, and disturbs us. We know those private regions of the heart where desires have their beginnings and the quiet anxieties of the spirit that express themselves in many ways that defeat us.

But there is something about hope, when it is grounded in the risen Christ, that is solid enough to sustain our lives and overcome skepticism and doubt. It *is* frightening, this hope, because we know that Jesus interrupts the mundane and comfortable in us and calls to us to move beyond ourselves and to accept a new agenda for living. We are led into a life of risk. The hope that is to be found in Jesus cannot simply be given a nod of recognition. It demands not only a contract from us, but also a covenant and a commitment. When we truly believe in this hope, it will order and shape our lives in ways that are not always predictable, not always safe, and rarely conventional, and it will protest with prophetic fury the sins of an inequitable health care system.

Hope gives us the gumption to lay claim to the strength of our faith and the power of God's love for us! We are drawn again and again to a God who gives us the comfort of the familiar landscape that enables us to find our way even in the darkness of sin and sorrows. Hope gives us the ability to recognize that no event in our lives, whatever its character, can imprison us. We refuse to scale down our aspirations to the level of the facts in our present situation because God is always calling us to move beyond the present to shape and mold a better tomorrow. We wrestle with the problems of health and health care until they open, until they yield, until they break down and disintegrate under the relentless pressure of our ability to hope and to live in that hope. This is what the resurrection is all about. Not even death is capable of telling us what it is that God has to say about life.

The events of our lives cannot make us prisoners unless we let them. There is misery abounding in our world. We cannot hide from inflation, from recession, from HIV/AIDS, from war, from responsibility. We can choose to say that someone else is more qualified and more knowledgeable about economic forecasts and global warming. We can be content to allow experts to debate the quality of our lives. We can wring our hands or, worse, turn our backs in indifference and callous disregard to the preaching of hate groups or the erosion of human rights. But this never relieves us of the responsibility we have to our generations and future generations to keep our hopes alive and vibrant. If we do not learn how to live out the hope that is our foundation, who is going to do it for us?

Hope, that which scares us and yet prepares us, gives us the wisdom to know that God is not through. Our task is to take the challenge that hope gives us—the joy along with the disappointment—and to work *with* God until our lives begin to pulse with something vaster and greater than anything we have known before. We are destined to reach for the skies and to embrace life with songs of joy and justice. Hope gives us the willpower it takes to look at all those people and situations that wish us harm and do us harm, and to decide that we are called to new life and not early death. Hope gives Black folks the stubbornness to survey our situations and work out a way of life that gives us health and growth despite the wearying paradox of our living.

With hope we do not give up, for we answer life *with* life. The responsibility for living with meaning and health and dignity ultimately rests within us—not with the hatemongers and scalawags of the world. Only a hope that is grounded in a faith that rests within God can see us through the miasma of living.

all who take hold of their disbelief
    and fashion a faith that does not let us go
    and holds us accountable to ourselves and to God
all who recognize the cost of hope
    and choose to live *in* it rather than circle it, dodge it, or turn from it
all who hope in Christ

have accepted a gift that will always challenge and always change us
it is a solid hope, a hope that will never fail us
    and never leave us alone and without support
when it's the spirit showering us with grace and hope and love
    then we are set free to serve
    and free others
with full hearts—we can do this
with a full ministry—God's church is never put to shame
    your sons and your daughters
    your young and your old
    your free and your slave
them is us
and *we* are the church
a church that can stand in the clearing
    and declare like toni morrison's character baby suggs, in her novel
    beloved,

> here in this place we flesh; flesh that weeps, laughs;
> flesh that dances on bare feet in grass. love it. love
> it hard.[29]

we are called to love ourselves
    to one another
    to love God hard
if we are to *live* out
    the pouring of God's spirit in our lives
we must reach out to our brothers and sisters
    and touch creation with our hearts and souls
the spirit will let us do much more
    but it will not tolerate much less
    and still allow us to name ourselves faithful
God's spirit is showering us
    will we stand in the midst of the flux
    seek forgiveness
        move on in faith
        and work to create a healthy life for us all
or will we wait
    for the trumpet blast
    and the swarm of locusts

Notes

1. Claus Westermann, *The Psalms: Structure, Content and Message*, trans. Ralph D. Gehrke (Minneapolis: Augsburg Publishing House, 1980), 32.

2. Paul Wayne Ferris Jr., *The Genre of the Communal Lament in the Bible and*

the Ancient Near East (Atlanta: Scholars Press, 1992), 10.

3. Graham S. Ogden and Richard R. Deutsch, *A Promise of Hope—A Call to Obedience: A Commentary on the Books of Joel and Malachi* (Grand Rapids, MI: Eerdmans Publishing, 1987), 23.

4. Walter Brueggemann, "The Formfulness of Grief," *Interpretation: A Journal of Bible and Theology* 31, no. 3 (July 1977): 265.

5. Farai Chideya, *Don't Believe the Hype: Fighting Cultural Misinformation about African-Americans* (New York: Plume/Penguin Books, 1995), 13.

6. Lewis W. Diuguid, "Marchers to Celebrate Surviving," *Kansas City Star*, October 14, 1995.

7. Ibid.

8. Ibid.

9. Ibid.

10. Ibid.

11. Chideya, *Don't Believe the Hype*, 14.

12. Ibid., 16.

13. Ibid., 16-17.

14. Ibid., 211, citing the National Institute on Drug Abuse, *National Household Survey on Drug Abuse: Population Estimates, 1991.*

15. Ibid.

16. Ibid., 213.

17. Ibid.

18. Ibid., 215.

19. Ibid., 215-16.

20. Ibid., 216.

21. Ibid.

22. Ibid.

23. Ibid., 219.

24. Ibid.

25. James H. Jones, *Bad Blood: The Tuskegee Syphilis Experiment*, new and expanded edition (New York: Free Press, 1993), 62.

26. Ibid., 64.

27. Ibid.

28. Quoted in ibid., 8.

29. Toni Morrison, *Beloved* (New York: Knopf, 1987), 88.

PART III

LOVES THE FOLK

12

WOMANISTCARE

Some Reflections on the Pastoral Care and the
Transformation of African American Women

Marsha Foster Boyd

What Is WomanistCare?

Hold your voice there, mister:
    I can speak for myself!
    Yeah, you're used to talkin' for me
        like I'm mute or deaf or plain
not here—
But
    I got somethin' to say and,
    since you've never been inside my
Soul,
    you just list'n awhile.
        I dream my walk
            everyday,
    and sometimes declare
        this just the way it is—
    I'm not backin' up or flinchin'
One inch.
    Seems every time I pause,
    You open your mouth ready to explain
    away my potential—
But,
    I can speak for myself, and,
    since you've never been inside my
Visions,
    you just pay attention.[1]

197

This poem, written by Valerie Bridgeman Davis, represents the essence of WomanistCare. WomanistCare is the intentional process of care giving and care receiving by African American women. It is the African American woman finding her place and her voice in this world. It is the bold expression of that woman caring for her circle, be it small or large. It is the expression of that woman influencing her circle, be it small or large. In this process, the focus is the holistic care of body, mind, and spirit in order that healing and transformation occur for African American women and their circles of influence.

This care is given and received generally in small group settings, be they spiritual or secular, and through the cultivation of friendships and interdependent relationships between and among African American women. It involves African American women finding their own places and their own voices in this world. It is the bold expression of African American women caring for their circles, be they small or large. WomanistCare is the varieties of expression of African American women as they influence these circles. In this essay, the focus is on the spiritual setting in which WomanistCare takes place.

Pastoral theology is "the practical theological discipline concerned with the theory and practice of pastoral care and counseling."[2] In the field of pastoral theology, which has evolved during the twentieth century, the voices of women are just beginning to be heard. In the foreword of *Women in Travail and Transition*, published in 1991, the editors state that the focus of the book is on white women. They write: "As editors, we hope that companion volumes will be written by nonwhite, ethnic, non-middle-class women within Western culture and by other women elsewhere throughout the world."[3] African American pastoral theologians and pastoral caregivers realized that something had to be done in order for the voices of African American women to be heard—that it was time for us to speak for ourselves. Thus, the publication of *Women in Travail and Transition* served as a catalyst for that work to begin.

Also in 1991, the first group of African American women in the pastoral care professions gathered in Lansing, Michigan, and coined the term "WomanistCare." The twelve of us represented five Christian denominations, lay- and clergywomen, social workers, pastors, associate pastors, clinical pastoral educators, professors, and hospital chaplains. The volume *WomanistCare: How to Tend the Souls of Women*, volume 1, is the result of the work done at that meeting. We came together very quickly, solicited the assistance of African American laywomen from local churches, and together formulated this volume, which explains the rudiments of the emerging discipline of WomanistCare.

WomanistCare speaks of the importance of narrative and voice in the healing and transformation process of African American women. In Bridgeman Davis's poem, it is a surprise to the unidentified "mister" not that this woman could speak for herself, but that she is demanding to direct the content of the conversation—content that is self-directed, not other-directed. WomanistCare encourages African American women to see themselves as the subject of conversation, no longer the object. A line is drawn as the African American woman claims her story and establishes her own boundaries. In WomanistCare, the telling of one's story and finding comfort and power in that story are essential for healing and transformation. WomanistCare speaks of the importance of one's personal and cultural history as well as the impact of one's family of origin on one's choice making; one's responses regarding racism, classism, sexism, and able-bodyism; and the other challenges in this world which impact us all.

Fundamental to a pastoral theology of WomanistCare, African American women's experience is the loom on which the weaving of personal transformation begins. This experience links African American women with all women of the African Diaspora, African peoples around the world. This story, which is both individual and collective, is the background upon which the dialogue is woven between those telling and those listening. After all, the image of weaving connotes warp and woof, two strands which by themselves can exist, but which woven together are stronger, more functional, and richer in color and texture. Through the telling and the hearing of this story, the reciprocal, interdependent relationship is honored, cultivated, and nourished. Through the re-creation of this collective story, African American women realize that WomanistCare is not new; rather, it has been a necessity for African American women throughout the centuries. WomanistCare simply represents the caregiving realities of African American women in contemporary societies.

In developing a pastoral theology of WomanistCare, one must examine the traditional images and roles used in describing those giving and receiving care within the context of the church. Traditionally, the images of the pastor as "shepherd" and the parishioners as "flock" are predominant.[4] WomanistCare is a response to this form of pastoral theology that is predominantly white, male, linear, and fraternal, and that traditionally lifts up such images as shepherd and servant as the primary means by which care is given and received.

These images engender at least discomfort and at most abhorrence and revulsion on the part of African American women, for reasons made clear in the writings of Katie Cannon, Jacquelyn Grant, Delores Williams, and others. Jacquelyn Grant wrestles with the image and metaphor of "servant" in her essay "The Sin of Servanthood and the Deliverance of Discipleship."[5] Grant indicates that this image is particularly oppressive to African American women, since they have been viewed as the "servants of servants" (white women).[6] Grant explores the viability of the image of "disciple" as a healthy one for women of color.

Part of what WomanistCare has done and is doing is working with another image that has been handed down through the discipline of pastoral theology and pastoral care, and that is the image of the "wounded healer" that was put forth by Henri Nouwen some thirty years ago. Womanist-Caregivers reject this image. To continue to dwell on the wounds that need to be healed for African American women keeps them debilitated, keeps them disempowered.

I offer the image of the "empowered cojourner" as a more appropriate one for African American women. To envision oneself as an empowered cojourner, one understands that through one's life, through one's hurts, through one's victories, one has power to cojourn with others.

The word "cojourner" was developed by Cecelia Williams Bryant.[7] Williams Bryant indicates that a "cojourner" is a person or persons whom "heaven has summoned to journey with us."[8] Cojourners are spiritual companions brought together on a common path for a particular time. "Cojourners witness a union that is birthed by an imprint of the Soul."[9] This image of the cojourner encourages us to work and walk together; and as we work and walk together, our community, our family, and our selves as individuals are able to be transformed. Indeed, as practitioners and teachers, those pastoral theologians involved in WomanistCare must continue to help women in both the church and the classroom forge and maintain healthy images. Thus, conversation between the academic world and the world of the church is vital.

A pastoral theology of WomanistCare involves several components. The first is clearly communication in all of its forms. Communication can be verbal, physical, and/or spiritual. For example, the visual and performing arts, craft making, sacred rituals are all considered part of the healing balm of WomanistCare. African American women can trace these healing elements to their African and Caribbean roots. As African American women engage in any of these forms together, the potential for healing is present. Women communicate their stories, pains, and triumphs as they create together.

Clearly, this communication goes beyond the one-hour-once-a-week counseling model found in traditional psychotherapy. Thus, traditional psychotherapy is but one means for African American women to communicate their issues and stories. The point is that this communication is not just verbal and does not necessarily involve a "trained professional" who determines when healing takes place. WomanistCare enables African American women to take their healing into their own hands through the communication of their needs among a supportive network of sisters. Since there is sometimes mistrust of the traditional counseling model, WomanistCare works to transcend its potential limitations among African Americans, regardless of class.

Another key element of communication is listening. WomanistCaregivers work at developing effective listening skills. As one engages in pastoral care, one realizes the privilege one is afforded to listen as another tells her or his story. A theology of WomanistCare, then, seeks to ensure that African American women are "listened into life." This is the power of listening.

Second, a pastoral theology of WomanistCare involves affirmation, validating and affirming the stories and the places of African American women. The woman in the Bridgeman Davis poem reminds us that "I can speak for myself!" This woman affirms for us that we have dreams and visions which must be articulated. She advocates active, assertive, and, some may say, aggressive affirmation, not navel gazing or star gazing: "I'm not backin' up or flinchin' / One inch."

Third, WomanistCare involves a confrontation between and among African American women and, as a result of those confrontations, a confrontation of structures and the strictures in our world. The purpose of confrontation in which African American women are called to engage is bridge building, so that those who come behind us will not have to go through what we have had to go through. The coming generation is to stand on our shoulders.

Fourth, WomanistCare involves accountability, women holding one another accountable for who we say we are and what we say we are about and, from that circle, moving forth to hold others accountable for who they say they are and what they say they are about. This is particularly important as African American women and Anglo women continue to try to forge alliances with one another. Bridgeman Davis reminds "mister" that "Seems every time I pause, / You open your mouth ready to explain/ away my potential." We women cannot do that to each other.

Fifth, WomanistCare involves healing. Hebrews 12:12 says, "Lift your drooping hands and strengthen your weak knees and make straight paths for your feet that what is out of joint might be put in place"; that lifting and straightening and strengthening is a part of the healing dimension of WomanistCare, so that we are able to help one another to overcome. As a result of these five components, a dual transformation takes place for the African American woman, in that as that woman is individually transformed, she in turns works to transform each circle in which she has influence.

"I dream my walk everyday," and I am surprised that we even have time for dreams and visions. Too many have been willing to explain away our potential. The spirit of the poem is the spirit that drives what we write about. It is a spirit that is born out of necessity, determination, survival/thriving. It is the spirit that calls forth life.

Notes

1. Valerie J. Bridgeman Davis, "Hold Your Voice There, Mister," in *WomanistCare: How to Tend the Souls of Women*, vol. 1, ed. Linda H. Hollies (Chicago: Woman to Woman Ministries, Inc., 1992), 18.

2. J. R. Burck and Rodney J. Hunter, "Pastoral Theology," in *The Dictionary of Pastoral Care and Counseling* (Nashville: Abingdon Press, 1990), 867.

3. Maxine Glaz and Jeanne Stevenson Moessner, eds., *Women in Travail and Transition: A New Pastoral Care* (Minneapolis: Fortress Press, 1991), vi.

4. See these early works in the field of pastoral theology: Charles E. Johnson, *The Minister as Shepherd* (New York: Thomas Y. Crowell Co., 1912); Seward Hiltner, *Preface to Pastoral Theology* (Nashville: Abingdon Press, 1958) and *The Christian Shepherd: Some Aspects of Pastoral Care* (Nashville: Abingdon Press, 1959); Paul E. Johnson, *Psychology of Pastoral Care* (Nashville: Abingdon-Cokesbury, 1953); and E. Brooks Holifield, *A History of Pastoral Care in America: From Salvation to Self-Realization* (Nashville: Abingdon Press, 1983). Even though he advocates use of the image in his book *Pastoral Care in the Church* (New York: Harper & Row, 1964), C. W. Brister states, "We have seen that this shepherd motif has become a stone of stumbling for some moderns who resent the idea of being viewed as part of a dumb flock, driven by herd instinct or maneuvered by a strong paternalistic leader" (19).

5. Jacquelyn Grant, "The Sin of Servanthood and the Deliverance of Discipleship," in *A Troubling in My Soul: Womanist Perspectives on Evil and Suffering*, ed. Emilie M. Townes (Maryknoll, NY: Orbis Books, 1993), 199-218.

6. Ibid., 200.

7. Cecelia Williams Bryant, *Kujua: A Spirituality of the Hidden Way* (Baltimore, MD: Akosua Visions, 1993).

8. Ibid., 35.

9. Ibid., 39.

13

Some Kind of Woman

The Making of a Strong Black Woman

Barbara J. Essex

"You better stop being so womanish! Bring me a switch! I'll show you how to act!" These are words I often heard from my mother. She believed her task was to teach me how to be a woman. Her southern roots dictated that she teach me how not to be bold, not to ask questions, not to rock the boat—this was for my safety and her comfort. But how could I be anything other than "womanish" when being so was in my genes?

I come from a long line of strong Black women; women who made choices and decisions outside the norm; women who worked farms without men; women who made livings without husbands; women who left inadequate and abusive men and forged on alone; women who by their examples opened up new possibilities for me. Sociologists would describe their lives as ones filled with hardship, menial jobs and poverty. What they fail to see in the lives of my great-grandmothers, my grandmothers, my mother, my aunts and my cousins is strength, beauty and the power of making "a way out of no way." The women who gave birth to me transformed society's norms into something that would work for them. In the face of oppression and pain, they made a life for themselves and for their children. They refused to be fenced in by narrow thinking and limited options. When there was no way, they forged a way. When they hit a brick wall, they tore the wall down, brick by brick. Therefore, I cannot help being "womanish"—it's in my genes!

This story is about my mother, Archie Mae Simmons Essex. She died one year and one month after my father died, twenty-eight days after my graduation from seminary and six days before my thirty-fourth birthday. Her story is one of movement—physical, emotional and spiritual. She moved from the country to the city and again to the country and to the city. She moved from shy little girl to sometimes awkward teenager to complex adult to mature and confident woman. She moved from wife and mother to woman of substance and power.

I learned about my mother's life through the stories she told. In conversations with my four siblings, we often begin our reminiscences with "Mama used to tell us . . ."

Mama used to tell us about her grandmother, whom we called Grandma. Arie Sanders was some kind of woman. At a young age, she married Jake Sanders. When the youngest of their eight children was six months old, Jake was struck by lightning and killed. Grandma instantly became a single parent, independent farmer and landowner. She raised her eight children without a husband. She worked the land and tended to the chickens and pigs without a man. No doubt there were folks who did not believe she could make it; the odds of her remarrying with eight children were slim. She wanted a life for her children and taught them wholesome values—hard work, courtesy, determination, faith and hope.

Grandma had a sense of humor that was infectious—many a summer day under the protection of her porch roof and many a summer evening with a chorus of crickets in the background, she would entertain us with stories of her childhood and young life in rural Demopolis, Alabama, always referred to as "the country." Grandma was unpretentious and opinionated. She was gracious and stubborn. She was a God-fearing, churchgoing woman who never complained or moaned about her situation. She buried her husband and a son; there was much sadness in her life. But she managed to go on without feeling sorry for herself. She did not encourage self-pity in her children. When asked how she made it, she always acknowledged a deep, abiding faith in God. I can recall her singing some gospel hymn in the morning, and I overheard her talking to God throughout the day. Faith was not something she picked up only on Sundays; faith was what she lived every minute of every day.

My family and I would return to the country each year to visit relatives. We always spent a couple of nights with Grandma. In those days, there was no electricity or indoor plumbing. During the day, we sat on the porch and talked. At night, we lit the kerosene lamps for light and most often went to bed early. One night, when we had all gone to bed, we were awakened by the blast of a shotgun! Grandma came in with a wide smile on her face, carrying a kerosene lamp. She declared with great pride, "I finally got that sly old fox. He's been sneaking into my henhouse, eating the eggs and killing my chickens. I got that son of a gun good!" Grandma was in her sixties when this happened. When she wasn't killing foxes, she raised vegetables and made quilts by hand. She received guests with warm hospitality—there was always "sweet bread" and something cool to drink at her house. We felt at home at Grandma's; we knew she was always happy to see us. She lived alone until her death and remained active, rational and wonderful. She did what she had to do. She was a strong Black woman!

Mama used to tell us about her mother, whom we called Big Mama. Corine

Sanders was some kind of woman. As one of eight children growing up on a farm, she had to work the fields with her mother and siblings. One day, one of the girls got sick. Corine was to escort her sister back to the house and put her to bed. Then, Corine was to return to work. But she never went back to the fields. She and her sister had conspired together to set up Corine's elopement with Eddie Simmons. At the appointed time, he drove by the house and picked up Corine and her suitcase, and off they went to be married. Shortly after that, they moved to Birmingham, the big city in Alabama. Against her mother Arie's wishes, Corine claimed her destiny and literally ran off with the man of her dreams. They had one child, Archie Mae. In the big city, Eddie worked at the steel mill and Corine worked as a domestic. She could cook up a storm—delicious and healthy meals, light-as-a-feather cakes and incredible dinner rolls were her trademarks. Her own home was immaculately clean and cozy. She had a number of "what-nots" collected on her various travels and received as gifts. She was a seam-stress par excellence and was the pianist for her church.

Grandpa Eddie died when my mother was eighteen years old. Big Mama remained single for more than twenty years before she married again. In those years, she worked hard and played hard. She was quite stylish, not at all looking like a grandmother. She must have gotten her storytelling ability from her own mother. Big Mama could tell a story and make you laugh and cry at the same time. She had a full-body laugh that filled a room and a charm that conquered everyone within a five-mile radius. She had a subtle way of teasing that made the object of her attention feel special. She was most eloquent in her stories about growing up during the Depression. Big Mama told us how Black folk just seemed to press on even during the hardest of times. Neighbors helped each other, and whatever there was was shared with others. She encouraged generosity and community. She was a savvy businesswoman who never got swindled. She was generous and kind, even-tempered and fair.

As my mother did with her grandmother, I spent my summers with Big Mama. She assigned certain chores to me and allowed plenty of free time. She encouraged me to use the library across the street and would quiz me on my readings. She encouraged my questions about life and religion. Big Mama took me seriously as a person. She was firm, patient and gentle. She never whipped me and always explained why what I did was wrong.

She encouraged me to be the best. She used to say, "You can be and do anything you want. Your color is not an obstacle. If you have a brain, you can do it all." And she practiced what she preached. She, too, did what she had to do. She was a strong Black woman!

Mama used to tell us how she met her future husband. Nathan M. Essex was "mannish," according to Grandma; he was a fast, charming, sweet-talk-ing boy. One day, Archie Mae was having lunch with friends at the John Essex High School in Demopolis when this brash Nathan came along and snatched a candy bar out of her hand. In mock anger, she demanded that he buy her another Baby Ruth candy bar. He bought her two, and the romance was on! Grandma warned her that nothing good would come of her liaison with Nathan. Archie Mae did not listen. On December 23, 1950, she and Nathan went to Meridian, Mississippi, where they were married in a simple civil ceremony. In 1952, Nathan left his wife and their infant daughter, Barbara Jean, to venture to Chicago, seeking a better life for all of them. In early 1953, he moved his small family to the South Side of Chicago.

Mama used to tell us how life was during those early days. Those were bittersweet days. Daddy worked hard and usually worked two jobs. Mama worked for a short time as a maid at a downtown hotel. Soon after, however, she became a full-time mother. Mama spent many days indoors, especially during the cold, hard winters. For entertainment, my parents would sponsor "quarter parties." These parties required twenty-five-cent admission, drinks were twenty-five cents and sandwiches were twenty-five cents. There was card playing, dancing and much laughter and fun. Mama would be busy days before the party—cleaning up, cooking, sorting phonograph records and just plain getting ready.

During the summer, life was even better. My mother, brother and I often spent our days shopping on Forty-seventh Street, then a thriving business district. At least once a week, we went to a doubleheader filmfest at the Regal Theater. After the movie and for the one admission price, we saw the up-and-coming stars perform. We thrilled to the performances of Jackie Wilson, the Contours, James Brown, Ruth Brown, Etta James and others. We often ate lunch out of picnic baskets on Drexel Boulevard. On the weekends, we got together with other relatives and friends for cookouts on the lakefront.

There also were bitter days. My mother had to deal with my father's infidelities. Could Grandma have been right about him? Mama had to deal with her loneliness. She had left her life in Alabama to follow her husband to a strange, big and sometimes scary city. Until other relatives migrated to Chicago and stayed with us for short periods, Mama had few people to talk to during the day. Many of her friends worked and envied her because her husband had enough wherewithal to "sit her down." Mama had to deal with her weight and her self-esteem. After the birth of each of her children, she never quite lost the weight she had gained. Her identity was wrapped up in her husband and her children—she was wife and mother. She had to deal with the stress of raising five children. She did not complain, but it was clear that she was not happy.

During the early 1960's, our home was a way station for other migrating relatives. At any given time, there were one or more cousins and their spouses sharing our apartment. They were young and curious about life in the big city. Mama became the elder sister/surrogate mother to these kinfolk. They asked her advice about all sorts of things, including sex and marital relationships. She did not spout clichés and platitudes. She spoke from deep places of loneliness, frustration, betrayal and forgiveness—all of which she lived. She always told the whole truth—the good, bad, ugly, joyful and painful. She was the queen, and this role suited my mother well. She never judged but was brutally honest and candid in her assessments. She never pried but responded when asked. There were a couple of cases of violent spousal abuse. My mother tried to empower the women to resist and to create something better for themselves. Most often, however, they remained in the abusive relationships. Even though my mother did not understand why, she sympathized with them as best she could. Several times, we were called to escort a beaten woman to the hospital. Eventually, the fighting couples were asked to leave. As these relatives conquered city and married life, their need for Mama's advice and support diminished. She seemed to be searching for something to do, someone to be.

More and more, Mama escaped by watching television—soap operas and baseball games were her favorite shows. It was difficult to talk to her when one of her shows was on. Forget about conversation if there was a baseball game on. She seemed to withdraw more and more. After a minor but scary car accident, she refused to drive. She depended on her husband, and later her children, to drive for her. She claimed that she was too nervous to drive. She was often short-tempered and sad.

She went through the motions: visiting school when needed, cleaning the house, cooking the meals, grocery shopping and doing the laundry. But there was something missing. Only since my mother's death have I learned to recognize and appreciate the strong woman she was and continues to be. By outside standards, her life was nondescript yet typical for her time—she married a good man who took care of her and their children. The marriage was not perfect; it may not have been all that she had hoped for, but she knew who she was in that marriage and never lost sight of that.

When I asked her about her life, Mama often shared two important choices she had made. First, she changed her name. Her birth name was Arthur Mae Simmons. She disliked this name immensely and, when she was able, she changed it to "Archie Mae." Those who knew her from childhood always called her Archie Mae! She decided to make a change and become who she wanted to be. She rejected the name given to her by her parents. She claimed the right to be called what she wanted to be called.

Second, when she was a child, she chose to move back to Demopolis. She spent the summers with her maternal grandmother, Arie Sanders. One year, she decided she wanted to live the life of a country girl on the farm. She often talked about how she loved the wide, open space of the country and the rhythm of farm life. Mama was a tomboy, and the country suited her well. She boasted about her ability to chop cotton and pitch bales of hay just like the boys. She talked about how well she fit in on the farm— her big hands, big feet and big bones were perfectly matched for the labor of working the land. In the country, she was surrounded by cousins who liked her for herself. In Birmingham, she was reminded that she was an only child and of the loneliness that brings. So she decided to stay in the country. Her parents took care of matters, and she began living in Demopolis. I do not know what level of resistance she met from her parents. Mama never indicated any great trauma about this. She made a decision and it was accepted by all. She lived in Demopolis until her husband moved her to Chicago.

These choices indicate that Mama had more control over her life than even she might have known. She made up her mind, and others accepted her choices. She was some kind of woman.

And so, it was always puzzling when she sought to make me conform! For many years, it seemed that I could never do anything right—there was always something wrong with my hair or my clothes. My homework was never neat enough, my grades never quite high enough. I always laughed too loud, or I was too nosy. Every minor mistake was magnified. I was reminded of my mistakes again and again. I was embarrassed in front of others and belittled for "not having the sense I was born with." For a long time, I thought my mother was mean and picky. These days, I wonder why she did the things she did—was she reliving her own childhood and its hurts? I wish I had been aware enough to ask her why she needed to whip me for the smallest infractions and what her real expectations of me were.

These days, I remember my mother as a strong Black woman. I watched her grow before my very eyes and did not recognize it as such. It was after one of my own acts of defiance that I noticed a change in my mother. One Saturday morning in 1968, I told Mama I was going to the library to study. This was not an unusual routine for me and there was no need for suspicion. Instead of going to the library, however, I went to LaTee's Barber Shop on State Street and told the barber to cut my hair into an Afro. After much resistance and my threat of taking my business and money elsewhere, the barber did as I asked. I returned home that afternoon with a short, bushy Afro. My mother took one look at me and went ballistic! Since she had stopped whipping me years before, her major threat was simply, "Wait until your father sees you! He's going to kill you!" And I was duly afraid.

When my mother asked why I cut my hair and why I was so secretive about my intentions, I replied that I wanted my hair to reflect who I was and that if I had asked for permission, she would have said no. That incident led to a long discussion about empowerment and controlling one's own destiny. My mother and I fussed and yelled—well, she yelled and I listened! But it opened up something special between us, and we both changed in ways that only now are becoming clearer.

Mama never quite grew to love the city; her heart seemed to belong to the country. She would longingly talk about life in the country and the "good old days." She spoke of the days when she had to fetch water from the nearby creek and chop wood for the stove. Those days seemed to represent a time and place that were safe and comfortable. She always knew what to do on a farm. It must have been terrifying for her to give up those open spaces to follow her husband to Chicago. It must have taken incredible courage and love for her to leave behind all that she knew to forge a new life. But she did.

Then something miraculous happened. Seemingly out of the blue, Mama lost weight and kept the weight off. She began wearing makeup and pretty clothes. When the children came home from school, Mama was greeted with, "Why are you dressed up? Where are you going?" Her reply would be, "I'm not going anywhere. I just want to look nice."

Mama began asking me what I learned in school, and she really listened. She began reading my books—together we read James Baldwin, Langston Hughes, W. E. B. Du Bois, Booker T. Washington, Marcus Garvey, Mary McLeod Bethune, Richard Wright, Helene Johnson, Gwendolyn Brooks, Nikki Giovanni, LeRoi Jones and June Jordan. We discussed and debated the merits and limitations of the Black Power movement and what it meant to be "Black and Proud." Before it was all over, my mother even wore an Afro! We watched Dr. King and the growing Civil Rights movement and projected the impact it would have on the lives of Black folk.

When I left home for college, my mother went back to work. She worked as a cashier in a bakery owned by some friends of ours. She came home each evening with stories of weird customers and new things she had learned. The laughter and sparkle returned to her eyes. She became more aware of business and applied for and got credit cards in her own name. She paid for her own bills with her own money. She joined a social club of other women and met on a regular basis with them. They planned outings just "for the girls." She talked about going back to school. All this she did over the protests of her husband, who wanted her to stay at home. She made her choices, and they were accepted by all. She was some kind of woman.

Even the birth of her fifth child did not stop her. She hired a baby-sitter and went back to work. I believe that my mother needed to work—on the job, she was more than Nathan's wife and our mother. She was a woman—attractive, witty, charming, graceful and fun. One day, I visited the bakery where she worked. I was amazed at how easily she went about her work and how she joked with customers, female and male. She was bold, beautiful, wonderful—the woman I wanted to be.

Mama used to tell us that her dream was to be a nurse; she would talk wistfully of the future she had envisioned for herself. She saw herself enjoying the finer things that life had to offer: travel, material things, financial security and fun. These and more she wanted to experience before settling down. Instead, she married, became a parent and dropped out of high school. She did not outwardly brood about her fate. She took stock and moved on to different dreams and hopes. Perhaps the act of defiance that led me to cut my hair reminded her of who she was. Perhaps she remembered Grandma and her independence and determination to make a life for herself. Perhaps she remembered Big Mama's strength in defying her mother to pursue her dreams. Perhaps she remembered her aunts and cousins who chose to live the way they wanted to live. Archie Mae stood in the legacy of strong Black women—women who established their own businesses at a time when women were not encouraged to be independent. They chose to marry or not to marry. There was no shame for those who chose to remain single; indeed, they flaunted their freedom and independence. They were not antimarriage, they simply recognized that there were options. They labored, earned their own money and depended on no one for financial support. Without being conscious of it, these women were role models. They created and cultivated their own values and virtues on their own terms. They did not seek legitimization from outside forces, they listened to their own voices. Despite the societal limitations on their freedom and autonomy, they made their own way in the world.

In many ways, my mother grew into her legacy—it takes a lot of tears and laughter to make a strong Black woman. Like many Black women, my mother cried a lot. She was misunderstood by those closest to her. She probably spent a good deal of time being depressed; we did not have a name for her moods and withdrawal—it was just the way she was. It is easier now for me to forgive her for not being the perfect mother. I realize now that her own childhood was not perfect. I will never know the depth of her pain. She sacrificed parts of herself for the sake of her family. Mama used to say that families stay together because the woman makes the compromises. It was clear that she did; yet she did not wallow in self-pity and victimization for long.

Like many Black women, Mama reached down deep within herself and found the strength and power that was always there. She searched herself and found again that sassy, brash, womanish girl who had changed her name and her place of residence just because she wanted to! Once she rediscovered herself, it was easy for her to pass that strong self on to her children.

She encouraged her children to think for themselves. We were taught to lead and not simply to follow the crowd. So it is no surprise that she pushed me to live my dreams first and to think about living others' dreams for me later. My mother was a stay-at-home mom for most of her life—but when I went away to college, my mother came into her own. She got herself a job, got herself some credit and got herself an identity beyond being my father's wife and our mother. She knew there were options; some were better than others, but they were choices nonetheless. What I am realizing these days is that my mother had been coming into her own her whole life! Her choices may have seemed feeble and too passive, but Mama was a powerful woman. At some point in her journey, my mother recalled the legacy of the women who gave birth to her—she claimed her name, claimed her life and claimed her "womanish" self! She took the cards she had been dealt and made something more to her liking, where she called the shots and others accepted her choices. It would have been easy for her to remain passive and miserable. It would have been easy for her to slip into a serious depression and remain victim. Instead, she took a stand for herself and reclaimed her legacy. She knew that no matter what, she could not let down the women who gave birth to her.

It seemed that each time one of her relatives died, Mama got stronger. She mourned the passing of Grandma but took on her abiding faith in God. She mourned the death of Big Mama but took on her understanding of Scripture at deep levels. She mourned the passing of her aunts and cousins but took on their spirits of adventure and determination. Through it all, Archie Mae seemed to rediscover the parts of her she had suppressed and sacrificed.

My relationship with my mother improved during those years. We became more than mother and daughter—we became friends. We spent "quality" time together, dining out, going to the theater and concerts and continuing our discussions about what we were reading. She encouraged me to "do my thing" on all levels—socially, professionally and spiritually. She never questioned my choices, although she must have wondered about my sanity more than once.

It did not seem to surprise her when I told her of my call to the ministry. She was supportive and proud. She sat through many a dull and fumbling sermon in order to show her support. Finally, I had gotten something right! I felt loved by my mother. Even though I knew she loved me, there had been times when I questioned that. In our conversations about religion and family, I learned about her doubts and insecurities. Even more, I learned about her power. Her choices may not have been the ones I chose, but without the choices she made, I would not have been empowered to make my own. By her example and through her heritage, I learned what it means to be a woman—strong, proud, courageous, bold, womanish!

My mother could never forget that she came from a family of strong Black women. When times were tough, she was reminded that there was something special in her blood. Archie Mae Simmons Essex knew she was surrounded by a great cloud of witnesses cheering her on. Arie, Corine and others bade her to stand up and be a woman. A real woman. And so she did. My mother—strong Black woman in life and in death! My mother—some kind of woman! I am proud to be her daughter.

14

Paul and the African American Community

C. Michelle Venable-Ridley

Historically, African Americans have not been afforded the luxury of reading. Only within the last 125 years or so have African Americans as free citizens had the legal right to learn to read.[1] Prior to that, the American slavocracy not only prohibited reading among slaves, but also employed aggressive, hostile measures to discourage free and enslaved Africans from seeking to learn to read. Because of this blighted aspect of American history, many contemporary African Americans view reading as an ominous act, one cloaked in mystery and danger.

Since enchained persons were not permitted to read, their exposure to information and ideas was primarily aural. What they knew and understood of the Bible, therefore, was communicated to them through word of mouth by means of public readings and sermons. Accordingly, then, the dominating slave culture communicated and rehearsed portions of the biblical text that accommodated and enforced the dehumanizing, hegemonic rule of the slavocracy. Hence, it became the task of enslaved African Americans to remember, repeat, and interpret fragments of the Bible's content that were in accordance with their own hermeneutic. Vincent Wimbush corroborates this by contending that meaning and significance were found in the telling and retelling, the hearing and rehearing of biblical stories—stories of perseverance, of strength in weakness and under oppressive burdens, of hope in hopeless situations.[2]

Howard Thurman's grandmother illustrates how many African Americans, depending upon the aural tradition, chose for themselves the texts they included in their biblical canon. Thurman writes:

> Two or three times a week I read the Bible aloud to her. I was deeply impressed by the fact that she was most particular about the choice of Scripture. For instance, I might read many of the more devotional Psalms, some of Isaiah, the Gospels again and again; but the Pauline

epistles, never—except, at long intervals, the thirteenth chapter of First Corinthians . . . With a feeling of great temerity I asked her one day why it was that she would not let me read any of the Pauline letters. What she told me I shall never forget. "During the days of slavery," she said, "the master's minister would occasionally hold services for the slaves. Old man McGhee was so mean that he would not let a Negro minister preach to his slaves. Always the white minister used as his text: 'Slaves, be obedient to them that are your master . . . , as unto Christ.' Then he would go on to show how it was God's will that we were slaves and how, if we were good and happy slaves, God would bless us. I promised my Maker that if I ever learned to read and if freedom ever came, I would not read that part of the Bible."[3]

Because of Thurman's grandmother's aural contact with the Bible, she was able to reject those portions of the biblical text that insulted her sense of dignity as an African American and as a woman. She likewise was able to embrace those sections of the Bible that affirmed her sense of self-worth as an enchained woman of color.

Thurman's grandmother's rejection of the Pauline texts demonstrates three ways in which the experience of oppression has influenced African American women's disposition toward reading Paul.[4] First, African American enslaved women, out of positions of domination and oppression, used biblical paradigms, images, and scripture references as tools of liberation. Their textual practice or use of New Testament sources can therefore be viewed as political strategy, for these enchained women's appropriation of the biblical text gives notice to their dogged and creative strength even in the midst of forced servitude. Second, shackled by forces of domination and death, Black bondwomen clung to the words of hope and promise in the biblical text to create a world of political resistance and Black selfhood. Third, a text cannot be understood apart from the world it creates in the imagination of the hearer. Its effects—social, emotional, psychological, and otherwise—are vital to any extraction of meaning, since that meaning has no productive existence outside its realization in the mind of the hearer. Hence, the hearer must act as cocreator of the work by supplying the portion of it that is not written but is only implied. This is extremely important, especially for enslaved women of African descent, who were not written about, written to, or written for. By placing herself at the center, the African bondwoman could create a range of interpretations that filled the "gaps" of the text in a way informed by her own historical context.

Within the African American religious community, then, the apostle Paul, both an enigma and an apostate, has often been ignored, disclaimed, and discredited by a cruelly skeptical audience. Nevertheless, it is quite impossible to offer an objective, holistic biblical exegesis without the thorough examination of the religious legacy of the man Paul. It is not my goal to redeem Paul for the African American community, but rather to provide a much needed corrective to the historiography that has so blighted the Pauline vision for African Americans, women, and especially African American women.

It is the purpose of this essay, then, to continue the search for religious direction and meaning within the African American community through a historical analysis of the biography—even identity—of the apostle Paul. Insofar as there is a distinctive Black religious consciousness[5] that considers the writings of Paul suspiciously and even with contempt, this work seeks to locate and reexamine those elements of the Pauline biography that create cognitive dissonance in the processes and development of African Americans.

African Americans have struggled for more than two centuries to reinterpret and revise a distorted gospel received from White Christians who held us in bondage for almost 250 years. The major task of this chapter, therefore, is to add a nuanced perspective—one detached from the assumptions and interpretations of the slavocracy—in three fundamental ways. First, it aims to continue the ongoing struggle to correct the distortions of the New Testament text; second, it attempts not to redeem but to reclaim the writings of Paul as a religious source for the African American community; third, it presents a holistic portrait of Paul—one that reintroduces the religious legacy, theology, call, mission, eschatological hope, and vision of Paul, the man and the apostle.

The Biography of Paul

Paul, a first-century non-Palestinian Pharisaic Jew, was born in the city of Tarsus, a naval installation in the Roman Empire around 5-15 C.E.[6] Born to a family of impressive Jewish heritage, Paul was named after the tribe's most illustrious member, King Saul.[7] "He was circumcised on the eighth day, of the people of Israel, of the tribe of Benjamin, a Hebrew born of Hebrews; as to the law a Pharisee" (Philippians 3:5).[8]

The date of Paul's birth is uncertain. However, he is referred to as a young man (*neanios*) at the stoning of Stephen (the death of Stephen cannot have been much before 31 C.E.; Acts 7:58);[9] and he calls himself an old man (*presbytes*) in Philemon 9, around 52-54 C.E. Correlating these points of reference with his meeting with Gallio (50-52 C.E.) in Corinth and his martyrdom under Nero (54-68 C.E.), we can estimate his birth at around 5-15 C.E.

Little can be ascertained about the birth, childhood, and early manhood of Paul. Christian literature, albeit extensive, provides insufficient data for reconstructing the life of Paul. Although half of the Book of Acts gives an account of Paul's career from the time of his persecution of the church through his imprisonment in Rome toward the end of his life, it nonetheless must be used cautiously as a supplement to the primary sources. There are several extrabiblical correspondences, like the Epistles of Paul and Seneca, the Letter to the Laodiceans, and 3 Corinthians, that others produced in the name of Paul, from which one may also infer secondary data on the apostle. However, these early Christian documents, highly legendary in character, are useful for reconstructing Paul's life in matters that are best regarded as debatable or unknown.[10]

Within the African American Christian community, the Pauline tradition has been enshrouded in controversy. Not only are Paul's letters often polemical and seemingly contradictory, but also his thought embodies the tensions of a multidirectional vector. Paul, therefore, holds a unique position in both early Christianity and the Black Church for three major reasons. First, Paul's letters are the earliest records of early Christianity in its embryonic stages. The gospels (Matthew, Mark, Luke, and John) were written after 68 C.E., while Paul's letters range in date from at least a decade before 60 C.E. Paul's missionary activity began around 37 C.E., a few years after the death of Jesus. This was a time of formation, questioning, and definition for the emerging Christian movement. The early Christians were seeking answers to questions such as, Who are we and what do we believe? What are the rules for our community? Who will be admitted into our community? and, How will those who do not adhere to our rules be handled? Many answers to these questions were sources of conflict and inspiration in Paul's letters:

> Closest attention has to be paid to the letters, for they are the most direct and earliest primary sources from the beginnings of Christianity. They were not intended as literature. Paul would have been doubly astonished that they should have a place in the "history of ideas," for he had no high opinion of philosophy, and he thought he was living at the end of history. On the other hand, they are not merely private letters. They are official correspondence, directed to a variety of immediate and urgent problems confronting the newly established Christian congregations in the cities of the eastern Mediterranean. For that reason they afford a most candid glimpse into the character of those congregations as well as of the man who founded them. And indirectly they provide precious hints about the form of Christianity which existed before his conversion and about the special school he shaped, which was destined to survive him.[11]

Paul wrote within a particular historical context—one characterized by the bustling atmosphere of the polis, multifarious religious movements, and diverse philosophies—to address the issues and concerns of first-century Christians. His writings were not directed to a monolithic society; nor were they intended for an eighteenth- and nineteenth-century White audience whose primary goal was to keep their Black slaves docile and obedient. Paul wrote to a specific group of people with a specific intent. Therefore, it is fraudulent historiography that equates the school of thought that emerged from the authentic Pauline texts with the gospel that resonated from the pulpit of the slaveholders.

> I was preaching to a large congregation on the Epistle to Philemon; and when I insisted on fidelity and obedience as Christian virtues in servants, and upon the authority of Paul, condemned the practice of running away, one-half of my audience deliberately rose up and walked off with themselves; and those who remained looked anything but satisfied with the preacher or his doctrine. After dismission, there was no small stir among them; some solemnly declared that there was no such Epistle in the Bible; others, that it was not the Gospel; others, that I preached to please the masters; others, that they did not care if they never heard me preach again.[12]

Second, Paul's letters provide the largest corpus of material written by one person in the New Testament:[13] "Letters attributed to him comprise a quarter of the New Testament, and another twelfth of its pages—most of the Book of Acts—is devoted to a description of his career."[14] Since the Bible is the greatest collective document of human liberation that has ever come out of human experience and the effort of God, contends Latta R. Thomas, it is imperative that the African American believing community wrestle with Paul and his writings.[15]

Third, Paul's letters have been used to support diametrically opposed views. For example, Galatians 3:28 and 1 Corinthians 7:21-24 hold exactly opposite views. W. A. Meeks argues that in Galatians 3:28, Paul downplays the importance of worldly social distinctions within the Christian community ("for you are all one in Christ Jesus"), whereas in 1 Corinthians, Paul urges slaves to seize the opportunity to attain freedom ("but if you can gain your freedom avail yourself of the opportunity"). Christianity was a polymorphous movement that constituted tensions in many directions. Paul embodied many of those tensions. No wonder his letters have stirred such controversy and debate.

Paul holds a precarious position in the Black Church. It is not only imperative to the agendas of reconciliation and reclamation that we understand the historiography that created the African American perception of skepticism, it is also necessary to see how the deconstructing of a distorted biblical message can assist in the pursual of human liberation. It is, therefore, essential that the gospel of the slavocracy and its devaluation of Black personhood be fully examined and justly reappropriated for the African American Christian community.

The Good News of Paul

The word *apostolos* or "apostle" appears in the New Testament with a general meaning of "messenger." According to Liddell and Scott, it does not mean the act of sending or, figuratively, the object of sending; it denotes a person who is sent, and sent with full authority.[16] In historical usage, the specific designation of the twelve disciples of Jesus has prevailed; however, Paul, calling himself the apostle to the gentiles, justifies this naming in terms of his call and commission from the risen *Kyrios* (Lord) (1 Corinthians 9; Galatians 1): "For I did not receive it from man, nor was I taught it, but it came through a revelation of Jesus Christ" (Galatians 1:12).[17] Paul's call prompts his mission and derives its authority directly from God's revelation (*apokalypse*) of his own son to him. Paul, maintaining this as proof of his election as an apostle, sets out to convince gentile hearers to participate in the marvelous process that changed his life.

Paul's activity of evangelization (i.e., his presentation of the *euangelion*, the "good news" of the glory of Christ [2 Corinthians 4:4]) became his way of announcing, preaching, his meaning of the Christ-event. Thus, Paul often speaks of "my gospel" (Romans 2:16), "the gospel that I preach" (Galatians 2:2), or "our gospel" (1 Thessalonians 1:5; 2 Corinthians 4:3) because he is cognizant of the fact that "Christ did not send me to baptize, but to preach the gospel" (1 Corinthians 1:17). He was fully aware that his commission to preach the good news among the gentiles was not a message peculiar to him or different from that proclaimed by those "who were apostles before me" (Galatians 1:17); "whether it was I or they, so we preach and so you came to believe" (1 Corinthians 15:11). Paul saw himself as the servant (*doulos*) of the gospel (Philippians 2:22) and thought of himself as set apart from his mother's womb for this task (Galatians 1:15; Romans 1:1), like the prophets of old (Jeremiah 1:5; Isaiah 49:1):

> The Damascus vision was the vision that gave him his calling, and it can be compared to the visions in which the prophets were called. Because of that vision he was unable to be silent about Christ, "for a necessity lieth upon me. For woe is unto me if I preach not the gospel" (1 Corinthians 9:16).[18]

Paul's gospel, his emphasis on the redemptive power of the cross of Christ, is central to the understanding of his theology. The Christ-event, Jesus' death on the cross and his resurrection from the dead, is the heart of the good news that Paul so eagerly preaches. "For Paul," write Norman Perrin and Dennis C. Duling, "this event is a powerful event, signaling that the final period of history has begun, that the end is imminent. It is therefore an eschatological event."[19] Hence, the gospel reveals the reality of a new age, the reality of the *eschaton*.

Joseph Fitzmyer adds another level of understanding when he writes, "To this apocalyptic nature of the gospel must be related Paul's view of it as 'mysterion,' 'mystery, secret,' hidden in God for long ages and now revealed—a new revelation about God's salvation."[20] Paul equates "God's mystery" with "Jesus Christ . . . crucified" (1 Corinthians 2:2). Paul, seeing himself as a "steward" dispensing the wealth of this mystery (1 Corinthians 4:1), reveals God's plan to bring humanity—gentiles as well as Jews—to share in the salvific inheritance of Israel, now realized in Jesus Christ.

In presenting the gospel as "mystery," Paul is suggesting that it is something that can be understood only in faith. The promise to Abraham was given with no strings attached. It was purely a one-sided gift, in that God was the only one to take initiative. The response of Abraham was faith: "Thus Abraham 'believed God, and it was reckoned to him as righteousness'" (Galatians 3:6). He did nothing to qualify or to earn merit. The promises of Abraham find their fulfillment in Christ. When a person is "in" Christ, then that person, too, inherits the promises of God. This great opportunity comes only by an act of faith in Christ Jesus. "A man is not justified by works of the law but through faith in Jesus Christ, even we have believed in Christ Jesus, in order to be justified by faith in Christ, and not by works of the law, because by works of the law shall no one be justified" (Galatians 2:16).

This comprehension of the world, then, making itself known through an apocalypse, a revelation of the resurrected Christ, gave birth to Paul's theological thought and shaped the contents of the gospel of Jesus Christ he so fervently preached. Paul's life-changing engagement with Jesus Christ not only reoriented his life, but also designated him the "apostle to the gentiles" (Romans 11:13). By means of his very personal, religious experience with the risen Christ, Paul's gospel, logic, and theology are shaped and expounded. Paul had indeed experienced a critical moment in the revelation of God's Son to him, and in the aftermath of that crisis, he reflected on the ways of God within the world inhabited by Jews and gentiles, in light of the disclosure of the risen Lord. Paul the Pharisee, then, became Paul the apostle and theologian.[21]

The "good news" of Paul was very different from the *euangelion* of the slavocracy. The apostle's message, one of hope and expectation in the *Christos*, embraced all the people of God, Jews and gentiles alike. It was not used or intended for the oppression, subjection, or control of any person, but rather as a resource that affirmed community coalescence and faith in the faithfulness of Christ. Paul's gospel gave identity both in the world, now quickly passing away, and, more importantly, in the *eschaton*, the soon-coming kingdom in which human liberation will overcome the hierarchy and oppression of the status quo. Paul's *euangelion*, therefore, projected an inclusive agenda of freedom and wholeness—one directed toward practical advice in everyday situations and committed to the attainment of emancipating power in matters of faith.

The liberating power of this eschatological domain, demonstrated partially in the present world and fully in the world to come, is attested to in many of Paul's writings. In Romans he demonstrates the impartiality of God (2:11). In 1 Corinthians, because of the quickly approaching end, he urges the community to remain as it is; however, despite the shortness of the time, Paul counsels slaves who have the opportunity to attain their freedom to do so. In 2 Corinthians, while revealing the transiency of the old dispensation of death under the law, Paul discloses the liberation and glory of a new covenant: "Now the Lord is the Spirit, and where the Spirit of the Lord is, there is freedom" (3:17). Perhaps the most vibrant declaration of Paul's affirmation of human liberation and disavowal of the status quo is found in Galatians 3:28: "There is neither Jew nor Greek, there is neither slave nor free, there is neither male nor female; for you are all one in Christ Jesus."[22]

The Gospel of the Slavocracy

Despite the agenda of liberation purported in Paul's writings, the bearers of the gospel of slavocracy purposefully used the scriptures ascribed to Paul as ideological tools in the devaluation of the sacredness of the slave's soul, body, and mind. By constituting what Riggins R. Earl Jr. calls "a hermeneutical circle of double negativity," White slaveholders used the gospel of Jesus Christ to teach their slaves internal and external self-disavowal: the slaves were "black of body" and "blacker of soul."[23] While this interpretive loop of self-debasement used the scriptures to prove the evilness and utter defilement of blackness and all of its associations, it also provided White men and women a justification for the dehumanization of their slaves.[24] This doctrine, requiring slaves to impugn themselves in both body and soul, not only affirmed the belief of White superiority and justified the enslavement of people of African descent, but also constituted the cornerstone on which the gospel of slavocracy was built.[25]

Although many questioned whether Black people had souls, most White clerics in the antebellum South felt commissioned by God to share the gospel with their slaves:

[We] by the providence and word of God are under obligation to impart the word of God to our servants. It may be added, that we cannot disregard the obligation thus divinely imposed, without forfeiting our humanity, our gratitude, our consistency, our claim to the spirit of Christianity itself.[26]

Slaves were taught to imitate Jesus, the exemplary servant of servants, in their daily interactions with their masters and with one another. If they chose to morally pattern their lives after Jesus, slaves were expected to view themselves as

God's innocent sufferers of history, to be led as sheep to the slaughter, enduring the cross and despising the shame. Slaves were told to practice the hospitable spirit of Jesus that typified his life. In their actions, slaves were to love their enemies, to feed them, to give them drink, and to make them their friends by love and kind treatment.[27]

The primary intention behind such a teaching was to shackle the slave, in the name of Jesus Christ, to the will and command of the slaveholder. It implied, therefore, that slaves could be saved only according to their master's functioning definition of "good works." Since reading was forbidden for slaves, this pedagogy was accomplished through oral instruction.

The sermon, providing a pedagogical method for instructing slaves, served two primary purposes: it reinforced the slave's dependency upon the slaveholder, and it provided a fertile ground for the proof-texting process that confirmed the absolute authority of the master. In short, it supplied a vehicle for the propagation of a distorted gospel, an attractive device for slave control. As a result, slavery became defended as an economic and social good— one ordained and sanctioned by the holy scriptures of God.

Slaveholders were blind to the "good news" of Paul's message. By selecting specific portions of the biblical text that seemingly supported their agendas, slaveowners preached a gospel of damnation and death to their slaves. Paul's affirmation of human liberation in this world and in the world to come, therefore, was neither acknowledged by the slave masters nor presented to enslaved Africans.

The writings of the Pauline tradition are the primary texts used in most of the sermons of the slaveholders. These texts were not only popular and useful for reminding slaves of their duties toward their masters, but they also served as a balm for the occasional eruptions of Christian conscience that suggested that perhaps slavery was wrong. Hence, sermons that urged slaves to obedience and docility were repeated quite frequently. In 1935, Frank Roberson, a former slave, paraphrased the type of sermon to which he and his fellow slaves were often subjected:

> You slaves will go to heaven if you are good, but don't ever think that you will be close to your mistress and master. No! No! There will be a wall between you; but there will be holes in it that will permit you to look out and see your mistress when she passes by. If you want to sit behind this wall, you must do the language of the text "Obey your masters."[28]

Harriet A. Jacobs, a North Carolina slave who escaped to the North in 1842 and published a slave narrative in 1861, provides the following rendition of a typical sermon preached to slaves:

> Hearken, ye servants! Give strict heed unto my words. You are rebellious sinners. Your hearts are filled with all manner of evil. 'Tis the devil who tempts you. God is angry with you, and will surely punish you, if you don't forsake your wicked ways. You that live in town are eye-servants behind your master's back. Instead of serving your masters faithfully, which is pleasing in the sight of your heavenly Master, you are idle, and shirk your work. God sees you. You tell lies.

God hears you. Instead of being engaged in worshipping him, you are hidden away somewhere, feasting on your master's substance; tossing coffee-grounds with some wicked fortuneteller, or cutting cards with another old hag. Your masters may not find you out, but God sees you, and will punish you. O, the depravity of your hearts! When your master's work is done, are you quietly together, thinking of the goodness of God to such sinful creatures? No; you are quarrelling, and tying up little bags of roots to bury under the door-steps to poison each other with. God sees you. You men steal away to every grog shop to sell your master's corn, that you may buy rum to drink. God sees you. You sneak into the back streets, or among the bushes, to pitch coppers. Although your masters may not find you out, God sees you; and he will punish you. You must forsake your sinful ways, and be faithful servants. Obey your old master and your young master—your old mistress and your young mistress. If you disobey your earthly master, you offend your heavenly Master.[29]

Charlie Van Dyke, also a former slave, expressly stated that "Church was what they called it but all that preacher talked about was for us slaves to obey our masters and not to lie and steal. Nothing about Jesus was ever said and the overseer stood there to see the preacher talked as he wanted him to talk."[30]

The texts ascribed to Paul and used by masters as tools of slave control (Ephesians 6:5-9; Colossians 3:22-24; 1 Timothy 6:1-2; Titus 2:9-10) were not actually written by the apostle. As many as six of the thirteen New Testament letters attributed to Paul were actually written by his companions and admirers. These are 2 Thessalonians, Ephesians, Colossians, 1 and 2 Timothy, and Titus. Only seven letters, judged undisputedly to be authentic Pauline letters, give us primary source material. Therefore, it is a slander to place Paul on the side of the slavocracy. In fact, when Paul does mention slaves, he does so affirmingly. For example, in 1 Corinthians 7:20-21, Paul says, "Everyone should remain in the state in which he was called. Were you a slave when called? Never mind. *But if you gain your freedom avail yourself of the opportunity*" (emphasis mine).[31] What this passage implies is that though Paul advises Christians to suspend all general plans since there are only a few remaining days, he finds the attainment of human freedom important enough to make it an exception to his prescriptive ethic. Marriage, divorce, circumcision, funerals, and business can all wait. However, it is not so with human freedom. Paul almost included it in the list of things to be put off, but he catches himself: "Well, never mind; but if you do have a chance to become a free man, use it" (v. 21, TEV).

So how did Paul come to be viewed with a hermeneutic of suspicion and skepticism in the African American community? This question, seemingly simple, points to an embittered history of Black pain and torture. On the one hand, it is quite easy to answer it by saying that the eisegetical renderings of the slaveholders painted a portrait of Paul that was antagonistic to how slaves valued themselves as embodied, sacred selves. On the other hand, it is a bit more disturbing and difficult to offer a solution that points to the absence of liberation in the analysis of the gospel.[32]

The apostle Paul emerged from slavery with a tainted identity. However, careful exegesis and nontendentious reading prove that the gospel of Jesus Christ preached by Paul was not entangled by the strictures of dehumanizing, oppressive, and racialized rhetoric. His pedagogy, directed toward development "in Christ," was pointed, urgent, and framed by his hope in the impending *Parousia*. Although Paul believed he was living in the "end times," he nonetheless found the liberty of persons from the throes of servitude and bondage of utmost importance. Therefore, as the African American community struggles for an agenda of Black liberation and wholeness, Paul's work, in many ways, does indeed provide liberating power and direction to that end.

The Eschatological Hope of Paul

Eschatology, derived from the Greek words *eschaton* ("last") and *logos* ("word" or "account"), pertains to teachings about the end times. It is the aspect of theological reflection concerned with the consummation of history. Paul describes himself as "one upon whom the end of ages has come," and sees the present as the juncture that not only exists because of the cross of Christ (1 Corinthians 1:17-18), but will also end at the coming of Christ from heaven (1 Thessalonians 2:19; 3:13; 4:13-18; 1 Corinthians 15:23-28).

Therefore, Paul's revelation of the Christ gave him a new vision of salvation history. Before the call, Paul saw human history divided into three distinct periods: (1) from Adam to Moses (the period without the law); (2) from Moses to the Messiah (the period of the law); and (3) the messianic age (the period when the law would be fulfilled). Paul's encounter with Christ led him to believe that the messianic age had already begun; it thus introduced a new perspective in salvation history:

> The eschaton, "endtime," so avidly awaited before, had already started (1 Cor. 10:11), although a definitive stage of it was still to be realized (as was hoped not too far in the future). The Messiah had come, but not yet in glory. Paul realized that he (with all Christians) found himself in a double situation; one in which he looked back upon the death and resurrection of Jesus as the inauguration of the new age, and another in which he still looked forward to his coming in glory, his Parousia.[33]

The end times refer to the messianic age, the last period in Paul's scheme of salvation history. Intense tribulation and various cosmic phenomena characterize this era. Joel 2:30-31 narrates: "And I will give portents in the heavens and on earth, blood and fire and columns of smoke. The sun shall be turned to darkness, and the moon to blood, before the great and terrible day of the Lord comes." This time of conflict and upheaval predicts great signs and wonders, intense persecution, and warfare between God's people and their enemies.

However, when Christ comes in glory, he will consume history by demolishing all evil and inaugurating a new age—an era that marks the supernatural triumph of God over demonic powers and even death: "Then comes the end, when he delivers the kingdom to God the Father after destroying every rule and every authority and power. For he must reign until he has put all his enemies under his feet. The last enemy to be destroyed is death" (1 Corinthians 15:24-26).

The second coming of Christ, the *Parousia*, means "arrival," "coming," or "presence" in Greek and refers to the coming of Christ in glory to judge the world and to redeem his people. The first preserved tradition of "second coming" in relation to the return to earth of the resurrected Jesus is found in Justin Martyr's *Dialogue with Trypho* (chapter 14), from the middle of the second century.[34] Yet the Christian expectation of the return of Christ at the end of history is traceable to the earliest traditional material in the New Testament, primarily 1 Thessalonians and 1 Corinthians.

In his writings, Paul draws upon the established belief of the early church that Christ would come again. In 1 Corinthians 16:22, Paul writes, "If any one has no love for the Lord, let him be accursed. Our Lord, come!" The enthusiastic liturgical formula "Our Lord, come!" originates from the Greek word *maranatha* which is a transliteration into Greek of two Aramaic words. Scholars understand Paul to be using an expression (*maranatha*) from the worship of the oldest Christian community in Palestine, and in this utterance ("Our Lord, come!") one sees that the earliest Aramaic-speaking Christians strongly anticipated the second coming of Christ.

For Paul, the Son of God will come at the *eschaton*, conquer the powers of evil, and supernaturally usher in a new era. It is because this "present evil age," the epoch ruled by the gods of this world, will give way for "the age to come," the supernatural realm of the power of God, that Paul seemingly lives on the boundary of two worlds, one passing away and one being born. "It may be said," writes Herman Ridderbros,

> that in Paul a "mingling of the two ages" takes place and that the advent of Christ is to be viewed as the "breaking through of the future aeon in the present." For him the future has become present time, and even when he speaks of the groaning of the creation and of the church in the present world, that is for him not a reduction, but a confirmation of the coming redemption (Rom. 8:13).[35]

Paul's eschatological hope, then, is encompassed by his obsession with the end of the world and the inauguration of a new age:

> I mean, brethren, the appointed time has grown very short; from now on, let those who have wives live as though they had none, and those who mourn as though they were not mourning, and those who rejoice as though they were not rejoicing, and those who buy as though they had no goods, and those who deal with the world as though they had no dealings with it. For the form of this world is passing away (1 Corinthians 7:29-31).

Paul's experience with the risen Christ and his resulting eschatological hope shaped his whole outlook on life. His new vision not only paved the way for a new type of eschatological theology that is most clearly explicated through the church's doctrine of the resurrection of Christ, but also filled his followers with an anticipation for the divine and powerful intervention of God. In *New Testament Eschatology in an African Background*, John S. Mbiti observes that,

> Beginning with the Resurrection of Jesus Christ, there is a marked movement in the New Testament, and in the life of the Church, towards a crescendo at the Parousia. Paul puts more weight upon the Resurrection than upon all the other eschatological realities. The doctrine and belief in it vividly colour the life, expansion, and thinking of the early Church. It is only in the light of the Lord's Resurrection that we can understand our own resurrection, and can hope for it with great anticipation and certainty (cf. Acts 23:6, Rom. 6:4 f., 1 Cor. 6:14, 17, 15:20 ff., etc.). It is the Resurrection of Jesus Christ which validates that of his followers; it is also His Resurrection which promises and guarantees the realization of human and cosmic resurrection.[36]

Because of Paul's unwavering confidence that the end was near, his teaching was urgent and compelling: "But we shall all be changed, in a moment, in the twinkling of an eye, at the last trumpet" (1 Corinthians 15:51-52).

Resurrection, a development from first-century Jewish eschatological literature, is a rising to life from death. Paul sees the resurrection of Jesus as an act of God that results in a complete transformation: "It is sown a physical body, it is raised a spiritual body" (1 Corinthians 15:44). Like many others before him, Paul saw Jesus' resurrection as a victorious triumph of God over death and over the spirit-rulers of this world. Colossians 2:15 says, "He disarmed the principalities and powers and made a public example of them triumphing over them in him."

The resurrection of Jesus differs in one crucial respect from the prevalent first-century Jewish expectation. Jewish anticipation was for a corporate resurrection—all of God's elect would be vindicated at the end of time. The resurrection of Jesus does not diminish the eschatological savor of this anticipation, but it does relocate the hope drastically. The resurrection of Jesus—that which happens to one person—is recorded as a historical event that has eschatological significance. Therefore, not only is the resurrection of Jesus a transformation, but it is also, as demonstrated in slave spirituals, the immediate cause for the transformation of a resurrection hope from a corporate, eschatological event to a personal, historical event with corporate, eschatological implications.

The Eschatological Theology of the Slave Spirituals

An eschatological theology provides an excellent point at which the African American community can reinitiate dialogue with Paul, for the Christianity that enslaved Africans adopted was clearly eschatological in that it deferred the present time in hopes of a soon-coming better day:

> We'll soon be free,
> We'll soon be free,
> We'll soon be free,
>   When de Lord will call us home.
> My brudder, how long,
> My brudder, how long,
> My brudder, how long,
>   'Fore we done sufferin' here?
> It won't be long (thrice)
>   'Fore de Lord will call us home . . .
> We'll soon be free (thrice)
>   When Jesus sets me free.
> We'll fight for liberty (thrice)
>   When de Lord will call us home.[37]

The African American spiritual, the earliest or one of the earliest narrative representations of the African American populace, offers the most profound expression of Black eschatological theology. The spiritual not only serves as a religious classic for the study and construction of Black religion as eschatological theology, but it also provides insight into how the collective imagination of the slave community gave expression to a worldview shaped by human domination and exploitation. The African American spiritual, then, is a result of the African American folk community's nascent attempt to come to grips with its forced exile in the New World under the terms of the prevailing ideology of evangelical Christianity.

According to the nineteenth-century slave narrative *Memoir of Old Elizabeth, a Coloured Woman*, enslaved Christians were not allowed to hold meetings on the plantation.[38] Therefore, they often congregated in secluded areas aptly called "hush harbors." At these secret gatherings, bondwomen and -men would pray, sing, "get happy," and praise the Christian God in ways that expressed the religion the slaves called their own. Indeed, it was the freedom of religious expression at the "hush harbors" that gave birth to the African American spirituals. The spirituals emerged as communal songs with traditional African melodies and rhythms.

> Us ole heads use ter make 'em on de spurn of de moment, after we wressle wid de Spirit and come thoo. But the tunes was brung from African by our grandaddies. Dey was jis 'miliar song . . . dey calls 'em spirituals, case de Holy Spirit done revealed 'em to 'em. Some say Moss Jesus taught 'em, and I's seed 'em start in meetin'. We'd all be at the "prayer house" de Lord's Day, and de white preacher he'd splain de word and read whar Ezekiel done say—
> Dry bones gwine ter lib again.
> And, honey, de Lord would come a shining thoo dem pages and revive dis ole nigger's heart, and I'd jump up dar and den and holler and shout and sing and pat, and dey would all cotch de words . . . and dey's all take it up and keep at it, and keep a-addin' to it and den it would be a spiritual.[39]

The singing style of the slave songs, uniquely colored by a cultural background whose roots lay in Africa, was distinctly marked by repetition, call and response, body movements, syncopation, hand clapping, foot tapping, and note slides. This style with its attendant structures of meaning is infused with an intensely personal faith orientation that places emphasis on the desire for freedom. This style has linkages to an African past and forms bridges to the American evangelistic tradition that allowed for the formation of an African American eschatological tradition as exemplified by the spiritual.

Slave songs reverberate with the sense of freedom:

> As the great day [of emancipation] grew nearer, there was more singing in the slave quarters than usual. It was bolder, had more ring, and lasted later into the night. Most of the verses of the plantation songs had some reference to freedom. True, they had sung those same verses before, but they had been careful to explain that the "freedom" in these songs referred to the next world, and had no connection with life in this world. Now they gradually threw off the mask; and were not afraid to let it be known that the "freedom" in their songs meant freedom of the body in this world.[40]

Freedom, an eschatological motif that embraces the dualistic notions of heaven and hell, good and evil, present and future, becomes a metaphor that expresses the dawn of a new time. It marks the demise of the dehumanizing stronghold of the slavocracy and ushers in a new age of human ennoblement and peace.

Many spirituals created by our enslaved ancestors are still sung in the Black Church today. These slave songs are timeless not only because they are the vocal expression of the Black woman's and man's faith and courage, but also because a religious style that emphasizes the ever-persevering struggle for freedom resists the bonds of oppression. This timelessness, which gave birth to a legacy of faith even in the cruel and embittered context of chattel slavery, is what makes the African American spiritual a liberating trope of an eschatological theology.

So, the African American spiritual, a narrative production of African cultural expression, remains central to an understanding of the American past and present. It parallels the writings of the apostle Paul in that both, seeking to make sense of their particular realities, present motifs of urgency, faith, and obedience—themes that reflect a classic and empowering eschatological perspective. For us, then, the survival of this eschatological tradition is not only the rattle of the bones of the ancestors, but the overflowing in us of a mighty river whose living water sustains and strengthens us.

Notes

1. During slavery, each slave state had a slave code. These codes were enacted not only to maintain discipline and to provide safeguards against slave rebellions, but also to establish the property rights of slaveholders. Fundamentally, the slave codes, barring a few differences in the severity of punishment in the Deep South and the Upper South, were much alike. Kenneth M. Stampp contends, in *The Peculiar Institution: Slavery in the Ante-bellum South* (New York: Vintage Books, 1989), that at the heart of every regulatory slave law was the requirement that slaves submit to their masters and respect all White people. As early as 1712, the South Carolina legislature passed a law which forbade the teaching of slaves to read or write under penalty of imprisonment, physical punishment, or monetary fine. The enactment of this law was the immediate cause for the passage of similar codes in Georgia, Louisiana, North Carolina, Tennessee, Kentucky, and Mississippi.

2. Vincent Wimbush, "Biblical Historical Study as Liberation: Toward an Afro-Christian Hermeneutic," *Journal of Religious Thought*, 42, no. 2 (Fall-Winter, 1984-1985), 10-11.

3. Howard Thurman, *Jesus and the Disinherited* (Nashville: Abingdon Press, 1949), 30-31.

4. Renita J. Weems asks, in the chapter "African American Women and the Bible," in Cain H. Felder's *Stony the Road We Trod: African American Biblical Interpretation* (Minneapolis: Fortress Press, 1991), how and why contemporary readers from marginalized communities continue to regard the Bible as a significant resource for shaping modern existence. She explores the rationale by which African American women, marginalized by gender, ethnicity, and often class, continue to regard the Bible as meaningful. By identifying the varying types of texts found in the Bible in terms of the voices and values of African American women, Weems challenges Black women to let their stories and lives dictate how they "read" the Bible. Her attempt to develop a critical hermeneutical method for dealing with African American women's issues provides a model for the way in which other problematic material in the Bible

(e.g., slavery, homosexuality, war, racism, and classism) can be assessed.

5. Black religious consciousness is the mind-set that considers preeminent the reality of Black suffering and the historical experience of Black people in a racist society. For a detailed discussion of the Black religious consciousness, see chapter 7 of C. Eric Lincoln and Lawrence H. Mamiya's *The Black Church in the African-American Experience* (Durham, NC: Duke University Press, 1990).

6. Tarsus, the major city and capital of Cilicia, situated in the northeastern section of the Mediterranean on the banks of the Cydnus River, was the birthplace and early residence of Paul. During the flourishing era of Greek history, Tarsus, "no mean city" (Acts 21:39, except where noted, the translation is the author's), was a place of commerce and of great cultural importance. Tarsus prospered under Alexander the Great, and as a member of the Seleucid Kingdom, it was under the rule of the Ptolemies for a period of time. However, in the civil war of Rome, Tarsus joined allegiance with Caesar, and Augustus made it a free city. Tarsus was a thriving industrial city. Therefore, many of the philosophies and religions prevalent throughout the Greco-Roman world were greatly varied. Mystery cults thrived there, and everywhere a process was afoot of syncretizing the old religions with the new ones. Religiously and philosophically, Tarsus and the entire late classical world was in a state of profound confusion.

Paul was born a citizen of Rome (Acts 21:39). As a Roman citizen, Paul had a forename (praenomen), a family name (nomen gentile), and an additional name (cognomen). Of these three names we know only his cognomen, Paullus. If we knew his nomen gentile, we might have some clue to the circumstances of the family's acquisition of citizenship, since new citizens usually assumed their patron's family name. Even though the circumstances in which Paul's family acquired Roman citizenship are obscure, New Testament scholars Wayne A. Meeks, Luke T. Johnson, Norman Perrin, and Dennis C. Duling contend that Paul more than likely inherited his citizenship from his father or some other ancestor who had done meritorious service for the Romans.

On more than one occasion—for example, at Philippi and some time later at Jerusalem—Paul appeals to his rights as a Roman citizen. The former time, he protested at having been beaten with rods by the lictors, attendants of the chief magistrates of Philippi, without being given a proper trial: "But Paul said to them, 'They have beaten us publicly, uncondemned, men who are Roman citizens, and have thrown us into prison; and do they now cast us out secretly? No! Let them come themselves and take us out" (Acts 16:37). On the second occasion, he invoked his rights in order to be spared a scourging for instigating a riotous outburst among the Jerusalem populace:

> But when they had tied him up with the thongs, Paul said to the centurion who was standing by, "Is it lawful for you to scourge a man who is a Roman citizen, and uncondemned?" When the centurion heard that, he went to the tribune and said to him, "What are you about to do? For this man is a Roman citizen." So the tribune came and said to him, "Tell me are you a Roman citizen?" And he said "Yes." The tribune answered, "I bought this citizenship for a large sum." Paul said, "But I was born a citizen." (Acts 22:25-28)

Even though Paul appeals to the rights and privileges of his Roman citizenship in these two situations, the loyalty of his parentage to the ancestral faith remains a mark of pride. Of himself Paul passionately boasts, "Are they Hebrews? So am I. Are they Israelites? So am I. Are they descendants of Abraham? So am I" (2 Corinthians 11:22): "And I advanced in Judaism beyond many of my own age among my people, so extremely zealous was I for the traditions of my fathers" (Galatians 1:14).

7. It was very common for first-century Jews who lived outside Palestine to have two names. Known as Saul in the Aramaic-speaking community, the apostle was most frequently called Paul, the Roman form of his name. In his writings the apostle calls himself Paulos, the name also used in 2 Peter 3:15 and from Acts 13:9 on. Prior to that in Acts he is called Saulos (e.g., 7:58; 8:1, 2; 9:1), the Greek form of Saoul. The latter spelling is found only in the Conversion Accounts (Acts 9:4,17; 22:7, 13; 26:14) and stands for the Hebrew Sa'ul, the name of the first king of ancient Israel (e.g., 1 Samuel 9: 2, 17; cf. Acts 13:21).

8. The scriptural translations are the author's, except where noted. Paul was a Pharisaic Jew of the Diaspora, the community of Jews who lived outside Palestine. The Pharisees were a Jewish religious party that flourished from the middle of the second century B.C.E. to the second destruction of the Temple in 70 C.E. One of the three major sects of Judaism (the other two were Sadducees and Essenes), the Pharisees were middle-class "laymen" who were committed to obeying the written and oral traditions of the Mosaic law (the Pentateuch, or the Five Books of Moses) as it was interpreted by the scribes. For a more careful discussion, see Shaye J. D. Cohen, *From the Maccabees to the Mishnah*, vol. 7, Library of Early Christianity (Louisville: John Knox Press, 1987); Peter J. Tomson, *Paul and the Jewish Law*, vol. 1, Halakha in the Letters of the Apostle to the Gentiles Series, Jewish Traditions in Early Christian Literature (Minneapolis: Fortress Press, 1990); Alan F. Segal, *Paul the Convert: The Apostolate and Apostasy of Saul the Pharisee* (New Haven: Yale University Press, 1990); and E. P. Sanders, *Paul and Palestinian Judaism: A Comparison of Patterns of Religion* (Minneapolis: Augsburg Fortress Publishers, 1977).

9. Acts is a secondary source and can be used only as a supplement to the primary Pauline materials. As problematic evidence, it can be used to verify the church's witness but must be used cautiously as testimony to the authentic Pauline letters. See Stanley B. Marrow, *Paul, His Letters and Theology: An Introduction to Paul's Epistles* (New York: Paulist Press, 1986); and Joseph A. Fitzmyer, *Paul and His Theology: A Brief Sketch*, 2d ed. (Englewood Cliffs, NJ: Prentice Hall, 1989).

10. See Dennis Ronald MacDonald, *The Legend and the Apostle* (Philadelphia: Westminster Press, 1983).

11. Wayne A. Meeks, *The Writings of St. Paul* (New York: Norton, 1972), xiii.

12. Charles C. Jones, *The Religious Instruction of Negroes in the United States* (Savannah: T. Purse Co., 1842), 126.

13. There are seven undisputed, authentic Pauline Epistles. They are Romans, 1 and 2 Corinthians, Galatians, 1 Thessalonians, Philippians, and Philemon. These letters are said to be authentic not only because of the agreement they show in content, vocabulary, modes of argumentation, epistolary form, literary style, theology, and sequence of events, but also primarily because they reflect the thought of the often contradictory but ever resilient apostle Paul.

14. Meeks, *The Writings of St. Paul*, xiv.

15. Latta R. Thomas, *Biblical Faith and the Black American* (Valley Forge: Judson Press, 1976). For candid discussions on the role of the Bible in the African Ameri-

230 C. MICHELLE VENABLE-RIDLEY

can community, see Cain H. Felder, *Stony the Road We Trod* and *Troubling Biblical Waters: Race, Class, and the Family* (Maryknoll, N.Y.: Orbis Books, 1988); Dwight N. Hopkins, *Shoes That Fit Our Feet: Sources for a Constructive Black Theology* (Maryknoll, N.Y.: Orbis Books, 1993); Emilie M. Townes, ed., *A Troubling in My Soul: Womanist Perspectives on Evil and Suffering* (Maryknoll, N.Y.: Orbis Books, 1993); Riggins R. Earl Jr., *Dark Symbols, Obscure Signs: God, Self, and Community in the Slave Mind* (Maryknoll, N.Y.: Orbis Books, 1993); and Lincoln and Mamiya, *The Black Church in the African-American Experience.*

16. Henry George Liddell and Robert Scott, *An Intermediate Greek-English Lexicon* (Oxford: Clarendon Press, 1988), 107.

17. Paul's call was not without preparation. As a Jew he was influenced by speculation about the future and looked forward to the coming of the Messiah. As a persecutor of the Christian church, Paul had heard the message of the disciples and had been impressed by their perseverance. Paul never explains his opposition to Christianity; however, after his call, Paul does not reject Judaism but, rather, combines the features of his Jewish nature with Christian principles. On several occasions he can and does speak about his past with pride, as he does in Galatians (1:14), Philippians (3:4-11), and 2 Corinthians (11:21-22). Indeed, in reflecting upon his Jewish past, Paul is able to consider it a former gain that is now a loss (Philippians 3:7-8). Furthermore, there is no evidence that Paul the Jew had a painful consciousness of sin; in fact, he is able to say that he was "blameless" in his Jewish life under the law.

In the New Testament, the word "conversion" or *metanoia* literally means "to repent," "to turn," or "to return." *The Greek-English Lexicon of the New Testament* (Johannes P. Louw and Eugene A. Nida, eds., vol. 1, 1988) says that *metanoia* means "to change one's way of life as the result of a complete change of thought and attitude with regard to sin and righteousness." Implied in this word is a complete change of course or direction. Therefore, inherent in the definition of "conversion" is the sense of one turning his or her back on an old situation to readily confront a new one. Conversely, the word "call" or *kaleo,* which implies a divine summons to a special vocation in God's plan of salvation, means "to urgently invite someone to accept responsibilities for a particular task, implying a new relationship to the one who does the calling." There is no sense of turning here, but rather a commission to come forth. *The Theological Dictionary of the New Testament* (Gerhard Kittel, ed., vol. 3, 1965) suggests that "the fact that God is the 'kalon' and that Christians are the 'keklaemenoi,' with no qualifying addition, makes it clear that in the New Testament 'kalein' is a technical term for the process of salvation."

The apostle's encounter with the resurrected Christ was not a conversion, it was a call. After becoming a Christian, Paul did not reject his Jewish past, for he was committed to Torah both before and after his encounter with the risen *Kyrios.* John G. Gager maintains that there was a "reversal or transvaluation of values" that led to a new understanding of himself as an apostle of the gospel to the gentiles.

Krister Stendahl, maintaining that the nature of Paul's commitment to Torah radically changed *but did not end,* argues also that Paul was called, not converted. Noting that there was a great continuity between "before" and "after," Stendahl observes that this instance does not involve the change of religion that is usually associated with the word "conversion."

However, Alan F. Segal, relying on Jewish material of Paul's time and on modern studies of conversion, suggests that Paul was both converted and called. In modern usage, the word "conversion" denotes moving from one sect or denomination to another within the same religion, if the change is radical. From the vantage point of mission, Paul is commissioned, but in terms of religious experience, Paul is a convert.

Paul's conversion experience is presented in the form of a call narrative, like that of the prophets (Jeremiah 1:4-10). This is seen from his most extensive account (Galatians 1:11-17), where the encounter involves two primary elements: the revelation of Jesus as God's Son and the commission to proclaim him to the gentiles. The Book of Acts recounts the conversion three times (9:1-19; 22:12-16; 26:4-18). These narratives emphasize supernatural occurrences: light and voices from heaven, and Paul's blindness; and recovery. For Paul, one thing is crucial: he saw the risen Christ (1 Corinthians 15:8); the Lord appeared to him (1 Corinthians 9:1). This vision not only led to the conviction that the crucified Jesus was the Messiah, but it also showed that the events of the end of history had started to unfold, that in these last days God was accomplishing his divine purpose through the crucified Christ, as power working in weakness (2 Corinthians 12:9).

While journeying to Damascus to persecute more Christians, Paul has an unexpected, revelatory experience with the *Christos*: "As I made my journey and drew near to Damascus, about noon a great light from heaven suddenly shone about me. And I fell to the ground and heard a voice saying to me, 'Saul, Saul, why do you persecute me?' " (Acts 9:3-4). This encounter, so profound and engaging, not only radically redirects his life, but also transforms him from a religious persecutor of Christianity to a persecuted advocate of the Christian faith.

By means of his experience with the risen Christ, Paul was able to look at the historical events which led to the birth of the Christian church from the inside. Those particular events he had initially regarded from the outside, for the church had already been in existence for probably three or four years when he became a Christian. What he gives us is an interpretation, in light of his encounter with the *Christos*, of a series of events in which he now saw a saving act of God, and which, so regarded, gave him a key to all history as divinely ordered.

18. Joseph Holzner, *Paul of Tarsus* (St. Louis: Herder Book Co., 1944), 43.

19. Norman Perrin and Dennis C. Duling, *The New Testament* (New York: Harcourt Brace Jovanovich, 1982), 197.

20. Fitzmyer, *Paul and His Theology*, 39.

21. See Arland J. Hultgren, *Paul's Gospel and Mission* (Philadelphia: Fortress Press, 1985), 4.

22. For an "alternative vision and Pauline modification" of Galatians 3:28, see chapter 6 of Elisabeth Schüssler Fiorenza's *In Memory of Her: A Feminist Theological Reconstruction of Christian Origins* (New York: Crossroad, 1990).

23. Earl, *Dark Symbols, Obscure Signs*, 22.

24. The so-called curse of Ham is one of the primary theological justifications for the enslavement of persons of African descent. In Genesis 9:18-27, Ham sees the nakedness of his drunken father, Noah. In an act of great shamelessness and filial disrespect, he leaves his father uncovered and goes to tell his brothers, Shem and Japheth, of Noah's condition. The two brothers go to their father and with filial reverence cover up his nakedness. Accordingly, then, Noah blesses Shem and Japheth and curses Ham. Ham and his descendants are damned to be slaves,

"hewers of wood and drawers of water."

According to Felder's, *Stony the Road We Trod*, the original narrative of Ham's error was reinterpreted in a fifth-century (C.E.) Midrash in which Noah says to Ham, "You have prevented me from doing something in the dark, therefore your seed will be ugly and dark-skinned." *Midrash Bereshith Rabbah* (London: 1939), 1:293, cited in Felder, 132; and Gene Rice, "The Curse That Never Was (Genesis 9:18-27)," *Journal of Religious Thought* 29, no. 1 (May 1980). Similarly, the Babylonian Talmud (sixth century C.E.) states that "the descendants of Ham are cursed by being Black and are sinful with a degenerate progeny." Ephraim Isaac, "Genesis, Judaism and the 'Sons of Ham,' " *Slavery and Abolition: A Journal of Comparative Studies* 1, no. 1 (May 1989). Into the seventeenth century the idea persisted that the blackness of Africans was due to a curse, and the idea reinforced and sanctioned the enslavement of blacks.

25. As did many of their theological forefathers, White slaveholders of the antebellum South manipulated and skewed Paul and his gospel to serve their own oppressive purposes. In the sixteenth century, the Protestant reformer Martin Luther told peasants, by means of scriptural manipulation and ecclesial authority, not to rise in opposition to their oppressions. "But when the uprising broke out, and the peasants took up arms, Luther tried to persuade them to follow a more peaceful course, and finally called on the princes to suppress the movement." Justo L. Gonzalez, *The Story of Christianity*, vol. 2 (San Francisco: Harper and Row, 1984). The theological tradition of spiritually emasculated clergy who urged the oppressed to be content, even happy, with their oppression was initiated long before the advent of the slavocracy, but it assumed embittered and cruel connotations in the context of chattel slavery.

26. Jones, *The Religious Instruction of Negroes in the United States,* 165.

27. Earl, *Dark Symbols, Obscure Signs*, 38.

28. Quoted in John B. Cade, "Out of the Mouths of Ex-Slaves," *Journal of Negro History* 20 (July 1935), 329.

29. Harriet A. Jacobs, *Incidents in the Life of a Slave Girl Written by Herself* (1861; Cambridge: Harvard University Press, 1987), 69.

30. Quoted in Albert J. Raboteau, *Slave Religion* (Oxford: Oxford University Press, 1978), 213-214.

31. Slavery was entrenched in the social order of Paul's world. Christian leaders did nothing to annul it. When Christian slaves in an Asian church community began to suggest that their freedom should be purchased from community funds, Ignatius of Antioch advised strongly against the proposal. He feared that they would become "slaves to lust" (Ign., Polyc. 4.3). Many of the church fathers advocated the principle of the equality of all humans, yet they argued that worldly distinctions of status should remain undisturbed.

As the church developed within the Roman Empire, it took for granted the persistence of slavery. During the early years of its formation, the church was powerless to change the institutions of the Empire and, in view of its eschatological expectations, hardly thought of doing so. Once the church became established, it transferred its revolutionary impulses to otherworldly expectations and sought to ameliorate rather than overturn prevailing social institutions. The church itself, adopting pagan practices, became a slaveholder. Augustine declared that slavery was a result of sin—a radical departure from Aristotle's teaching that some people were born to be slaves. But this doctrine had the effect of conditioning

Christians to expect the persistence of slavery until the distant consummation of the kingdom of God.

32. The willful misinterpretation of the biblical message is a symptom of a cancerous human malady. It not only points to the imbalance and fundamental conflict between faith and truth—that is, the basic discontinuity between theory and praxis—but it also relegates the Black identity to anonymity and irrelevance by racializing the gospel of Jesus Christ that Paul was committed to preaching.

33. Fitzmyer, *Paul and His Theology*, 31.

34. Justin Martyr, *Justin Martyr, the Dialogue with Trypho* (New York: Macmillan, 1930), chapter 14.

35. Herman A. Ridderbros, *Paul: An Outline of His Theology* (Grand Rapids, MI: Eerdmans, 1975), 53.

36. John S. Mbiti, *New Testament Eschatology in an African Background* (London: Oxford University Press, 1971), 163-164.

37. Quoted in Raboteau, *Slave Religion*, 248.

38. *Memoir of Old Elizabeth, A Coloured Woman* (Philadelphia: Collins, 1863).

39. Quoted in Jeannette Robinson Murphy, "The Survival of African Music in America," *Popular Science Monthly* 55 (1899), 660-672, reprinted in Bruce Jackson, ed., *The Negro and His Folklore*, 328-329.

40. Booker T. Washington, *Up from Slavery* (New York, 1901), reprinted in *Three Negro Classics* (New York: Avon Books, 1965), 39.

15

Daring to Speak

Womanist Theology and Black Sexuality

Kelly Brown Douglas

Renee Hill, a self-identified lesbian and womanist theologian, has boldly recognized that womanist theologians have imprudently ignored the issue of sexuality. Hill says:

> Christian womanists have failed to recognize heterosexism and homophobia as points of oppression that need to be resisted if all Black women . . . are to have liberation and a sense of their own power. Some womanists have avoided the issue of sexuality and sexual orientation by being selective in appropriating parts of [Alice] Walker's definition of womanism. This tendency to be selective implies that it is possible to be selective about who deserves liberation and visibility.[1]

In *The Black Christ* I have also acknowledged womanist theologians' failure to engage sexuality issues, as well as our tendency to ignore that part of Walker's womanist definition which clearly refers to a womanist as one who "loves other women, sexually and/or nonsexually."[2] When this reference was noted by a womanist religious scholar, it was done so for the purpose of denouncing gay/lesbian lifestyles. Womanist ethicist Cheryl Sanders argued against the appropriateness of the womanist nomenclature for Christian theological and ethical discourse, primarily because of its inclination to "affirm and/or advocate homosexual practices."[3] What is going on? Why is even womanist theology—a theology which is touted by some as providing one of the most holistic visions for human life and freedom—so hesitant to address sexuality concerns? Why are womanists, who so aptly criticize Black male and feminist theologians for their failure to

234

comprehend the complexity of Black women's oppression, so disinclined to confront heterosexism?

Because our theological concerns emerge not in a vacuum but from life experience, I need to clarify, before I continue, why the issue of homophobia/heterosexism and the failure of womanist theology to deal with this problem concerns me. Over the last several years I have lost no less than fifteen friends and acquaintances to AIDS. I ministered to and/or did the funerals for a number of these persons. No loss had greater impact upon my life and theology than when my longest and closest friend, Lloyd, succumbed to complications from AIDS. It was through my relationship with Lloyd that I really began to understand the alienation that Black AIDS survivors, especially gay survivors, feel in relation to the Black church community. His death changed the direction of my theological explorations. Initially I intended to explore "right relationships" between Black women and men. But one day, in the middle of delivering a lecture on that topic, I was struck by something deep within me that, for the sake of Lloyd and others like him, moved me to broaden my theological discussion. From that moment on, I have felt compelled to break the theological silence concerning the profound heterosexism/homophobia present within the Black church and community.

Black churches have gained a reputation for being slow in constructively responding to the AIDS crisis. Though AIDS has become the number one killer of Black men between the ages of twenty-five and forty, Black churches have appeared reticent to become involved in HIV/AIDS education and outreach programs. Some Black churches have been hostile in their treatment of those living with HIV and AIDS. In spite of evidence that suggests otherwise, too many in the Black church community continue to consider AIDS a "gay" disease. The AIDS crisis, therefore, has brought stridently to the surface the homophobia present in the Black church communities.

Many Black church people have unabashedly proclaimed that "they" (i.e., homosexuals with AIDS) had no business engaging in the sinful behaviors that would lead to AIDS. Some Black preachers have reminded their congregations that homosexuality is a sin and that, though we are to love the sinner, we must hate the sin. A pastor of one of the most prominent Baptist churches in Washington, D.C., is quoted as calling homosexuality an "abomination," though his church is reputed as "the place to be" among Black homosexuals. When asked about this apparent inconsistency, he responded, in reference to his gay parishioners, "If they don't know [my position], it is because they either can't read or can't hear."[4]

Because Lloyd was quite simply one of the best human beings I have ever had the pleasure of knowing, I could not quietly accept that Black churches had any cause to castigate him or label him an abomination. I did not understand how a church community that regularly boasts of its prophetic stance in relation to racial justice issues could be so unjust in its treatment of persons living with HIV/AIDS, particularly gay/lesbian persons. So I began to search for a word from God. I wondered what the God of Jesus Christ might be saying to the Black church community as we face the challenges of AIDS, and, more pointedly, what might God be saying to us in relation to the matters of sexuality, that is, homosexuality, that the AIDS crisis has caused to surface.

I began my theological reflection by turning to see if womanist theologians had begun to critically respond to Black churches' homophobia/ heterosexism. I was jolted by our theological silence. Were we content to join the ranks of "Black feminist" writers who in the past have been criticized for ignoring Black lesbian concerns?[5] Where were our prophetic theological voices? How could we expect Black churches to respond effectively to the AIDS crisis if their theologians were avoiding and ignoring attendant matters? These concerns bring me to this essay. This essay represents the preliminary stages of my efforts to break the silence. It will explore why womanist theologies have not effectively dealt with matters of sexuality and why these theologies must do so.

Why Have We Been Silent?

If who we are, that is, our life experience, helps to determine our theological questions and concerns, then it also circumscribes those questions and concerns. Our social, historical, cultural and political particularities can free us to address certain problems, or they can prevent us from doing so. What does this mean theologically? It means that theological silence in relation to a certain crisis is not necessarily God's silence. Perhaps more significantly, a particular theological response is not necessarily God's response. A response or even a lack of response is often more reflective of the theologian than it is of God.

I believe that God's revelation does have meaning and significance in relation to issues of sexuality (i.e., heterosexism/homophobia) as they affect the Black community—in spite of the virtual silence of womanist (and Black) theologians on these matters. So again, why have these theologians tended to ignore and avoid matters of sexuality? Perhaps our silence reflects our history as Black people. Paula Giddings aptly notes, "It is [African Americans'] historical experience that has shaped or, perhaps more accurately, misshaped the sex/gender issues and discourse in our community."[6]

The Black historical experience is indeed one that has rendered sexuality effectively a taboo issue in the Black community. Cornel West observes that historically, Black institutions such as families, schools and churches have refused "to engage one fundamental issue: Black sexuality. Instead, they [run] from it like the plague. And they obsessively [condemn] those places where black sexuality [is] flaunted: the streets, clubs, and the dance halls."[7] Giddings broadens the observation by noting that discourse which includes gender *and* sexuality is "the last taboo in the Black community."[8]

To be sure, the Black community, like the White community, has inherited Victorian standards and has been influenced by the contemporary "religious right" in ways which make public sexual discourse an uncomfortable and uneasy topic. But there appears to be an even greater "dis-ease" with Black sexuality for both Whites and Blacks. This "dis-ease," in large measure, stems from the complex nature of Black oppression, that is, from White supremacy/White racism. West affirms the inextricable link between racism and sexuality when he says, "It is virtually impossible to talk candidly about race without talking about sex."[9]

White Racism and the Vilification of Black Sexuality

The denigration and exploitation of Black sexuality have been the fuel for White racism. If French philosopher Michel Foucault is correct in his analysis of sexuality, the vilification of Black sexuality in a White racist society is inevitable. Because sexuality is the "axis" where the human body and reproduction come together, Foucault argues that it is one of the primary tools of power. He suggests that to secure and maintain power over a population of people requires the regulation of their bodies and reproductive capacities. Such regulation can be achieved through the conscientious deployment of sexuality, primarily through sexual discourse. Foucault explains: "The deployment of sexuality has its reason for being, not in reproducing itself, but in proliferating, innovating, annexing, creating, and penetrating bodies in an increasingly detailed way, and in controlling populations in an increasingly comprehensive way."[10] Foucault further argues that sexuality, as an instrument of power, is an essential tool by which distinctions can be made between classes and groups of people. Indicting people for possessing a depraved and bestial sexuality provides justification for treating them inhumanly. Essentially, to impugn the sexuality of another bolsters one's own claims to superiority, while also (as will be shown later) controlling another's sexual discourse.

An insidious attack upon the sexuality of Africans and other non-European peoples was certainly a device used by the White European intruders into Africa and America. Historiographers John D'Emilio and Estelle Freedman point out:

> Ever since the seventeenth century, European migrants to America had merged racial and sexual ideology in order to differentiate themselves from Indians and blacks, to strengthen the mechanisms of social control over slaves and to justify the appropriation of Indian and Mexican lands through the destruction of native peoples and their cultures. In the nineteenth century, sexuality continued to serve as a powerful means by which white Americans maintained dominance over people of other races.[11]

With the earliest intrusion of Europeans into Africa, myths were generated about African peoples' libidinous and lustful nature. Perhaps because Europeans, particularly the English, encountered apes and Africans at the same time, their slanderous myths easily equated the sexual habits of apes with those of Africans. One fifteenth-century writer on the subject advanced that "men that have low and flat nostrils, [i.e., the Africans] are Libidinous as Apes that attempt women."[12] Even more perverse myths developed as English intruders into Africa alleged sexual activity between apes and Africans. As scholar Winthrop Jordan properly notes, "By forging a sexual link between Negroes and apes . . . Englishmen were able to give vent to their feelings that Negroes were lewd, lascivious and wanton people."[13]

While sexual denigration was aimed at both Black women and men, particular gender-specific stereotypes emerged to further support the most preposterous lie—the inherent supremacy of White men and women. Black women were highly sexualized beings, according to the ideology of White racism. Their passions were uncontrollable, and their sexual appetite was insatiable. Their sexual behavior defied standards of decency. White racist doctrine regarded Black women as "Jezebels" "governed almost entirely by their libidos."[14] One southern female contributor to a popular nineteenth-century periodical exemplifies such beliefs:

> Degeneracy is apt to show most in the weaker individuals of any race; so negro women evidence more nearly the popular idea of total depravity than the men do. They are so nearly lacking in virtue that the color of a negro woman's skin is generally taken (and quite correctly) as a guarantee of her immortality . . . And they are evidently the chief instruments of the degradation of the men of their race . . . I sometimes read of a virtuous negro woman, hear of them, but the idea is absolutely inconceivable to me . . . I cannot imagine such a creation as a virtuous black woman.[15]

The "debased" Black woman served as a perfect foil for the Victorian image of the chaste White woman. It provided White men with justification for "protecting" the innocence of "their" women by placing them on a pedestal and relegating them to the home, out of harm's way. The widely accepted notion that Black women were completely without virtue also permitted White men to sexually abuse and rape Black women with impunity. And, most insidiously, the claims that Black women were sexual reprobates provided the fundamental proof of Black men's sexual perversion. Black women were deemed responsible for the depravity of the entire Black race.

As suggested in the preceding comments by the southern female writer, Black women were blamed for the lascivious and bestial nature of Black men. According to the "tenets" of White racism, it was impossible for Black men to possess any capacity for sexual propriety not only because of their blackness, but also because they were raised by morally depraved women. White racist theory went on to suggest that Black men, by necessity, harbored a "savage" and lewd sexual drive so as to satisfy the ravenous sexual needs of Black women. This insipid thinking culminated in the depiction of Black men as sexual predators and rapists of White women. Racist ideology suggested that Black men lusted after White women because these men longed to experience that which Black women could not provide—female virtue and purity. Giddings describes one nineteenth-century writer as suggesting that "it was the white women's qualities, so profoundly missing in black women, that made black men find white women irresistible and 'strangely alluring and seductive.' "[16] This portrait of Black men as rapacious provided an excuse for the thousands of lynchings that took place during the nineteenth century, as lynching was purportedly the punishment for those (Black men) who threatened in any way the chastity of White women.

While these fraudulent myths concerning Black women and men helped to justify African enslavement and White superiority, they also forged a culture of White fear of, yet fascination with, Black sexuality. The fear is evidenced by the type of legal and extralegal methods used to prevent "miscegenation" and to keep Black people in their place as slaves of society, even after chattel slavery ended. These methods, such as castration, lynching, and rape, were all sexual assaults upon Black bodies. The White fascination with Black sexuality is exemplified by the many studies of Black sexuality which appeared during the eighteenth and nineteenth centuries and by the public displays made of Black genitalia, especially the genitalia of Black women.[17]

That this White culture of fear and fascination continues to be vibrant, even while it exploits Black sexuality, is quite evident. It was exposed by the unnecessary public spectacle the United States Congress and mass media made of Anita Hill and Clarence Thomas during Thomas's confirmation hearings for the Supreme Court. Throughout the hearings, which were broadcast from gavel to gavel on every major television network, White Americans acted as voyeurs into the sexual behavior of two Black people. Many White Americans were no doubt able to confirm their deep-seated beliefs in Black people's sexual deviance as White male senators "dutifully" extracted from Hill every vulgar detail of Thomas's sexual harassment. The stereotypes of Jezebel Black women and rapacious Black men were "verified" for White America on national television by a select Senate committee.[18]

The circus-like attraction to the O. J. Simpson trial, as well as the curious judicial example made of Simpson, further evidences the prevalence of a White culture of fear and fascination in regard to Black sexuality. For many White Americans, it seemed that Simpson's guilt or innocence was less a factor than making clear that he, as a Black man, would have to pay the price for being sexually involved with a White woman, let alone for abusing and killing her. The specter of race and sex pervaded the entire, internationally broadcast Simpson fiasco.

Most insidiously, some of the theories concerning the origins of AIDS also reveal the pathology of White culture that surrounds Black sexuality. Giddings poignantly notes:

> That respectable journals would make connections between green monkeys and African women, for example, or trace the origins of AIDS to African prostitutes—the polluted sexual organs of Black women— reveals our continued vulnerability to racist ideology. It tells us that concepts of racial difference ... can still be used as weapons of degradation, and that the idea of difference turns on sexuality, and sexuality in this culture is loaded with concepts of race, gender, and class.[19]

Given the long history of White racist culture demeaning Black sexuality, how have Black people's responses to their own sexuality been affected?

The Impact of Racist Sexual Exploitation on Black People

Black sexuality, in its various expressions, is not simply a reaction to or a reflection of White racism. It exhibits the rich, complex mosaic of who Black people are. Black people did not come from Africa as blank slates. They came to America possessing a dynamic culture, intricate worldview and delicate patterns of relationships. They utilized this African heritage to carve out a reality and a culture in America which affirmed their humanity. Deborah Gray White, John Blassingame and others have noted that even under the tyranny of slavery, enslaved Black men and women maintained a strong sense of family and definite moral codes in regard to intimate relationships. The work of historians such as these has debunked notions of the absent slave family and slave promiscuity.[20]

It would be dishonest, however, to suggest that White racism has not had an impact on Black sexuality. It has. Its most penetrating impact has been upon Black sexual discourse. The Black church and community have been most reluctant to engage issues pertaining to sexuality. The fear that such discourse might only affirm the stereotype that Black people are obsessed with sexual matters no doubt inhibits the discussion. Likewise, a history of having their sexuality exploited and used as a weapon to support oppression also prevents the Black community from freely engaging with sexual concerns. Yet while the refusal to engage in sexual discourse has been a survival strategy, it has also functioned to foster attitudes, behaviors and structures within the Black church and community that threaten Black life and wholeness.[21]

Open and frank discourse can provide an opportunity for people to critically examine their attitudes and practices. Without that discourse, harmful perspectives may flourish unchecked and unexamined, eventually becoming the foundation for standard practices. So, while the Black community may believe that refraining from public discourse on sexuality protects the life and wholeness of Black women and men, it actually has had the opposite effect. Several examples will illustrate the point.

As Paula Giddings has noted, the Black community has yet to fully examine the disturbing findings of Leon Dash's book *When Children Want Children*. In this book, Dash examines the issue of teenage pregnancy. Through penetrating interviews with teenagers, he attempts to discern, among other things, what is behind the very high incidence of teenage pregnancy within the Black community. His findings are provocative and certainly worthy of sustained discourse and reflection. But significant segments of the Black community appear more concerned that Dash dared to publicly reveal his findings than they are about what he found.[22]

Even as many Black teenagers continue to engage in unprotected sex and as Black babies, at a rate disproportionate to the rest of society, continue to be born infected with the AIDS virus, candid discussion about sexuality and about ways of expressing one's sexuality is still avoided. Black church leaders have responded to the crisis of teenage pregnancy and unsafe sexual practices by simply telling teenagers to abstain from sexual intercourse. This is not an adequate response to such a complex issue. The sexual practices of many Black teenagers should compel Black community and church leaders to openly explore, with Black teens, healthy and life-enhancing ways for teens to express their sexuality. At the same time, Black community and church leaders need to find effective means to change the social conditions in which too many Black teenagers are trapped, that serve only to nurture life-threatening behaviors, sexual or otherwise.

The unwillingness to participate in sexual discourse also leaves unexamined male-female relationships and gender oppression within the Black community. The perceptions of what it means to be a man or to be a woman have been shaped by the ideology of a White patriarchal, racist culture. Unfortunately, these tainted perceptions of masculinity and femininity have too often interfered with Black male-female intimacy. Patricia Hill Collins explains:

> Much of the antagonism African-American women and men feel may stem from an unstated resentment toward Eurocentric gender ideology and against one another as enforcers of the dichotomous sex role inherent in the ideology. Eurocentric gender ideology objectifies both sexes so that when Black men see Black women as nothing more than mammies, matriarchs, or Jezebels, or even if they insist on placing African-American women on the same queenly pedestal reserved for white women, they objectify not only Black women but their own sexuality.[23]

By and large, the Black community has been reluctant to scrupulously explore the depth and intricacies of Black heterosexual relationships. When Black women, particularly literary artists, have ventured into this forbidden terrain, they have been attacked for "airing the dirty laundry" of the Black community.[24] Of course, it needs to be underscored that the attack upon these Black women is not simply because of the issue they have raised, but also because they are *women*. Again, even the gender oppression and misogyny virulently present within the Black church and community cannot be adequately addressed if the community is unwilling to participate in open and sustained discourse about Black sexuality. The multifarious nature of sexism is inextricably connected to matters of sexuality. To avoid sexual discourse is to circumvent a comprehensive analysis of Black male-female relationships as well as of gender oppression. To paraphrase Cornel West, it is virtually impossible to talk about relational and gender concerns without also talking about sex.

Finally, the issue which brought me to this discussion is homophobia/heterosexism. It is perhaps erroneously believed that the Black church and community are more homophobic and heterosexist than other communities. Recent research suggests that this is not likely the case.[25] However, given the Black community's own history as an oppressed people, it is highly objectionable that this community and church would self-righteously, and without shame, participate in another's oppression. They have done this in regard to gay and lesbian persons.

While the Black community was not willing to accept White racist biblical notions that Black people were a cursed and sinful people simply because they were Black, it has been far too amenable to notions that gay and lesbian persons are sinful abominations simply because of their sexual preference. As scientific and medical studies abounded to explain Black people's "affliction" of color, studies also abound to explain the "affliction" of homosexuality. Unwilling to accept such studies about themselves, far too many Black people utilize the findings of dubious studies on homosexuality to affirm their homophobic/heterosexist attitudes and practices. How is it that this hypocritical behavior has been able to exist with relative impunity within the Black community?

From a denial of the existence of homosexuality in the Black community to the belief that homosexuality is a European phenomenon somehow foisted upon African peoples, the Black church and community have avoided a profound discussion concerning homophobia/heterosexism. Why has this discussion been so particularly burdensome and not forthcoming?

In a White racist, patriarchal society, Black men and women are afforded very little privilege. If Black men enjoy male privilege in relationship to Black women, then Black women possess no privilege at all. Novelist Zora Neale Hurston's literary description of Black women as "the mule of the world" captures this point.[26] Yet sexuality provides a place of privilege for both Black women and men. In a White racist, patriarchal society, Black women and men can move to the center by seizing heterosexual privilege. They can marginalize instead of being marginalized. They thus oppress gays and lesbians by utilizing the very tool of power that has been used against them: sexuality. Barbara Smith explains, with particular reference to Black women: "None of us have racial or sexual privilege, almost none of us have class privilege, [so] maintaining 'straightness' is our last resort."[27] When one links the desire to enjoy some form of power and privilege with the tenacious reluctance to discuss sexuality, then any extensive critique of homophobia/heterosexism seems virtually impossible. But without such an analysis, dehumanizing and deadly homophobic/heterosexist structures and practices are allowed to fester within the Black church and community. Barbara Smith puts it plainly: "The oppression that affects Black gay people, female and male, is pervasive, constant, and not abstract. Some of us die from it."[28]

It is clear, then—from teenage sexuality, male-female relationships, sexism and heterosexism—that the lack of sexual discourse in the Black community has contributed to life-threatening and oppressive conditions for Black men and women. The time for a Black sexual revolution has come. The Black community can no longer allow White racist culture to deploy our sexuality through its shrewd control over our sexual discourse. The sexual silence must be broken.

If the task of the theologian is not simply to reflect its community's thinking but also to be prophetic in relation to it, then Black and womanist theologians cannot abandon their prophetic role. They, especially womanists, are compelled to break the silence concerning Black sexuality.

One Womanist's Response

Womanist theology boldly professes its profound concern for the "survival and wholeness of [the] entire [Black] people, male *and* female."[29] Wholeness refers to at least four aspects of Black life: (1) It involves individual wholeness as women and men strive to be healed spiritually, psychologically, emotionally and physically from the wounds of their complex oppression. (2) It means community wholeness as the community strives to overcome the barriers that divide it against itself as a result of being oppressed and of harboring oppressive systems and structures. (3) It implies the Black community's freedom from their multifarious oppression. (4) It is a dynamic process in which the community is actively engaged in a struggle toward its own wholeness. As this essay has shown, the Black church's and community's posture toward sexuality thwarts the very wholeness which womanist theology claims to promote.

The mandate for womanist theologians is explicit: they must break the tacit conspiracy of silence concerning sexuality. This necessitates that womanist theology engage the kind of socio-political and religiocultural analyses which would face this issue head-on. These analyses should clarify the pernicious connection between White racism and Black sexuality. In so doing, they should explore the various ways in which this connection has impeded Black men's and women's wholeness. A womanist sociopolitical analysis, for instance, will elucidate the points of power and privilege enjoyed in a patriarchal, racist, classist and heterosexist interlocking system of oppression. It will examine how sexuality is employed as a tool to garner and maintain that privilege and power. This womanist analysis will also forthrightly name the ways in which Black women and men deploy sexuality as a weapon of privilege, if not of power. In this respect, a womanist religiocultural analysis will be employed to reveal how White culture has utilized the Bible to denigrate Black people and to impugn their sexuality, and how the Black community has used religion and the Bible in a similar manner against gay and lesbian persons.

While womanist theologians are certainly constrained by their goal for Black wholeness to audaciously and boldly deal with Black sexuality, they are also compelled by Black faith to do so. Black people's faith is centered on a God they have come to know in their intense struggles to survive and to be whole. This God has been One who, out of the depths of oppression and sure and certain death, has called forth and sustained Black life. This God has also been an empowering and liberating presence. Essentially, by their journey with God through slavery and the other tyrannies of White racism, Black Christians have come to know a God who is provider, liberator and sustainer of life. Black people thus confess out of their own faith journey the one God who is triune: Creator, Redeemer (Jesus) and Holy Spirit. In this respect, Black Christians witness to a God who is internally relational. At the same time, while recognizing the different functions of God the Creator, Jesus and the Spirit, Black people have traditionally made little distinction among the three. God and Jesus, especially, are seen as one. This perhaps has been Black Christians' way of testifying to the fact that though their roles are different, God, Jesus and even the Spirit are of profoundly equal significance as they sustain and empower Black men and women in their life struggles. It would seem, then, that Black faith witnesses to a God in internal relationships of equality, reciprocity and mutuality, where each divine "person" is needed to complete the whole *and* is respected for its particular gift. It is this God in whose image Christians claim to be created. It is therefore this God whose image Christians are obliged to reflect in their living. This means that womanist theologians are further required by the faith of Black people to articulate a theology which transforms the Black church and community so that they become places that nurture respect, equality, reciprocity and mutuality for *all* people. For this to happen, womanist theologians have to engage in sexual discourse. Such discourse is the essential beginning of wholeness for the Black church and community and, hence, the essential beginning of the Black church and community reflecting the image of God.

If womanist theologians dare to open the door to candid sexual discourse, they can begin to unravel and grasp the nuanced complexity of Black people's lives and oppression. This would be the first step to creating a community and church where the "entire people"—male and female, gay and lesbian—can possess life and wholeness.

[handwritten: forward candid sexual discourse]

Notes

1. Renee L. Hill, "Who Are We for Each Other? Sexism, Sexuality and Womanist Theology," in *Black Theology: A Documentary History, Vol. 2: 1980-1992*, ed. James H. Cone and Gayraud S. Wilmore (Maryknoll, New York: Orbis Books, 1993).

2. Alice Walker, *In Search of Our Mothers' Gardens: Womanist Prose* (San Diego: Harcourt Brace Jovanovich, 1983).

3. Cheryl Sanders, "Christian Ethics and Theology in Womanist Perspective," *Journal of Feminist Studies in Religion*, vol. 5, no. 2 (Fall 1989), 90.

4. See Keith Boykin, *One More River to Cross: Black and Gay in America* (New York: Anchor Books, 1996), 128-131.

5. See the discussion and mutual criticisms concerning this issue in Barbara Smith, ed., *Home Girls: A Black Feminist Anthology* (Brooklyn: Kitchen Table: Women of Color Press, 1983).

6. Paula Giddings, "The Last Taboo," in *Race-ing Justice, En-gendering Power: Essays on Anita Hill, Clarence Thomas, and the Social Construction of Reality*, ed. Toni Morrison (New York: Pantheon Books, 1992), 442.

7. Cornel West, *Race Matters* (Boston, Beacon Press, 1993), 83ff.

8. Giddings, "The Last Taboo."

9. West, *Race Matters*, 83.

10. Michel Foucault, *The History of Sexuality: An Introduction*, vol. 1 (New York: Vintage Books, 1990), 107.

11. John D'Emilio and Estelle B. Freedman, *Intimate Matters : A History of Sexuality in America* (New York: Harper and Row, 1988), 86.

12. Quoted in Winthrop Jordan, *White over Black: American Attitudes toward the Negro, 1550-1812* (Chapel Hill: University of North Carolina Press, 1968), 30.

13. Ibid., 32.

14. For more on the ideology of the Jezebel in the antebellum South, see Deborah Gray White, *Arn't I a Woman?* (New York: Norton, 1985), 29ff.

15. Quoted in Giddings, "The Last Taboo," 444.

16. Ibid., 451.

17. See, for instance, Sander L. Gilman's discussion in "Black Bodies, White Bodies: Toward an Iconography of Female Sexuality in Late Nineteenth-Century Art, Medicine, and Literature," in *Race, Writing, and Difference*, ed. Henry Lewis Gates Jr. (Chicago: University of Chicago Press, 1987), 223-261. Note especially Gilman's discussion of the notorious nineteenth-century display made of a young South African woman, Sara Bartmann.

18. See the thorough and insightful analyses of these hearings in Morrison's *Race-ing Justice, En-gendering Power*.

19. Giddings, "The Last Taboo," 458.

20. See, for instance, White's *Arn't I a Woman?* John Blassingame, *The Slave Community: Plantation Life in the Antebellum South*, 2nd ed. (New York, Oxford

University Press, 1979); Eugene Genovese, *Roll, Jordan, Roll: The World the Slaves Made* (New York: Vintage Books, 1976); and Herbert Gutman, *The Black Family in Slavery and Freedom, 1750-1925* (New York: Vintage Books, 1977).

21. The term "wholeness" will be more completely defined later in this essay.

22. Leon Dash, *When Children Want Children: The Urban Crisis of Teenage Childbearing* (New York: Morrow, 1989).

23. Patricia Hill Collins, *Black Feminist Thought: Knowledge, Consciousness, and the Politics of Empowerment* (New York: Routledge, Chapman and Hall, 1991), 186.

24. Note, for instance, the response to Ntozake Shange's *for colored girls who considered suicide/when the rainbow was enuf,* or to Alice Walker's *The Color Purple* and Terry Macmillan's *Waiting to Exhale.*

25. See, for instance, Boykin's discussion in *One More River to Cross,* esp. chapters 4 and 5.

26. See Zora Neale Hurston, *Their Eyes Were Watching God* (New York: HarperCollins, 1990).

27. Barbara Smith, "Toward a Black Feminist Criticism," in *All the Women Are White, All the Blacks Are Men, but Some of Us Are Brave: Black Women's Studies,* ed. Gloria T. Hull, Patricia Bell Scott, and Barbara Smith (Old Westbury, New York: Feminist Press, 1982), 171.

28. Smith, "Introduction," *Home Girls,* xlvii.

29. Walker, *In Search of Our Mothers' Gardens,* xi.

16

"How Can We Forget?"

An Ethic of Care for AIDS, the African American Family, and the Black Catholic Church*

Toinette M. Eugene

Aid of AMERICA
by Imani Harrington[1]

Small bones crushed by the foot of racism
will be placed in an archaeologist's grave
precious red wet eyes run deep
with blood dripping staining our bodies
onto canvasses to be hung in a dying gallery
blending colors of pain-o-sorrow-o-grief
into the heart open lonely space of a mother's mouth
crying for the loss of her child
the rich sweet acrid taste of a mother's love
has been lost in this war

I am/we are/they are
you are now it a veteran in AMERICA
with the aids of AMERICA
crossing life's war
combating a disease infiltrated
with the aid of AMERICA

*Editor's Note: This essay uses figures from the 1995 midyear edition of the HIV/ AIDS Surveillance Report of the Center for Disease Control. Readers should consult the most recent edition of this report for current figures for the year in which they are reading this essay.

When you make your living at night under the red light
girl you will be charged
with the aids of AMERICA
hissing chimes the men throw dimes to slide
on your wet body your blood line is a crime
you are a black woman in AMERICA without a face or a voice

stop the denying lesbians do die
with the aids of AMERICA
until you are dead and gone every thing you do
will be wrong
with the aids of AMERICA

How can we forget what it means to lay down
on a pissy homeless bed with cardboard
hanging
over cold black heads lynching fear
Bein' a black woman in this country is to look
at the racist virus that's got you, us and me
like the black blood that dripped off southern trees

Little children will suffer from a never
to be gotten disease
with the aids of AMERICA
again the old red/white and blue stands true
for who's got who
with the aid of AMERICA
with the aids of AMERICA

Prolegomena to an Ethic of Care for African American Families Suffering with AIDS

By the end of 1994, neither of the two most recently published and most credible works relating the deadly disease of AIDS to the American Catholic Church[2] and to ethics and religion[3] mentioned at all the progress of this disease as it affects African Americans. The reasons for this lack are both inexcusable and incredible—unless one takes into account that racism and sexism are deeply rooted and causal in slowing the availability and effectiveness of research. One must factor the fearsome ideologies of heterosexism and classism above all as responsible in major ways for supporting and sustaining homophobic religious attitudes, and for delaying and limiting ministerial responses related to this disease[4] as it affects African American men, women, families, and communities of faith.

This essay is an attempt to address the ethical and theological problems connected to responding to AIDS and the African American family; to discuss the role of African American women within this complex, culturally problematic situation; and, finally, to begin to explore a womanist ethical praxis whereby the Roman Catholic Church present and ministering in the African American community might respond more effectively and pastorally to the crisis of AIDS as it manifests itself in African American families.

To understand the implications of AIDS in an ethical and theological context, we must first look at the sociological situation into which AIDS has been introduced for women and people of color, particularly African Americans. For significant numbers of these population groups, socioeconomically they are in the lower strata. There are many barriers that impede access to the means by which they could improve their quality of life, particularly education and/or an increase in economic level.

Recent research confirms that the dominance of the infrastructures of these social sins means the devaluation of people of color and of African Americans in particular. The 1992 report from the president's Commission on AIDS revealed that 21 percent of the total population accounted for 46 percent of the people in the United States living with AIDS. African Americans constituted 12 percent of the United States population and nearly 30 percent of AIDS cases. Hispanics/Latinos constituted 9 percent of the population and 17 percent of the AIDS cases. The most recent statistics continue to rise, with Blacks and Hispanics/Latinos accounting for 48 percent of reported AIDS cases. The increase for Blacks to 30 percent of cases is the cause.[5]

The 1989 age-adjusted HIV-related death rate among Black males was three times that of White males. African American females were nine times more likely to die of HIV than White females. The commission believed that the trends suggested that this disproportionate impact was likely to continue. In all likelihood, the end-of-the-year figures for 1995 in the United States will reveal that the percentage of youths who have been or will be left orphaned by the HIV epidemic will be 17 percent of children and 12 percent of adolescents. In hard numbers, in 1991, 32,400 children, adolescents, and young adults were orphaned by AIDS. By the end of 1995, the numbers will be from 72,000 to 80,700. By 2000, the estimates are 125,000 to 146,000.[6]

In her 1995 book, *In a Blaze of Glory*, womanist ethicist Emilie M. Townes noted that:

> the African American community is the most disproportionately represented with respect to HIV/AIDS. Beginning in 1990, AIDS became the leading cause of death for Black men between the ages of thirty-five and forty-four and the second leading cause of death for Black men and women between the ages of twenty-five and thirty-six. Of the AIDS cases, 78 percent are adult men (thirteen years or older), 19 percent are adult women, and 3 percent are pediatric (children

younger than thirteen years) . . . Black children have accounted for 54 percent of all the reported pediatric AIDS cases in the nation. Ninety-four percent have been due to perinatal transmissions from mothers infected with HIV. Four percent have been due to hemophilia-related blood products or the receipt of an HIV-contaminated blood transfusion. The mode of the remaining 2 percent cannot be determined.[7]

Given these statistics, it is extremely curious and critical that no mention is made of an ethical response to this social analysis by the American Roman Catholic hierarchy, which is in many ways rightly touted as in the forefront of the pastoral care movement, and which has also made prominent official pastoral statements refuting racism, sexism, and classism as they are manifested in the African American community.

The American Catholic Church, like much of American culture, is struggling with the question of what AIDS means. The American church hierarchy has drawn upon the Catholic tradition of social justice and a rich repertoire of myths, symbols, and rituals in constructing the meaning it ascribes to this disease. At the same time, unlike the process they employed when formulating their pastoral statements on the economy or on the question of nuclear war, the bishops did not formally dialogue with homosexual leaders as they developed their construction of AIDS.[8]

The result is a mixed message—calls for compassion and social justice for persons with AIDS issued simultaneously with condemnation of the values of groups most influential in the larger American AIDS discourse—that has compromised the American church hierarchy's ability to participate credibly in the larger American discourse on AIDS. The concurrent omission of failure to communicate with the African American community, which suffers disproportionately from AIDS, further compounds their conundrum. Richard L. Smith, in *AIDS, Gays, and the American Catholic Church*, makes the following pointed observation:

> Yet the American hierarchy's construction of the AIDS epidemic cannot be necessarily said to represent those of other sectors of the American church. Like so much of the American culture at large, the American Catholic church shares in the current polarization between orthodox and progressive viewpoints. In this polarized situation, other voices vie with the bishops in seeking to make some sense out of this tragedy. The voices that prevail will, in the end, decide what AIDS means from a Catholic viewpoint.[9]

In this essay, I contend, from my perspective as an African American Roman Catholic social ethicist, that some of those voices not yet in dialogue with the American Catholic hierarchy must be pastoral and health care givers identified as respected and dedicated members present and active in the midst of the Black civic and religious communities. Whether they hold highly visible positions with a chancery office or work quietly at the bedsides of Black persons dying from the disease, these men and women could be said to represent an even more powerful voice than that of the bishops. They are what the Italian theorist Antonio Gramsci and subsequently the philosopher Cornel West referred to as the "organic intellectuals" who perform an essential mediating function in the clash of conflicting social groups.[10]

"Little Children Will Suffer from a Never to Be Gotten Disease"

Larry, Brenda, and Ivan, fifteen, ten, and five years old respectively, are the children of an African American woman with HIV-positive status, more commonly known as AIDS.[11] Their father is gone, and it is very likely their mother will die within five years. While Larry will hopefully be in college by then, Brenda will be a teenager and Ivan a preteen, without their biological father and mother. Right now, the family is living in a community house for homeless people infected with the HIV virus. The children may be able to stay even after their mother dies, but nothing is guaranteed.[12]

Carmen, another African American, is thirty-nine and has used drugs since she was sixteen. She has three children. Her two young sons live with her sister, and Carmen and her thirteen-year-old daughter, the only person close to Carmen who knows she is infected with the virus, live in an old tenement building. When Carmen found out she had contracted the virus, she "cursed everyone. I think I even cursed God . . . But on the whole, I'm not really a bad person. At least I don't think so."[13]

Greg is an African American man. He used to live in the same home as Larry, Brenda, and Ivan, but was asked to leave. He also is infected with the AIDS virus and very often is tired and weak. When he got hold of a friend's few hundred dollars (money supposed to be used for medication), he spent it on drugs, breaking the rules of the house. Before Greg began living with the virus, he was a professional dressmaker, working for people such as Jacqueline Kennedy Onassis. Greg became infected after using a dirty needle.

AIDS is threatening the survival of the African American family. As Beth Richie says in her essay on AIDS,

AIDS, in many ways, is like every other health, social and economic crisis that black people have faced for generations. What is alarmingly different about AIDS is the severity of the infection and the particularly repressive political timing of the emergence of the disease. The combined effect of all these elements leaves the Black community in an extremely vulnerable position. AIDS has the potential to cripple Black people in a way that few other health or social forces have since slavery.[14]

While we are used to looking at the numbers of individuals dying from AIDS, this is too simplistic a view to take with the African American population. AIDS, a disease connected to other social problems, is putting African American individuals, families, and values at risk. Children such as Larry, Brenda, and Ivan; women such as Carmen; and men such as Greg are all living with AIDS. All of these people may be stigmatized as dirty and undesirable, but in an African American context they are valuable parts of a whole, members of a family.

To turn away from the harsh realities of AIDS among African Americans is at the same time to turn away from the African American family. When the American Roman Catholic church addresses AIDS and all that the disease brings with it, the Church is addressing the African American family "where they are at," it is embracing children, women, and men as valuable and wanted, and, finally, it is returning to its traditional and historical role as prophet and leader in times when no one else cares for African American people in a comprehensive, holistic, and hospitable manner.

AIDS and African American Families:
"Small Bones Crushed by the Foot of Racism"

As is the case with many other social realities, the problem of AIDS is worse for African Americans than for those of the dominant culture. The HIV virus is directly tied to homelessness, poverty, unemployment, and inadequate health care. As these basic dynamics of day-to-day life disintegrate, families are left with practically nothing to live on and must struggle to survive. Further, institutions which are supposed to serve as resources most often do the opposite, instead misleading and dehumanizing the very people they are said to serve.

As lives are threatened, so are human and Gospel values. In the face of AIDS, families are sometimes forced to break apart, to give up children to unknown social workers, to live on the streets, to steal money for drug addictions, to ask for financial and other resources, and to assume many other positions which have the power to rob African Americans of their independence and humanity. Three of the "Nguzo Saba" themes, or "Seven Principles," which seem especially in danger are unity, self-determination, and purpose and creativity.

The other most obvious value indicators at risk are the ongoing existence of the extended family as a primordial form of socialization for African Americans, social achievement factors, and the transmission of the foundations of Christian and Catholic faith and beliefs.[15] Death is a direct way of breaking up families. Also, as more women are infected, as AIDS is increasingly connected to homelessness, and as children are born with the virus, families are asked and sometimes forced to split up, nearly always by dominant social structures. Beth Richie comments: "The extended family support system which is characteristic of most black communities has been drained."[16]

Children, highly valued and cared for in African American families, are being removed from their parents and sometimes from larger extended families. In Carmen's case, her social worker wants her to give her daughter away, but Carmen has so far refused. She has already given her two young sons to her sister. Suzanne Hill, a clinical social worker at Beth Israel Medical Center in New York City, imparts her own experience:

> We see grandparents and relatives fighting over the children of AIDS patients. For example, a dying mother wants her sister to have her children . . . or maybe her next door neighbor who has been taking care of them for years and knows them well, and loves them. But the children's father, serving a sentence on Riker's Island, doesn't want them to go either to her sister or to the neighbor. He wants the children, he'll be getting out soon, he says. But he might not have seen these children for years! So the courts are involved and the children suffer . . . and often the person who is least equipped to take care of the children gets them.[17]

In this case, the family members are pitted against each other, and children become limited goods. While African Americans value their children, White social institutions have forced these children to be displaced and have forced the cultural family value of joy in numerous children to be gravely misplaced.

The loss of family unity is connected to the lessening degree of self-determination among African Americans living with AIDS. Self-determination is a value prized and acted on among African Americans; historically, African Americans have spoken and acted for themselves, often in opposition to the mainstream society. This ability to determine one's life, to make choices and carry them through, is almost impossible for African Americans with AIDS. For a person infected with the virus, the basics of housing, food, and clothing cannot be taken for granted. In cities, many African Americans with AIDS are homeless and living on the streets.

For any human being, to be without a home is demeaning, and it seems especially unethical in a country as wealthy as the United States. In addition to lack of housing, self-determination is made more difficult as the disease progresses. As weight goes up and down often, clothing no longer fits. Frequent sweating and vomiting mean increased laundry costs and more time spent on doing laundry. Preparing a meal or taking a bath can become, at the minimum, a two- or three-hour process. Essentially, a person has less and less control over his or her body, the most basic of all human functions.

Finally, as self-determination is made nearly impossible, purpose and creativity are almost always out of the question. When parents are unable to perform even the basic functions of feeding themselves, passing values on to children seems impossible. Although African Americans have often been able to quote the folk proverb "God can make a way out of no way," this becomes more and more difficult and discouraging with the problems of AIDS. Further, children are affected whether or not they have the virus. The African American Kwanzaa values of building and developing our community and doing always as much as we can, in order to leave our community more beautiful, are especially hard to pass on. For children to believe that they are wanted and that they belong is primary, yet even this is not guaranteed.

One must be careful, though, of an overly simplistic analysis. Before going on, I would like to comment briefly on the tensions and survival skills which arise in African American families with AIDS. One tension involves how and which choices are made. The choices African Americans make may be different than expected by dominant structures and institutions. One example of this is an infected African American woman having children. It is easy for the policy makers and those holding positions in dominant secular institutions to simply say, "Stop having kids." In African American (Roman Catholic) families, however, children (born or unborn) are wanted and valued; further, the "birth of a child may also serve as a social bond to a continuing relationship with a Black male, who, because of the scarcity of [Black] men, is a precious commodity."[18]

Even in the midst of risk, this crisis brings out the inherent strengths in African American families and values. Even as mothers and fathers die, grandmothers are raising children themselves. Even as institutions do their best to dehumanize people, African Americans still struggle to retain a sense of self-worth and dignity. Carmen—an unemployed woman, a single mother, a drug user of twenty-three years, a heroine and crack addict, and a one-time prostitute—somehow remembers that all of this is not her fault. As she daily makes trips on foot to different social agencies (sometimes she spends up to six hours a day doing this), she cares for and loves her daughter, giving the thirteen-year-old a sense of belonging. And, as she and many African American women have said before, "on the whole, I'm not really a bad person. At least I don't think so."

So, talking only about the disintegration of values is dangerously misleading to dominant and African American communities. As Carmen so clearly tells us, "I'm not really a bad person." Even as the Black community "has always and will always do its utmost to solve its problems," when these problems are so wrapped up in racism, sexism, and classism, the Black community is not enough.[19] When trying to understand the reality of AIDS among Black families, the Roman Catholic Church, its leaders, and its members must be honest and knowledgeable about where racist institutions end and the African American family begins, and about where these are inseparable.

Problems of the HIV virus are connected to other African American realities, such as homelessness, drug abuse, financial problems, and unemployment. Like all of these social ills, AIDS is subtly and powerfully connected to institutions. How systems and government agencies do or do not respond to African Americans with AIDS has much to do with how these families deal with the disease. As we can see from people like Carmen, when systems make housing, unemployment, and shelter difficult, if not impossible, it is African Americans who are impacted. As Lawrence Gary clearly points out in his introduction to *Black Men*, "Racist institutions need not be headed by racists nor designed with racist intentions to limit Black choices ... *The restrictive consequence is the important fact* rather than formal intentions" (italics added).[20]

AIDS and African American Women: "You Are a Black Woman in AMERICA without a Face or a Voice"

African American women—faceless and voiceless women—are women whom Audre Lorde says most of America has learned to hate. Yet these are women who have never accepted or let pass the dominant culture's erasure or hate, women who know what survival and celebration are about, women who endure the cycle of victim, survivor, and resource, women who have not forgotten what it means to be family. It is these women who have the most to offer their communities yet who also are the most at risk. Richie notes,

> A black woman's health needs are likely to be considered secondary to the needs of her children, her partner, her community or the convenience of the health care system. She is treated as a risk to others rather than in need of assistance herself.[21]

Recognizing this paradox of supporter and woman-at-risk is a beginning, a start, in addressing the threat AIDS poses particularly to African American women, and in learning from them some ways of survival, survival of both lives and values.

Even as general statistics are cited, it should be noted that African American women are rarely the focus of studies on persons with AIDS. Information and discussion about and for HIV-positive African American women are difficult to find. They are often grouped with White women or Black men but rarely addressed as their own group. Because of this difficulty in obtaining information on Black women as subjects, the following few paragraphs will be limited. In the future, there must be more work done on African American women with AIDS. It should also be pointed out that the estimates available on women with AIDS vary greatly, in part because of the Center for Disease Control's "failure to count many of women's HIV-induced illnesses as AIDS."[22] In looking at how the virus is transmitted to African American women, statistics are difficult to find. What we do know is this:

> Of the 3,668 cases of AIDS reported in American women in the single year ending November 30, 1989, 51 percent are attributed to transmission by intravenous drug use; 32 percent are attributed to hetero-

sexual transmission; 9 percent to transfusion; and 9 percent to "unde-
termined means of acquiring infection" . . . The higher rate of "unde-
termined" risk in women is assumed to reflect heterosexual transmission in which the woman is not aware of her partner's risk-taking
behaviors.[23]

However, it seems appropriate to question even these statistics, as the
very definition for AIDS may likely be unfair to women, and as it is almost
certain that not all African American women with the HIV virus were reported to the Center for Disease Control.

When one begins to look further into the reasons for sexual transmission
to African American women, one runs into the issue of sexuality in the African American community. Many African American men who are in relationships with African American women do not identify themselves as gay men
but do engage in sex acts with other men. This reluctance to identify themselves as gay may stem from the discomfort some African American communities feel with homosexuality and also from the early identification of
AIDS with bad behavior, which, as mentioned earlier, has too long been a
stereotype pinned on African Americans, especially African American men.

In her essay "Black Prostitutes and AIDS," Gloria Lockett, herself an African American woman who worked as a prostitute for nearly two decades,
discusses sex work and the realities of the HIV virus. According to Lockett,
most of the prostitutes infected with the HIV virus became infected through
IV drug use or were partners of IV drug users. Where studies have been
done (mainly in major cities), there is always a "direct correlation between
prostitutes with HIV and the prevalence of IV drug use."[24] In some cities,
the infection rate among prostitutes is 50 percent. COYOTE, an organization based in San Francisco which advocates on behalf of prostitutes, "reports that up to twenty percent of black women [over a sixty-five- to sev-
enty-year life span] have turned to prostitution to pay the bills—about
double the rate of the general population."[25]

This high number of sex workers, who enter the industry to pay for
basic survival needs, demonstrates how the economic system and lack of
social support have hurt African American women with AIDS in this country. Carmen, mentioned earlier in this essay, is one example. She was first
introduced to drugs (the cause of her infection) by her oldest son's father.
When she found out she was infected, she soon lost public assistance and
her apartment. She has been waiting for months for public support but
receives none. Vickie Mays and Susan Cochran make clear that the perception of and response to AIDS among African American women must be seen
in light of these women's context:

Competition for these women's attention includes more immediate
survival needs, such as obtaining shelter for the night, securing
personal safety or safety of their children, or interfacing with the

governmental system in order to obtain financial resources. For women who often, realistically, feel powerless to change the external realities of their lives—where they live, how much they earn, or the system's rules for getting financial supplements—AIDS may be of relatively low concern. In addition, even if AIDS is perceived as a relevant danger, women may not readily have the means to reduce their risk.[26]

With this in mind, one may begin to understand the complexities in responding to the needs of African American women with AIDS. They are nearly always higher at risk, economically worse off, more alienated from support systems, and given less attention than White women or African American men. In spite of all this, African American women, as they have done historically, are helping themselves and their communities. Carmen regularly volunteers at New York City's Minority Task Force on AIDS. Dr. Mitchell, an African American woman doctor in Harlem, is clear about her agenda of working with women infected with the HIV virus: "I don't deal with middle class women. My population is basically poor, Black women, whom I identify with because their surroundings are my origins. I come out of public housing. I am a Black woman. There by the grace of God go I."[27]

Beth Richie points to the National Black Women's Health Project, the California Prostitutes' Education Project, and Kitchen Table: Women of Color Press as organizations which are addressing how to combat AIDS. African American values are continued by these women, even as they themselves have AIDS. Larry, Brenda, and Ivan's mother (the children mentioned at the start of this essay) may still have problems with drugs, but when Sunday comes around, for most of the day the whole family is at a Catholic Church that ministers effectively in the Black community.

Carmen has told her daughter about her disease, and, according to some, she has told her too much. But perhaps for Carmen this is an issue of self-determination, telling her daughter what she needs to survive. Even as Carmen struggles with drugs, unresponsive social service agencies, and having to give her two youngest sons to her sister, she still tells the interviewer, "I'm doing twenty times better than I was," and finds her own place for unity and community on the block where she lives.

Gloria Lockett is also confident about the significance of African American women in the midst of this disease: "As a former prostitute, I know we can be excellent AIDS prevention educators and vital resources to the black community as it struggles with the AIDS epidemic." She points out that in opposition to prevailing sexual attitudes, African American women who have worked as prostitutes, and others who have known them, "are less likely to carry cultural stereotypes about prostitutes" and thus, it would seem to follow, about people infected with AIDS. Black sex workers have sometimes had more money than their peers and, as benefactors to other

African Americans, have won the respect of their communities. Prostitutes are "experts on sexual matters," often knowing the ins and outs of AIDS infection and ways to deal with culturally particular and sensitive issues such as how African American women can get their partners to wear condoms. As Lockett concludes her essay, "The risk [of AIDS] is too great to exclude them [Black prostitutes] from this struggle."[28]

Finally, a relatively recent article in *Ms.* magazine features conversations with Black women who either are infected or work with people who are infected with the HIV virus. Carolyn, a mother and a grandmother of two, lives in Detroit. When she first found out she was infected, she was set back, but after some help from her pastor, she was able to get focused again. She criticizes the dehumanization the system does to a person with AIDS, and is appreciative of her AIDS support group. Now, she is doing outreach: "We pass out condoms, take surveys, do STD and HIV presentations in schools, correctional centers, churches, drug rehabilitation centers, and girls' homes. I feel great because I can tell people that I'm HIV-positive, and, yes, you can live with this virus."[29]

Bernice Thompson's son died from AIDS in 1984. Her son's sickness "stopped my world. I did nothing else. Everything was Charles." After her son died, Bernice had to deal with undertakers who "didn't want the body because they knew he had AIDS." After he died (her husband had died in 1969), she "got sick. I was in a mental hospital." But one day, she heard the word "AIDS" and went to the AIDS Action Committee to volunteer. She explains her involvement:

> They told me I couldn't be a buddy because I couldn't take care of myself, but they found me something easier to do, stuffing envelopes. Then one day they put me on the front desk—I was so afraid, I was really down. It's sad what society does to you. But the people at AIDS Action took me by the hand. It's hard to see the people at AIDS Action who are sick. I've been there, and I know what they're going through. Then that's why I tell them jokes and I want to make them laugh and to know that I love them.[30]

"To know that I love them"—to help them feel valued and important, and that they belong—and "You can live with this virus" reflect the traditional and Afrocentric ethical values of self-determination, purpose, and creativity. "Educators and vital resources to the black community" mirror the Afrocentric value indicators of collective work and responsibility. "I'm doing twenty times better than I was" conveys the faith that I'm making it, I'm surviving, I'm O.K. Bernice, Carolyn, Gloria, and Carmen—all African American women, all women living with the HIV virus, all women who are victims, survivors, and resources. These women reflect the same kind of tenacity that the late Sister Thea Bowman exhibited in her illness and which can continue to serve as a witness of African Americans to the Roman Catholic Church as it makes efforts to understand and to participate in the ministries of healing and hope.

These women have held on to their Afrocentric value system through times of sorrow and times of celebration, and they know what it means to be family, each in her own way and context. It is in these women's experiences—as victims, survivors, and resources—that one can see the work of God. They know that their respective families are in danger, and they are responding as they are able. It is not a question of whether the African American family and its values will survive, but how. The last section of this essay will discuss some reasons and ways for the Roman Catholic Church to enter more effectively into the realities of African American families and AIDS.

African American Families, AIDS, and the Black [Catholic?] Church: *"How Can We Forget?"*

For African Americans, the historic Black Church has been the one place which has not been able to forget the fate of its suffering and struggling members. The historic Black Church has not forgotten its people, has not forgotten what it means to be a child of God, has not forgotten what it is to be African American in a Euro-American-dominated society. The historic Black Church has not forgotten the significance of a history of slavery and exploitation, has not forgotten what its families need. When no one else and no other institution has had time, resources, energy, or concern, the historic Black Church has. African Americans who are also Roman Catholic can partake in and claim this underside of largely unrecorded history as an important part of our heritage as Black Catholic people, according to the diligent spirituality and scholarship offered by church historian Cyprian Davis.[31] Moreover, as Wallace Charles Smith says in his book on the church and the African American family,

> The church has been the central authenticating reality in their lives. When the world has so often been willing to say only "no" to these people, the church has said "yes." For Black people, the church has been the one place where they have been able to experience unconditional positive regard.[32]

The historic Black Church, different from White churches, has less readily separated body and soul, spirit and material, spiritual and physical nourishment. It has historically been, and presently is, available and supportive when without that support and availability, the family might break. In fact, when a person had no family, no one with whom to belong, the church often provided (and provides) that family, that sense of belonging. This active role of provider and sustainer existed from the start with the African American Church in the United States:

The Black church in America developed out of the deprivation and oppression experienced by the slaves. In so doing, the black church existed as a support system for the oppressed at society's breakpoints. Without question the worst breakpoint in this slavocracy was the separation of family members from one another. Mothers, fathers, sons, and daughters were consistently sold away at the masters' whims. The church evolved as a new family for those who were continually being uprooted from their original families.[33]

In short, "How can we forget?" serves, in some ways, as a theological starting point for the African American Church. Remembering—its history, its people, its role as an instrument of God—is what it does best, better than societal institutions and better than many other churches.

For the most part, African Americans with AIDS have been forgotten. They have been ignored, by the media, by health services, by social service agencies, and by most of society. Families are being broken up, parents and children are dying, and values are at risk. Once again, however, in a situation the rest of society refuses to pay attention to, the African American Roman Catholic expression of church can respond to the needs of its people. It can respond as a church which knows God as justice-maker and liberator and as a caretaker of families affected by AIDS, and which is a place for education and dialogue. Although some might charge the Black Church with being conservative and not adequately dealing with issues of sexuality, these kinds of criticisms do not recognize the full potential and reality of the African American Church. As Harlon Dalton points out,

In practice, the African American church has proved adaptable, pragmatic, and even crafty when need be . . . Time and time again, the church has demonstrated its awareness of the variability of human existence and the fragility of the soul under siege. Time and time again, the church has been responsive to the needs, spiritual and nonspiritual, of the community.[34]

This adaptability, pragmatism, and craftiness will all be important as African American churches, including those representing, leading, and serving Black Roman Catholics, begin to confront AIDS. Being infected with the HIV virus is a spiritual, physical, emotional, mental, and sociopolitical reality. Perhaps more than any other form of oppression or disease, it is all-encompassing. Hopefully, the Black Church in all of its dimensions and denominations will not forget that its families are dying from AIDS and that because of this, the whole body suffers.

As AIDS impacts African American families, there are clear and strong issues of Afrocentricity which the church has always been responsive to. AIDS is a disease which threatens Black women, men, and children everywhere. The statistics for people affected in the United States appear earlier in this essay; in Africa, the numbers are even more staggering. The World Health Organization estimates that of the approximately 3 million cases of AIDS in women and children, about 80 percent of them are in sub-Saharan Africa, and in some cities, 40 percent of thirty- to thirty-four-year-olds are infected: "In one section of Uganda, there are reports of some 40,000 children orphaned, many as a result of this epidemic."[35]

An increased awareness of AIDS in churches in the United States will mean a more global concern and knowledge of the threat that the same disease poses to other Africans. In this sense, AIDS will be more understood in its entirety. African Americans will see how AIDS and the world's lack of response are failures that affect Blacks everywhere, not only in this country.

Another reality is that as AIDS endangers Blacks everywhere, the disease is threatening a race of people. Specifically in the United States, African Americans have long had to deal with the real possibility of genocide and with the frustration of trying to continue and maintain Afrocentric values and beliefs when societal institutions are in some ways threatening not only their culture and way of being but their very existence. Harlon Dalton, in his essay on the Black community and AIDS, brings up the term "genocide." He acknowledges it can be a powerful conversation stopper but also asserts that it is an issue the African American community raises. Dalton explains: "In its strong form, the term *genocide* reflects the genuine suspicion of many that the AIDS virus was developed in a government laboratory for the express purpose of killing off the unwanted."[36] Dalton says that he does not believe this is true, but at the same time, he understands "full well where the question comes from and recognize[s] that it must be heard."[37] Another way of understanding the issue of genocide is in the face of the federal government's seeming willingness to let AIDS spread "as long as it was confined to populations that straight White America would rather do without."[38] Finally, genocide can refer to dominant society's disregard, indifference, and subordination to the Black community's vital interests. Genocide and the larger society's treatment of AIDS must not be dismissed, especially as African Americans are asking the hard questions. Anytime its people have been at such great risk, the church has responded, and as the threat of AIDS grows, hopefully the same will happen.

AIDS threatens the existence of African Americans and the *way* African Americans are able to exist. The issue is not whether African Americans and their values will be able to survive, but how. The church has always been with African Americans "where they are at," and this is the Catholic Church that African American families living with AIDS need. Children are orphaned, parents are unable to care for themselves, families are homeless, young men are even further cast out, and young women are unable to be mothers. The physical, mental, emotional, and spiritual strength of African American men, women, and children, which is the lifeblood of the Church, is being depleted among those living with AIDS.

The Church has been there before, with its people where they are, and the cry for compassion and solidarity continues. African American families with AIDS are God's children in a largely silent world. As an institution which cares about its families and values, including families with AIDS, the Roman Catholic Church in the Black community has the potential to be a powerful listener and a bold speaker.

Being a powerful listener and a bold speaker is not a new role for the African American Church. In African American churches, God has been a justice-making God, a God who shows preference, a God who pays attention when and where nobody else does. African Americans know a God who is in relation with self and with creation. They know about adoption, about being adopted into the family of God through the Lord's Supper, and other tangible ways that the church has become extended family. For many African Americans, Jesus is a friend, a cosufferer, and a covictor. In light of the Afrocentric value of wellness, Jesus is a model for being well.

In his book on the African American church, Smith states clearly that the Black Church is an inclusive community, an adoptionist community, and a hopeful community. It is a community that recognizes the basic human dignity and image of God in all people; that embraces, first of all, its own children and, in some cases, children that are not its own; and that believes in the goodness and faithfulness of God. It is a church that, in the spirit of its African heritage, celebrates all life, however that life comes (i.e., being illegitimate, having a single parent, or being of mixed race). It is a church that is struggling with mutuality, that takes seriously the commandment to love our neighbor, and that celebrates and responds to being made in the image of God. As Wallace Charles Smith explains,

> In the church . . . persons may be moved to see that being made in the image of God mandates the abnegation of sexual role stereotypes and encourages a mutual responsibility which affords nurturing for the young, protection for the aged, and belonging for the homeless.[39]

It is clear that the institution of church as God's people in community knows what it means to suffer and knows what it takes to respond. The African American Church is already miles ahead of many institutions in being able to provide for the spiritual and physical needs of its families with AIDS. Although there are some obvious areas to which the church is not able to minister (for example, AIDS research, funding of health services, and similar areas that the government is responsible for), there are areas in which the church can, powerfully and boldly, speak with and stand for its people.

Three areas in which the Roman Catholic Church has a preeminent role in ministering to African Americans with AIDS are as caretaker, educator, and prophet. The idea of the church as caretaker has already been partially addressed. The African American church has always been a church that provides a family when there is none, establishes a sense of belonging when one feels he or she doesn't belong to anyone or any place. As more and more children become orphaned, as more and more men and women lose partners and spouses, and as more and more families are split apart because resources are not available, the church can provide a safe place, a place where people are welcomed and cared for. The Roman Catholic Church in the Black community must take its concrete presence more seriously in this regard.

For children now living with people not in their extended family, the church might be a place where members knew their parents and can help the child remember those parents in a hopeful way. For those infected with the HIV virus, the church might be a place where they feel accepted as they are, loved, and valued. Even as their health deteriorates and they feel a lesser sense of self, the church might "help them make a way out of no way" through members volunteering to spend an afternoon with the person living with AIDS. Most likely, the Catholic Church already provides nourishment for those working in public service institutions dealing with people with AIDS, as they are drained mentally, physically, emotionally, and spiritually in their jobs.

For Larry, Brenda, and Ivan, children of a mother with the HIV virus, the church may be a place where they can see positive male role models. For Carmen and her daughter, the church may be a place where they leave their harsh tenement and drug-infested neighborhood and remember themselves as children of God in a supportive and celebrative community of people. For Greg, perhaps the hardest to reach, the church might be a place that makes a job referral or provides a male friend not involved with drugs or living on the street. In all these ways and more, African American churches can en-courage people living with AIDS; care for children, women, and men where they are; and em-power families to hold on to their values and self-identity.

The church as educator is a complex and difficult role, because the American Catholic bishops have not overtly sought to be informed by or to speak in consonance with the African American community that is suffering from AIDS. Church education has much to do with the background and present context of a church's members, their views of the Bible, the neighborhood it is in, and the pastor's ideas of ministry. Further, AIDS among African American families is only recently beginning to be discussed in mainstream society, and a troubled history and misrepresentation of the HIV virus has left African Americans, as a race, feeling guilty, angry, and blamed for the AIDS epidemic. Talking about AIDS means talking about sexuality, a topic difficult to broach in any church setting. It means talking about relationships between men and women, about morality and ethics in a world where everything is rapidly changing.

Where mainstream society has failed in trying to communicate basic facts about AIDS, its transmission, and how to avoid it, the church has much more chance to succeed. The African American Church can also begin to address and encourage Afrocentric perspectives on such hard topics as sexuality and other issues which the dominant society has always hurtfully and inadequately tried to define for African Americans. For a church as concerned about its families as the African American Church has proved to be, education seems a difficult but natural response.

Before a response to AIDS and African American families can be realized by churches, two primary obstacles must be dealt with: dispelling the myths blaming African Americans for the origin and spread of AIDS, and addressing issues of morality and AIDS, specifically drug use and homosexuality. As was mentioned earlier, Black people are often made to feel guilty for the AIDS epidemic, and anger about this misappropriation among African Americans is justified and understandable.

Before effective education can happen, the church must be clear that African Americans are not to be blamed for the origin or spread of AIDS but must take responsibility for AIDS in their own communities. When AIDS is seen as a reality which impacts the African American family in significant ways, "black people [can] reconceptualize AIDS as not something White America is insisting we deal with but rather as a set of issues we ourselves want to take on."[40] When the African American community is ready to begin confronting AIDS and its families, education will be much more effective.

Another obstacle to education on AIDS in churches is connected to issues of morality. As Dalton affirms, "the black community has been slow in responding to AIDS [because] many of us do not want to be associated with what is widely perceived as a gay disease."[41] Dalton notices that some Black communities have "knowingly and sometimes fully embraced their gay members," but often homosexuality is a hidden factor: "It is all right if everybody knows as long as nobody tells." Dalton proposes that the way in which the African American community has dealt with homophobia results from gay men and lesbians representing the weak male and domineering female images that the Black community is trying to shake. Dalton's conclusion seems relevant to the Roman Catholic Church in particular: "To address it [the issue of homosexuality] successfully, we may have to take on such larger issues as the social construction of gender and the nature of male-female relations."[42]

Drug abuse is another obstacle in dealing with AIDS. Dalton points out that when a needle-exchange program was proposed in New York City, a few African American community leaders were supportive, but most were extremely vocal against the program. This problem extends beyond the Black community; much of the reluctance among African Americans to confront issues of drug abuse results from White society's association of Blacks as pathological, deviant, or diseased. Dalton makes the point:

> For us, drug abuse is a curse far worse than you can imagine. Addicts
> prey on our neighborhoods, sell drugs to our children, steal our

possessions, and rob us of hope. We despise them. We despise them because they hurt us and because they are us. They are a constant reminder of how close we all are to the edge. And "they" are "us" literally as well as figuratively; they are our sons and daughters, our sisters and brothers. Can we possibly cast out the demons without casting out our own kin?[43]

The historic Black Church has often been the one and only institution which sees the problems of its people yet does not cast its people out. It is often the one and only institution which remembers that all people are made in the image of God and are thus worthy of respect. If drug users are simply written off and cast out by the Roman Catholic Church (as they are by nearly every other institution), AIDS will continue to be an epidemic in the African American community. Rather, by accepting and giving all African Americans a sense of belonging, by recognizing and being clear about the connections of drug abuse to a much larger and more powerful systemic racism, the Black Church will continue its tradition as an adoptionist church, a church that provides family when there seems to be none. As Evelynn Hammond helpfully makes clear,

> The most disappointing aspect . . . is that by focusing on individual behavior as the cause of AIDS and by setting up bisexuals, homosexuals, and drug users as "other" in the black community, and as "bad," the national black media falls into the trap of reproducing exactly how white society has defined the issue. But unlike the situation for whites, what happens to these groups within the black community will affect the community as a whole . . . If people with AIDS are set-off as "bad" or "other"—no change in individual behavior in relation to them will save any of us. There can be no "us" or "them" in our communities.[44]

Once these obstacles of homosexuality and drug abuse are begun to be dealt with (and this will be a long, perhaps never finished, process), then education on AIDS has more of a chance of success. One priority is to make basic AIDS education (how it is transmitted and avoided) available, especially to youth. Too often, this education has been culturally insensitive and unrealistic. The education that has occurred has mainly come from White institutions (for example, the media), and, as Mays and Cochran say, "when someone of authority on the screen talks about the risk of AIDS, this individual is a White male, not an ethnic minority member."[45] In this sense, in being able to educate its own people, the Catholic Church in the presence of its Black members is already a resource full of potential.

As the Roman Catholic Church in the African American community begins to make basic information available, this will most likely quickly get into issues of sexuality. The Roman Catholic Church in the African American community has always been a supporter of its families, but at the same time it needs to deal with issues of mutuality and sexuality. As Beth Richie points out, AIDS is forcing Black communities to deal with sexuality and to address the religious and cultural narrow-mindedness and myths that plague Black adult relationships. For the most part, the dominant society has viewed African Americans as more promiscuous, irresponsible, and illegitimate than itself when it comes to sexuality. Accepting and not demystifying these images is especially hurtful as the number of African Americans infected with the HIV virus increases: "In the face of these damning images of black women's sexuality [and, one could say, that of black men, too], the community has become defensive and hesitant to openly discuss any issue related to sexuality."[46]

Unfortunately, racism has been able to turn Black sexuality into Black sexism, and vertical power is impacting horizontal relationships. One manifestation of this in connection with AIDS is that many African American men are involved with other men but consider themselves heterosexual. Thus, they do not tell their female partners about their involvement with other men, and the women become infected. Further, when talking to African Americans about ways to guard against AIDS, too often solutions have been narrow and unrealistic, setting up high expectations without providing options for the changed behavior required to fulfill those expectations.

Hammond points out that an *Essence* article talks about how women contract AIDS but does not mention men's bisexuality or homosexuality:

> The implication is again—just don't have sex with those people if you want to avoid AIDS. It avoids discussion of the prevalence of bisexuality among black men, and consequently the way that AIDS will ultimately change sexual relationships in the black community.[47]

Ways to prevent AIDS as advocated by the Roman Catholic Church must be connected to community response and not only individual behavior. If the church advocates monogamous, traditional relationships, how should heterosexuals respond when, in the African American population, women far outnumber men? Mays and Cochran argue that risk is an unavoidable reality of being young. If this is true, how will Catholic churches in the African American community educate and guide youth to take risks that avoid HIV infection? In short, ethical education about AIDS and how it is transmitted will have to be "presented in [their] appropriate context— that of an *interpersonal decision-making framework*" (italics added).[48] Mays and Cochran are both psychologists, and they emphasize that changes in behavior are linked to personal identities, psychological issues, social networks, and cultural norms. Again, the Roman Catholic Church in the African American community is perhaps the most understanding and aware of these realities and thus is a natural place for an educative response to AIDS.

If drugs and sex are sources of employment and income for African

Americans, can the church help with providing safer places of financial support? Studies have shown that among Black college students, "almost 50% of sexually active Black women worr[y] very little or not at all about getting AIDS."[49] Among African Americans, AIDS is still seen primarily as a White, gay men's disease. The Catholic Church has much to give in dispelling that myth and in providing viable alternatives for men, women, and children who are at risk.

Finally, in the process of education, the Roman Catholic Church in the African American community can begin to address Afrocentric values and beliefs about God and human sexuality, moving away from hurtful, individualistic, act-centered ideas of sin and toward holistic, communal ways of being together as embodied communities. In the past, tradition and the Bible have been the norm for ideas about sexuality. Now, more and more, experience is also becoming relevant to an ethic of sexuality and relationship. African American experience is a particular, oppressed experience. It is an experience that survived slavery and now contends with a pervasive racism.

Forming an ethic of sexuality and relationship that is particular to African Americans means looking at how Black men, women, and children understand gender roles and identities, as well as orientation issues.[50] In the past, sin has been perceived as oriented around a sexually wrong act. Sexuality has been antithetical to and disconnected from salvation. Racist myths about African American men and women say that distrust and disrespect have driven a wedge between Black women and men, and that this wedge accounts for the Black community not being able to mobilize as it used to. This kind of theology is not helpful or empowering for the African American community. It stands in the way of African American men and women relating mutually, and cuts them off from a holistic, faithful theology of sexuality coming out of African traditions and beliefs.

As notions of sexuality become more connected to experience, the sexuality of African American men and women will be connected to how they know God, interpret religion, and live out their faith. Jesus valued and modeled human sexuality and also offered a challenge to societal norms. He did not condemn, but, rather, when a woman was accused of adultery, he went beyond the law of Moses and said to the gathered people, "Let the one who is without sin among you be the first to throw a stone at her." As people left quietly until no one but the woman and Jesus were left, Jesus said, "Neither do I condemn you; go, and do not sin again" (John 8:3-11 Jerusalem Bible). With this as example, sexuality is intrinsic to a person's and a community's relationship to God. Sin is not an individual act, but an alienation from our divinely intended sexuality.

As children of God, we are embodied persons meant to be in relationship: "And the Word became flesh, and dwelt among us, full of grace and truth" (John 1:14). Jesus calls us not servants, but friends. Wallace Charles Smith says of Black theology that "the incarnation was the critical starting point for the articulation of the faith."[51] Rather than relationships keeping us from God, relationships are part of our faith, part of being a Christian community. As African Americans respect different choices, a more faithful and holistic theology will be lived out. Black love has always been an agent of Gospel liberation, and has historically enabled African Americans to look beyond their suffering, to believe in their self-worth, and to value all, born and unborn. Marriage has always been a commitment beyond all others, a place where love becomes not possessive, but creative and mutual. Friendship and love become the glue that holds relationships together.

In the midst of all of this, being aware of sexuality and celebrative of an embodied humanity will help dispel myths and hurtful, act-centered theologies. African beliefs about relationships will be remembered and held up as examples of being together. Moving from individualistic to holistic notions of sexuality will not be easy. It will require open discussions, a willingness to risk, and a commitment to a process. At the same time, in the face of the increasing threat of AIDS to the African American family, this movement will enable people to deal with prevention issues as a community and will empower churches both to lower the risk of AIDS in their communities and to encourage a growing awareness of Afrocentric values and worldviews.

Finally, the Roman Catholic Church in the African American community has always been a prophet in the wilderness, a voice when there was none. In addition to internally providing a support system for families in crisis, long before the government was involved in welfare, the Catholic Church in the Black community was feeding the hungry both materially and educationally. As it has done with other issues of racism and oppression, the Catholic Church must "go public" in more prophetic ways, breaking the silence about AIDS and the destruction it is wreaking on African American families.

"Justice is not cheap. Justice is not quick. It is not ever finally achieved."[52] Even so, the church in the Black community must continue its witness to an ineffective and callous society. As more and more churches become involved in confronting and educating on issues of AIDS with their congregations, they can serve as resources to other churches, building coalitions and resource banks. At the end of the introduction in his book on the Black Church and African American families, Wallace Charles Smith says:

> As God's children, blacks understood the nature of the church to be the performance of these rituals which cemented family members to each other and to God . . . The mission of the church was reaching out to those in need. Blacks have always been mission-minded . . . In its missionary outreach the black church modeled a concept of sufferers reaching out to fellow sufferers. Reaching out was inclusive . . . Men, women, and children suffered equally; so the church reached out comprehensively. Single mothers, orphans, widows, and widowers were all sought to come out as they were . . . The consummation for

black people will be the final overcoming. It will be at that time that the little Jesus boy of whom they have sung will return. The Holy Spirit's power that they felt when they shouted will have all creation shouting.[53]

Mothers are single, children are orphans, and men and women are losing their partners. People are suffering. AIDS, as a disease which is causing African American families to cry out for help, is a Gospel issue, an issue of justice and compassion. It is an issue about which the Roman Catholic Church in the African American community has much to say, and much to do. It is an issue which calls that church to be prophetic, a witness to the larger society and to its own families.

As racism continues to plague African American families, as the dominant society fails to be responsive to its destruction of the valuable human resource of African American peoples, as people and families continue to die from AIDS, the Catholic Church must be present in all of that suffering. It has been and will continue to be an institution that resists status quo values and inaction, that resists assimilation, that provides alternatives and hope for its people. As more and more African Americans are left without a home, physically or spiritually; as more and more families are broken up; as more and more of God's children are cast out, the Catholic Church in the African American community can be an institution that provides a home, creates family, and brings in those who have been cast out.[54] As larger communities and systems continue to ignore the reality of AIDS, continue to deny the pervasiveness of racism, and continue to turn away from large portions of the population, the church can hold those larger communities and systems accountable to their people.

The concept of power brokers enters into the arena here. African Americans traditionally look to the clergy in their community as leaders and advocates on their behalf, because the clergy have received advanced education and are capable of advising them on what course of action to take in a given situation.[55] They may be the most influential members of the community, able to articulate the needs of the members, in addition to being moral trendsetters. Even where the spiritual leaders are members of the dominant culture yet serve the African American community, they may all the more be viewed as the interceders between the community and the power structure.

The role which the church as an institution has played as provider of values and moral standards serves an important function for the community it represents. This means that there is a voice that can articulate the community's views and needs in the larger arena. Furthermore, it has meant a support system and a place for consultation, if the need should arise. This has been very important for members of the community who perceive themselves as powerless and unable to control their lives or to impact the system.

Consequently, confronted with AIDS, many members of the Black and

Hispanic/Latino communities have turned to their religious leaders for advice and direction. This disease, however, also requires an inquiry into behaviors often considered immoral by many clergy. Homosexuality and intravenous drug use are considered by some as illnesses to be treated, and frank discussions of how to reduce one's risk or how to talk to one's family about these lifestyles, in addition to a diagnosis of AIDS, will present a real challenge to many clergy.

The relation of clergy to women and to their role in the definition and defense of women's rights and needs raises a number of questions and issues. One of the basic concepts that has been reinforced by many clergy is that of the strong nuclear family unit, based on the traditional model of the dominant middle-class White culture, a model that is fast eroding in the United States. The reality that presents itself in the African American community, however, is that of an increasing number of single-parent-headed households with women as the sole supporting adults. The role of African American women in these new configurations is in conflict with the accepted but pseudo norm of the dominant culture, and indeed of traditional and contemporary papal and magisterial teaching and idealism.

Women have assumed more responsibility for financial support of the family unit. They have not provided all the resources effectively to carry out this task, though. In addition, many support systems are not in place to help them successfully carry out these responsibilities. Such programs as day care, job training, educational assistance, and affordable health insurance are not readily available or accessible. The lack of these resources contributes to maintenance of a significant number of women at the lower end of the economic spectrum. This means that the children of these households are also locked into poverty. The fact that a large proportion of these women are people of color underscores the seriousness of the situation. Women may feel even more of a lack of control over their circumstances and a resignation to the situation.

The role of clergy serving the African American community in addressing these issues has not been perceived as a vigorous one. It appears that these issues have taken a back seat to those affecting the large community. Even though the issues of poverty, access to services, and equality have been in the forefront for Catholic clergy and the teaching magisterium, especially within the last two decades, the special needs of women of color are not singled out or examined for their particularity and cultural uniqueness, which require different pastoral and ministerial understanding and applications.

An even bigger dilemma is now emerging for clergy. As community leaders, they are being sought and approached by public health officials to become partners in providing education and development of services for the communities they represent. This means that the issues of church and state as separate entities must be addressed, especially in terms of the message to be transmitted. There must be an examination of the issues of prevention and what they mean for those considered at greatest risk. The role of the Roman Catholic Church and its clergy in the future will have to be weighed carefully, since it is this designated group that is directly responsible for providing policy and doctrinal guidelines.

For African American women, men, children, and for people of color in general, there is the immediate need for clergy and administrators to provide the services for which they have become best noted in their community—leadership, advocacy, prophetic moral praxis, and companionate care. Further, the attitude with which clergy approach their roles in AIDS intervention and in partnership with public health officials to provide effective education and to develop supportive social services for those affected by AIDS, must reflect a pure moral sense of duty to one's community, not a punitive and judgmental attitude.

It is also apparent that the impact of AIDS on the entire society and the way in which it affects all aspects of the system of services utilized by its members need to be addressed by Catholic clergy and the institutional church, but the larger context must also be considered. It may be necessary to change the way these services are delivered, so they can be more responsive to the needs of the community. The roles of leadership and advocacy must be continued and expanded to foster these changes and to improve the quality of life for all those affected by AIDS.

As "Little children will suffer from a never/to be gotten disease," as "Small bones [are] crushed by the foot of racism," as African American women are women "in AMERICA without a face/or a voice," and as "AIDS has the potential to cripple black people in a way that few other health or social forces have since slavery,"[56] the Catholic Church in the African American community must ask, "How can we forget?" How can we forget that children are dying, that women are dying, that men are dying? How can we forget that our communities are again, on another level, being threatened?

The Black Roman Catholic Church is not an institution that forgets. It is an institution that cares, shows preference, and takes in when everybody else has pushed out. It is an institution that remembers—remembers its roots, remembers its mission, and remembers its families. As a remembering, reconciling, and caring institution and a symbolic extended family, the Roman Catholic Church in the African American community can prophetically, and as a people made in the image of God, be with its most vulnerable members as they die from or suffer and live with AIDS.

Notes

A large debt of gratitude and an expression of profound appreciation must be expressed to Jennifer S. Simpson, Ph.D. (Cand.), my research assistant, without whom this paper could not have been developed and produced.

1. Imani Harrington, "Aid of AMERICA," in *The Black Women's Health Book: Speaking for Ourselves*, ed. Evelyn C. White (Seattle: Seal Press, 1990), 187-88. Imani Harrington is an HIV-positive Black woman who was a victim of sexual assault and

is recovering from drug addiction [editor's note].

2. See Richard L. Smith, *AIDS, Gays, and the American Catholic Church* (Cleveland: Pilgrim Press, 1994).

3. See Kenneth R. Overberg, SJ, ed., *AIDS, Ethics, and Religion* (Maryknoll, N.Y.: Orbis, 1994).

4. See J. Gordon Melton, ed., *The Churches Speak on AIDS: Official Statements from Religious Bodies and Ecumenical Organizations* (Detroit: Gale Research, 1989). The introductory essay, "The Contemporary Debate in the Churches on the AIDS Crisis," describes the churches' response as reaching beyond the homosexual issue and attempting to keep moral issues concerning sexual behavior in focus. This essay, in particular, notes that "apart from the condom debate within Roman Catholicism, the churches have proposed a variety of programmatic responses . . . [and] that the Roman Catholic Church has taken the lead in developing educational programs for the secular community" (xix).

5. National Commission on AIDS, *The Challenge of HIV/AIDS in Communities of Color* (Washington, D.C.: Government Printing Office, 1992), 4.

6. Alan Bavley, "Who Will Care for the Children Left by AIDS?" *Kansas City Star* (January 23, 1994), A-1, A-13.

7. Emilie M. Townes, *In a Blaze of Glory: Womanist Spirituality as Social Witness* (Nashville: Abingdon Press, 1995), 82-83.

8. United States Catholic Conference Administrative Board, "The Many Faces of AIDS: A Gospel Response," in *Origins* 17:28 (December 1987): 481-89.

9. Richard Smith, *AIDS, Gays, and the American Catholic Church*, 87.

10. Quinton Hoare and Geoffrey Nowell Smith, eds. and trans., *Selections from the Prison Notebooks of Antonio Gramsci* (New York: International Publishers, 1971); Cornel West, *Keeping Faith: Philosophy and Race in America* (New York: Routledge, 1993), 882-84.

11. The terms "HIV virus" and "AIDS" do not have the same meaning. AIDS refers to the last stage of the illness which sometimes affects people infected with the HIV virus. In this essay, I will use both terms, because being HIV-positive (infected with the HIV virus) results in AIDS, and because so many African American families are infected by the HIV virus and AIDS. For a more thorough discussion of terms and definitions, refer to the essays in "Section I: The HIV Virus and Its Epidemiology," in *The AIDS Reader*, ed. Nancy F. McKenzie (New York: Meridian Books, 1991).

12. Some information, experiences, and stories in this essay are taken from a Catholic Worker house in Chicago, very close to sixty-fifth and Woodlawn. The house ministers to HIV-positive neighborhood people. The names I use to refer to people in this house have been changed.

13. Brenda Wilson, "All Things Considered," National Public Radio, May 14 and 15, 1991.

14. Beth Richie, "AIDS in Living Color," in White, *The Black Women's Health Book*, 183.

15. See my unpublished doctoral dissertation, "Black Catholic Belonging: A Critical Assessment of Socialization and Achievement Patterns for Families Black and Catholic" (Ph.D. diss., Graduate Theological Union, 1983).

16. Richie, "AIDS in Living Color," 184.

17. Quoted in Ernest Drucker, "Drug AIDS in the City of New York: A Study of

Dependent Children, Housing, and Drug Addiction Treatment," in McKenzie, *The AIDS Reader*, 174.

18. Vickie Mays and Susan D. Cochran, "Issues in the Perception of AIDS Risk and Risk Reduction Activities by Black and Hispanic/Latina Women," *American Psychologist* 43:11 (1988), 953.

19. Marian Wright Edelman, *Families in Peril: An Agenda for Social Change* (Cambridge: Harvard University Press, 1987), 19.

20. Lawrence E. Gary, "Introduction," in *Black Men* (Newbury Park, New Jersey: Sage Publications, 1981), 13.

21. Richie, "AIDS in Living Color," 185.

22. Peg Byron, "HIV: The National Scandal," *Ms.*, January/February 1991, 26.

23. Kathryn Anastos and Carola Marte, "Women—The Missing Persons in the AIDS Epidemic," in McKenzie, *The AIDS Reader*, 193.

24. Gloria Lockett, "Black Prostitutes and AIDS," in White, *The Black Women's Health Book*, 189.

25. Ibid., 190.

26. Mays and Cochran, "Issues in the Perception of AIDS Risk," 951.

27. Wilson, "All Things Considered."

28. Lockett, 189-92.

29. "Voices," in *Ms.*, January/February 1991, 30.

30. Ibid., 32.

31. Cyprian Davis, *The History of Black Catholics in the United States* (New York: Crossroad, 1990).

32. Wallace Charles Smith, *The Church in the Life of the Black Family* (Valley Forge: Judson Press, 1985), 14.

33. Ibid., 22.

34. Harlon L. Dalton, "AIDS in Blackface," in McKenzie, *The AIDS Reader*, 127.

35. Marcia Ann Gillespie, "HIV: The Global Crisis," *Ms.*, January/February 1991, 21.

36. Dalton, "AIDS in Blackface," 136.

37. Ibid.

38. Ibid., 137.

39. Wallace Charles Smith, *The Church in the Life of the Black Family*, 56.

40. Dalton, "AIDS in Blackface," 129.

41. Ibid.

42. Ibid., 133.

43. Ibid.

44. Evelynn Hammond, "Race, Sex, AIDS: The Construction of 'Other'," *Radical America* 20 (1987):32.

45. Mays and Cochran, "Issues in the Perception of AIDS Risk," 951.

46. Richie, "AIDS in Living Color," 184.

47. Hammond, 33.

48. Mays and Cochran, "Issues in the Perception of AIDS Risk," 952.

49. Ibid., 951.

50. See Toinette Eugene, "While Love Is Unfashionable: Ethical Implications of Black Spirituality and Sexuality," in *Sexuality and the Sacred*, ed. James B. Nelson and Sandra P. Longfellow (Louisville: Westminster/John Knox Press, 1994), 105-12.

51. Wallace Charles Smith, *The Church in the Life of the Black Family*, 17.

52. Edelman, *Families in Peril*, 107.

53. Wallace Charles Smith, *The Church in the Life of the Black Family*, 18f.

54. See Toinette Eugene, "African American Family Life: An Agenda for Ministry within the Catholic Church," *New Theology Review* 5:2 (May 1992): 33–47.

55. See James H. Harris, *Black Ministers and Laity in the Urban Church: An Analysis of Political and Social Expectations* (Lanham, N.Y.: University Press of America, 1987).

56. Richie, "AIDS in Living Color," 184.

17

"A Conscious Connection to All That Is"

The Color Purple *as Subversive and Critical Ethnography**

Cheryl Townsend Gilkes

Believing with Max Weber, that man is an animal suspended in webs of significance he himself has spun, I take culture to be those webs, and the analysis of it to be therefore not an experimental science in search of law but an interpretive one in search of meaning.

Clifford Geertz[1]

No one is exempt from the possibility of a conscious connection to All That Is. Not the poor. Not the suffering. Not the writer sitting in the open field.

Alice Walker[2]

Experience is messy . . . When human behavior is the data, a tolerance for ambiguity, multiplicity, contradiction, and instability is essential . . . We must constantly remind ourselves that life is "unstable, complex, and disorderly" . . . everywhere.

Margery Wolf[3]

*An earlier version of this essay was presented to the Womanist Approaches to Religion and Society Group at the Annual Meeting of the American Academy of Religion in Chicago, Illinois, on November 21, 1994. The author would like to thank Emilie Townes and Constantine Hriskos for their comments and encouragement. The essay is written in loving memory of my great-aunt Mary Elizabeth Burns Lloyd (1880-1978), who was raised in Macon, Georgia, and witnessed a lynching next door to her house at the age of five.

The threads of spirituality and Black feminist humanism are tightly intertwined throughout *The Color Purple*.[4] The intersection of spirituality and human emancipation is the source of the great popular appeal of the book, especially among women. Many critics, however, miss this element entirely. Hypersensitive male critics often dismiss the book as Black male bashing. Not a few Black readers, even sympathetic ones, worry that White readers will presume that Celie's disordered and unhappy life is typical of most African American families. But for the many readers who take seriously the womanist perspective proffered by Alice Walker, the centrality of spirituality is obvious.[5] The endurance of the book, in spite of the critical ambivalence with which it is regarded, is a testimony to the profound statements found on its pages.

In the tenth anniversary edition of *The Color Purple,* Alice Walker expresses her own dismay that a book that began "Dear God" was not immediately grasped "as a book about the desire to encounter, to hear from, the Ultimate Ancestor."[6] For Walker, her book was a "theological work examining the journey from the religious back to the spiritual." For most of us, the initial joy in reading the book was connected to the great revelation wherein Celie discovers through the love of a good woman named Shug that God is not an old White man with long White hair but can be found in "the color purple." Shug insists, "God ain't a he or a she but an It":

It ain't a picture show. It ain't something you can look at apart from anything else, including yourself. I believe God is everything, say Shug. Everything that is or ever was or ever will be. And when you can feel that, and be happy to feel that, you've found It (190).

In spite of the temptation to connect this way of thinking about God to a variety of movements offering ways of thinking about God and to Walker's own emphasis on the importance of "the Spirit," I am not going to dwell on the theological dimensions and contributions of *The Color Purple*. Instead, I wish to point to the way this work of fiction can be read as a subversive and critical ethnography. Although the book is not an ethnography in the technical sense and is not what many anthropologists would consider "anthropologically correct," the book does do what anthropologist Margery Wolf stresses are important consequences of ethnography, the inscription of a culture into respectful existence in the modern world and the assertion that any group of human beings is "suspended in" what Clifford Geertz calls "webs of significance."

The Color Purple is about these webs of significance and their complexity within a people and among peoples who are often dismissed from the human family. Embedded in a society whose material and symbolic dimensions are suffused with racism, African Americans are repeatedly dismissed as a people without a history and without defensible norms, values, customs, and traditions. To philosophers and social scientists, African Americans in the United States are a people incapable of constructing culture and community because of either their nature or the destructive consequences of their oppression. Alice Walker places her protagonist in a matrix of conflicted social relations constrained by the sociohistorical realities of racial oppression and the diverse resistances and accommodations that this oppression elicits. Walker's Black people in all of their tragedies and comedies are creative, resourceful, and constantly evolving, and they enable one another in their evolutions and transformations.

Walker's thick description of the social world of creative, resourceful, and developing Black people forms what I call subversive and critical ethnography. This paper explores *The Color Purple* as subversive and critical ethnography that offers a prophetic critique of oppression and its consequences. I point out minute details of the material conditions and the social relations that are embedded in Walker's text. I pay special attention to the way in which Walker centers the lives and experiences of women in the emerging class relations within the African American community. Although the book is most often read as a novel about a poor (meaning in-poverty) Black woman, Walker provides unusually thick description of the private milieu and structural ambiguities that gave rise to those whom Evelyn Brooks Higginbotham identifies as "the female talented tenth" in the late nineteenth and early twentieth centuries[7] and whom Stephanie Shaw points to as the Black professional women workers of the Jim Crow era.[8] Walker also describes the conditions from which such African American women had to cut themselves "loose" in order to save their lives and eventually the lives of others. Beyond the description, explanation, and interpretation of a "poor" Black woman caught in a web of exploitative relations, there is also the process of transformation and change that makes possible the lifting and the climbing that became the personal watchwords and public ideologies of Black women's struggles for personhood and social change in their homes, communities, clubs, and national organizations.

This essay is a "reading" of *The Color Purple* through a sociologist's eyes. For sociologists, the problems of social stratification and the complexities of class often represent the initial questions they address. In this essay, the complexities of social class are a critical focus. Walker not only depicts social class complexities and ambiguities within an oppressed people, but also connects one woman's experience of these complexities and ambiguities to the larger world in which they are embedded. Like an anthropologist of the William Lloyd Warner persuasion, Walker wonders through the voice of Celie what subjective notions of social class and position can mean in one person's life. Walker highlights the importance of the discovery of agency, resources, and social position through a variety of experiences in the life of one Black woman, poor by her own definition, who insists, "I'm pore, I'm Black, I may be ugly and can't cook, a voice say to everything listening. But I'm here" (205). Finally, Walker's sociological vision is important for understanding and interpreting African American women's history, particularly their history of consciousness of and connection to the external structures that shape their oppression, not only in rural Georgia but in the "modern world system." Walker's description of connectedness in *The Color Purple* anticipates her assertion of connectedness as a "womanist" who is "committed to survival and wholeness of entire people, male *and* female."[9] It is with a prophet's eye that Walker sees points of complicity and resistance in the micro-order of the African American experience that are connected to and have consequences for that larger world. Walker does not ignore the oppression of the White world, with its lynchings and violence toward Black people, but she puts it in perspective, expressing her faith and hope in the ability of Black people to constitute and construct lives that persist in subverting oppression through the healing and uplift of one another.

The Doctor Aunt and Persistent Misreadings

The complexities of social class leap from the very first page of Alice Walker's controversial, misunderstood, and terribly misperceived novel *The Color Purple*. Celie begins her correspondence with God, attempting to explain her transition from "a good girl" to someone in search of "a sign letting me know what is happening to me" (1). Celie's mother, after refusing to engage in sexual relations with her husband because of her fragile physical condition and her fear of pregnancy, goes "to visit her sister doctor over Macon." This little detail signals webs of social relations in early-twentieth-century Georgia that are grounded in the emerging complexities of African American intragroup class relations and a larger political context of exploitation and vulnerability. There is a connection, through this aunt who is a doctor, between Celie and the Black professional class that emerged during the rise of Jim Crow. The daughters of landowning farmers contributed disproportionately to the educational leadership during this period, and the community often, according to Stephanie Shaw's analysis, sponsored these women's mobility from the farm to the college in order that they might "uplift the race."[10] Disadvantaged communities that were unable to defend all of their daughters often made choices for a few women that were simultaneously empowering and constraining.

With the reference to Macon, we become part of the movement between the countryside and the town, and eventually the city, that women were making at the time in far larger numbers than men. Men, especially men without land, were more firmly tied to the land than were women.[11] Some of the men who emerged as educational leaders during this period describe personal struggles that arose in their homes because their fathers did not feel the family could afford to lose their labor if they went away to school.[12] For landless families, the positions available in the town or city for women and girls sometimes provided the only cash that the family ever had. For families with resources, such as land, the desire to educate daughters so that they would not be trapped in rural labor or domestic service also coincided with the historical needs of the Black community.

Alice Walker, an artist with an amazing critical vision, possesses a profound understanding of the complexities of African American social experience. It was not until I found myself listening to the controversies over the novel that I realized that a wealth of ethnographic detail is overlooked by many, if not most, readers of Walker's novel. Through several years of experimentation with the novel, I have found it is valuable for challenging students to grapple with the complexities of African American women's experience, particularly the various strands of experience that can be woven together and whose participants do interact in a number of contexts within the African American community. *The Color Purple* is built on an amazing wealth of detail about the lives of African American women in the South and the connections between those lives and the larger world. Not only is there complex detail, there is also an engagement with the messiness of experience and the connectedness of that messiness to things that are also grand and glorious.

The controversies over the novel also obscure, mask, and mystify the larger sociohistorical context of the novel. The novel was most often labeled "the story of . . . a poor, barely literate Southern Black woman who struggles to escape the brutality and degradation of her treatment by men." Although it is a complex novel, male critics often reduced it to one major theme, "the estrangement and violence that mark the relationships between Miss Walker's Black men and women."[13] The controversies over the depiction of the relations between Black men and women and a related subtheme, the state of the Black family, began almost the day the novel was published. The tensions continue to this very day, with many people still complaining that Alice Walker, the author, is too hard on Black men.

The sociologist in me was drawn to this book. Regardless of the impassioned arguments complaining that its depiction of African Americans focused on the negative, and in spite of the protests and complaints that conflate the book with every negative point of view on the Black family, the book told me much I needed and wanted to hear about the life of Black people in the Jim Crow South as they struggled in a variety of ways against the forces of politics, history, economics, and cultural humiliation—the elementals of racial oppression—to exercise hope-filled agency.

There is within the novel a complex sociological and ethnographic imagination. Ethnography aims to provide "an account of a culture emphasizing descriptive detail and offering an interpretive framework within which to understand the meaning of the details presented."[14] Ethnography at its best is the respectful, careful inscription of a people's culture and community into the written record of human existence. I have come to view *The Color Purple* as a subversive and critical fictional ethnography (or ethnographic novel) about the lives of women who represented the foundations of the Black middle class in the South. In a society that offers nothing but disrespect and flat images in its manifestations of racism, an ethnography of Black people that grasps complexities, presents a nuanced humanity, and offers a critique of oppression is subversive of that society. Ethnography is a written account of an anthropologist's or a qualitative sociologist's participation in and observation of a culture. Alice Walker as ethnographer provides, in the tradition of Zora Neale Hurston, what Henry Louis Gates calls a "speakerly text,"[15] a text that allows us to *hear* the voices of those who persistently constitute and construct culture and who carve out discursive spaces somewhat free from the intrusions of the oppressors.[16] Ethnography provides descriptive detail organized in an interpretive framework, and *The Color Purple* offers an interpretive framework that takes seriously the intersection of spirituality and humanism in the African American response to oppression.[17]

A critical approach to culture involves identifying the stresses, strains, contradictions, and antagonisms that constrain and motivate the participants, particularly in a situation of inequity and oppression. Such a critical perspective seeks to identify the forces within and without a culture that may, particularly in situations of colonial oppression, deform or assault certain aspects of social organization, such as kinship, economics, religion, and politics, and that may prevent the meeting of basic social and individual needs. Regardless of the political or self-reflexive standpoint of the anthropologist, sometimes the simple act of writing the culture and its members into existence can be an act subversive of the inhumane consequences of marginalization and domination. *The Color Purple* carefully details the webs of significance and connectedness that shape and constrain the lives of Black landowning families in the Deep South during its most violent and repressive period of history.

Poorness and Blackness are so fused as interacting terms in American social consciousness that the class complexities of Walker's novel are largely overlooked by hostile reviewers and sympathetic readers alike. We call Celie "poor," and Celie calls herself "poor." However, there is land and there is food, and Alice Walker's "poor" pay far more, morally and psychically, for their material advantage than can ever be imagined. If there was ever an answer to the question as to whether Black elites or members of "the Black middle class" were oppressed, Walker seems to answer with a resounding "Yes."

Yet within this world that Walker describes, there is also hope. It is this hope that moves us beyond critical ethnography and takes us into the realm of prophetic critique. Contained within this world is powerful God-talk. This God-talk directs us to decenter our thinking from "this old White man," our image of God "in the White folks' bible" (189). Our ability to see our own culture with its strengths and possibilities for change requires a shifting of vision away from White power. Shug admonishes Celie:

You have to git man off your eyeball, before you can see anything a'tall. Man corrupt everything, say Shug. He on your box of grits, in your head, and all over the radio. Soon as you think he everywhere, you think he God. But he ain't. Whenever you try to pray, and man plop himself on the other end of it, tell him to get lost, say Shug. Conjure up flowers, wind, water, a big rock (189).

This God-talk subverts the constraints and denigrations of White Western hegemony, because it challenges every prevalent Western notion of God and reaffirms what African Americans have always recognized about the God of the Bible and the God of Abraham, Isaac, Jacob, Harriet Tubman, Sojourner Truth, W. E. B. "DuBoyce," Amanda Berry Smith, and Bessie Smith: "God is a Spirit and they that worship [It] must worship [It] in Spirit and in truth."[18] Walker consistently points to the way in which "the Spirit" is a source and resource for Black women of different classes and statuses and gives them voice for themselves and others. This love of the Spirit, a central tenet in Walker's definition of "womanist," is something represented in her work as a value and an experience that crosses boundaries of class and color.

The time period of the novel, from the late nineteenth century through the first half of the twentieth, is full of contradictions and enigmas. The violence leveled against the former slaves and their families was unprecedented. Every effort toward their political participation was met with a myriad of creative strategies to exclude them. The predatory sexual activities of Whites were so great that one writer argues that the raping of colored women was "as common as the fish in the sea."[19] Yet at the same time, Black Americans worked with White philanthropists and missionaries to build colleges, universities, and schools for Black youth. Women in the various Black denominations, the same women who were raising money for schools and preachers' salaries, challenged the male supremacy of their church bodies, either by carving out new spaces in the form of missionary societies and auxiliary conventions or by creating new denominations or new roles in the emerging Sanctified Church.[20] By 1896, when the Supreme Court enshrined "separate but equal" as the right of states to establish segregation, Black women had developed a network of more than two hundred clubs working on the problems of survival, participation, and social change that confronted the Black community.[21] That network of clubs became a socioreligious movement called the National Association of Colored Women's Clubs whose motto was "Lifting as We Climb."[22] How could women, caught in the oppressive web of experiences and structures that characterized the horrendous constraints on the African Americans in the rural South, construct a movement that educated a nation within a nation, institutionalized women's public leadership, challenged racism, fostered internationalism, and reached across the ocean to reclaim their African kinship? The novel *The Color Purple* provides an ethnography of the personal dimensions of women's experience that is a partial answer; it is both a description of suffering and its organization of experience and an account of spiritual rebellion and transcendence.

The Doctor Aunt and the Lynched Daddy

One can read many accounts of the ways in which Black people were cheated, terrorized, and otherwise coerced into giving up land that a small proportion of freedmen and -women owned at the end of slavery and during Reconstruction. The Black masses were, for the most part, a landless peasant class, and every effort was made to keep that class landless and subject to all sorts of political and economic controls. Roger L. Ransom and Richard Sutch have argued that the sharecropping system that developed in the rural South was the outcome of a dynamic class struggle between former slaves seeking economic autonomy and political personhood, and former slave owners working to reinstate slavery.[23] Those Black families that acquired land and retained it did so in a milieu that saw the economic independence of Black men and their families as a provocation to murder. This is the motivation that Ida B. Wells-Barnett identified as the basis for lynching in the South, a motive masked by the myth of the Black rapist.

One wonders why Celie's mother left home to visit her sister, leaving Celie and the other children alone with her husband. At the beginning of the novel, we readers do not know that Celie's "father" is really her stepfather. And we do not know that the title to the land and the house is in her mother's hands and not her "father's." This stepfather never gets control of the property; he manages, through an ironic accommodation to White power, but he never owns.

The plaintiveness and moral poverty of Celie's situation often overshadow the little details that signal the ambiguity and complexity of social class. First of all, when Celie marries, she brings her own linens and her own cow. Ownership of a cow was a critical component of economic independence and implied a level of self-sufficiency that made a big difference. James Comer, writing about the experience of his mother's family and the little details of economic life that allowed her to survive in the rural South, pointed to his mother's ownership of a cow as a critical element in the family's economic survival that loomed as large as land ownership.[24] Fannie Lou Hamer's father's escape from sharecropping to renting was short-lived because hostile Whites poisoned the family mule. The critical importance of ownership of farm animals to economic position in the rural South cannot be overstated.

After Celie's marriage to Mister, we meet his sisters, Kate and Carrie. They like Celie and are quite critical of Mister's treatment of her and his late wife. From the exchange between Celie and the sisters, we learn about the complexity of Celie's household and the considerable skill that she has brought to this marriage. We also learn how hard Black property-owning women must work "to keep a decent house and a clean family" (19). Failures of effort and discipline lead to households full of children with "colds, they have flue, they have direar, they have newmonya, they have worms, they have the chill and fever. They hungry. They hair ain't comb. They too nasty to touch" (19). Celie is diligent, disciplined, and very hardworking, and the sisters convince Mister to buy Celie some clothes. Celie, of course, wants to buy the "color Shug Avery would wear" (20). Although she wants a red dress, Celie eventually chooses blue. She writes (to God):

> I can't remember being the first one in my own dress. Now to have one made just for me. I try to tell Kate what it mean. I git hot in the face and stutter.
> She say, It's all right, Celie. You deserve more than this (21).

The custom-made dress and the interaction between Celie and Mister's sisters are the kind of details that point to class position and, at the same time, depict the varieties of female presence in that class and the tensions associated with being a woman of that class. When Kate and Carrie become a threat to Mister's untrammeled oppression of Celie, they are sent home. Celie is admonished to struggle: "You got to fight them, Celie . . . You got to fight them for yourself" (21). Part of Celie's eventual emancipation process involves her discovery of the resources that she and her sister Nettie possess. In spite of the assaults to her personhood that sexual molestation and marriage bring, the ennobling elements of Celie's world—education, spirituality, and humanism—persist as positive life forces.

We also discover that the vulnerabilities and personal damages Celie and Nettie experience are also the consequences of lynching. The isolated and highly ambiguous position of Celie's family comes about because her Daddy was lynched. Everyone in a Black community knew that no one deserved lynching.[25] However, the terror of lynchings was effective precisely because communities were placed in such a state of fear that the normal funerary rites were impossible. Lynchings immediately smashed the supports that follow normal deaths—the comforting hands, the sharing of food, the celebration of life, and the promises of help toward healing in the future. Lynchings and, by extension in Alice Walker's world, other forms of deadly violence are so wrenching that they destroy the opportunity for the basic human interactions that sustain the community. We learn that Celie's lynched Daddy was buried in an unmarked grave, and the fear and the terror were so great that Celie's mother never said a mumbling word about their biological father to her children. Not only did a lynching terrorize an entire community (usually as an assault on an independent and advantaged Black man, as Ida B. Wells-Barnett persuasively demonstrated), but the lynching also ripped away the protections and controls that made a normal and liberating family life possible. We learn later that perhaps

Celie's mother married this man for protection. And protection she has, as we see him go hunting with a group of White men from the community, after which we find pregnant Celie vomiting and dressing game.

Overall, one realizes that the problems faced by both Celie's family and Mister's family are tied to the terror attached to Celie's father's death and the scandal attached to Mister's first wife's death. Both families are isolated from the larger community, one of the most effective and dangerous consequences of terror and violence. Celie's family is particularly isolated. With a sick mother, Celie points out, "Don't nobody come to see us" (2). Actually, the local schoolteacher, Addie Beasley, does come and try to persuade Celie's stepfather to send Celie back to school. She relents in her pleadings when she realizes that Celie is pregnant.

The novel is written in such a way that one has to "look back and wonder" about many of the details that are there all along. The small detail that Celie's mother's sister is a doctor over in Macon signals the beginning encounter with a wide range of late-nineteenth-century and early-twentieth-century Black women who populated the towns and cities of the South. These same women also were the "farmers' daughters" who sought higher education and became the army of Black schoolteachers who were responsible for the great surge of literacy in the Black community after the Civil War.[26] When Mister comes to ask for Nettie, Celie's stepfather, monster that he is, refuses, saying, "I want her to git some more schooling. Make a schoolteacher out of her" (7).

Significant class ambiguities abound within this family. The story takes place among families who have material resources and access to literacy. Furthermore, in the first few pages we discover that in spite of the moral degradation and ambiguity attached to Celie's stepfather, even he upholds and affirms the value of education and the importance of women educators. And it is clear that somewhere deep down in all of this sickening misery, there is an understanding that education is a liberative pathway, especially for women.

A Novel of Black Women's History

Appreciating the full power of the novel depends upon one's familiarity with the organizations and activities of African American women in the United States at the end of the nineteenth century. I discovered that having undergraduate students read a wide variety of texts in my "African American Women and Social Change" course and then having them reread the novel elicited a much thicker description of the people and activities. The students recognized that many of the distinctive features of African American women's history in the United States are present throughout the novel and indeed contribute to the survival and transformation of the person presented as victim.

As a novel of Black women's history, *The Color Purple* engages the sociological imagination, described by C. Wright Mills as the intersection of history, biography, and social structure.[27] Sometimes that intersection is subtly presented. It was several readings before I realized that Celie's aunt is a doctor, one of those African American women at the turn of the century who struggled with the intersection of "the personal troubles of milieu" and "the public issues of structure" in their lives to achieve against the odds. African American women at the turn of the century had generated a social movement that articulated the ethics of lifting as we climb. Without a nuanced understanding of the club movement's origins and practices, the movement and its ethic can seem elitist and has been criticized as such.[28] However, at the end of the nineteenth and the beginning of the twentieth centuries, an important leadership class emerged, an intellectual elite of teachers and preachers, that was largely centered in the cities and towns, especially the Black college cities and towns, of the South. In Atlanta, Nashville, Hampton, and Tuskegee, women who were faculty members and wives of faculty members organized for the Black communities surrounding them and extended the services and learning of the colleges and universities to the wider community.[29] Places like Tuskegee utilized the needs of the wider community and its Black professionals to find placements for its students, especially its nurses-in-training.[30] We know, from a variety of accounts, that migration to southern cities was heavily female, and some have highlighted the pattern of migration during this period as "the farmer's daughter" effect. For poor and uneducated women, migration was often flight from physical and sexual violence. For a very few who entered the world of entertainment, there were notable stories of actual escape from horrendous physical abuse. Josephine Baker's stories of life in East Saint Louis offer some chilling examples.[31]

Walker's novels have always been about women and their social worlds. All of her work evinces a sharp sociological eye for the operation of class, status, gender, and color within the African American experience. Her novels are about constraints, consequences, and the struggle to transcend. *The Color Purple* looks both at constraints internal to the Black community and at the larger forces that produced those constraints. Women in the late nineteenth and early twentieth centuries were forced to make some terrible choices in their lives. Besides the facade of respectability attached to the few who seem to have escaped the horrors Celie faced, there is a world of pain and suffering attached to many more who did not.

Walker brings through the pages of the novel a parade of Black women, especially educated Black women, who represent significant points along the time line of Black history in the United States and the world. The role of schoolteachers as prophetic and instrumental leaders inspires long discussions. Bernice Johnson Reagon, in an essay pointing to the importance of diverse women in her community in shaping her life, writes extensively about Mamie Daniel, the schoolteacher who came to her community and brought improved health and broader cultural exposure along with literacy.[32] This teacher, Mamie Daniel, organized the entire community to participate in the children's education. They built a theater and a playhouse and organized trips for the children. Reagon thought as a little child that Mamie Daniel was old, but she later learned that Mamie Daniel was only in her twenties. Mamie Daniel was not unlike other members of that army of young women who taught throughout the South. Many of these women trained for the mission fields at places like Spelman College and spent their summers teaching school in rural communities.[33] Walker connects Celie's life with these kinds of women. We not only meet Miss Beasley, who comes to plead for Celie's attendance at school, but we then meet Corrine, the first woman Celie has ever seen use actual cash in an economic transaction.

Cash money is a small but critical detail in this story. When telling Nettie where to go to escape Mister, Celie tells her to find Corrine precisely because she had handled cash money. The ambiguities of cash are at the nexus of much racial oppression in the late nineteenth and early twentieth centuries. For the most part, a lack of cash kept African Americans in the position of a debtor class. Poll taxes could not be paid without cash, and in those areas of the South where Black people could vote if they paid their poll taxes, families went without eating to have that money. Bail could not be paid without cash. The lives of African American women, the poor and the not so poor, were tied to their participation in the labor force in ways that provided access to cash for their families—for parents and siblings as well as husbands and children. For most rural Black people, economic life was mired in farm tenancy, sharecropping, and contract labor situations. Sometimes, as in the case of Sofia, Celie's daughter-in-law, the criminal "justice" system allocated the workers for domestic and farm work. In a letter to Nettie, Celie tries to explain whom she saw working as "the mayor's maid." Celie writes:

> The mayor and his wife and a lot of other white people get labor free from the jailhouse by pretending a colored person jumped on them or cussed them out so they had to have them locked up. After they're locked up these same white people come up to the jail and get them out and make them work for them for nothing. It's just like slavery, except they sign a paper with the sheriff. They call it contract labor (193).

In the early decades of the twentieth century, Black people had no cash for poll taxes, bail, and material goods unless some, usually female, member of the family found work that provided cash. Women could be released from farm labor, especially young, unmarried women, more easily than skilled men and older skilled women. Although bootlegging, prostitution, and other "shady" pursuits were conduits for cash, aside from domestic work the only real honest and honorable option for women was teaching school. Everybody in Black communities, even Mister, understood those harsh realities. Therefore, if the route of escape through education was open, there was a cultural consensus that women should take it.

In the course of telling Corrine's story, Walker connects us with Spelman and its history of missionary and teacher training.[34] We know we are in the world of the talented tenth when we meet "Dr. DuBoyce" on the Spelman campus. Nettie, in her letter to Celie, places these women in the context of African American history and world history, writing:

> [Spelman] was a very interesting place . . . Started in a church basement, it soon moved up to Army barracks. Eventually these two ladies were able to get large sums of money from some of the richest men in America, and so the place grew. Buildings, trees. Girls were taught everything: Reading, Writing, Arithmetic, sewing, cleaning, cooking. But more than anything else, they were taught to serve God and the colored community. Their official motto was OUR WHOLE SCHOOL FOR CHRIST. But I always thought their unofficial motto should have been OUR COMMUNITY COVERS THE WORLD, because no sooner had a young woman got through Spelman Seminary than she began to put her hand to whatever work she could do for her people anywhere in the world. It was truly astonishing. These very polite and proper young women, some of them never having set foot outside their own small country towns, except to come to the Seminary, thought nothing of packing up for India, Africa, the Orient. Or for Philadelphia or New York (231-232).

In her discussion of Spelman and its community work, Walker also deconstructs the false consciousness surrounding color that characterized this community and others like it and, in the process, connects the history of these talented women with the history of the oppression of Native Americans of the southeastern United States. Walker identifies the source of the false consciousness of color in the prurient interests and sexual violence of White power. That false consciousness not only deformed the self-understanding of Black people about their substantial Native American heritage, but also operated powerfully in the world of Shug Avery and the blues queens of the twentieth century.[35] While Sofia is incarcerated, Squeak's color and her family history of sexual oppression become a site on which the eventual liberation of Sofia is mapped. The dialectic of kinship, even an unspeakable kinship, becomes a resource for ending Sofia's incarceration. Liberation by any means necessary sometimes means the subversion of indignities for a higher purpose. In the process of liberating Sofia, however, Squeak/Mary Agnes is raped by her White uncle, the warden. Although not part of the more visible and honorable segments of the lighter-skinned Black elite, Shug Avery and the other blues queens represent a critical group of women whose freedom was meaningful to the larger

Black community. Their opportunities to shake themselves loose from oppressive reality were disproportionately tied to their skin color. According to Daphne Duval Harrison, "Complexion and hair that approximated White standards of beauty continued for decades to be plus factors for women who sought stage careers as singers, chorus girls, or actresses."[36]

In spite of the colorism and cultural politics that shaped their marginal positions in the Black community, Shug is a blues singer, and blues singers, particularly the blues queens of the 1920s, are a vital segment of African American women's history. Education was one motivation for women to leave the farms and towns and migrate to cities. Opportunities in the entertainment industry were another. Women of both genteel and peasant upbringing sought careers as blues singers and entertainers. Most women were the same age as Celie, twelve, fourteen, and sixteen, when they ran away to become stars. Walker's novel gives us some idea of what they may have been running from, not only with regard to the oppression and degradation visited upon them by Whites but also with regard to the problems of coming of age sexually in an oppressed Black community and the limited opportunities for the most exploitative work.[37]

Evelyn Brooks Higginbotham points out that the church women of the talented tenth engaged in a "discursive effort of self representation" that opposed the humiliation of the "social structures and symbolic representations of White supremacy," identifying this self-representation as the "politics of respectability." Further,

> The politics of respectability emphasized reform of individual behavior and attitudes both as a goal in itself and as a strategy for reform of the entire structural system of race relations . . . Such a politics did not reduce to an accommodationist stance toward racism, or a compensatory ideology in the face of powerlessness . . . The Baptist women emphasized manners and morals while simultaneously asserting traditional forms of protest, such as petitions, boycotts, and verbal appeals to justice.[38]

While church women generally and Baptist women particularly were "privileging respectability and particularly the capacity and worthiness of poor, working class Black women for respect" at the same time that they were emphasizing "a critical message . . . namely that self-esteem and self-determination were independent of contexts of race and income,"[39] the blues women were engaged in a different set of oppositional practices that often drew the wrath of the church.

The blues women, queens and empresses to their audiences, were engaged in a politics of elegance. Although they did not reject outright the politics of respectability, their lifestyles and the contents of their singing did not garner the approval of the church community. The discussion of Shug Avery by Mister's respectable sisters reflects this disdain:

Shug Avery, Shug Avery, Carrie say. I'm sick of her. Somebody say she going around trying to sing. Umph, what she got to sing about. Say she wearing dresses all up her leg and headpieces with little balls and Lassies hanging down, look like window dressing (20).

Later, when Shug Avery is sick, no one wants to offer her a place to stay. Her estrangement from her parents becomes apparent, and the women at church claim that she is afflicted with "some kind of nasty woman disease." Her alienation from the church is even more pronounced: "Even the preacher got his mouth on Shug Avery . . . He talk about a strumpet in short skirts, smoking cigarettes, drinking gin. Singing for money and taking other women mens. Talk about slut, hussy, heifer and streetcleaner" (41).

Celie, on the other hand, reflects the response of those who filled the audiences of tent shows, juke joints, and theaters when she writes, "I think what color Shug Avery would wear. She like a queen to me so I say to Kate, Somethin purple, maybe little red in it too" (20). Later, when "Shug Avery is coming to town," the anticipation of her presence briefly provokes a new civility in the relationship between Celie and Mister. Mister gets all dressed up, and Celie tells him how nice he looks. Mister actually appreciates her opinion. Celie then spends the day walking around with an announcement of Shug's performance in her pocket. Celie's description reflects the emotional impact these women had on their communities:

Shug Avery standing upside a piano, elbow crook, hand on her hip. She wearing a hat like Indian Chiefs. Her mouth open showing all her teef and don't nothing seem to be troubling her mind. Come one, come all, it say. The Queen Honeybee is back in town.

Lord, I wants to go so bad. Not to dance. Not to drink. Not to play card. Not even to hear Shug Avery sing. I just be thankful to lay eyes on her (25).

These women who were "like a queen" to their audiences wore beautiful jeweled gowns and dresses when they sang. According to Harrison, "they raised the status of Black women entertainers to a new height and were adored at home and abroad for a brief moment in history."[40] In a way that the church women could not, the blues women engaged in the messiness of life, the disrespected underside of African American women's experience. Further,

The blues women . . . brought to their lyrics and performances new meaning as they interpreted and reformulated the Black experience from their unique perspective in American society as Black females. They saw a world that did not protect the sanctity of Black womanhood, as espoused in the bourgeois ideology; only White middle- or

upper-class women were protected by it. They saw and experienced
injustice as jobs they held were snatched away when White women
refused to work with them or White men returned from war to reclaim
them. They pointed out the pain of sexual and physical abuse and
abandonment. They sought escape from the oppressive controls of
the Black church but they did not seek to sever their ties from home,
family, and loved ones. They reorganized reality through surrealistic
fantasies and cynical parodies.[41]

In a way, the discursive practices of blues women were as prophetic as
those of the church women. Blues women, Harrison points out, "were able
to capture in song the sensibilities of Black women—North and South—
who struggled daily for physical, psychological, and spiritual balance."[42]
They gave voice to the troubles that people experienced in an oppressive
social structure at the same time that they provided an alternative vision
of Black women—a rich elegant one—in a world that insisted on their poverty and humiliation. Often, the language of the biblical prophets was harsh
and shocking as it addressed the consequences of apostasy and oppression. At the same time that these women embodied opposition to the cultural humiliation, they spoke forthrightly of the troubles endemic to their
lives: "Alienation, sex and sexuality, tortured love, loneliness, hard times,
marginality, were addressed with an openness that had not previously existed."[43]

The Color Purple allows us to see the variety of women who embodied
the diverse experiences that made the lives of women in the South, particularly women associated with landowning families, complex and ambiguous. Their relative affluence and the image of moral authority that affluence represented made these women and their families especially visible
targets of White supremacy. Although there is no solid reference to Celie's
and the other characters' family histories during slavery, a substantial proportion of landowning families in the late-nineteenth- and early-twentieth-
century South were from families that had been free before the Civil War.[44]
Historian Adele Logan Alexander, exploring the historical connections
within her own family, provides a portrait of free women of color in rural
Georgia. She writes:

> Although such people . . . were not slaves, doubts still remain as to the
> extent of their freedom, its source, and even its legitimacy. These so-
> called "free" men and women of color frequently dwelt in an ill-defined
> penumbra between bondage and freedom.[45]

The Color Purple helps us to understand the limited extent of freedom and
the oppressive continuities between slavery and freedom that remained.
Even without a large discussion about slavery and the roots of Celie's,
Shug's, Mister's, or Sofia's family, Walker is able to extend the discussion of

the slightly advantaged Black family in the South. The most important point that both Alexander and Walker make is that these families did not exist in a vacuum. The constraints imposed by White power were significant, historically constructed, and devastating. The personal consequences of historical oppression were overt, violent, and fraught with injury.

"But I Don't Never Git Used to It"

There are multiple manifestations of oppression in the lives of Black people. Walker reveals these oppressions and their intersections in the everyday lives of rural Black people, in the operations of larger systems of violence and exploitation, and in the political economy of an imperialist world system.[46] We see the ambiguity of Black dependency in a context of White supremacy. We see the violence used to enforce that system and its reverberations throughout the community as it latches onto false moral visions and pretensions to respectability. We see the basic, everyday humiliations that come in the form of White harassment of all Black people regardless of their class or precisely because of their class. We see the difference between White paternalism in Christian missions and Black communalism in their differing approaches to Christian missions. We see the way in which the expanding international colonial order often heightened contradictions on mission fields, producing a cloud of witnesses who could speak against the brutality and cultural genocide of colonialism. Walker constructs a world where the poor Black person who is *here* is connected to "all that is."

In the process of naming oppressions, Walker also links the near-destruction of Sofia with her husband's violence against her and with Celie's collaboration with that violence, a collaboration not disconnected from her own victimization. It is a "dry bones in the valley" phenomenon wherein the interconnections of oppression cannot be ignored. As the family comes together to rescue and reclaim Sofia, the family must manipulate the history of sexual exploitation that has shaped Squeak/MaryAgnes's story (193-194). In her own act of liberation, Celie reminds Harpo that "If you hadn't tried to rule over Sofia, the White folks never would have caught her" (195).

Thus, through the lives of women, fully credible lives when seen in the context of African American women's history, we see the way in which oppression breeds and feeds oppression. The roots of what Deborah King calls Black women's "multiple jeopardy"[47] are carefully described, contextualized, historicized, and then subjected to very creative criticism. Walker does not accept the received wisdom of disconnections between Black people of different classes; the simplistic dichotomy between the house slave and the field slaves, or more accurately their descendants, is unacceptable. Walker reiterates the voices of Mary Church Terrell and Ida B. Wells-Barnett when she points to the real targets of lynching and then explores its consequences in the lives of the women left behind. Lynching and rape are no longer issues of male suffering contrasted with female suffering; they are interconnected and interlinked, and they shape the personal worlds of several generations. Both lynching and rape function together as an assault on "the survival and wholeness of entire people, male *and* female." Walker also protests against the tendency to dismiss the suffering of privileged Black people, especially those whose color distinguishes them from the masses. To be loved for one's color is also an aspect of dehumanization that is dialectically linked with the self-hatred among Black people manifested in antipathy toward dark people. In a manner similar to that of the biblical prophets, Walker points out that brothers' mistreatment of their sisters and women's collaboration with violence against other women have consequences that can literally, as through Celie's and Nettie's letters, stretch across oceans. The book's ethnographic vision provides a cautionary tale about judgments that dismiss and therefore disconnect members of the community as either privileged or disreputable. What Higginbotham calls "the politics of respectability," when carried too far, can be hazardous to communal health.

Every aspect of suffering in Walker's multifaceted model of oppressions is also a site and an opportunity for resistance and subversion. The pretty, light-skinned blues woman can articulate the suffering of the masses of women. The unspeakable kinships between Black and White people can sometimes be manipulated to sustain life—always a revolutionary act in a death-dealing system. The woman labeled hussy and heifer from the pulpit is the one with the spiritual vision for raising the dead. Even the most dissolute sinner man is able to share a vision of empowerment through educated women. No matter the limited comfort zones that are carved out of segments of personal experience; people, Walker points out, are never really comfortable with suffering. The fact that people "don't never get used to it" is a catalyst for activism or, at least, for the support of someone else's.

Finally, Walker demonstrates that it is important to provide those who seem to be "the least of these" a vision of something, if only just a sign, beyond the boundaries of one's own personal pain and suffering. The book begins because Celie, ever the obedient daughter, doesn't tell anyone about her troubles but God. But her world grows. She acts to save her sister and in the process begins to save herself. She hears the prophetic voice of the blues woman. Her sisters-in-law urge her to fight. The reflexive process grows. She repents and reconciles through the production of a quilt. Celie's humanity grows. And, eventually, there is rebellion, resistance, and a new order. What Walker tells us in the opening pages of her book is that our journey and our connectedness by way of Celie's story to an oppressive world order that can be described, named, and challenged all happen because one sexually abused, pregnant fourteen-year-old "don't never git used to it" (1). In the process, Walker also lifts up the significance of African American women's history for the liberation of the entire community. The entire community must be constantly challenged not to become complacent with oppression and not to develop strategies of internal and internalized oppression that further reinforce the power of larger, more alien structures in all our lives. Ultimately, the resistance to oppression, the saving and sustaining of lives, and the persistent humanizing of community are problems of the Spirit and of our spiritual freedom. Nettie, assessing the impact of her experience in Africa on her life, writes to Celie:

> God is different to us now, after all these years in Africa. More spirit than ever before, and more internal. Most people think he has to look like something or someone—a roofleaf or Christ—but we don't. And not being tied to what God looks like, frees us (256).

The critical dimensions of Walker's ethnography challenge us to recover the details of our everyday existence in all their messiness in order to understand fully our humanity. The subversive dimensions of her ethnography seek to free us to reshape and to liberate our communities and our existence. We are products of our history, but our spiritual journeys also make us shapers of history—historical subjects—who have the power to challenge and reshape the world beyond our immediate milieu.

Notes

1. Clifford Geertz, *The Interpretation of Cultures: Selected Essays* (New York: Basic Books, 1973), 5.

2. Alice Walker, "Preface to the Tenth Anniversary Edition," *The Color Purple*, 10th anniversary ed. (New York: Harcourt Brace Jovanovich, 1992), xi.

3. Margery Wolf, *A Thrice-Told Tale: Feminism, Postmodernism, and Ethnographic Responsibility* (Stanford University Press, 1992), 129.

4. My use of the terms "Black feminist humanism" and "humanism" is taken from Patricia Hill Collins, *Black Feminist Thought: Knowledge, Consciousness, and the Politics of Empowerment* (Cambridge: Unwin Hyman,1990), 37. She insists that Black feminist thought comes from a wide variety of sources in Black communities, and one of its distinguishing features and connecting threads is what she calls the "recurring humanist vision" of Black women that insists that "Black women's struggles are part of a wider struggle for human dignity and empowerment."

5. See Alice Walker, *In Search of Our Mothers' Gardens: Womanist Prose* (New York: Harcourt Brace Jovanovich, 1983).

6. Alice Walker, *The Color Purple*, xi. All quotations from the novel are from the 1992 tenth anniversary hardcover edition of the book, and page numbers are henceforth provided in the text. Misperceptions about the book are exacerbated because of some of the terrible miscastings in the movie based on the book. In order to demonize Celie's stepfather more dramatically, for example, he is played by an actor whose age, color, and demeanor are not the same as those presented in the book.

7. Evelyn Brooks Higginbotham, *Righteous Discontent: The Women's Movement*

in the Black Baptist Church, 1880-1920 (Cambridge: Harvard University Press, 1993).

8. Stephanie Shaw, *What a Woman Ought to Be and to Do: Black Professional Women Workers during the Jim Crow Era* (Chicago: University of Chicago Press, 1996).

9. Walker, *In Search of Our Mothers' Gardens*, xi.

10. Stephanie Shaw, *What a Woman Ought to Be and to Do: Black Professional Workers During the Jim Crow Era* (Chicago: University of Chicago Press, 1996).

11. Walker points out, through the relationship between Mister and his father, that being the son of a large landowner was not the same as being a large land-owner. Mister's father is a very domineering and oppressive presence who imposes on Mister the kinds of relations that Mister imposes on Celie.

12. See, for example, Benjamin E. Mays, *Born to Rebel: An Autobiography* (New York: Charles Scribner and Sons, 1971).

13. Henry Louis Gates Jr. and K. A. Appiah, eds., "Introduction" in *Alice Walker: Critical Perspectives Past and Present* (New York: Amistad Press, 1993), 16, 17.

14. Lynn Davidman, *Tradition in a Rootless World: Women Turn to Orthodox Judaism* (Berkeley: University of California Press, 1991), 53.

15. Henry L. Gates Jr., *The Signifying Monkey: A Theory of Afro-American Literary Criticism* (New York: Oxford University Press, 1988) xxv-xxv, 112.

16. I believe that the ethnographic continuity between Alice Walker and Zora Neale Hurston is no mere accident. Zora Neale Hurston has been criticized for her "ethnographic intrusions" into the text by Eric Sundquist, in *The Hammers of Creation: Folk Culture in Modern African-American Fiction* (Athens, GA: Mercer University Press, 1992). However, the description of African Americans as cultural and cultured beings is the mission of both novelists as they inscribe the humanity of Black people into the Western consciousness. For White people or any people affected by White Western racial hegemony, ethnography must be part of a writer's mission.

17. See Wolf's discussion in *A Thrice-Told Tale*.

18. This is a restatement of the King James Version of John 4:24 with emendations consistent with Shug's description of God as "It." See Walker, *The Color Purple*, 190.

19. Julie Dash, with Toni Cade Bambara and bell hooks, *Daughters of the Dust: The Making of an African American Woman's Film* (New York: New Press, 1992).

20. See Higginbotham, *Righteous Discontent*; Jualyne E. Dodson, "Class Consciousness and Resistance of Southern African Methodist Episcopal Women" (Typewritten manuscript, 1989); Jualyne E. Dodson and Cheryl Townsend Gilkes, "Something Within: Social Change and Collective Endurance in the Sacred World of Black Christian Women," in *Women and Religion in America: Volume 3: The Twentieth Century*, ed. Rosemary Radford Ruether and Rosemary Skinner Keller (San Francisco: Harper and Row, 1986); and Gilkes, " 'Together and in Harness': Women's Traditions in the Sanctified Church," *Signs: Journal of Women in Culture and Society* 1985, 11 (4).

21. See Stephanie Shaw, "Black Club Women and the Creation of the National Association of Colored Women," in *"We Specialize in the Wholly Impossible": A Reader in Black Women's History* (Chicago: University of Chicago Press, 1995).

22. For further discussion, see Marcia Y. Riggs, *Awake, Arise, and Act! A Womanist Call for Black Liberation* (Cleveland: Pilgrim Press, 1994); and Elizabeth Lindsey Davis, *Living as They Climb: A History of the National Association of Colored Women*

(Washington, DC: Moorland Spingarn Research Center, Howard University, 1933).

23. Roger L. Ransom and Richard Sutch, *One Kind of Freedom: The Economic Consequences of Emancipation* (New York: Cambridge University Press, 1977).

24. James P. Comer, *Maggie's American Dream: The Life and Times of an American Family* (New York: New American Library, 1988).

25. Harold Garfinkle, in *Studies in Ethnomethodology* (Englewood Cliffs, NJ: Prentice Hall, 1967), and others have pointed out that what "everybody knows" represents the central, taken-for-granted aspects of culture. People construct their behavior in everyday life with reference to what "everybody knows"—those things that "go without saying."

26. W. E. B. Du Bois, *The Gift of Black Folk* (Millwood, NY: Kraus-Thomson Organization, 1975 [1924]).

27. C. Wright Mills, *The Sociological Imagination* (New York: Oxford University Press, 1959).

28. See Higginbotham, *Righteous Discontent.*

29. See Cynthia Neverdon-Morton, *Afro-American Women of the South and the Advancement of the Race, 1895-1925* (Knoxville: University of Tennessee Press, 1989).

30. See Thadious M. Davis, *Nella Larsen, Novelist of the Harlem Renaissance: A Woman's Life Unveiled* (Baton Rouge: Louisiana State University Press, 1994).

31. See Josephine Baker, *Fighting for Life* (New York: Arno Press, 1974).

32. Bernice Johnson Reagon, "My Black Mothers and Sisters, or On Beginning a Cultural Autobiography," *Feminist Studies* 1982, Spring, 8 (1): 81-96.

33. See Higginbotham, *Righteous Discontent.*

34. The work of historian Sylvia M. Jacobs is vitally important for understanding the roles, relationships, and responses of African American women who worked as missionaries in Africa. See Sylvia M. Jacobs, *Black Americans and the Missionary Movement in Africa* (Westport, CT: Greenwood Press, 1982). People like Mary McLeod Bethune and Mamie Garvin Fields also trained to work overseas. Bethune was told by the Presbyterian Church that there were no openings for Negroes in Africa.

35. See Daphne Duval Harrison, *Black Pearls: Blues Queens of the 1920s* (New Brunswick: Rutgers University Press, 1988).

36. Ibid., 32.

37. In my classes I also use the film *Wild Women Don't Have the Blues*, which provides enough information on blues singers' class backgrounds to make the point about the mix of women who sought careers on the stage. Those who were more advantaged were better able to manage their own lives and to hold on to their money. See Christine Dall, *Wild Women Don't Have the Blues*, produced by Carole Van Felkenburg and Christine Dall, 58 min., California Newsreel, 1989, videocassette.

38. Higginbotham, *Righteous Discontent*, 186-187.

39. Ibid., 191.

40. Harrison, *Black Pearls*, 14.

41. Ibid., 64.

42. Ibid., 221.

43. Ibid.

44. See E. Franklin Frazier, *The Black Bourgeoisie: The Rise of a New Middle Class* (Glencoe, IL: Free Press, 1957).

45. Adele Logan Alexander, *Ambiguous Lives: Free Women of Color in Rural Georgia, 1789-1879* (Fayetteville: University of Arkansas Press, 1991), 7.

46. In *The Everyday World as Problematic: A Feminist Sociology* (Boston: Northeastern University Press, 1987) and *The Conceptual Practices of Power: A Feminist Sociology of Knowledge* (Boston: Northeastern University Press, 1990), Dorothy E. Smith, a feminist sociologist, suggests that the problematics of everyday life are the starting point for a critical perspective on the world and its power structures.

47. Deborah E. King, "Multiple Jeopardy, Multiple Consciousness: The Context of a Black Feminist Ideology," *Signs: Journal of Women in Culture and Society* 1988, 14 (1): 265-295.

Contributors

Karen Baker-Fletcher is associate professor of theology and culture at Claremont School of Theology. She is the author of *A Singing Something: Womanist Reflections on Anna Julia Cooper.* She is also the coauthor of *My Sister, My Brother: Womanist and Xodus God-Talk,* with her spouse, Garth KASIMU Baker-Fletcher. She is a preacher and the mother of three children.

Marsha Foster Boyd is associate professor of pastoral care and counseling at United Theological Seminary in Dayton, Ohio. She is the first African American woman to receive tenure there. She is also the first African American woman to receive the Ph.D. in religion and the personality sciences from the Graduate Theological Union in Berkeley, California. Dr. Boyd was ordained in the African Methodist Episcopal Church in 1978. She works to build bridges between the seminary community and the African American Church.

Teresa L. Fry Brown is an assistant professor of homiletics at Emory University's Candler School of Theology in Atlanta, Georgia, and associate pastor of St. Paul African Methodist Episcopal Church in Lithonia, Georgia. She has a Bachelor and a Master of Science degree in speech pathology and audiology and a Master of Divinity. Her doctoral dissertation, "God Don't Like Ugly: The Intergenerational Transmission of African American Spiritual Values by Grandmothers and Othermothers as Depicted in African American Women's Literature from 1960 to the Present," was written for the University of Denver and Iliff School of Theology program in religion and social transformation.

Kelly Brown Douglas is associate professor of theology at Howard University Divinity School in Washington, D.C. She is the author of *The Black Christ.*

Barbara J. Essex is an ordained United Church of Christ minister and a ministry consultant who has pastored and served on the staff of several dynamic and exciting churches in the Chicago area. She believes that faith and works are inseparable as we seek to be faithful disciples of Jesus Christ and to serve this present age of rapid change. Her mission in life is to work with pastors to empower the laity to be more effective leaders and stewards; to assist congregations in developing strong programs for all members; and to work with other agencies and organizations to provide quality resources for effective ministry. Her clients include the United Church of Christ Board for Homeland Ministries, the Presbytery of Chicago, Hartford Seminary, the Alban Institute, and, many churches and seminaries across the nation. She has served as Associate Executive for Community

Ministry and Social Witness with the Presbytery of Chicago (Presbyterian Church, USA) and as project associate for Hartford (Connecticut) Seminary's Leadership Education Program for regional and national executives of churches, ecumenical agencies, and seminaries, and she has taught Hebrew Scripture (the Old Testament) in Hartford Seminary's Black Ministries Certificate Program. She currently serves as the administrative director of the Pacific School of Theology/Hartford Seminary National Religious Leadership Program funded by the Lilly Endowment, 1997-1999. In addition, Essex is the author and producer of several church education resources, a frequent preacher at church-related functions, and a frequent speaker at national and regional consultations and conferences. She has received numerous awards for her work throughout the United States.

Toinette M. Eugene develops womanist social ethics from her perspective as a Roman Catholic scholar. She educates within a community context for a more peaceful, ecological society of peoples who are diverse racially, culturally, and denominationally. She is Associate Professor of Christian Social Ethics at Garrett-Evangelical Theological Seminary and a member of the graduate faculty of Northwestern University in Evanston, Illinois. Her forthcoming books are *Lifting as We Climb: A Womanist Ethic of Care* and *Balm for Gilead: Pastoral Care for African American Families Experiencing Abuse*, coauthored with James N. Poling.

Cheryl Townsend Gilkes is the MacArthur Associate Professor of African American Studies and Sociology at Colby College (Waterville, Maine) where she directs that college's African American Studies Program. She is also an associate minister at the Union Baptist Church in Cambridge, Massachusetts. Her articles have appeared in journals and anthologies on women, sociology of religion, and the African American religious experience.

Diana L. Hayes is an associate professor of theology (with tenure) at Georgetown University and serves as adjunct faculty for the Master of Theology in Black Catholic Studies program at Xavier University in New Orleans. Her area of specialization is systematic theology with a particular emphasis on Black liberation and womanist theologies. She is presently engaged in research and writing on an African American understanding of God and on the development of a contextual theology for the United States, and is the author of numerous articles. Her books include *Trouble Don't Last Always: Soul Prayers*; *Hagar's Daughters: Womanist Ways of Being in the World*; and *And Still We Rise: An Introduction to Black Liberation Theology*.

Cheryl A. Kirk-Duggan is director of the Center for Women and Religion and assistant professor of theology and womanist studies at the Graduate Theological Union in Berkeley, California. Kirk-Duggan has a Bachelor of Arts in voice and piano from the University of Southwestern Louisiana, a Master of Arts in voice from the University of Texas at Austin, a Master of Divinity from Austin Presbyterian Theological Seminary, and a Doctor of Philosophy degree in religion, with special emphasis in theology and ethics from Baylor University. Kirk-Duggan is a member of the American Academy of Religion, the American Society for Aesthetics, the Colloquium of Violence and Religion; Sigma Alpha Iota; the Society for Christian Ethics; the Society for the Study of Black Religion; the Society of Biblical Literature; and Golden Key. She is listed in *Who's Who in the World*; *Who's Who in America*;

and *Who's Who in Black America*. Her books include: *African-American Special Days*; *Exorcising Evil: Theodicy and African American Spirituals—A Womanist Perspective*; and *It's in the Blood: A Trilogy of Poems Harvested from a Family Tree*. Her current research includes violence and religion; humor, faith, and religious experience; female gangs, sororities, and social organizations; and the milieu of popular media as a praxeology for constructive and narrative theology.

Rosita deAnn Mathews, an ordained minister, is the director of pastoral care at the VA Medical Center in Northampton, Massachusetts. She is the first African American woman to hold this position in any veterans hospital in the nation. She was awarded the Outstanding American Baptist Chaplains Award, 1995-97, for her work in medical ethics and patient rights. She has been awarded grants for academic study in Greece, Rome, and the Middle East. A native Detroiter, she is a graduate of the University of Michigan and the Southern Baptist Theological Seminary and has also done postgraduate work at Princeton Theological Seminary. She leads gospel singing workshops in the Northeast. This chapter is dedicated to her brother Art "Archie" Mathews (1955-1996) who died from complications caused by diabetes.

Mozella G. Mitchell is a native of Meridian, Mississippi, who grew up in Memphis, Tennessee, and was educated at LeMoyne College, receiving a B.A. in English in 1959. She received an M.A. in English language and literature from the University of Michigan at Ann Arbor in 1963; an M.A. in religious studies from Colgate Rochester Divinity School, with a Black Church studies and Ethics concentration, in 1973; and a Ph.D. degree in literature and theology from Emory University in 1980. Her dissertation, on Howard Thurman, was published under the title *Spiritual Dynamics of Howard Thurman's Theology*. She has also published an edited collection on Howard Thurman, titled *The Human Search: Howard Thurman and the Quest for Freedom*, as well as other books and many articles in journals and magazines. Her latest book is *New Africa in America: Religious and Social Traditions among Black People in Meridian, Mississippi, and Surrounding Counties*. Mitchell has taught in colleges and universities for many years, including Alcorn A & M College, Owen Junior College in Memphis and Norfolk State University in Norfolk, Virginia. Presently, she is professor of religion at the University of South Florida, where she has been on the faculty for fifteen years.

Rosetta E. Ross is an ordained elder in the United Methodist Church. She received a Ph.D. in Christian social ethics from Emory University in Atlanta, Georgia. She is assistant professor of ethics at the Interdenominational Theological Center in Atlanta.

Linda E. Thomas is an assistant professor of theology and anthropology at Garrett-Evangelical Theological Seminary in Evanston, Illinois. She has published articles on religion and healing in the Republic of South Africa and on womanist perspectives in the United States. She is currently writing a book about healing rituals in African-initiated churches in South Africa.

Emilie M. Townes is an associate professor of Christian social ethics and Black Church ministries at Saint Paul School of Theology. She is editor of

A Troubling in My Soul: Womanist Perspectives on Evil and Suffering and the author of *Womanist Justice, Womanist Hope* and *In a Blaze of Glory: Womanist Spirituality as Social Witness*. She is currently writing a book about health and health care issues in the African American community.

Mary M. Townes is distinguished professor emerita and doctor of humane letters (*honoris causa*) of North Carolina Central University (NCCU) in Durham, North Carolina. In the forty-four years she was employed at NCCU, she served as the dean of the College of Arts and Sciences (the position from which she retired), the chair of the biology department, and the dean of the School of Graduate Studies. She also served as special assistant to the chancellor. Townes holds a master's degree in public health education and a Ph.D. in zoology (cell physiology). Her daughters, Emilie and Tricia, are extremely proud of her.

C. Michelle Venable-Ridley, a native of Pulaski, Virginia, completed a Bachelor of Arts from the University of Virginia, a Master of Arts in religious studies from Howard University, and a Master of Arts in religion from Temple University. She received a Ph.D. in New Testament literature and languages from Temple University in 1995. As a womanist New Testament scholar, she not only seeks to uncover the hermeneutical connections between the experience of slavery and the reading of the Bible, but also actively deconstructs the learned stereotypes, myths, and assumptions of race, class, and gender. Venable-Ridley is assistant professor of religious studies at Morningside College in Sioux City, Iowa.

Delores S. Williams is the Paul Tillich Professor of Theology and Culture at Union Theological Seminary in New York. She is an active Presbyterian laywoman. In addition to her many articles, she is the author of *Sisters in the Wilderness: The Challenge of Womanist God-Talk*.